The Masada Myth

The Masada Myth

COLLECTIVE MEMORY
AND MYTHMAKING
IN ISRAEL

Nachman Ben-Yehuda

THE UNIVERSITY OF WISCONSIN PRESS

The University of Wisconsin Press
114 North Murray Street
Madison, Wisconsin 53715

3 Henrietta Street
London WC2E 8LU, England

Library of Congress Cataloging-in-Publication Data
Ben-Yehuda, Nachman.
    The Masada myth: collective memory and mythmaking in Israel /
Nachman Ben-Yehuda.
        424 p.   cm.
    Includes bibliographical references and index.
    ISBN 0-299-14830-0 (hardcover: alk. paper).
    ISBN 0-299-14834-3 (pbk.: alk. paper)
    1. Masada Site (Israel)—Siege, 72–73—Historiography.
    2. Masada Site (Israel)—Siege, 72–73—Influence.   3. Zionism.
    4. Heroes—Israel—Mythology.   5. National characteristics, Israeli.
    I. Title.
    DS110.M33B46   1995
    933—dc20   95-13543

To Vered Vinitzky-Seroussi, Einat Usant,
Anat Kaminer, Yossi Bar-Nachum, and Iris Wolf,
whose help, enthusiasm, and support
made this study and book possible

Brave and loyal followers!

Long ago we resolved to serve neither the Romans nor anyone other than God . . . The time has now come that bids us prove our determination by our deeds. At such a time we must not disgrace ourselves. Hitherto we have never submitted to slavery . . . We must not choose slavery now . . . For we were the first to revolt, and shall be the last to break off the struggle. And I think it is God who has given us this privilege, that we can die nobly and as free man . . . In our case it is evident that day-break will end our resistance, but we are free to choose an honorable death with our loved ones. This our enemies cannot prevent, however earnestly they may pray to take us alive; nor can we defeat them in battle.

Let our wives die unabused, our children without knowledge of slavery. After that let us do each other an ungrudging kindness, preserving our freedom as a glorious winding-sheet. But first, let our possessions and the whole fortress go up in flames. It will be a bitter blow to the Romans, that I know, to find our persons beyond their reach and nothing left for them to loot. One thing only let us spare—our store of food: it will bear witness when we are dead to the fact that we perished, not through want but because . . . we chose death rather than slavery. . . .

Come! While our hands are free and can hold a sword, let them do a noble service! Let us die unenslaved by our enemies, and leave this world as free men in company with our wives and children.

From the speeches of Elazar Ben-Yair,
last Sicarii commander of Masada,
persuading his people to kill one another.
Source: Josephus Flavius.
The translation into modern English
is from the brochure distributed by the
Israeli National Parks Authority.

Contents

Illustrations

Tables

Acknowledgments

A CONSIDERABLE PERIOD of time typically elapses from having the first research ideas about a topic until a book is in print. In this case, the project began sometime during 1986 or 1987. Almost eight years elapsed between the germination of the first ideas and the actual publication of the book. Hence, this book, like many others, although written by one person, has many parents. These include people I talked to before and during research and writing, friends and colleagues who provided both much-needed support and constructive challenges and criticism. I would like to use this opportunity to thank all those that I remember and whose help, company, and comments really made a difference.

My first gratitude is to Etti, Tzach, and Guy, whose love, devotion, and dedication enabled me to transform this project from an idea into a book.

Israel and Hanna Tamari have always been there to listen. Israel's constant challenge and pure curiosity were a delightful experience I learned to love tremendously. Gideon Aran, Michal and Yossi Ashkenasi, Moshe and Illana Brendell, Robert Brym, Ofra Elad, Michael Faiga, Louis Greenspan, Zali Gurevitz, John Hagan, Baruch Kimmerling, Aliza Kolker, Cyril Levit, Robert Paine, William Shaffir, Ya'acov Shavit, John Simpson, Ilana Silber, and Yael Zerubavel all provided essential help, support, constructive criticism, and good advice.

I am very grateful to the undergraduate and graduate students in my department who took my empirical research seminars about the Masada myth and with passion devoted much of their time to the project. The discovery of the real nature of the Masada myth indeed whetted their intellectual appetite, as it did mine. It is a pleasure to admit that, overall, the undergraduates' work was far superior to the graduates.' I hope they all remember the Friday at the end of the course, when we drove to Masada early in the morning and each student read his or her paper on top of the mountain. So involved were we in the study group that we missed the last cable car and had to climb down on the "snake path." The students did very well; it was I who once or twice slid on my behind. Whenever I have used any of the students' ideas or results, I have fully referenced them in the notes. I am very grateful to all of the students who gave me permission to use parts of their fascinating works.

I would like to express particular gratitude to my research assistants, without whose help none of this would have been accomplished. Einat Usant and Vered Vinitzky-Seroussi helped me begin the project. Then Anat Kaminer—with amazing and unsurpassed energy, insight, and devotion—kept it going. When Anat had to return to her kibbutz, Yossi Bar-Nachum continued the research. Finally, the energetic Iris Wolf helped and pushed me to finish the study. Without her enthusiasm and determination, this work would have probably waited another year or more to be completed. I am very grateful to them all. As we all agreed, this research was quite an experience for us.

The Yad Tabenkin (Ramat Efal) archive, the *Haaretz* archive, the Hebrew University libraries, and Machon Jabotinski provided indispensable help. Israel's National Parks Authority very graciously supplied us with statistics and documents.

I thank the spokesman unit of the Israeli Army (Israeli Defense Forces, or IDF) for giving us all the help we needed and wanted in "digging" out the reality of the involvement of the IDF in Masada, particularly the role of the armored units in swear-in ceremonies.

Grants from Machon Eshkol and the Shaine Institute, in the faculty of Social Science, and from the Israeli Foundations Trustees made this work possible. John Simpson, the convener of the June 1992 annual meeting of the Canada-Israel Social Science Exchange, gave me the first opportunity to present the preliminary findings of my study, in Toronto. The comments I received there were very useful.

This is also the proper opportunity to express my deepest gratitude to John Simpson for his warmth, friendship, and continuous support during my last two projects.

I am very grateful to Barry Schwartz's invitation to visit him for two days in November 1992 in North Carolina. His hospitality and company are a memory I treasure. It was my first opportunity to tell him—in some detail—about the earliest results of this study. His comments were indispensable.

Many thanks are due to the many archaeologists, some at Hebrew University, who gave us so much of their time for interviews: Joseph Aviram,

Dan Bahat, Meir Ben-Dov, Amir Drori, Avi Eitan, Gideon Foerster, Shmaria Guttman, Gila Hurvitz, Aharon Kampinski, Moshe Kochavi, Micha Livne, Menachem Magen, Ze'ev Meshel, Ehud Netzer, David Osishkin, Yoram Tzafrir. Let me emphasize here the obvious, that whatever is written in this book is my full and sole responsibility and is in no way intended to reflect (or not to reflect) their views regarding Masada.

My intellectual debt to Erich Goode and Ronald A. Farrell for their continuous support and their superb advice and comments is an experience I have come to cherish in the deepest sense of the term.

Neil Zwail's editorial suggestions taught me an important lesson in writing. I am delighted to be in his debt for doing such a fine job. Thanks also to Ellen O. Setteducati for her meticulous editorial comments.

Last, but most certainly not least, it is a pleasure indeed to acknowledge my profound gratitude and appreciation to Rosalie M. Robertson, my University of Wisconsin Press editor, for her support, kindness, advice, and patience, as well as a delightful sense of humor that was so very bright even over a distance of thousands of miles. I am very grateful to Raphael Kadushin, Elizabeth Steinberg, and Gardner R. Wills from the Press for all their help and good advice.

The first two aerial photographs of Masada, as well as the illustration on the cover were taken by Albatross, aerial photography, Tel Aviv. I am very grateful to Albatross (and particularly to Sarah Peleg's endless patience and warm help) for their permission to reproduce these photographs. The remaining photographs are reproduced here by permission of the 1963/4 Archaeological Excavation Expedition to Masada, the Institute of Archaeology, Hebrew University, and the Israel Exploration Society. I am very grateful to Professor Ehud Netzer and Professor Gideon Foerster, who were instrumental in granting the permission to use these beautiful photos. I am also very grateful to Dubbi from Tafsar L., Jerusalem, whose skills in optical digital scanning made it possible to reproduce these pictures.

Prologue: Masada—A Chronology

TYPICALLY, A CHRONOLOGY of events is found in an appendix. However, because this book is structured along the lines of the different cultural manifestations of the Masada mythical narrative in different areas, a nonsequential time presentation may be created. To help overcome that, I felt that a chronology of Masada, at least of most of the important events, should be placed at the beginning of the work. This chronology, obviously, emphasizes the Jewish Israeli aspect.

40 to 4 B.C.: Masada is being built.

66 A.D.: The Jewish Great Revolt begins. A group of Jewish rebels takes the fortress from the Roman garrison.

73 A.D.: Masada falls. A Roman garrison is stationed there for an unknown period of time. Later, Christian monks live there.

1800s to early 1900s: Masada is visited by a number of non-Jewish travelers and visitors. Most of them identify the place correctly and file reports about the visits (some reports include maps and charts).

1912: First tour to Masada by Jews from the gymnastic group of "Maccabi" in Jerusalem (Illan 1968:10).

1920s: The Berdyczewski–Achad Haam debate mentions Masada as a case of Jewish heroism.

1923: Josephus Flavius is translated from Greek into Hebrew by Dr. Y. N. Simchoni.

1922 to 1925: The first trips to Masada are made by various individuals and groups from Jerusalem and Tel Aviv.

1927: Yitzhak Lamdan publishes the full version of his *Masàda* (which he began writing during 1923–1924).

1933: Shmaria Guttman climbs to Masada with two colleagues and is persuaded that Masada must become a national symbol. "Brit Habirionim," which uses Sicarii symbols, meets its demise.

1934: The Jewish National Fund is involved in an attempt to purchase Masada for a hefty sum of money (Weitz 1962:7–12).

1940: Lehi, headed by "Yair" (named after Elazar Ben-Yair, Masada's last Sicarii commander), is created.

1941: Shmaria Guttman climbs to Masada again.

1942: Shmaria Guttman' seminar of guides takes place on Masada. The "plan for the North" is debated (between 1940 and 1942).

1942 to 1948: Masada is visited more and more frequently by youth movements; members of the prestate, underground Hagana/Palmach go there regularly.

1948: Soldiers of the Israeli army, mostly recruits to the armored units but others too, climb regularly to Masada. Youth Movements and schools make Masada a preferred destination for their annual trips. This situation lasts into the 1970s.

1949: Masada is under Israeli sovereignty. A new path to Masada is paved by the Israeli army (Nahal units blast the way through rocks).

1950: One thousand youth from the Gadna climb to Masada.

1953: The snake path to Masada is exposed.

1955 to 1956: The first archaeological excavations at Masada take place including the first exposure of Herod's palace.

1950s: The Sodom–Ein Gedi road opens (the car road from the Dead Sea beach to Masada was paved in 1956).

1958: The snake path is widened by volunteers from youth movements. A youth hostel opens near Masada.

1960: Helicopters begin flying tourists regularly to Masada. Shmaria Guttman excavates and restores one of the Roman army siege camps.

1962: A new road to Masada is opened. A plan to build a cable car to Masada is debated, and a landing strip for light airplanes is built near Masada, to be opened and operating in 1964. The strip will be upgraded by 1966 into Bar Yehuda Airfield.

1963 to 1965: Yigael Yadin's main excavations and reconstruction of Masada take place.

1963: Fifteen human skeletons are discovered on Masada.

1964: Hundreds of cats are "brought" to Masada to "kill" snakes (a fabricated prank committed by some members of the archaeology expedition to Masada and published in the daily papers). Israel issues a series of Masada stamps.

1966: Many activities about Masada take place, including a Masada exhibition in the Israeli museum.

1967 to 1968: The building of the cable car to Masada is further debated.

1967: The *Jewish Spectator* maintains that there was no suicide on Masada.

1969: Israel Eliraz and Joseph Tal's opera is presented on Masada. The bones of twenty-seven humans found on Masada are brought to burial in an official state ceremony.

1970: The building of the cable car to Masada begins. The Arad-Masada road is completed. A huge ceremony is held on Masada by 2500 Jewish students as an act of identification with Soviet Jews.

1971: The cable car to Masada is operational. Stewart Alsop, *Newsweek*'s commentator, accuses Golda Meir of having a "Masada complex."

1972: An impressive sight-and-sound show begins at Masada.

1973: A few official ceremonies are held on Masada, including a 1900-year commemoration of the fall of the fortress. The debate about the "Masada complex" continues.

1974: Recruits to Israeli armored units are still sworn in on Masada.

1979: The movie *Masada* is being shot.

1981: The movie *Masada* is shown by ABC.

1988: The Israeli Philharmonic Orchestra plays Mahler's Symphony no. 2 on Masada as part of a social extravaganza.

1992: The Israeli police take steps to prevent a drug party on Masada.

1993: An exhibition about Masada, commemorating thirty years since the 1963 excavations, is initiated by the Hebrew University Department of Archaeology, the Israel Antiquities Authority, and the Society for the Study of Eretz Israel and Its Antiquities.

Part I

The Puzzle and the Background

Chapter One

Introduction:
The Research Puzzle

HOW DOES ONE develop a sociological interpretation for an important belief system that turns out to be based on a series of deceptive and very biased (even falsified) claims? Moreover, what should one do when this belief system turns out to be not only an important building block for the development of receptive young minds but also a cornerstone of an entire nation?

The so-called Masada mythical narrative is such a belief system: a fabricated moralistic claim. The startling discovery of its falsehood descended upon me in 1987. However, while the sociological interpretation presented in this book is based on an Israeli experience, it would be a grave mistake to assume that such a mythology and deviant belief system constitutes a cultural idiosyncrasy, typical of Israel only. On the contrary, such myths and deviant beliefs are characteristic of many cultures. Hence, the sociological lesson embedded in this particular tale has wide-ranging ramifications, as we shall indeed see later.

THE PERSONAL ANGLE

The beginning of the story is innocently interesting. In 1987 I was involved in a long-term research project concerning political assassinations by Jews in Palestine and Israel (see Ben-Yehuda 1993). During the research, I became increasingly interested in the question of whether there were Jewish groups that advocated—and practiced—political assassinations.

One Friday I was reading a fascinating paper by David Rapoport (1984) in which he compared three groups of assassins: the Thugs in India, the Islamic Assassins, and the Jewish "Zealots Sicarii." The Sicarii were a group of Jews that flourished during the time of what has

3

Masada, looking southeast. The three levels of the northern palace are very clear, as are the storerooms and bathhouse. In the low background, one of the Roman siege camps, surrounded by a wall, can be seen very clearly. Another such camp is close to it but more difficult to discern.

become known as the Jewish "Great Revolt" against the Romans (66–73 A.D.). This group advocated the use of assassinations and terror and put these tactics into practice as well. It is probably the only known Jewish group up until 1940 that had such an explicit ideological commitment resulting in a corresponding practice. It does not take much to consider the Sicarii a "bunch of assassins." One can imagine my amazement, indeed indignation, at Rapoport's statement that this "bunch of assassins" perished on top of Masada. I still vividly remember reading this and skeptically thinking, "Here is another American who wants to tell *me*, the Israeli, what happened on Masada." After all, I "knew" what happened on Masada. I learned it in school, in the army—I climbed to the top of Masada. I *knew* that there was a group of Jewish freedom fighters who fled Jerusalem, after its destruction by the Roman

Imperial Army in 70 A.D., to Masada. There, they staged the final fight against that army. When the Romans were about to conquer the fortress, all these heroic Jewish freedom fighters chose to commit collective suicide rather than surrender to Rome and become slaves or die in some strange and painful ways (e.g., in the arena). But to think that these Jewish freedom fighters were in fact a group of detested assassins? "Ah," I thought, "this is a bunch of bull." However, trained as a social scientist, I became very curious as to how Rapoport could possible have made such an obvious mistake. I checked his references and saw that his major source was Josephus Flavius, who is considered to be *the* main historical source concerning the period. It being Friday, a very short workday in Israel, I rushed to the library just before it was to close for the weekend. I managed to grab from the shelves the English and Hebrew versions of Josephus Flavius. I returned to my office already formulating in my head the letter I would have to write Rapoport, protesting his mistake. Because Hebrew University was shutting down at around noon, I went home with the two versions of Josephus. I spent that weekend frantically reading the relevant parts from both versions. To make a long story and a painful weekend short, let me state that on Saturday night I *knew* that Rapoport was right and I was wrong.

Emotionally, this was not an easy conclusion to reach. To put it mildly, I felt cheated and manipulated. I tried to reconstruct in my own mind how, during my formative years, going through the Israeli socialization process, I acquired "knowledge" about Masada that was not only wrong but also very biased. And, mind you, Masada is not just a story. Masada provided, certainly for my generation of Jewish Israelis, an important ingredient in the very definition of our Jewish and Israeli identity. Now, what was I supposed to do when it turned out that such a major element of my identity was based on falsehood, on a deviant belief?

THE PROFESSIONAL ANGLE

Once the anger and resentment of having been manipulated subsided, I did the obvious thing for a social scientist to do: I decided to research the Masada mythical narrative. My motivation for this inquiry most certainly had a very strong professional element in it, but it also had a very strong personal element. First, studying the Masada mythical narrative could easily give us a clue as to how a myth (which could be conceptualized as a deviant belief system) is created, why it is created, by whom, under what circumstances, how it is diffused into the population, how the

Masada, looking southeast. Clearly visible are the three levels of the northern palace with the storehouses on top. The spur on which the Roman siege ramp was built is to the right. Below the northern palace one can see the entrances to the caves and water cisterns.

suspension of natural disbelief in such a fantastic story is created, how it is maintained, etc. Second, my own personal reaction really puzzled me. Why was I so angry? As we shall see in later chapters, I observed this type of anger again and again when I confronted fellow Israelis with the real Masada narrative (that of Josephus Flavius). This anger has an important lesson hidden in it. The angry response indicates, of course, that some raw and very sensitive nerve is stimulated by the confrontation of Jewish Israelis with the conflict between the Masada mythical narrative and the original, nonmythical narrative. The emotion of anger, provides a good indication of a strong socialization of an attitude toward a symbol. Thus, this particular emotion is seen here not only as a propelling motivation but also as an important indicator for social relations.

I have been interested in the ways in which deviant belief systems are formulated and in their operation (e.g., the European witch hunts and deviant sciences and scientists [1985]; politics and deviance [1990]; political assassinations and their justifications [1993]; and moral panics [Goode and Ben-Yehuda 1994]). Moreover, as my professional interests crystallized, I found myself being more and more involved in natural histories and much more so in the theoretical perspective of constructionism. The Masada mythical narrative is a superb illustration of a process of social constructionism; hence, delving into Masada using a natural-history perspective looked like a natural extension of my work up to that point.

Thus I began a long and fantastic voyage into the past, a study in the "archaeology of knowledge," to use Foucault's terminology. The length of the process was due to many factors. At one point, the research was put on hold for a considerable period of time after a very powerful and painful 1987 interview with Shmaria Guttman, one of the men who created the myth.

This research showed me, again, that the main intellectual, cultural, and political debate in Israel is not so much about the country's future or present but rather about the interpretation and social construction of what is considered to be its past and the impact of particular constructions on the present and future. During my quest, I also discovered a few fascinating facts, among them that protests against turning Masada into a myth had been made, sometimes very loudly, to no avail. Also, I could observe how Masada was turning from a symbol for a central national ideology into a tourist attraction that uses the myth for some very down-to-earth economic purposes. And yet this transformation of Masada clearly indicates a major change in Israeli society, a change we shall discuss in chapter 11.

MYTH

So far, I have used the word *myth* in a rather open-ended fashion. Let me therefore clarify a few preliminary issues about the concept. I will return to the concept in much greater depth in chapter 13, where I will analyze the data gathered for this research in the context of the concept of "myth." Moreover, it is important to emphasize that the words *Masada myth* are very common in the way many Israelis now refer to Masada.

Mythologies are "entities" we are all supposedly familiar with. But are we really? What exactly *is* a mythology? What is a myth? Beyond the numerous and varied definitions of *myth* or *mythology* (and we will get into this too in chapter 13), myths share one common characteristic. It seems that the invocation of the word *myth* implies something that is not quite true, something whose relation to facts or to an objective reality is problematic at best. Thus, there is an implication of a lie or perhaps even of a manipulation in the use of the term. A mythical account implies some sort of a deviation from what most of us will accept as "truth."

And yet, the use of myths creates another reality: a reality in which that myth may be taken as a guiding light for daily conduct—a self-fulfilling prophecy, if you like.

All cultures have myths. Moreover, these myths have played a crucial role in some fundamental processes of nation building and in some powerful symbolic realms for a variety of cultures. Although myths deviate from reality, such deviation can be thought of as positive. Hence, examining the role of myths in cultural processes is a rewarding challenge for sociologists and anthropologists alike.

JOSEPHUS FLAVIUS AND THE MASADA MYTHICAL NARRATIVE

What *is* the Masada mythical narrative? We shall delve into the myth and the reality in detail in the rest of the book, but it is important to show here, even briefly, the essence of the myth-reality contrast so that we have a good grasp of what it is. The exclusive basis for determining whether the Masada mythical narrative is indeed a myth is the comparison of what we think we know with the only known history, written by Josephus Flavius. Without Josephus there is not much we know about Masada.

Josephus Flavius

Although I shall discuss Josephus at length in the next chapter, what he tells us, in a very brief form, is as follows.

During the days of the Second Jewish Temple, the Jews revolted against the Roman conquest of Israel. The initiative of a small number of people, the Jewish revolt against the Roman empire was doomed to fail. What has become known as the Great Revolt was in fact a majestic military and political failure by the Jews, culminating in disaster and the destruction of the second Temple. Masada was the last remnant of that doomed revolt.

At the time of the revolt, several ideological-political groups existed among the Jews. Two of these groups were the Zealots and the Sicarii. The Sicarii's distinct feature was their use of political assassinations against both Romans and Jews. The Sicarii were disliked and were driven out of Jerusalem not by Romans but by other Jews a long time before the Roman army put the city under siege and destroyed it. The Sicarii fled to Masada. Thus, the group on top of Masada was a group of assassins, not Zealots. During their stay on Masada, the Sicarii raided nearby (Jewish) villages, killed the inhabitants, and took their food to Masada. They were responsible for a terrible massacre of presumably innocent women and children at Ein Gedi. Jerusalem was destroyed in 70 A.D., but the siege on Masada in 73 A.D. only lasted four to eight months. Thus, there was no active battle for three years. In fact, according to Josephus Flavius there were *no* battles around Masada, except the siege and the day before the collective suicide. Thus, despite the typical depiction of a furious, pitched battle, there is no evidence that any battle was fought between the Jews and the Romans during the short siege. Indeed, there are indications that the Sicarii were none too eager to fight the Romans. Clearly, the Sicarii on Masada were not convinced that they should kill themselves, and a major persuasive effort had to be invested to make them kill one another—and murder the noncombatant children and women who were on Masada—in preference to being captured. Moreover, not all of the 967 Sicarii on Masada died; 7 survived.

It is not too difficult to see that Josephus's original narrative does not convey heroism. Rather, it is obvious that the Masada mythical narrative, a clear heroic myth, was a construction. The heroism in the Masada myth had to be created. It is simply not justified by Josephus.

The Masada Mythical Narrative

The full meaning and magnitude of the myth will be presented in part three of this book, following the examination of the details of its different manifestations in part two. This order of presentation is designed to achieve a better understanding and appreciation of the myth. However, while it is somewhat premature to present the myth at this stage, it will not be beneficial to continue with the presentation without discussing, even if only briefly, the myth so that we know what it is that we discuss. Most modern Israelis would describe Masada as a fortress on a remote mountain near the Dead Sea. They would then state that at this site, a small group of Jewish warriors (or freedom fighters or, more typically, "Zealots") fought to the bitter end against overwhelming odds and a *much* larger Roman army. When these "Zealots" realized that there was no hope, they committed collective suicide so as not to lose their freedom to the Romans. Once I hear this stereotypical narrative I tend to ask a few more specific questions. First, I ask if there was anything particularly distinguishing about this group of Jews. Most often the answer is no. Second, I ask how many people committed suicide on top of Masada. The numbers given have a wide range, but the typical answer places the number of these "Jewish warriors" at around 250–350 people. Third, I ask specifically about the context. Most respondents maintain that there was some sort of revolt against the Romans and that those "Jewish warriors" escaped from Jerusalem after it was conquered and burnt by the Romans. Requesting more details about the nature of the revolt or its dates usually yields nothing. Likewise, most respondents either have no knowledge of the length of the Roman siege on Masada or assume it lasted a long time. Most respondents I talked to had visited Masada. Hence, respondents generally do not know whether there was anything special about these Jewish warriors, from where they came (some would, however, claim that these warriors were the survivors of the Roman siege and destruction of Jerusalem), how long the Roman siege on Masada lasted, how the warriors on Masada survived (in terms of, say, food), or how the decision to commit suicide was made. Typical are the following descriptions.

The first is taken from a person who has become identified with Masada in the most intimate way: Yigael Yadin. At the time a prominent archaeologist at Hebrew University, Yadin headed an eleven-month archaeological expedition during two seasons of excavations in Masada, from October 1963 to May 1964 and from November 1964 to April 1965. Yadin wrote one of the most influential books about Masada (1966), and here is what he has to say about the Masada story (pp. 11–13):

> The rock of Masada, at the eastern edge of the Judean desert with a sheer drop of more than 1,300 feet to the western shore of the Dead Sea, is a place of gaunt and majestic beauty. It is also the site of one of the most dramatic episodes in Jewish history. In the 1st century AD Palestine was under the occupation of the Romans, who had overthrown the Jewish Maccabean kingdom in the middle of the previous century. Periodic rebellion by the inhabitants, who sought to

regain their freedom and sovereignty, had been quickly crushed. But in the year 66 AD the Jewish revolt flared up into a full-scale country-wide war, which raged with fierce bitterness for four years, the Romans having to bring in legion after legion in reinforcements to suppress the insurgents. In 70 AD the Roman general Titus conquered Jerusalem, sacked the city, destroyed the Temple, and expelled the bulk of the Jewish survivors from the country.

One outpost alone held out till 73 AD—the fortress of Masada. According to the 1st-century historian Josephus Flavius, the first to fortify this natural defensive position was 'Jonathan the High Priest', and there was controversy among scholars as to which Jonathan he had in mind. But there was no controversy at all about the man who turned Masada into the formidable fort it became: King Herod the Great. Between the years 36 and 30 BC, Herod built a casemate wall round the top, defense towers, storehouses, large cisterns filled ingeniously by occasional rain water, barracks, arsenals and palaces. It was these fortifications and buildings which served the last band of Jewish fighters in their struggle against the Romans some seventy-five years after Herod's death.

At the beginning of the 66 AD rebellion, a group of Jewish zealots had destroyed the Roman garrison at Masada and held it throughout the war. They were now—after the fall of Jerusalem—joined by a few surviving patriots from the Jewish capital who had evaded capture and made the long arduous trek across the Judean wilderness, determined to continue their battle for freedom. With Masada as their base for raiding operations, they harried the Romans for two years. In 72 AD, Flavius Silva, the Roman Governor, resolved to crush this outpost of resistance. He marched on Masada with his Tenth Legion, its auxiliary troops and thousands of prisoners of war carrying water, timber and provisions across the stretch of barren plateau. The Jews at the top of the rock, commanded by Elazar Ben Yair, prepared themselves for defense, making use of the natural and man-made fortifications, and rationing their supplies in the storehouses and cisterns.

Silva's men prepared for a long siege. They established camps at the base of the rock, built a circumvallation round the fortress, and on a rocky site near the western approach to Masada they constructed a ramp of beaten earth and large stones. On this they threw up a siege tower and under covering fire from its top they moved a battering ram up the ramp and directed it against the fortress wall. They finally succeeded in making a breach. This was the beginning of the end. That night, at the top of Masada, Elazar Ben Yair reviewed the fateful position. The defensive wall was now consumed by fire. The Romans would overrun them on the morrow. There was no hope of relief, and none of escape. Only two alternatives were open: surrender or death. He resolved 'that a death of glory was preferable to a life of infamy, and that the most magnanimous resolution would be to disdain the idea of surviving the loss of their liberty.' Rather than become slaves to their conquerors, the defenders—960 men, women and children—there-upon ended their lives at their own hands. When the Romans reached the height next morning, they were met with silence. And thus says Josephus at the end of his description:

> And so met [the Romans] with the multitude of the slain, but could take no pleasure in the fact, though it were done to their enemies. Nor could they do other than wonder at the courage of their resolution, and at the immovable contempt of death which so great a number of them had shown, when they went through with such an action as that was.

Yadin's 1966 book (in Hebrew and English) provides a more expanded view of the Masada mythical narrative.

Two other books with a more or less detailed explication of the Masada mythical narrative were also published, in English, by Pearlman (1967, for general audiences) and Yadin and Gottlieb (1969, for young readers). Furthermore, if the reader consults other readily available English sources, such as the *Encyclopaedia Judaica* ("Masada," vol. 11:1078–1092) or the *Encyclopedia of Zionism and Israel* (1971, "Masada", pp. 809–811), that reader will find a nice replication of the Masada mythical narrative there too. An even better illustration of a full and impressive version of the Masada mythical narrative (although less accessible) is Lapide's deceptive article in a 1964 issue of the *Jewish Heritage*. Among other things, Lapide calls the Sicarii "Jewish patriots" and tells the readers that "for years the Romans tried to storm the fortress, and each time they were beaten back" (p. 29). To describe this as "fiction" is a compliment. "Fantasy" would probably be a better term.

The same journal published a longer account about Masada in 1967. This account also reflected the Masada mythical narrative but in a more attenuated form (Harker 1967). In what has become an almost ritualistic fashion, Aberbach (1967) added in that issue a follow-up article about Josephus Flavius.

Another example is provided in a 1985 booklet called *Facts about Israel*, published (in English) by the Israeli Ministry of Foreign Affairs, Information Division. The short paragraph describing Masada appears on page 22 of the pamphlet, following an aerial photo of Masada, in a chapter called "Roots" and thus emphasizes the importance of Masada. This 1985 "official" version is very close to the Masada mythical narrative, much more so than Yadin's carefully worded "description." That an official organ of the state of Israel chooses to mention Masada as a part of the "facts about Israel" is interesting in itself. This is how this official document describes Masada (p. 22):

> Masada (70–73 ce)
> Nearly one thousand Jewish men, women and children who had survived the fall of Jerusalem refused to surrender to Rome. They took over King Herod's fortress on the steep rock-mountain of Masada by the Dead Sea. For three years they managed to hold their own against repeated Roman attempts to dislodge them. When the Romans finally broke through, they found that the Jews had committed suicide so as not to surrender to the enemy.

The interesting thing about the above two illustrations is how they construct and present the Masada mythical narrative—for example, by choosing to ignore selected facts. Among the ignored parts is the nature of the "Jews" on Masada. Yadin refers to them as "Zealots," and the 1985 document neutrally refers to them as "Jews." The word *Sicarii* disappears. The Ein Gedi massacre is gone. The terroristic nature of the Sicarii is gone. Both narratives, with different degrees of deception, manage to hide the fact that the Sicarii arrived at Masada a long time before the siege on Jerusalem was completed, and both convey the impression that the people on top of Masada were the last remnants of the Jerusalem fighters. This pattern is to be repeated again and again, and these passages actually give us the clue to how the myth was created.

It is not too difficult to see that the Masada mythical narrative has a large number of specific manifestations, but most narratives tend to converge around a rather standardized and stereotypical account, which I refer to as the "Masada mythical narrative." In essence it assumes the following form: The leaders of the Great Revolt belonged to a group of Jews referred to as Zealots. The Roman imperial army crushed the revolt and conquered and destroyed Jerusalem together with the Second Temple. The Zealots who survived the siege and destruction of the city escaped to the fortress of Masada, a difficult-to-reach stronghold on top of a mountain near the Dead Sea. The Romans reached Masada too. They surrounded the fortress and put it under siege. After three years of a heroic battle by the few Zealots against the huge Roman army, the Zealots on top of Masada realized that there was no more hope. They faced a grim future: either be killed by the Romans or become slaves. They thus decided to kill themselves, a heroic death, rather than become slaves. When the Roman soldiers entered Masada, they found there only silence and dead bodies.

Masada has thus become a symbol for a heroic "last stand." In the words of the famous Israeli chief-of-staff and politician Moshe Dayan (1983:21):

> Today, we can point only to the fact that Masada has become a
> symbol of heroism and of liberty for the Jewish people to whom it
> says:
> Fight to death rather than surrender;
> Prefer death to bondage and loss of freedom.

The Masada mythical narrative played a crucial role in the crystallization of a new individual and collective identity for generations of Israeli Jews between the early 1940s and the late 1960s.

Clearly, the popular, widespread Masada mythical narrative has some elements of truth in it, but in the main, what most people I asked think they know about Masada is quite different from what Josephus tells us. The popular narrative of Masada, no doubt, constitutes a myth or a deviant belief. This popular narrative takes a very long, complex, and at some points unclear historical sequence and reduces it to a rather simple and straightforward heroic narrative, characterized by few clear themes. This heroic narrative emphasizes that a small group of heroes who survived the battle of Jerusalem chose to continue the fight against the Romans to its bitter end (collective suicide) rather than surrender.

As we can see, the Masada mythical narrative is very different from the only true account we have—that of Josephus Flavius. The myth was created by consistent omissions of major facts and by additions and fabrications of facts that do not exist in Josephus's account. Documenting and analyzing this process of omissions and additions will constitute a major part of this book.

RECENT SOCIAL SCIENCE EXPLANATIONS

There have been a few attempts to develop explanations for the Masada mythical narrative within the social sciences. However, in contrast to the huge amount of literature concerning Masada in other disciplines, the number of explanations that use a discourse close to that employed in the social sciences is not great.

One of the first scholars that took a very sharp position on the Masada narrative was Bernard Lewis (1975). Lewis unquestionably belongs to the social constructionist perspective in collective memory. He maintains that the Masada modern narrative is a case of what he calls "invented history."

Shargel (1979) has presented us with what is probably the first elaborate attempt to understand Masada in a social science discourse. Shargel states that the Masada mythical narrative is a political myth, based on a specific historical event. She then uses a functional analysis, based on Durkheim's and Malinowski's works, to argue that the Masada myth played a crucial role in Israeli society, mostly that of social legitimation and integration. In essence, Shargel's functional interpretation seems to have stood the test of time well. That the Masada mythical narrative was used to create cohesion and social integration, or, in Becker's (1986) terminology, to make people "do things together," is more obvious today than ever before.

Yael Zerubavel's dissertation (1980) compared two heroic Israeli narratives: those of Masada and Tel Hai. Although not strictly a social science discourse, this is most certainly a very impressive work. It involves a comparative analysis of myths of heroism in Jewish Israeli society: how they emerged, how they were dealt with, and their meaning, all from a perspective of folklore studies.

Bruner and Gorfain (1984) make an argument similar to Shargel's. They state that the Masada narrative helped to foster integration, encapsulate ideology, and create social order. Their interest, however, lies in Dialogic Narrative theory, and, hence, they apply a comparative perspective to question the credibility of Josephus Flavius (pp. 64–65).[1]

Schwartz, Zerubavel, and Barnett (1986) examine how the Masada narrative was revived after years of "forgetting," from a perspective of collective memory. The paper gives a tremendous weight in this process to Lamdan's poem (very much in the spirit of Lewis's 1975:8 argument).

Dan Bitan, a graduate student at Hebrew University, has been studying for years now the various heroic myths, including Masada, that were developed in the Yishuv (Jewish community in Palestine) and in Jewish Israeli society, mostly by members of the secular Zionist movement. Bitan's work places the Zionist quest for symbols of heroism within the emerging new nonreligious Jewish identity in the Yishuv and Israel—in his terminology, the new "Zionist mentality."

Positioned between the studies of history and those of memory and from a collective memory perspective, Paine (1991, 1994) continues the argument begun by Bruner and Gorfain (1984). He suggests that there are actually two Masadas: the 73 A.D. Masada and the twentieth-century Masada. He states that the two narratives are quite different.

French historian Pierre Vidal-Naquet has argued—very persuasively— that the Masada mythical narrative, as Israelis and others "know" it, is a fabrication and a myth (1983, 1991). In this sense, Vidal-Naquet shares Lewis's (1975) view, and he clearly belongs to the social constructionist perspective in collective memory. Moreover, Vidal-Naquet questions the credibility of Elazar Ben-Yair's speeches. He implies that there may be a strong element of fabrication there too.[2]

Finally, Anita Shapira's 1992 book is focused on the debates within secular Zionism over the legitimization of the use of force. In this most fascinating book, Shapira discusses Masada in two lengthy sections. In one she describes Masada briefly, within a few youth movements (pp. 426–433). This discussion is part of a larger section about what she calls "Masada—as a heroic myth" (pp. 421–33). One of the main arguments Shapira makes is that, indeed, the invocation and use of the Masada story was intended to legitimize the use of force by secular Zionists.

METHODOLOGY

Choice of a Myth

When looking at the sociology of myths, one can either choose to focus on many myths, perhaps using that magical (and mythical) phrase "cross-cultural comparison," or delve in depth into one particular myth in one specific culture. The latter approach seems to be the more powerful. Furthermore, it may be better to focus on a central myth than on some esoteric one. In this way, our understanding of how a myth is created, as well as of the role of myths in societies, will be magnified.

This study indeed focuses on one central myth in one culture: the Jewish culture that developed up to 1948 in Palestine and was continued after 1948 in the state of Israel. The Masada mythical narrative is not confined to Jewish Israel; it has diffused into most of the literate middle-upper class of the Western world (and not only there).

Documenting the Myth

How do we know what *is* the Masada mythical narrative? One needs to ask at least two questions here. The first is "What *is* the 'story' most Israelis know about Masada?" and the second question is "How do we know what they know?" Answering these two questions is not a simple matter.

The most obvious way to find the answer to both questions is to ask Israelis what they know and how they know it. In the prevailing methodological wisdom, one has to take a so-called representative sample of the population and ask some questions. This method looks suspiciously like a "survey," and most Israeli bureaucrats who occupy positions of power in various research institutes (at least those I know) tend not to approve of what they view as "surveys." However, a much more serious problem is that even if such a survey would have been approved, it would have given us good information only about the time in which the survey was conducted. Even if we were to try to bypass this problem by using methods that could give us meaningful longitudinal information, (e.g., cross-sectional methods), we would still be left with problematic information. Moreover, a very large part of the critical population (or a representative sample of them) for this study who lived in the 1920s, the 1930s, and the early 1940s cannot—for all practical purposes—be surveyed any longer. So using what might look like a "survey" was an idea I discarded very early in the research.

Curiosity does not die easily, however, so, knowing all the limitations and problems, I did not stop asking people. I attempted to utilize every opportunity in which I had contact with a large group of people, to ask them about what they knew concerning Masada and how. I was fortunate (at least in this respect) to teach the "Introduction to Sociology" courses in the Department of Sociology and Anthropology at the Hebrew University for four years, as well as some very large classes on the sociology of deviance and of drug abuse. All three courses, combined, had an annual attendance of about 550 students a year. I asked the students in those classes, four years in a row, what they knew about Masada. Their "knowledge" was very different from mine. Moreover, I began to take advantage of social gatherings of friends to ask the same questions. In some cases, I even asked these questions of friends in the U.S.A. and Canada, while I was visiting those countries. Thus, in the last four or five years I ended up asking thousands of people about Masada—young and old, well-educated and noneducated, in Israel and abroad. For many, I have become "Mr. Masada." The conclusion I reached from all this questioning was rather clear. The story that was usually given was quite stereotypical. I can only urge you, the reader, to try this instructive exercise too.

Although interesting and fascinating (and yielding some valid and useful results), this method of asking nonrepresentative "samples" is very limited. It is impressionistic, based on anecdotes and on nonrepresentative respondents, and it is biased. In spite of all this, as a starting point for illustrations and as a source of *limited* information, this method was adequate. However, the weaknesses from which this method suffers can drive even a half-decent methodologist into a frenzy. Fortunately, there *is* another way, derivative of contextual constructionism, to approach this problem. It is not problem-free, but it is much better than the approach above.

The key to this alternative approach lies, first, in viewing the Masada mythical narrative as a deviation from Josephus and, second, in the question we ask, preferably along the time continuum: *What* do Israelis know about Masada, and *how* have they acquired this knowledge. These are questions relating to how what looks like a myth developed.

Finding a more appropriate methodology to answer these questions is easier. The way to do it is, first of all, to ask how have Israelis, myself included, and others acquired our "knowledge" about Masada? Masada and the history of the Jewish Great Revolt are part of the history textbooks in Israeli high schools. The Israeli army brings soldiers to visit Masada; Israeli youth movements take youngsters to visit Masada too. Moreover, Masada has been used in the media quite frequently in different periods as a national symbol of heroism and as a symbol for the "last stand." That understood, the next step is rather obvious. It involves listing the agencies and agents of socialization in Israel and checking how they have presented Masada. It made sense to begin our search with a time period coinciding with what is considered the renewal of modern Jewish life in the land. That period began in the last three decades of the nineteenth century and lasted until what is usually called by historians the first wave of Jewish immigration to Palestine, or "the first Aliya" (1882–1903). In this way we do indeed have a long time perspective, as well as a realistic hope of answering both questions: what and how.

Thus, the appropriate methodology in this case lies not in taking surveys but in looking historically at how the social construction of the Masada mythical narrative took place and where, area by area.

To document the myth historically, I mapped all the possible routes leading to any socialization attempts concerning Masada. I interpreted the word *socialization* in the broadest possible way to include all forms of information. What I ended up with was an in-depth examination of a number of areas. This strategy is reflected in part two of the book, in a discussion of how and when the myth was created by Shmaria Guttman (Yigael Yadin's excavations of Masada are described in chapter 3). Then I discuss how Masada was presented in youth movements, pre-state underground groups, the Israeli army, textbooks for schools, the media and tourism, and the arts. For example, we checked textbooks from the beginning of the century through 1991, when the research effort ended. Thus, we were able to create a very thorough, reliable, and cinematic picture of the myth. We analyzed texts (e.g., textbooks or the printed media coverage of Masada) whenever we could get them, and we conducted open interviews when there were not enough texts or when the texts were not explicit (e.g., in the arts or in the Israeli army). More than once both methods were used (e.g., when focusing on youth movements). Interviews were very easy to obtain; not one of the people we asked for an interview refused.

In this way we had a real longitudinal look at how Masada was represented during about half a century. This examination was done very meticulously, as we shall see, and constantly compared the myth to Josephus Flavius's original narrative.

Because the playing with words and expressions, as well as the sequencing of the events, were major ingredients in the construction of the myth, in the presentation in the book I tried to use as many quotes as I felt justified in using so that the direct experience and fascinating flavor of the myth and its environment would be retained (particularly in chapter 7). Unfortunately, most of those expressions are in Hebrew. I hope that my translations kept that flavor. In the quotes, all bracketed inserts are mine.

Another method I used consisted of driving to Masada, joining different tour groups, and listening to how the tour guides were explaining Masada to the tourists on the site. Typically, I asked the tour guide if it was OK for me to stand on the side and listen, promising that only passive listening was involved. I was never refused. Whenever it was possible I tried to talk to the guides. As we shall see in the chapter on tourism, the way many of these guides gave their tourists the Masada mythical narrative was fascinating, but more fascinating was how they undid the suicide.

Results

The end result of using the above methodologies was twofold. First, we had a very clear answer as to *what* the mythical narrative about Masada was (and to what extent exactly it deviated from Josephus Flavius's original account). Second, we had a very clear answer as to *how* that mythical narrative was created, in maximum detail. These two research achievements, to the best of my knowledge, have not yet been attained in any other research concerning similar topics. Thus, when collection of the data was completed, the riddle presented earlier was solved.

CONCEPTUALIZING THE ANALYTICAL FRAMEWORK

Solving the puzzle of the Masada mythical narrative requires a sound analytical framework. Although the in-depth analytical discussion is located in part three, the infrastructure of the theoretical orientation must be laid out and conceptualized here so that the rest of the book will be understood and interpreted from this conceptualization.

This theoretical framework is divided into two broad categories. The first is the general theoretical conceptualization from which this book was written. This category is based on contextual constructionism and a natural history approach. The second category is divided into two questions. The first is why and how we interpret the creation of the Masada mythical narrative. The answer will be based primarily on concepts developed in the area of collective memory. The second question is how exactly the Masada mythical narrative was created. The answer here will be based on Allport and Postman's (1945, 1947) model of leveling, sharpening, and assimilation.

General Theoretical Framing

In recent years, a theoretical distinction has developed within different areas of sociological research, including the sociology of social problems and of deviance, between the so-called "objective" and "constructionist" views.[3] The "objective" view is a variant of the positivist approach, quite close actually to functionalism. It assumes that "deviance" (or, more generally, "social issues and problems") constitutes an "objective" and measurable reality and, particularly, that it consists of objective conditions and harm. The "constructionist" (also referred to as "subjective" or "relativist") approach maintains that deviance does not present the characteristics of a so-called objective reality and that it is the result of collective social definitions of what some organized members of a culture view as problematic, harmful, or dangerous conditions. That is, the nature of what is and what is not, defined as reality (in this case, deviance, or social issues or problems), is not a result of some objective conditions but is rather a social construction of different cultures. As Goode puts it: "To the subjectivist, a given condition need not even exist in the objective sense to be defined as a social problem" (1989:328).

This controversy, of course, goes deeper than this debate. The argument here is really about what we view as the nature of reality. That is, is there a real, objective reality "out there" (à la Plato's famous cave), or is it that all we have are only images and all we do is relate to these evasive, changing, and elusive images? This problem is particularly acute for construction theory. As we shall see below, modern construction theory offers a solution for this problem.

Both Best (1989) and Goode (1989) point out that there are two variants of the constructionist perspective. First, there is strict constructionism (e.g., see Best 1993); second, there is contextual constructionism. As Goode (1989:328–329) notes, the first variant argues that the expert, or scientific, evaluation of deviance as such simply represents one "claim-making" activity out of many such activities. This view argues that scientific claims are also socially constructed, as are other claims, and can be studied as such. The second variant argues that while deviance and social problems are the results of "claim-making" activities, the so-called "objective" dimension can be assessed and evaluated by an expert, on the basis of some scientific evidence. Sociologists working from this theoretical perspective typically contrast the "objective" and the "constructed" versions of reality. Contextual constructionism offers a solution for the problem focusing on the nature of reality. It sets the defining parameters of reality and hence provides the researcher with a powerful analytical docking anchor.

The theoretical view taken in this book is that of contextual constructionism. I shall use Josephus, like works on moral panics (e.g., see Ben-Yehuda 1986; Goode 1989; Goode and Ben-Yehuda 1994), as that "objective" narrative. For my purposes, Josephus Flavius's credibility and reliability are a side issue.[4] I take Josephus Flavius as my departure point and compare the Masada mythical narrative to his version of the events. There can hardly be a question that, as compared to Josephus's account, the Masada mythical narrative constitutes a major deviation. The myth is based on omissions of some major facts and on the fabrication of others. We shall watch, in detail, how, why, where and when the deviations from Josephus Flavius were made. This strategy was totally dictated by contextual constructionism.

In fact, the very structure of this book is based and reflects contextual constructionism. The first part charts the factual basis, and the second part details the social construction of the facts. The contrast between the two is discussed fully in the third part of the book.

The other analytical and methodological emphasis I shall use is that which has become known as "natural history." On the one hand, this approach is close to what David Matza described as an "appreciational" position (1969). This position calls for a sensitive stance on the part of the researcher. It means being faithful to the natural process and events as they happened, to the different values and positions of the different actors, including the moral entrepreneurs. We need not agree with what we observe, but we must try to recreate (and reconstruct) the social world as those participating in it experienced it, in the natural sequence of events. Although the perspective of contextual constructionism limits the use of "appreciation," it nevertheless enables utilization of the approach. On the other hand, "natural history" means that we have to examine a social phenomenon from its birth through its peak flourishing phase to its demise. Obviously, this can be done only if the developmental sequence of that social phenomenon is indeed coherent with this pattern. This emphasis is in total agreement with contextual constructionism.

Since the Masada mythical narrative is based not only on a text but also on visitation of the site, we shall examine that aspect too: who visited Masada, when, why, how.

The Role of Collective Memory

Without a doubt, the most relevant theoretical framework within which this study has to be conceptualized lies squarely within the major theoretical concerns of the study of *collective memory*. Two approaches have developed in this area. One approach is rooted in social constructionism. It states that the past is socially constructed in the present so as to fit the needs of the present. In this approach, collective memory is an invention of the present, and there is a marked and strong *discontinuity* between the past and the present. This approach challenges the assertion that there is an "objective" past. The second approach is opposed to the first. It states that there is a *continuation* between the past and the present and that the past shapes our understanding of the present. This approach accepts the existence of an "objective" past.

For a long time these two approaches challenged one another, with a clear advantage to the first. Barry Schwartz, in his 1991 work, reviewed these two approaches and suggested that they "can be seen as special cases of a broader generalization that relates both change and continuity in the perception of the past to immediate human experience" (p. 234). That is, he claimed that these approaches are not contradictory and that one may integrate them both into a coherent interpretation that emphasizes both continuity and discontinuity. It is my intention to test Barry Schwartz's integrative hypothesis, directly, explicitly, and meticulously, in this study. As we shall see in chapter 13, the hypothesis was fully confirmed. In this way, this study helps to solve a major theoretical issue in the area of collective memory by confirming Schwartz's hypothesis.

The Masada mythical narrative influenced millions of Israelis, including major figures in the Israeli political and military elites, to develop a sense of new identity both individual and national. Furthermore, it helped them to develop a strong and mystical connection with what these Israelis thought were Jewish heroic warriors almost two thousand years ago. It thus gave these new Israelis a sense of continuity with the distant past and with acts of supreme heroism. It gave them a powerful and awesome example to identify with. Moreover, in the face of some Palestinian and Islamic militants' claim that the Jews do not belong in the Middle East, that they are a foreign imposition, the identification with Masada affirms the Jewish claim for legitimacy to this land. Thus, it is not just heroism in the face of possible extermination or wretched slavery by the enemies of the Jews; also, this is an important historical event that places Jews in the Middle East nearly two thousand years ago, in the heroic role of fearless and fierce warriors for their homeland. As we shall see shortly, during the early 1940s, this process of identity building was most crucial. It continued to be important until the late 1960s and then declined.

Moral Entrepreneurship and Identity

The perspective of collective memory helps us understand the nature of the development and acceptance of the Masada mythical narrative. Using and enriching this theoretical perspective will be supplemented by an analytical discussion in two other areas: one, the moral entrepreneurship that served as the base for the invention of the Masada mythical narrative, and two, the development of particular personal and national identities as a consequence of accepting the meanings of the Masada mythical narrative.

Methodological Framing

As I indicated above, much of this research was devoted to comparing the way Masada is presented in different contexts to what Josephus Flavius tells us. An easy analogy would be a photocopying or recording process. Each copy is compared to the original on some major points. In each comparison we can determine how faithful the copy is to the original. The research question here is what theoretical framework to use to explain how the Masada mythical narrative was actually created—not why but how.

A few studies in the social sciences have tried to answer similar questions: for example, Berkowitz's (1971) work, which examined how accurately different textbooks reported about one particular experiment. The findings were that the accuracy was not very good. Berkowitz's study used for its interpretation of the data one classical study in the social sciences, that of Allport and Postman (1945, 1947) concerning rumors. Allport and Postman, in the basic research design, showed one person a slide or a picture and asked that person to tell another person what the picture was about. The second person was not exposed to the original information but was asked to pass on the description to a third person, and so on. Transmitting information in this fashion was conceptualized to imitate a process of rumors.

Like Berkowitz, I found the work by Allport and Postman very relevant. The important aspects concern the model they suggested to explain the way the information was transmitted from one person to another.

Basically, they found out that complex and long messages were reduced to simple and short messages and that the content of the messages changed. They identified three basic processes working in the process of transmitting the information: leveling (the significant reduction in the amount of information and its simplification), sharpening (as the message became shorter and simpler, its contents became sharper), and assimilation. This process includes a number of subprocesses, all dealing with the way information was subtracted and added to the original message to make the message coherent and make it conform to a theme.

As we shall see in part three, chapter 12, the model developed by Allport and Postman and the concepts of leveling, sharpening, and assimilation are to become central to my explanation of the processes that were used to actually *create* the Masada mythical narrative. These concepts will provide us with a powerful analytical tool with which we can understand *how* the myth was created.

INNOVATIONS OF THIS RESEARCH

It is quite obvious that the amount of academic, popular, and journalistic work concerning Masada, in relation to Josephus Flavius and otherwise, is huge. It is also clear that many people have become convinced that a Masada mythical narrative was created. Indeed, Shavit's (1992) observation that "more texts were written in the last decade criticizing the 'Masada Syndrome' than heroic texts" is probably true. That the Masada narrative as most of us "know" it (and as most of Zerubavel's [1980] interviewees probably "knew" it) is deceitful and cleverly fabricated so as to transform a sad and tragic historical narrative into a heroic tale is also not a new "discovery."

The new perspectives of the present research, not found in other studies, are both theoretical and empirical. This study takes a major controversy in the sociological study of collective memory and uses the Masada mythical narrative to show how, in fact, this controversy can be resolved. The solution suggested here supports, in the strongest way, Barry Schwartz's proposal to integrate the "continuous" and "discontinuous" perspectives into one unified interpretation. Moreover, the theoretical perspective proposed here has expanded the analytical framework of collective memory into a discussion about time and history. This perspective suggests that the controversy in the sociological study of collective memory was created because of the way in which we conceptualize the "past." The whole work is based on contextual constructionism and presented in a "natural history" style of research.

On the empirical side, this work will analyze, in detail, how the Masada mythical narrative was actually created. This will be accomplished by measuring, area by area, the deviations from the original narrative as provided by Josephus Flavius. Such a painstaking and meticulous examination has never been carried out before. This methodology places the Masada mythical narrative under a very powerful magnifying glass. Thus, we will be able to establish, in detail and with great accuracy, which elements from Josephus's original narrative were retained, which were discarded, and which were added, and we will be able to determine when and how the myth was created and culturally transmitted. This also means that we can identify those responsible for creating the mythical narrative, as well as their motives for doing so. The powerful empirical analysis presented here simply does not exist elsewhere. It was exactly this detailed analysis that enabled us to determine that Schwartz's analytical suggestion was the best way to solve the theoretical contradiction in the sociological study of collective memory.

The social construction of the Masada myth has not only been interpreted as a written narrative. Alter's (1973) warning that one needs to be careful in relying on a written historical narrative as a base for myth creation is only partially valid. The construction of the Masada mythical narrative involved a very strong and powerful *social* element and was not only literary. This social element was the ritualistic experiential trek and climb to Masada itself. Both elements—the literary fictional fabrication, which was added to a few true historical ingredients, and the social ritual of the pilgrimage to Masada—combined to create the Masada mythical narrative.

To the best of my knowledge, both the type of empirical methodology and the specific theoretical approach used here have never been used before in this way in the literature concerning Masada, Josephus Flavius, or the 66–73 A.D. Great Revolt.

Looking at the Masada myth from a sociological point of view, it is important to answer these questions:
1. What exactly *is* the Masada myth?
2. How and why was this myth created? How was it diffused? How did it decline?
3. What was the impact of the myth?

In what follows, I shall provide the sociological "story" of the Masada mythical narrative, as I have discovered it. I invite you, the reader, to join me in this fascinating, sometimes painful and aggravating story.

In the first part of the book, we delve into the historical "story" of Masada. Regardless of myth, fabrications, and manipulations, what do we *really* know? Following that, a few words must be said about the source of our knowledge about Masada, that is, Josephus Flavius. In this part we shall basically learn the Masada narrative as Josephus Flavius presented it.

The second part charts the myth. Here we shall acquaint ourselves with how the myth was created and how it has been presented and diffused into society. This part is the contrast to part one: the original narrative (part one) vs. the mythical narrative (part two). The myth would be presented in this part area by area in which the myth exists.

In the third and last part of the book I shall discuss the findings of this study in light of the analytical framework. The major thrust of the interpretation will be the social construction of the Masada mythical narrative as a problem in the field of collective memory. However, the discussion will also focus on a few other relevant issues: the nature of time and of the past, mythmaking, moral entrepreneurship, and identity. The analysis will emphasize a natural history approach, as well as contextual constructionism.

Finally, let me point out that a longitudinal look at the Masada mythical narrative in a natural history perspective provides us with a fascinating opportunity of looking at part of the history of Israel, as well as its ethos as a state, from a unique and very revealing point of view. Looking at the Masada story from 66 A.D. until 1993 gives a powerfully enchanting and awesome view indeed.

Chapter Two

The Historical Events
of Masada

IN THE YEARS 66–73 A.D., the so-called Great Revolt of Jews against the Roman Empire, whose army occupied Judea at the time, took place.[1] The Romans responded with full force—they burnt Jerusalem to the ground, destroyed the second temple (70 A.D.), and reconquered the land with brutality. The Great Revolt became one of the most traumatic events in the collective memory of the Jewish people. It was a period of brave and proud men and women who stood up for their national and religious rights and tried to free themselves from foreign rule. But the result of their revolt was failure, and the heroic effort ended in the disastrous large-scale bloodshed of the Jews at the hands of the Roman imperial army. The Masada myth (Shargel 1979) and the enigma of the Sicarii are direct remnants of that period. No understanding of modern Israel can be achieved without understanding this sad, heroic period.

A major source for this period is Josephus Flavius. However, Josephus has become a controversial figure, and his writings are not free from bias and are considered problematic by many—albeit less so today than a few years ago.

JOSEPHUS FLAVIUS

The amount of work concerning Josephus can easily fill a decent-sized bookshelf.[2] For two thousand years his enigmatic figure and monumental works have glared at and challenged us.

Joseph Ben-Matityahu, later known as Josephus Flavius, was born in Jerusalem in 37 A.D., to a priestly family. He was not an enthusiastic supporter of the Great Revolt. However, when the Great Revolt began, he became the commander of the Galilee and was charged with the important responsibility of defending it. In 67 A.D. the major fortress in the Galilee, Jotapata (Yodfat), fell. The last few survivors, including Josephus, decided to commit suicide. Josephus managed to trick the others, and he and another person remained as the last ones alive. At that point, Josephus persuaded the other man that they should both surrender to the Romans, which indeed was what they did. Josephus was apparently a skillful man, and he struck up a relationship with the commander of the Roman forces, Vespasian. Josephus supposedly told him, among other things, that he would become emperor. Vespasian indeed later became the Roman emperor. Regardless of how accurate this story is, it is clear that Josephus went to Rome, where he became a Roman citizen and an official historian. He married four times and probably died sometime after 100 A.D. (see, e.g., note 2 and Feldman 1984, 1986; Hades-Lebel 1993; Simchoni 1968).

His history of the Jewish war lies at the center of this work. One must remember that Josephus was a problematic figure, and his history was probably influenced by a complicated set of interests. For many Jews, he was regarded as a traitor, and for this he was hated. As a historian for the Romans, he had to write a history that would satisfy his masters. As a Jew, he had his own identity and need to justify his acts. Hence, it is not difficult to see that nothing is simple with Josephus's narratives.

According to Y. N. Simchoni, the first translator of Josephus into modern Hebrew (the original modern Hebrew translation was published in 1923), the *Wars of the Jews* was written not before 75 A.D. and not later than 79 A.D. That is five to nine years after the completion of the Roman military campaign against the Jewish Great Revolt (1923:11). It seems that most researchers agree that Josephus was not physically present during the Roman siege of Masada and that his narrative is thus based on secondary processing of primary sources. Josephus most probably used the reports (*commentarii*) and/or diaries written by the military Roman officers who had taken part in the Masada siege. As Gill (1993) points out, Josephus Flavius's reliance on these sources may have caused him to be innocently misled by the Romans in his description of Masada (or to be deliberately deceptive). Nevertheless, Josephus Flavius also adds explicitly that one of the two women survivors from the Masada collective suicide gave the Roman soldiers the details about the fateful last night of the Sicarii on Masada. I will say more about this later in the chapter.

It must be emphasized, however, that virtually all of what we know about the period and the relevant events surrounding it is based on Josephus Flavius's writings (see e.g., Ladouceur 1987). He is, fortunately or unfortunately, the main—and in most respects the only—source. If Josephus had not written a history, there would "be" no Masada, Sicarii, revolt, etc. In Aberbach's words, "Without him, the history of the last two centuries of the Second Commonwealth could be reduced to a few pages—and a good part of that would be legendary" (1985:25). Yadin, who headed the most intensive archaeological excavations of Masada in the 1960s, states dryly that "the only source for the history of Masada is the writings of Josephus Ben-Matityahu" (1970:374). Indeed, the interpretation of the archaeological findings in Masada "makes sense" only if one knows Josephus Flavius's account (see Ladouceur 1987). These findings do give support to some of Josephus's statements (e.g., a Roman siege on and break into Masada, the architectonic findings) but not to all of them (e.g., the mass suicide [the riddle of the "missing" 960 skeletons was not yet solved], the burning of Masada). In this regard we are "lucky," in the sense that we have only one major blueprint for the events in question. That makes life for this researcher very easy. After all, it is very easy to find any deviation from that one source.

Therefore, it must be reiterated that the accuracy or validity of Josephus's writings is *not* being judged, tested, or challenged in this work. I take the narrative of Josephus *as is*. The analytical puzzle of this work is not whether Josephus's narrative is accurate or not (or to what degree)[3] but how some modern Israeli interpreters (and some non-Israelis) changed and molded Josephus's original narrative; were these changes systematic, and if so, why? This strategy is very much like checking how faithful copies are to the original. Hence, the many arguments about the validity and accuracy of Josephus's narrative are simply irrelevant to this work. In this respect, I find Erelli's 1983 account very relevant: "Either we disqualify Josephus's testimony altogether, regardless of whether or not it suits our national needs, or we accept it as it is" (p. 185. See also Feldman's review on Josephus's reliability as a source for Masada 1984:772–789).

In what follows I shall try to describe Masada and the Sicarii, mostly according to Josephus.[4] I trust that my description is faithful to that source. In my own narrative, I tried, as much as I possibly could, to avoid relying on any interpreters other than Josephus.

Two points require emphasis at this stage. First, the events and processes I describe took place almost 1,900 years ago; hence, not all the details are completely clear.[5] Second, some points are unclear in Josephus too. In those few cases in which I was not quite sure about the narrative, I tried to check with later interpreters of Josephus. Whenever

An aerial view of the western palace, before reconstruction, looking south. Remnants of the casemate wall can be seen to the right (west) of the palace. On the left bottom corner of the picture, the remnants of the Byzantine church are visible. This palace is very close to where the Roman breach to Masada took place; its lower right (west to north) edge "touches" the end of the natural spur on which the Roman legion built its siege ramp. The western palace is the largest structure on Masada. The fact that Josephus Flavius does not mention this palace is a strange omission—an indication, perhaps, that he never was on Masada, or that part of his manuscript is missing (note 3, chapter 2).

30

One of the rooms in the western palace, displaying a beautiful mosaic.

I used interpretations, a full reference is given and explained. However, I did make an effort to use these later interpretations mostly for clarifying what appear to be facts and not for reaching my own conclusions or interpretations.

Furthermore, different interpretations of Josephus's writings obviously exist, and the question of which is the better one can easily keep a lifetime career flourishing (see, e.g., Feldman 1984, 1986). As we shall see later, the question of the different interpretations is of crucial theoretical and empirical importance. It was the systematic and deliberate choice of one interpretation over others that helped the Masada myth come into existence.

THE SITE

Before delving into the Masada narrative, let me provide, very briefly, some basic geographical and ecological information about Masada itself.

Masada is a mountain fortress nearly one hundred kilometers southeast of Jerusalem, about a ninety-minute drive from the capital. This rocky mountain is located about two kilometers from the west shore of the Dead Sea and about seventeen kilometers south of Ein Gedi, in one of the world's hottest places (daily temperatures between the months of May and October range typically between thirty-three and forty degrees centigrade). The height of the mountain is about 320 meters from top to bottom. On its top there is a diamond-shaped flat plateau. Its long axis is about 645 meters, and its widest axis is about 315 meters (Livne 1986).

The mountain itself is very steep and is accessible by foot either by climbing the eastern "snake path" (the preferable way) or by means of the spur on which the Roman siege ramp was built from the west side. There is also a Swiss-built modern cable car that makes reaching the top of Masada from the east side very easy.

The name of the mountain and fortress in Hebrew is *Metzada*. The word *metzada* is a derivative of *metzad* or *metzuda,* literally meaning a fort, fortress, or stronghold. The translation of *Metzada* to Greek is Masada (Simchoni 1923:513). The Greek translation was retained in English, and so *Metzada* has become popularly known as Masada. Throughout the text I tried to remain faithful to the Greek translation, because that is how non-Hebrew-speaking people know the name.

Josephus describes Masada and tells us that "upon this top of the hill Jonathan the high priest first of all built a fortress and called it Masada; after which the rebuilding of this place employed the care of King Herod to a great degree."[6] While researchers are not sure who exactly this Jonathan was,[7] the identity of Herod is beyond doubt. It is obvious from the majesty of the structures on Masada that they were designed and built by Herod's engineers and builders. Being where it is and what it is, Masada could have been used for a number of purposes: as a refuge from enemies (and Herod had quite a few of those), as a place to host preferred guests, as a prison, or as a place to hide precious treasures or friends. Josephus himself states that Masada was built "by our ancient kings, both as a repository for their effects in the hazards of war, and for the preservation of their bodies at the same time."[8]

Caldarium, the hot room, part of the Herodian bathhouse, looking west. This is one of the more impressive buildings on top of Masada. As Ehud Netzer points out, its construction is better than average for Masada. The short pillars carried a floor (a remnant of which can be seen on the lower left side), under which heat was flowing. The arched doorway is part of the original structure and led from the Tepidarium (warm room) into the Caldarium. The picture was taken before reconstruction, and provides an additional manifestation of the lavishness of Herod's construction, so evident in the northern palace as well.

> Herod prepared this fortress on his own account, as a refuge against
> two kinds of danger; the one for fear of the multitude of the Jews,
> lest they should depose him and restore their former kings to the
> government; the other danger was greater and more terrible, which
> arose from Cleopatra, Queen of Egypt, who did not conceal her
> intentions, but spoke often to Anthony, and desired him to cut off
> Herod, and entreated him to bestow the kingdom of Judea upon her.[9]

The remnants of Herod's massive and awesome buildings are very easily visible to anyone visiting Masada today. As we shall see shortly, Masada was conquered by the Roman tenth legion in 73 (or 74) A.D. A great amount of destruction was caused then both by the Jewish rebels on top of Masada and by the Romans.

Masada, contrary to what many may think, was not an unknown place or a "lost site." Following the Roman conquest of the fortress, a Roman unit was left there. It is not known until when exactly the Roman soldiers kept their presence there. During the Byzantine period (fifth and sixth centuries A.D.), some monks settled in Masada. Masada appears in sixteenth-century maps of the area, and during the nineteenth century it was mentioned and identified correctly by quite a few tourists and researchers. Many of these researchers and tourists left, in their reports, paintings of the site, as well as detailed descriptions and diaries of their visit.[10]

Many young Jewish groups (particularly soldiers) used to trek during the whole night through the small but dangerous Judean desert and climb Masada just before sunrise.

Standing on top of this big, barren, dry, yellowish plateau and looking at this harsh moonlike landscape at a very early hour of the morning, tired and with a cold desert breeze striking one's face in the heavy silence of the desert, gives one a very eerie feeling. There almost seems to be a sort of mystical presence on the top of the mountain.

The very effort involved in getting to the top of the mountain and the extraordinary site and atmosphere combine to create a very suggestive, almost hypnotic state of mind. The experience of being on Masada in itself can be a very powerful and persuasive one. It is hardly, if at all, matched by any other site in Palestine before 1948 or in Israel after 1948. The dreary and shocking narrative of the Jewish Great Revolt and the tragic end of the Sicarii are somehow in full harmony with the harsh, dry, desolate terrain and the remote mountain with the doomed fortress on its top. Thus, it is not difficult at all to realize how the environment of Masada supports the horrendous historical narrative of a doomed and bloody revolt. Moreover, it appears that the ecology and geography of Masada have not changed significantly since the days of the Great Revolt. Hence, the sites and landscape seen today are probably, more or less, the very same sites and landscape seen by the Sicarii and Romans too.[11] Travelers to Masada are told about this amazing fact, and the impact of this knowledge obviously adds to the credibility of the narrative.

This atmosphere is very conducive to the suspension of disbelief. I know because, like hundreds of thousands of Israelis, I was there, more than once, in carefully orchestrated dramatic ceremonies. Thus, the combination of a concocted heroic myth and an environment that very easily lends itself to support the drama was simply unbeatable. Socialization agents of the emerging and crystallizing Jewish state and society in Palestine and Israel did not fail to notice that.

THE NARRATIVE

The Masada narrative is not a discrete, unrelated event. It must be understood within the relevant context; otherwise it has no meaning.

The Masada narrative is interwoven with the story of the Jewish Great Revolt and much more with the more specific story of the Sicarii.

One may begin by dating the Great Revolt to the year 6 A.D., when the Romans wanted to carry out a census in the province. One of the main objectors to the census was Yehuda from Gamla (also identified as Yehuda from the Galilee), who, with Zadok Haprushi, kindled the fire of resistance. They developed and spread what Josephus called the "fourth philosophy". The first three philosophies were those espoused by the Essenes, the Sadducees, and the Pharisees. The fourth philosophy emphasized the value of freedom, and its adherents felt allegiance only to God. It seems reasonable to assume that Yehuda was killed by the Romans, but the "fourth philosophy" apparently did not die with him and continued to spread in the land. It probably became the ideology of the Sicarii and was identified with the aspiration to be free of and totally resistant to the rule of the Roman Emperor (see Feldman's review 1984:655–67).

We first find the name Sicarii mentioned by Josephus in connection with events that took place between 52–62 A.D. The name *Sicarii* derives from the word *sica,* meaning a small dagger, which the Sicarii supposedly carried beneath their robes and which they used to knife and assassinate those whom they viewed as their opponents in Jerusalem, especially during the holidays. One of their very first victims was Yonatan Ben-Hanan, the former high priest. Thus, while the Sicarii were involved in quite a few indiscriminate terror activities, they did not shy away from committing acts of discriminate political assassinations. The Sicarii also took hostages, whom they exchanged for their own people who had been caught by the Romans.

In 66 A.D. the Sicarii, headed by Menachem (or Manahem in the English transliteration), captured Masada.[12] Taking some armaments from Masada, they went to Jerusalem, where they helped conquer the upper city. They set fire to the house of Hanania, the high priest, and burned the central archives where the legal, business, and financial documents and notes were kept. Hanania and his brother Hizkiahu were killed, as were a host of Roman soldiers who surrendered. These acts not only signified the beginning of the Great Revolt but also helped to divide the Jews into "zealots" and "moderates". It appears that the "fourth philosophy" adopted by the Sicarii was also accompanied by what we might call today "socialistic ideas."

Menachem, who was the leader of the Sicarii in Jerusalem, was killed by members of Elazar Ben-Hanania's group, who killed other Sicarii as well. The rest of the Sicarii, headed by Elazar Ben-Yair (a relative of Menachem), fled to Masada, where they remained. Josephus states that Ben-Yair "acted the part of a tyrant at Masada afterward."[13]

The Sicarii in Masada, according to Josephus, attacked the settlement of Ein Gedi (at the foot of the mountains nearby Masada), chased the men out, and killed the women and children—about seven hundred people in all and possibly more. In addition, Josephus mentions that the Sicarii also robbed and destroyed other nearby villages.[14]

According to Josephus, after the fall of Jerusalem, Lucilius Bassus was sent as legate into Judea and continued to suppress the remains of the Jewish Great Revolt. He first took the fortress Herodium and continued to put a siege on Macherus.[15] Josephus reports a real siege and fierce battles around Macherus till that fortress too surrendered. Following that military success, Bassus marched to the forest of Jarden, where refugees from Jerusalem and Macherus were hiding. In the battle that ensued, all Jews in the Jarden forest were killed. At an unknown date, after the taking of Herodium and Macherus, Lucilius Bassus died (possibly at the end of 72 A.D. See Simchoni 1923:512), and Flavius Silva succeeded him as procurator of Judea. Realizing that only one last fortress, Masada, remained with Jewish rebels from the Great Revolt, Flavius Silva decided to finish that last remnant too.[16] It is thus very clear that the siege on Masada was not laid immediately after the fall of Jerusalem in the summer of 70 A.D.

In any event, the tenth Roman legion, now receiving its orders from Flavius Silva, was on the march again, this time against the rebels, the Sicarii, of Masada.

It is important to emphasize that while Josephus Flavius may be vague sometimes about the types of people in particular places, when he describes the siege on Masada, his use of the word *Sicarii* is very consistent in his book.[17] For example: "There was a fortress of very great strength not far from Jerusalem, which had been built by our ancient kings. . . . It is called Masada. Those that were called *Sicarii* had taken possession of it formerly."[18]

According to Josephus, the Roman army built a circumvallation wall around Masada so that none of the besieged could escape. A series of military camps for the soldiers was also built around the mountain. Having completed these, Flavius Silva ordered his tenth legion to build a siege ramp up to Masada on the western side of the mountain. The remnants of the wall, the camps, and the ramp are easily visible today. In Gill's recent geological work (1993), he argues that the Roman artificial siege ramp was actually built on a natural spur. If so, the Roman effort in building the ramp was not very impressive. When the ramp was completed, the Roman soldiers effectively used their battering rams, which were put on the ramp, to hit the wall of Masada and destroy part of it. Thus, the wall of the fortress was breached. At that point, the Sicarii in Masada hastily built another wall, this time a soft wall made from wood and earth filling. This wall could absorb the ramming energy of the machines without yielding. However, the Roman soldiers set fire to the second wall and destroyed it too. Clearly, this signaled the end for the Sicarii in Masada.[19] Their choices were clear. They could try to escape, fight to the inevitable end, surrender, or commit collective suicide. The first choice, at this stage, may have been really hopeless. Surrender meant slavery for the women and children and painful, humiliating, shameful, and strange deaths for the men. Although there were on top of Masada 967 people (only 7 of whom survived), a safe guess is that only a few hundred were actually capable of fighting, the rest being women and children and others who apparently could not fight. Elazar Ben-Yair selected the last option, a choice that was not easy. He had to make two fiery speeches to persuade the reluctant people to agree to be killed or to kill themselves. The two speeches succeeded, and the Sicarii killed one another and themselves.

The account provided by Josephus does not mention the role of the women and children in the decision to die. Were the women consulted? What about the children? Even the hesitations after Elazar Ben-Yair's first speech are attributed to the "soldiers." It thus seems safe to assume that the decisions were probably made by men from the dominant social category on Masada (the Sicarii) and that the men killed everyone, including the women and children. The Sicarii on Masada left no choice for anyone who may have been reluctant. The seven survivors had to hide themselves.

Only two women and five children who were in hiding survived the massacre:

> Yet, was there an ancient woman, and another who was of kin to Elazar, and superior to most women in prudence and learning, with five children, who had concealed themselves in caverns under ground . . . and were hidden there when the rest were intent upon the slaughter of one another. These others were nine hundred and sixty in number.

When the Roman soldiers entered Masada,

> the women heard this noise and came out of their underground
> cavern, and informed the Romans what had been done, as it was
> done; and the second of them clearly described all both what was
> said and what was done, and the manner of it.[20]

The Roman breach of the wall and the collective suicide took place on
the evening and night of the fifteenth of Nisan in 73 A.D.[21] When, on the
next day, the Roman soldiers entered Masada, they were met with utter
silence.

What then are the main elements of the Masada narrative?

1. Masada was part and parcel of a much larger Jewish revolt against
the Roman oppressors. That revolt ended in a disaster and a bitter defeat
for the Jews. Masada was only the final defeat in the much larger suppres-
sion of that revolt.[22]

It is also interesting to note that Josephus Flavius implies very clearly
that only a few minority groups of fanatics drew the Jews into a hopeless
revolt. Many modern researchers (see, e.g., Menachem Stern's works)
tend to reject this claim. They feel that the revolt against the Roman Empire was popular and widespread. Moreover, a sober look at the military
situation at that time leaves one with some gloomy thoughts. The Roman
Empire of the first century A.D. was at its peak of power, extending from
Britain to Mesopotamia and controlling anywhere between twenty-five
and twenty-nine fully armed, well-supplied, battle-ready legions—an awesome military might for those times. At the time of the Great Revolt, the
Roman consular legate (perhaps "high commissioner" in our terminology) in Syria was considered the most important (because of the threat of
a military challenge on the southeastern flank of the Roman Empire). He
had at his disposal four legions (not to mention the three legions that
were stationed in Egypt and those that could be—and were—brought
from other places). The logic of and justification for deciding to challenge
that kind of military might must make an intelligent person think hard.

2. Different ideological groups of Jews existed during the time of the
revolt. Of those, four are singled out as important. It appears that the two
most relevant groups are the Sicarii and, much more so, the Zealots, who
apparently carried the main burden of the revolt. Josephus makes a clear
distinction between these two groups. Throughout Josephus's books, the
connection between the Zealots and the Sicarii is not always entirely
clear, but when Josephus discusses Masada, his use of the word *Sicarii* to

describe the Jewish rebels who were there is quite consistent (see Stern 1973; Feldman 1984:655–67).

3. The Masada fortress was taken over by force probably by the Sicarii (headed by Manahem) in 66 A.D., prior to the beginning of the revolt. In fact, this very act may have symbolized and marked the beginning of the Jewish Great Revolt.[23]

4. The Sicarii in Jerusalem were involved in so much terrorist activity against Jews and others that they were forced to leave the city way before the Roman siege there began. They fled to Masada. There, under the command of Elazar Ben-Yair (a "tyrant" in Josephus' terminology), they remained (possibly with other non-Sicarii who may have joined them) until the bitter end, when most of them agreed to kill one another.

5. While the Sicarii were in Masada, it is clear that they raided nearby villages. One of the worst of these raids was the attack on Ein Gedi. According to Josephus, the Sicarii on Masada attacked Ein Gedi in the following ferocious manner: "They came down by night, without being discovered . . . and overran a small city called Engaddi:—in which expedition they prevented those citizens that could have stopped them, before they could arm themselves and fight them. They also dispersed them, and cast them out of the city. As for such that could not run away, being women and children, they slew of them above seven hundred." Afterwards, the Sicarii raiders carried all the food supplies from Ein Gedi to Masada.[24]

6. There are different versions about how long the siege of Masada lasted. Josephus does not discuss this issue. However, it is very obvious that the siege of Masada did *not* begin immediately after the destruction of Jerusalem. First, Herodium and Macherus were conquered; then Bassus died and was replaced in command by Flavius Silva. Silva had to gather his forces and only then launched the final attack on Masada. All these processes took time. Most researchers seem to accept that the siege and fall of Masada only took a few months, probably from the winter of 72–73 A.D. till the following spring—a matter of four to six (maybe eight) months (see note 21). Moreover, this conclusion is supported by Gill's (1993) recent geological work. It implies that the massive siege ramp on the west side of Masada is based on a huge natural spur. If so, then the Roman army did not have to build the ramp from the bottom of the mountain but only to add the actual ramp on top of that natural spur. This means that constructing the ramp took significantly less effort and time than previously assumed.

7. Whereas in Josephus Flavius's account of the siege of Jerusalem he

describes rather courageous raids made by the Jewish defenders of Jerusalem against the Romans, no such descriptions are available for the siege on Masada. This is a significant omission because after Jerusalem fell, the Roman army went on to conquer three other fortresses. One was Herodium, which fell rather quickly. The other was Macherus, where the Jews put up a courageous fight too, including raids, against the Roman army. Moreover, Josephus had a clear interest in presenting the heroic fight by the Jews to show just how much *more* heroic was the Roman army that conquered them. His failure to mention any active fights or resistance (or raids) by Masada's defenders against the Romans is not insignificant. Thus, while the impression one typically gets is that there was a war around Jerusalem—fights, battles, and struggles—no such impression is projected about the Roman siege of Masada. In other words, there really was no "battle" around Masada.

Furthermore, this most puzzling failure to mention a battle or fights around Masada is supplemented by four additional pieces of information.

First, as mentioned earlier, when Josephus describes the Roman siege and capture of another contemporary formidable fortress, Macherus, we read again of fierce fights and struggles.[25]

Second, Josephus states specifically that although forces headed by Simon the son of Giora joined the "robbers who had seized upon Masada" and both forces "ravaged and destroyed the country . . . about Masada," the people on Masada would not join Simon's forces to do "greater things" because they were used to living in Masada and "were afraid of going far from that which was their hiding place." Simon and his forces were apparently not afraid and continued their fights, to the point when "many . . . were obedient to him as to their king."[26] Eventually, Simon and his forces ended up in the besieged city of Jerusalem, fighting the Romans (as well as other factions of Jews, including the Zealots in the city). Simon was captured by the Romans, brought to Rome, and killed there.[27]

These last two pieces of information strengthen the impression one gets about the lack of a "fighting spirit" among the rebels on Masada. Third, and in a strange way, the suicide narrative to be discussed next may support the above impression, too. Those on top of Masada *could* have killed the nonfighting personnel in the fortress, and then the fighting force *could* have gone out to battle the Romans to the bitter end. However, they did not choose to do so. Instead, they killed each other. It is interesting to note that hundreds of years later, in 953 A.D., Josippon (to be mentioned in a later chapter) indeed changed the Masada narrative in exactly this way. In his imaginary version, the Masada warriors killed the noncombatant personnel and went out to fight the Roman soldiers till the last person was dead. Obviously, this *is* a more "heroic" end than the one provided by Josephus. Indeed, both Zeitlin (1967:262) and Hoenig (1970: 14; 1972:112) point out that the Sicarii did not fight.

We must remind ourselves at this point that there *are* plenty of historical examples of real, remarkable, and heroic "fighting to the last"—for example, Leonidas and his three hundred Spartans at the pass of Thermopylae (480 B.C.); the last stand at the Alamo (1836)[28]; the readiness of the American commander of the 101st Airborne Division in Bastogne to "fight to the end" during the German counterattack in the Ardennes in 1944[29]; the heroic stand of the U. S. Marines on Wake Island in 1941[30]; the Jewish revolt in the Warsaw Ghetto (1943), against all odds; and the death of the Biblical Samson together with his enemies. Thus, even using a strictly Jewish analogy, when the Sicarii were faced with the choice, they picked suicide over the destiny of Samson.

What Josephus has to say about the suicide is that after the Romans entered Masada and discovered the dead bodies, "nor could they [the Romans] do other than wonder at the courage of their [the Sicarii] resolution, and at the immovable contempt of death which so great a number of them had shown, when they went through with such an action as that was."[31] The absolute resolution and courage of the Sicarii and their act of collective suicide in Masada raised, apparently, much respect and wonder among the Romans and in Josephus Flavius. Indeed, it should. But the analytic jump from "respect" to "heroism" is *not made* by Josephus. It was socially constructed. Indeed, on p. 603 Josephus makes this comment about the Sicarii killing one another: "Miserable men indeed they were!"

Finally, the implication from Magness's fascinating 1992 work is that if there were "battles" around Massada, they may have been confined to the last stage of the siege only. Magness refers to "the mystery of the absence of projectile points at Masada remains" (p. 66) and, describing the possible late phase of the siege, states:

> Under covering artillery fire, the Roman forces dragged the battering
> ram up the ramp and broke through the wall that Herod had
> constructed around the top of the mountain. The Roman auxiliary
> archers added covering fire to that of the machines as the forces
> ascended the ramp. The Zealots certainly returned the fire with
> everything at their command, including bows and arrows
> manufactured during the last days of the siege of Masada (1992:67).

Magness's paper leaves the distinct sense that the major weight of the siege and battle on Masada may have been carried out not by the more prestigious units of the Roman tenth legion (the legionaries) but by the much less prestigious auxiliari troops:

> The soft arrowheads from Masada indicate that there was a major contingent of auxiliari troops at Masada and/or that the Zealots had armed themselves in the manner of auxiliaries, with bows and arrows. . . . Strangely, the excavators seem to have found no projectile points of the kind that would have been shot by legionaries from torsion bows . . . [i]n contrast to the situation in Gamla . . . where numerous projectile points were uncovered. (p. 64)

The evidence for heavy fighting around Masada is simply not there. The unpleasant impression that one gets from all this is that the Sicarii on Masada, so adept at raiding nearby villages, were not really good fighters and, in fact, avoided opportunities to fight. They may not have believed the Roman army could reach them, and they may not have fought well during the siege. As it became clear that the end was approaching, they may have hastily put together some defense activities, but that may have been too little and too late. Finally, they did not even "fight to the end" and preferred suicide. If this deduction is valid, then the resulting conclusion is unavoidable, that is, that the history of the Roman siege on Masada does not convey a very heroic picture at all.

8. Josephus specifically states that the people on Masada committed suicide. Moreover, Josephus points out, in particular, that Elazar Ben-Yair had to make two speeches to persuade the people to commit that suicide. He even "quotes" those speeches at length. The implication, obviously, is that the Jewish rebels on Masada were originally quite reluctant to commit themselves to collective suicide.

Moreover, Josephus states that there were close to a thousand Sicarii on top of Masada. These people were not all warriors. There were women and children there and perhaps other noncombatants. How many actual fighters were there is unknown. Although Josephus Flavius does not state the specific size of the tenth Roman legion, which carried out the siege on Masada, it is safe to assume that it was probably composed of a minimum of six thousand soldiers (the estimate found in the literature).[32] These numbers cast the phrase "the few against the many" in a somewhat different light.

9. It is imperative to emphasize that there were seven survivors from the collective suicide. This is an important point because the details about

that last night of the Sicarii on Masada were provided by one of the two women survivors.

Thus, when we look at the main ingredients of Josephus Flavius's narrative about both the Great Revolt and Masada, a portrait of heroism in Masada is simply not provided. On the contrary, the narrative conveys the story of a doomed (and questionable) revolt, of a majestic failure and the destruction of the Second Temple and of Jerusalem, of large-scale massacres of the Jews, of different factions of Jews fighting and killing each other, and of collective suicide (an act not viewed favorably by the Jewish faith) by a group of terrorists and assassins whose "fighting spirit" may have been questionable. Moreover, and specifically for Masada, the implication from Josephus is that not only was the nature of the rebels problematic but their lack of fighting spirit as well. Josephus implies that the tenth Roman legion came in and put a siege around Masada. That siege took a few months only and was not accompanied by any major fighting. When the Romans managed to enter the fortress they found seven survivors and the remains of the Jewish Sicarii (and perhaps some non-Sicarii too) who had committed collective suicide. This act itself, clearly, instilled in both the Roman soldiers and Josephus a respect for those rebels.

From the Roman military perspective, the Masada campaign must have been an insignificant action following a very major war in Judea— sort of mop-up operation, something that the Roman army had to do but that did not involve any special military strategy or effort.[33] Josephus Flavius's narrative raises the immediate question of how such a horrible and questionable story could become such a positive symbol. After all, the heroism in the Masada narrative and in the context is not at all self-evident or understood.

JOSEPHUS'S CREDIBILITY—INTERPRETATIONS

Clearly, Josephus Flavius's account of the Great Revolt does not leave the reader (and certainly not an Israeli Jew) indifferent. The narrative is both awesome and inspiring. However, since Josephus is virtually the *only* detailed source concerning the period, his credibility and the soundness of his version are constantly being challenged. Furthermore, the accounts Josephus Flavius provides are not always complete. Thus, the academic debate concerning the interpretation of his works fills up the bookshelves— and not only in regard to the Masada mythical narrative. What *exactly* happened during the Great Revolt is a riddle waiting to be unraveled. The problem is that without the discovery of new and independent sources concerning the period or the revolutionary development of a time machine, we are totally dependent on Josephus's narrative.

Various scholars, as well as other commentators, have tried over the years to suggest different interpretations of Josephus. In this chapter, I shall briefly mention some of them. Of course, for our purposes, many of these debates are marginal because we are interested in deviances from Josephus that were made to create the Masada mythical narrative. However, some of these professional-academic interpretations do touch on the Masada mythical narrative, and in this particular regard it is worthwhile to acquaint ourselves with a number of these debates.

The Masada affair and Josephus Flavius's writings have inspired many arguments and debates.[34] The riddle in Josephus Flavius's narrative boils down to a simple question: just how credible *is* it? Should we trust him on each and every account? It is almost impossible to answer this question. However, different people have taken the original narrative and examined it very critically.[35]

Popular Knowledge of Josephus

One work I would like to mention in this context is that of Yael Zerubavel (1980). A major theme in Zerubavel's work revolves around the 120 interviews that she conducted in Israel concerning perceptions of Masada and related issues. She maintains that not one of her interviewees had any doubts about the credibility of Josephus Flavius's story and that a "more skeptical attitude towards this source would have undermined the tremendous impact of Masada" (1980:61–62). This is a strange statement indeed. The question that needs answering is, *What* knowledge exactly did these interviewees possess? Was it Josephus's original account or the Masada mythical narrative? Judging from the findings discovered in the present research, my guess is that they knew and did not question the Masada mythical narrative and were not aware of or knowledgeable about the original narrative by Josephus Flavius.

As we have seen, the original narrative by Josephus was twisted quite considerably. A more critical attitude toward Josephus Flavius would probably not have made a difference. It *was*, in fact, a critical view toward Josephus (by Klosner and Guttman, for example) that, indirectly, gave rise to the creation of the Masada mythical narrative. Shmaria Guttman was never too pleased with the issue of suicide and tried to refute it; he was also critical about the massacre at Ein Gedi. Yadin, obviously, was not too thrilled with the Sicarii and, in fact, he preferred to use the name "Zealots." Indeed, it is my suspicion that had the full version of Josephus been provided faithfully, no myth would have been created. The original narrative does not convey a message of unquestionable heroism. Such heroism was *added* to it.

Although Josephus's basic account is of defeat, disaster, and mass suicide, the Masada mythical narrative turned all of that upside down and into a heroic "last stand" and a moral victory. These constructions could result only from a critical reading of Josephus.

Sicarii vs. Zealots

Obviously, the question regarding the *nature* of the rebels on Masada is crucial. Josephus Flavius is quite consistent in describing them as Sicarii, and this is no compliment. The debate over whether these rebels were Sicarii or Zealots dominates a good part of the literature (see, for examples, Lewin's 1976 and Kasher's 1983:299–388 reviews). Regardless of this debate, there is no escaping the fact that in his description of the Masada affair, Josephus Flavius is more consistent than in any other part of his work in identifying the rebels on Masada as Sicarii.

The Suicide

The most salient and problematic issue about the Masada affair seems to be that of the suicide. The suicide issue has created many feelings of uncertainty and discomfort. The reasons are complex. First is the feeling of unease about the act itself. Second is the act's implication of the lack of a fight. Third is the recitation of Elazar Ben-Yair's two speeches. This complex set of reasons raises many questions indeed.

Clearly, the suicide issue has drawn most of the fire. How do we explain this? On the one hand, when taking a look at Jewish history, one can find both justifications for and other cases similar to this one. On the other hand, there are some good reasons to believe that, culturally, it is not exactly "natural" for Jews to commit an act such as this.

To begin with, Judaism, as a religion, does not favor murder or suicide. Murder is strictly forbidden in the Ten Commandments, and although the issue of suicide is not explicitly discussed, according to later Halachic interpretation, it is not a preferred or honorable way of dying. Judaism, in other words, is not a religion that worships death.

There is one case, however, in which suicide may be allowed, and that is within the context of what is referred to as Kiddush Hashem, or, in other words, Judaic martyrdom.[36] Under very specific circumstances, it is acceptable for Jews to die willingly. Such is the case, for example, if the alternative is a religious conversion.

It is claimed that Josephus Flavius cannot be trusted on this point. It is argued that he could not possibly have known the speeches he quotes; that suicide was a Graeco-Roman practice, not a Jewish one; and, finally, that he simply fabricated the suicide story.

Thus, as we shall see later in the chapter about tourism and Masada, there are tour guides who "undo" the suicide by denying that there was any suicide on Masada. In a similar fashion we find Heller (1968:33) referring to the death scene in Masada as a "murder" scene. However, while many argue that the death scene on Massada should be considered an act of Kiddush Hashem, that is, of justified martyrdom, Frimer (1971) points out that many more deny that. Much ink has been spilled on this issue, and still there is no consensus on the matter.

Also raised in the literature repeatedly is the denial that there was a suicide on Masada at all. Authors point out that Josephus Flavius cannot be trusted on this particular point. Thus, Weiss-Rosmarin (1966, 1967), Cohen (1982, 1988), Yadin Roman (1987:72), and others all question the credibility of Josephus Flavius regarding this point and suggest that his account concerning the suicide is at best inaccurate and at worst a fabrication. Alas, what is one to do when Josephus states very explicitly that the rebels on Masada killed one another?

Flusser (1993) is not among those who deny the suicide. In a persuasively argued paper he states that those Jews living at the time of the suicide viewed it as a self-inflicted death sentence, intended to expiate the crimes committed by the Sicarii. Flusser views this position as consistent with other and similar cases, as well as with contemporary ideologies and moral stands.

Fighting in Masada

We have already noted that Josephus Flavius does not mention any battles around Masada or raids by the Sicarii on the Roman army. This is a strange and significant fact indeed. The impression one gets is that the Sicarii were not very belligerent, not interested in actually fighting the Romans. A few scholars have focussed their criticism exactly on this point. These are Zeitlin (1967) and Hoenig (1970, 1972), both of whom point out that, indeed, the Sicarii did not fight. In Israel, both Kedar (1973, 1982) and Rotstein (1973) have joined this view. Zerubavel (1980:118–21) also notes that a minority of her interviewees (20 percent) said that this issue in the Masada narrative was problematic for them.

Additional Criticisms

If much of the criticism so far discussed has been based on a strict reading of Josephus Flavius, other forms of criticism have "invented" new scripts for the Masada story. Obviously, in doing so, these critics need to question the validity and credibility of Josephus's account. In fact, they are basically doing what the mythmakers did—only in the opposite direction. They tend to focus on the few puzzles in Josephus's account. One glaring example is his quote of Elazar Ben-Yair's two speeches. As we have said, Josephus was not present at Masada, and the question of how he knew exactly what Elazar Ben-Yair said remains open.

In any event, there are a number of challenges concerning Josephus Flavius's version. Alter cautions us against taking Josephus Flavius "as is." But it is one thing to be wary and another thing to completely discard Josephus's account and suggest a different narrative.

Weiss-Rosmarin (see her 1966 and 1967 works) *does* offer a different narrative. She accuses Josephus Flavius of mass fabrication. In her lengthy nonacademic papers, which—one must add—are argued very powerfully and persuasively (that is, if one accepts her assumptions), she basically challenges both Josephus Flavius and Yigael Yadin. She states that Josephus himself is guilty of fabrication and Yadin is guilty for believing him. According to Weiss-Rosmarin, no one committed suicide on Masada. She claims that there was a battle at Masada, that the Sicarii did not commit suicide but rather fought, and that some of them even managed to get away. The thesis presented by Weiss-Rosmarin received much criticism and is not usually accepted (see Gordis 1968; Orlan 1969a; Feldman 1973).

It is also interesting to note that it was not only Weiss-Rosmarin, in the *Jewish Spectator,* that was interested at the time in Masada. During 1968–1969 a few papers also appeared in the U.S.A. Jewish weekly *Hadoar* arguing with Zeitlin's interpretations, as well as with other details (e.g., see Gordis 1968; Orlan 1969; Rosenthal 1968a, 1968b).

The suicide issue was raised again, in 1992, by Schwartz and Kaplan. Although quite ignorant of the literature concerning the suicide on Masada, they both argue that Josephus cannot be trusted and that there probably was no suicide at all. Stern (1989), one of the most knowledgeable researchers of the period, discusses both of Elazar Ben-Yair's speeches, as well as the suicide.[37] Although it appears that Stern may have some doubts about the speeches, his position concerning the suicide is not one of disbelief.

In summary, it seems safe to assume that Josephus Flavius was not an eyewitness to the Roman siege of Masada. Although the question regarding his sources of knowledge about what happened on Masada remains open, it also seems safe to assume that whatever his sources were, most of them were probably secondary. Thus, there are a number of inaccuracies in his description (see also note 3). However, as I pointed out earlier, the problem with the Masada mythical narrative was not focused on these inaccuracies as a base for the mythical narrative but, rather, on the social narrative. It was a very particular interpretation of Josephus Flavius's narrative that gave rise to the mythical narrative.

THE GREAT REVOLT IN PERSPECTIVE: THE "ALTERNATIVE"

The Jewish Great Revolt against the Romans raises some interesting and important questions, two of the most interesting being whether or not, in a very long historical perspective, the rebellion was justified and whether there were other alternatives. These are very difficult questions, and, obviously, answers to them tend to be stained with mild to wild speculation.

As a result of what can be seen as Josephus Flavius's betrayal in Yodfat (Jotapata) and his defection to the Romans, he has been viewed by many as one of the worst traitors in Jewish history. What is regarded as his act of betrayal is even more marked because of his high position not only as commander of Yodfat but also as having been in charge of the ineffective defense of the Galilee. But what can one do when this man wrote the only book available about the period? It is a strange situation indeed that so many Jews must form an opinion about the behavior of Jews during those fateful years from information provided by a Jew who is viewed by many as a person who betrayed his own people.

However, Josephus Flavius was not the only one guilty of betrayal. Another rather famous man defected from the Jewish camp to the Romans and is generally not viewed as a traitor. That man was Rabbi Yochanan Ben-Zakai, who, like Josephus Flavius, lived and died during this cataclysmic period for the Jewish people. Ben-Zakai escaped from Jerusalem (probably in 69 A.D., in the middle of Vespasian's spring offensive in the north) and found refuge with the Romans.[38]

Like many other contemporary Jews, Yochanan Ben-Zakai kept a healthy and sober degree of skepticism in the face of increasing levels of military-political activism, zealot fervor, and false messianism. Clearly, he was not a fan of either the Zealots or the Sicarii and questioned the wisdom of challenging the might of the Roman empire. Discussing Yochanan Ben-Zakai not only raises possible alternatives to the Great Revolt but also provides an unavoidable comparison to Josephus Flavius.

Like Josephus Flavius, Ben-Zakai disagreed with many of the stated goals of the Jewish Great Revolt. Being in his sixties when he defected, he apparently found a common language with Vespasian (who was more or less his age), chief commander of the Roman military machine that was crushing the Jewish rebellion (and on his way to becoming the Roman Emperor). Vespasian granted Ben-Zakai his wish to establish a small center, with a few wise Jews, to study and continue developing spiritual Judaism. The place Ben-Zakai was sent to was Yavneh. There he was successful in establishing a renewed branch of spiritual Judaism. As so many point out, despite his defection, Ben-Zakai is definitely *not* considered a traitor. His way led to a renewed type of Jewish life, and his challenge of the decision of the rebels to confront the Roman Empire is frequently presented as an alternative to the rebellion. Apparently, both Ben-Zakai and Josephus Flavius objected to the rebellion against the Romans. Ben-Zakai did not hide his views from the beginning (see Stern 1984:320–45). Whereas Josephus Flavius left Judaism altogether, went to Rome, and adopted a Roman lifestyle, Ben-Zakai remained Jewish to his last day.

Many people take Ben-Zakai as an illustration of what could have been the alternative to a rebellion against the Romans, that is, instead of decimation and destruction on a mass scale, a renewed meaningful Jewish life that enabled Jews to fulfill their religious and cultural aspirations without endangering that which was most cherished by them.[39]

Chapter Three

Excavations of Masada

MASADA IS NOT just a historical event. There is also a story behind the actual identification of the site itself.

PRE-1940 MASADA

As Yadin (1966:231–46; 1970:374–75) and Livne (1986:123–28) point out, the first identifications of the site were already made in 1838 by Robinson and Smith, who had traveled in the area. However, they did not actually climb the mountain. In March 1842 the American missionary S. W. Wolcott and his English painter W. Tipping climbed to Masada (rather easily via the Roman siege ramp). From that time on Masada enjoyed a continuous stream of visitors, who made some significant discoveries about different aspects of the fortress, its water supply system and so forth. It is commonly agreed that the most important study of Masada in that period was made by the German scholar Adolf Schulten, who spent a whole month on Masada in 1932. As Yadin states: "It is his plans that laid the foundation for the future study of the ruins" (1966:243).

With the increased interest in Masada in the 1920s and even more in the late 1930s and early 1940s by Jews from the Yishuv, especially by Shmaria Guttman, an obvious desire to excavate the ruins of Masada began to crystallize. This interest received a boost when, in 1944, Joseph Breslavski published a booklet summarizing the work done by researchers of Masada up to that point in time. This booklet served as a guide for the many travelers to Masada in the decade following its publication (Livne 1986:128).

MASADA AFTER 1940

From the 1940s on, most interest in excavating Masada came from Jewish residents of the land. First it was focused in enthusiastic amateurs and

Excavations and reconstruction of storerooms on the top northern section of Masada, looking north.

later on in professional archaeologists. As Yadin (1970:374) points out, the most important contribution in this area was made by Shmaria Guttman. As Guttman relates in the next chapter, during his many different climbs to Masada he made various small discoveries that whetted his appetite for more work. He reported his trips to different archaeologists, trying to get them interested in excavating Masada. Guttman and Azaria Alon checked the water supply system, which was built by King Herod.[1] Ze'ev Meshel and Micha Livne were the first to publish, in 1953, more or less accurate plans of the structures found in the northern slopes and stairs of the mountain, making the correct identification of Herod's palace as described by Josephus Flavius (Yadin 1970:375; Livne 1986:128). A summary of all the known and available research about Masada was published in 1953–1954 (in Hebrew) by the Israeli Society for the Research of Eretz Israel and its Antiquities (Livne 1986:128). The above research efforts, made mostly by enthusiastic and interested individuals, culminated in some major discoveries and in a start to unraveling some of the mystery that shrouded Masada.[2]

These sporadic research efforts also had another very major impact. They created much impetus among professional archaeologists and other formal archaeological institutes in Israel—namely the Israeli Society for the Research of Eretz Israel and its Antiquities, the Hebrew University, and the Israeli government Antiquities Department—to initiate a survey-excavation of Masada. Thus the work done by the first few local Jewish amateurs and professionals served as a catalyst to raise and crystallize interest in Masada as a legitimate site for continued professional archaeological research (Yadin 1970:375; note 2).

As we shall show in the next chapter, Shmaria Guttman was the first "moral entrepreneur" in the transformation of Masada into a national myth. His entrepreneurship began to show fruits already in the 1940s with youth movements and later on with his drive to interest Israeli archaeologists in excavating Masada.

EARLY EXCAVATIONS

The professional archaeological interest in excavating Masada was expressed in two efforts, during two different periods.

The first effort took place in 1955 and 1956. The first archaeological excavation party was headed by Michael Avi-Yonah, Nachman Avigad, Yochanan Aharoni, Immanuel Dunayevski (an architect), Joseph Aviram, and, of course, Shmaria Guttman. All except Guttman were professionals. They worked on Masada for about ten days in March of 1955. The major goals for this expedition were a thorough survey of all the visible remnants on Masada and an actual excavation in the northern Herodian palace. Exactly one year later, in March of 1956, Yochanan Aharoni and Shmaria Guttman returned for an additional period of ten days to continue excavating the palace and carry out a small but important excavation in one of the storage areas. These two early expeditions uncovered some important discoveries and allowed for the accumulation of important field experience.[3]

In the early 1960s Shmaria Guttman made a few more interesting discoveries at Masada. He was involved in the excavation and reconstruction of Roman camp A, and he discovered, with much precision, the location of the "snake path." He also found the "snake path" gate to Masada and excavated and reconstructed it (Guttman 1964).[4] All of these excavations helped to prepare the groundwork for the most intensive archaeological excavations at Masada in the early 1960s, headed by Yigael Yadin.

As Guttman told me, at the beginning Yigael Yadin was not interested in excavating Masada. Yadin thought that Masada was a Herodian fortress where criminals were sent. Guttman was not the sort of person to let

A closer view of the three levels of the majestic northern palace, looking from top down and south. The photo was taken while the excavations were taking place and before reconstruction. The huge supporting walls for the lower level of the palace are seen, as well as the enigmatic circular middle level. On top, the storerooms and large bathhouse are clearly visible.

that just pass. He knew that if he could persuade Yadin to invest an effort in Masada, then some major excavations could be made. At that time, Yadin's power, connections, and prestige were such that he could make the dream of excavating Masada a reality. In fact, Yadin acknowledges Guttman's key role when he writes in his book that Shmaria Guttman "greatly advanced the study of Herod's water system: and finally, it was he who spurred the scientific institutions in Israel to undertake the excavations at Masada" (1966:245). Netzer too notes that Shmaria Guttman was "the first and the head for the research about Masada" (1990:185).

The continued pressure from Shmaria Guttman, as well as what was viewed as the exciting and successful results of the previous expeditions, encouraged Yadin to take the next step, the intensive excavations of Masada in the early 1960s (Netzer 1990:187).

Although Shmaria Guttman's initiative in the 1930s and 1940s achieved spectacular results in creating social commitment to Masada by some very crucial groups and individuals, Yadin's excavations of Masada in the early 1960s had an even more spectacular impact, this time worldwide (see also Feldman 1984:763–65).

YADIN'S EXCAVATIONS

Yigael Yadin (see Silberman 1993) was born on March 21, 1917, in Jerusalem. He was the son of a famous archaeologist, Eliezer L. Sukenik. He joined the Hagana (a pre-1948 Jewish underground group) in 1933 and was given various commanding posts in the organization. In 1947 he was appointed officer of operations and planning. This was an important position in view of the 1948 War of Independence. Following the establishment of the state of Israel in 1948, Yadin was appointed chief of staff of the newly created Israel Army in 1949, a position he held till 1952. From 1952 on, he devoted his professional life to archaeology at Hebrew University. He received his Ph.D. from that university in 1955 for his work on the scroll of the War of the Sons of Light against the Sons of Darkness (one of the Dead Sea scrolls). From 1955 on, Yadin taught at Hebrew University, where he received his professorship in 1963. Prior to 1977 Yadin formed and headed a new political party, Dash (Hamiflaga Ledemocratia Veshinui, "Party for Democracy and Change"), which won an impressive victory in the elections of that year and was able to put a large number of members in the Knesset. Yadin's party joined the coalition government headed by Menachem Begin, and Yadin became the deputy prime minister. However, Dash eventually disintegrated. Yadin died on June 28, 1984.[5]

A close look at the lower level of the northern palace, looking south.

The archaeological excavations of Masada, under the guidance of Professor Yigael Yadin, took place in two periods. The first was between October 1963 and May 1964 and the second between November 1964 till April 1965—all in all, about eleven months of excavations. The excavations constituted a major logistical effort at that time. Thousands of volunteers from Israel and from all over the world came to help in the excavations. The Israeli Army assisted this gigantic effort too by contributing means and volunteers (remember that before his academic career Yadin was chief of staff of the Israeli Army). All sources about the excavations point out that the logistics of the operation were immense indeed, involving, among other things, taking care of food, water, housing, and equipment—all at a time when not even half-decent roads to Masada existed.[6]

Yadin had at his disposal on any given day about two hundred volunteers who were actually involved in the excavations. However, these volunteers kept changing every two weeks or so. This turnover meant that, eventually, thousands of Israelis and non-Israelis alike participated in both the experience of the excavations and the exposure to the "Masada tale" in the most intimate and direct way.[7] Although it is difficult to estimate the economic cost of the excavations, it seems safe to assume that the overall cost, in today's (August 1992) terms, was around two million U.S. dollars. The British newspaper *The Observer* assumed patronage of the excavations. Much of the money needed came from outside Israel, through Yadin's connections and *The Observer*'s support. A few families lent monetary support too: Mrs. Miriam and Mr. Harry Sacher, the late Mrs. Mathilda and Mr. Terence Kennedy, and Mr. Leonard Wolfson and the Wolfson Foundation (Yadin 1966, 1970; Yadin and Gottlieb 1969). The direct monetary support from within Israel was minimal, but different organizations in Israel (e.g., the Israeli Army) contributed either manpower or equipment.

It is interesting to take a look at a contemporary Hebrew-language Israeli newspaper for some information about the excavations. According to *Maariv* (p. 18, May 3, 1964), about two hundred to three hundred volunteers from thirty-three countries (including Israel) worked at Masada. Yadin stated that the excavations cost, in 1964 terms, about six hundred thousand lirot. He estimated the entire cost of the excavations at about two million lirot.

According to Silberman (1989:89): "Due to their efforts and their discoveries, Masada became the most famous project in the history of Israeli archaeology, and—perhaps second only to the clearance of the tomb of Tutankhamen—the most publicized excavation in the twentieth century."

During (and after) the period of the excavations, the burning furnace of the myth received, of course, additional fuel. The topic was discussed intensely on the Israeli radio, in the newspapers (see the chapter about Masada and the media), and among the public. For a whole generation of Israeli Jews the experience of participating in the excavations and of digesting the myth became a fixed and permanent ingredient of their identity as Israelis.

Moreover, because of the large number of volunteers from outside of Israel and the foreign press coverage, the world focused its attention on the excavations as well. The publication of Yadin's book about Masada in 1966 kindled the fire of debate once again as the book created much interest among intellectuals and laypersons alike.

The end result of the work was that "we excavated 97 per cent of the built-on area of Masada" (Yadin 1966:203). Much of the excavated structures and artifacts were reconstructed too. The architectonic findings revealed, again, the majesty and beauty of the Herodian buildings. However, the excavations did not confirm or refute many of the important aspects of Josephus Flavius's narrative, that is, except for the facts that there was a fortress called Masada built by Herod, that the Romans put a siege around it, that they built a siege ramp, and that they were effective in winning. The questions regarding the Sicarii, the suicide, Elazar Ben-Yair's speeches, the massacre at Ein Gedi, and the length of the siege, as well as a few others, still remain unanswered to this day.[8] Most archaeologists I spoke to feel that the reliability of Josephus Flavius's general description was proven good (see, e.g., Netzer 1990:193, 195).

One of the most interesting and curious findings was of some ostraca with inscriptions of names; one had the name Ben-Yair on it. The most seductive interpretation of the ostraca (developed by Yadin—1966:195–97) is that they were the lots used by the Sicarii to help decide who would die first. This interpretation hinges on Flavius's statement that

> they then chose ten men by lot out of them, to slay all the rest; every one of whom laid himself down by his wife and children on the ground, and threw his arms about them, and they offered their necks to the stroke of those who by lot executed that melancholy office; and when these ten had, without fear, slain them all, they made the same rule for casting lots for themselves, that he whose lot it was should first kill the other nine, and after all, should kill himself. Accordingly, all those had courage sufficient to be no way behind one another, in doing or suffering; so, for a conclusion, the nine offered their necks to the executioner, and he who was the last of all, took a view of all the other bodies, lest perchance some or other among so many that were slain should want his assistance to be quite despatched; and when he perceived that they were all slain, he set fire to the palace, and with the great force of his hand ran his sword entirely through himself, and fell down dead near to his own relations.[9]

Another result of the excavations—and this is an interesting question for the sociology of science—was that many of the young archaeologists that worked with Yadin in the excavations of Masada developed future careers in archaeology and related fields. A few even achieved some very prominent positions in their fields. Thus, these excavations (and Yadin's support) may have served as a turning point that enabled a generation of young and new Israeli archaeologists to develop impressive professional careers (see also Livne 1986:130). However, whether this particular hypothesis is valid requires separate research.

Before, during, and after the excavations, Yadin emerged as Mr. Ma-

An ostracon found on top of Masada, magnified
in size. The words "Ben Yair" are clearly visible.
Yadin felt that this ostracon could have been one
of the "lots" that the Sicarii on Masada used to
decide who would kill whom. Ben-Yair, of course,
was the last Sicarii commander of Masada.

sada. We have already read earlier what he had to say about Masada, but
let us examine here another passage, this time in chapter 15 of his 1966
book, where he discusses "the defenders of Masada" (p. 197):

> It is thanks to Ben-Yair and his comrades, to their heroic stand, to their
> choice of death over slavery, and to the burning of their humble chattles
> as a final act of defiance to the enemy, that they elevated Masada to an
> undying symbol of desperate courage, a symbol which has stirred hearts
> throughout the last nineteen centuries. It is this which moved scholars
> and laymen to make the ascent to Masada. It is this which moved the
> modern Hebrew poet [Lamdan] to cry: "Masada shall not fall again!" It
> is this which has drawn the Jewish youth of our generation in their
> thousands to climb to its summit in a solemn pilgrimage. And it is this
> which brings the recruits of the armored units of the Defense Forces of
> modern Israel to swear the oath of allegiance on Masada's heights:
> "Masada shall not fall again!"

However, Yadin systematically ignores Josephus's insistence that the
rebels on Masada were the Sicarii. Yadin uses the term *defenders* but

much more frequently *Zealots*. Likewise, he ignores the massacre at Ein Gedi, the lack of battles and fights, the choice that the Sicarii on Masada had to fight to the end (a choice pointed out in Weiss-Rosmarin's 1967 article as well), and the fact that Massada was virtually repressed by Orthodox Judaism, because of, among other things, the suicide angle (and has definitely not "stirred hearts throughout the last nineteen centuries").

If Shmaria Guttman began the main push for the Masada mythical narrative in the 1940s, Yigael Yadin continued this push in the 1960s. He most certainly used his very high credibility as former chief of staff and professor of archaeology at Hebrew University to bulldoze his overhauled version of Josephus Flavius concerning the events in Masada. Moreover, unlike Guttman, Yadin was a natural media person. His appearances on radio and in the printed media were on a mass scale. He interviewed very well, projecting the image of a very articulate, poised, self-assured, authoritative man. He was exactly the type of person that gave the impression that he "knew what he was talking about." His projection of the overhauled version of Josephus, no doubt, helped "sell" the myth tremendously. Indeed, Silberman points out that "Yadin's genius was his ability to draw people into a web of mythmaking, into a deeply felt communal consciousness" (1993:284). He added that "the drama of the Masada excavations and the virtuoso brilliance with which Yadin conveyed the discoveries to the public made the project as much an exercise in patriotic inspiration as in scientific research" (1993:288).

It is interesting to note that Yadin was originally quite reluctant to get involved in the excavation of Masada (e.g., see Silberman 1993:273–74; interviews with Guttman in 1987 and 1993; interview with Joseph Aviram, December 1993). He was busy in other projects, according to Aviram and Silberman, and did not see the importance of excavating Masada, according to Guttman. The efforts to persuade Yadin were, however, successful, and he did get involved in the project.

Furthermore, it is noteworthy and significant that the name Yadin chose for his book in English, *Masada: Herod's Fortress and the Zealot's Last Stand*, is not identical to the name of the book in Hebrew, "Masada: In Those Days—at This Time." The original Hebrew phrase is *Metzada: Bayamim hahem bazman haze*. The key words are the last four. These words are lifted, verbatim, from the narratives Jews use at Hannukkah to denote the miracle of that holiday. Among other things, it may be taken to imply that the same miracles that happened *then* may happen *now*, again an attempt to bridge, by utilizing this interesting rhetorical device, an abyss of close to two thousand years. I cannot resist

The northern section of the casemate wall, surrounding Masada, looking south. The remnants of the synagogue are visible in the lower half of the picture (square building with elongated stone "stairs" for seating). The two long rooms attached to the synagogue are visible in the lowest part of the picture (north).

Remnants of the southern *mikveh* (ritual bath) with ritual immersion pool, looking east. This *mikveh* is part of the casemate wall. On the right side of the picture, looking down from Masada, one can see the remnants of three Roman army siege camps, surrounded by walls.

the cynical comment that both titles of the book project, vividly, Yadin's bias. The Zealots, at least according to Josephus Flavius, were not on Masada, and I am still puzzled about the Hanukkah-Masada connection, for what was the "miracle" of Masada?

As if to magnify the Masada mythical narrative, Pearlman published in 1967 a book in which the Masada mythical narrative is given a full exposé, with much praise to Yadin.

Indeed, the authors of the first volume of the final report of the Masada excavations state that "perhaps no other archaeological endeavor in Israel has attracted such widespread attention as the excavations of Masada" (Aviram, Foerster, and Netzer 1989a:ix). Moreover, to drive the point even further, the authors of the volume quote Feldman too:

Masada and its surrounding, looking east. On the left side (north) of Masada the three levels of the northern palace are visible. We can see the natural spur on which the Romans built their siege ramp, leading to the top of the doomed fortress, connecting to Masada somewhat lower than the top, near the western palace. On the lower left side (northwest) of the picture the large Roman army siege camp is clearly visible, with a smaller camp within it. Yadin suggested that this might be the camp of the commander of the Roman legion at that time—Flavius Silva. Near it, to the right, is another Roman army siege camp, and yet another one can be seen on the distant, eastern side of Masada.

> No single event in the history of the second Jewish commonwealth has occasioned more discussion in recent years than the fall of Masada, the mausoleum of martyrs, as it has been called. . . . The spectacular discoveries in the excavations of Masada by Yadin in a nation where digging is a veritable form of prayer have made Masada a shrine for the Jewish people.[10]

There was a very significant delay in publishing the final results of the excavations. Although some early reports were made available,[11] the final reports began to come out only after Yadin's untimely death, and they are still being processed in the early 1990s. Between 1989 and 1991 (almost twenty-six years after the excavations), three volumes summarizing parts of the final reports were published.[12]

ARCHAEOLOGY AND HISTORY AS POLITICS

The topic of archaeology in the context of politics, particularly in Israel, came to academic (and nonacademic) attention in recent years. Discussing the excavations of Masada and not commenting on this issue is simply impossible.

Already in 1966 Moses Finley wrote, in his review of Yadin's book, that Masada is a prime example of the politics of modern archaeology. The clear implication that archaeology can be used for political purposes received another boost in the 1980s.

During 1986 an accusation was made that Israeli archaeologists and historians distort facts for political purposes.[13] An echo of this debate could be heard again in both the English language weekly *Newsweek* and the Hebrew language daily *Haaretz* during 1992.

The May 18, 1992, issue of *Newsweek* (p. 38) carried a fascinating article about how history is taught to Israelis. The major criticism was that this teaching is focused on the most negative aspects of that history, with an emphasis on the persecution of Jews, at the expense of periods of Jewish renaissance and an explanation of the true complexity of the history of the Jews. The article implied that Israelis learn a "whining [or kvetching] history." Thus, Moshe Dayan (1983:21) discusses Masada in the context of Jews being massacred and claims that killing Jews from the days of the Great Revolt on was a pattern: "In one country after the another, the Jews have met a similar fate." In fact, Narkis (1983) draws a direct line from Masada to the Holocaust. The "Masada complex" (to be discussed in chapter 13) fits very well into this critique. While Bartal (1992) tried to show that the *Newsweek* article was too simplistic and biased, Raz-Krakotzkin's (1992) critique of the studies of history in Israel supported implicitly the critique voiced in *Newsweek*. Raz-Krakotzkin argued that the study of Jewish history in Israeli schools has been reduced to a study of Zionism, emphasizing national power and aggressiveness as crucial factors.

It is not easy to discuss this very important debate and remain neutral; let me, therefore, say something about the debate. To begin with, I find Bartal's criticism of the article in *Newsweek* justified. However, I find the *Newsweek* article very valid and focused too. Of course, it is virtually impossible to expose all the complexities in a one-page article, but there is no question in my mind that the article touched on a very important problem, and Raz-Krakotzkin's paper obviously supports *Newsweek*'s critique.

One question to which I have no answer is whether it was possible and realistic to expect a state in Israel's circumstances to have a balanced and humane program for studying history. This special circumstance is reflected in the ongoing perception of an immense threat to the very survival of the state and results in the tremendous investment of national resources in security (to the point where some refer to it as a "garrison state"). Can a balanced or objective program for the study of history be put into effect in a state where the specific selection of what is considered the "appropriate history" to learn is dictated by political and national considerations as those are determined by the current minister of education?

The general problem here, I feel, can be divided into two issues. The first is the *reason* for carrying out a study, any study, in sociology, history, archaeology, or another area. Much like Weber, I feel that the reason for curiosity is a secondary issue (albeit important in terms of motivation). That many Jews in Israel are interested in archaeology for what they see as political and national reasons, is, I think, very legitimate. Two essays are relevant and important in this context.

Shavit (1986) points out that the central place archaeology (in the broader sense of the term, including history) occupies in shaping the national modern historical consciousness is undisputable.[14] One can say, tongue in cheek, that to substantiate national claims one had better start digging.[15] Shavit's paper testifies that archaeology was in the midst of various ideological debates (e.g., biblical archaeology). As he points out, recruiting archaeology for the service of Zionism is a later development. The involvement in archaeology had these goals:

1. To confirm the Biblical historical description, particularly from the time of conquering the land by the Israeli ancient tribes.
2. To prove the continuity of the Jewish settlement in Eretz Israel, as well as its size.
3. To emphasize the attitude of the Jewish settlers to the land, as distinguished from the attitude of the non-Jewish settlers.
4. To emphasize the "down-to-earth" side of the Jewish life in Eretz Israel.
5. To give the new Jewish presence [in the land] a new and deep structural historical meaning.
6. To provide the new Jewish presence concrete symbols from the past, [symbols] that can be transformed into symbols of historical legitimization and presence (1986:54).

As Shavit points out, most of the deep and intense public excitement was created by archaeology that focused its efforts precisely on the period of the Second Temple (and not, for example, biblical archaeology). It was this period that could—and did—provide the symbols that the moral entrepreneurs for the newly emerging national Zionist Jewish identity needed the most (Shavit 1986:54). Masada was certainly a major ingredient in this process.

Geva (1992, 1994) focuses on Biblical archaeology in Israel. Geva knows Yadin's work in Hatzor well, and her paper very strongly supports the claim that biblical archaeology was used by Zionism to help legitimize the establishment of the state of Israel. According to Geva, this use of biblical archaeology helped to transform it from an independent scientific field into an ideology and to degrade its quality. The issue raised here for the sociology of science is truly fascinating.

However, the reasons for the interest in archaeology do not say much about the quality of that research. Thus, the second issue is whether the reason for doing the research "colors" the data collection, the interpretation based on the data, and so on. If such coloring indeed takes place, then it definitely provides a basis for the accusation implied by Geva's (1992) work.

That the reason for the interest in Masada, beginning with the initiatives of Guttman and continuing with Yadin's work, was ideological-political is clear. Yadin made some unmistakably ideological-political statements before, during, and after the excavations. For example, in an interview he gave to *Bamachane* published March 18, 1969,[16] he stated:

> The public's interest in the antiquities of the land is . . . almost phenomenal. . . . This big interest does not stem from interest in archaeology as such. Everyone feels and knows that he is discovering and excavating findings and artifacts from the days of his fathers. And every finding bears witness to the connection and covenant between the people and the land. From this aspect, the archaeological research added an important national dimension. There is an element of curiosity as far as the unknown is concerned. There is the wish to decipher the past. This is a natural tendency that most certainly helped the revival of interest in archaeology. But as far as Israel is concerned, it seems to me that the factor I mentioned—the search and building of the connection to the people and the land—must be taken into consideration. [Archaeology] in my view reinforces the Hebraic consciousness, let us say—the identification and the connection with ancient Judaism and Jewish consciousness. (23(26)14–15)

What Yadin says is quite explicit. The tremendous interest in Israel in archaeology that he mentions was not confined to Yadin's era as an archaeologist or to the time he was interviewed. As we saw earlier, Shavit (1986) documented that the interest in archaeology could already be witnessed in the 1930s.

It is not too difficult to understand that secular Zionism, dealing with the difficult—really unprecedented—idea of a whole people returning to its homeland after almost two thousand years of living elsewhere, was only too happy to be interested in and support a scientific endeavor that could, potentially, validate and reinforce its moral claim to the land (against increasing Arab resistance, one must add). Moreover, the possibility of discovering ancient Jews that had worked the land, were fierce fighters, and were willing to live and die for the land is a rather healthy antidote for the traditional and stereotypical anti-Semitic view of Jews in Europe as parasitic, lazy, unwilling to "get their hands dirty," and unable to fight, among other things. Because the political and social leadership of the Yishuv (Jewish community in Palestine) and Zionism at that time came from Europe, the temptation of relying on archaeology for these two purposes (connection to the past and countering anti-Semitic images) must have been simply irresistible.

Furthermore, Shapira (1992) pointed out that the use of the Masada mythical narrative also helped to solve a debate within the Yishuv. That debate revolved around the question of legitimizing the use of violence and force by secular Zionists. The Masada mythical narrative was most certainly utilized to give credence to the idea that using force was indeed justifiable (pp. 45, 269, 421–433).

These ideas put some major parts of Israeli archaeology, certainly up to the 1960s, in the context of supporting the process of a new nation building in Israel (more on this in chapter 13). Indeed, in July of 1994 a social organization called the "Council for a Good Eretz Israel" (together with Maariv, El Al [Israeli airlines], and EMI, the association of Israeli performing artists) declared special festivities giving distinctive recognition and appreciation to Israeli archaeologists for their contribution to "expose the secrets of the land, its antiquities and heritage" (Maariv, July 22, 1994, p. 7). Just to have a meaningful comparison, let me point out that no such recognition was ever offered to, say, Israeli physicists, mathematicians, biologists, economists, or sociologists. In fact, if I am not wrong, only Israeli archaeologists have had this honor bestowed on them. Considering the above discussion, this should really come as no surprise.

That Yadin had a real personal and national interest in Masada is obvious. That he helped spread the Masada mythical narrative is obvious too (see also Silberman 1993:270–93 and Benziman 1994). Both he and Guttman *knew*, no doubt, the original narrative yet chose to tailor their version to what they felt were personal and national needs. However, did that basic motivation cause Guttman and/or Yadin to falsify findings of the excavations, or did their view affect the physical results of their excavations? The answer must be no. Yadin was so careful with the findings that the daily meetings of his staff of archaeologists were recorded and later transcribed. That, as Magness (1992) pointed out, was very unusual and helpful. In fact, Yadin and Guttman must have been quite disappointed that the findings did not confirm in an unequivocal way the narrative provided by Josephus Flavius (see, e.g., Ladouceur 1987:109). So again we can see that motivation to conduct a study is separated from the actual scientific findings and that scientific findings can be separated from interpretations of these findings. The warping of the historical narrative for both Guttman and Yadin was not at the level of the excavations or the findings themselves. It was at the level of the *interpretation* (that is, the social construction) of the findings. The process of how exactly that was done certainly provides an interesting future puzzle for a separate study in the sociology of science.

Let me illustrate this point with just one example. As noted earlier, Yadin and the archaeologists excavating Masada held a daily evening meeting at which they discussed the work and findings of the day. On November 26, 1963, the remains of three skeletons were found in the northeastern part of the lower terrace of the northern palace, a place the archaeologists marked as "locus 8." Below is the English translation of the daily protocol of the meeting of the archaeologists discussing the find.

> Dr. Haas: Three skeletons were found in locus 8 . . . one of a woman. . . . This is a woman aged seventeen to eighteen and there is also there a skeleton of a child aged eleven to twelve. . . . The third skeleton . . . is first of all a man, and his age is between twenty and twenty-two, quite young too.
> Yadin: . . . It is obvious that the child and woman cannot be a mother and a son because of the age difference, so if there really was a family here, the man could possibly be the father of the child. . . . In those periods—YA HABIBI!—there is a plus-minus of a year. . . . Here you make it twenty-three and there ten and everything is OK. . . . The man and the woman can certainly be a pair! But the son is not from this woman. . . . Could be her or his brother.

In 1966, Yadin wrote in his book (Hebrew version) that they found

> the remains of three skeletons. One skeleton was that of a man in his
> twenties, who was perhaps one of the commanders of Masada. . . .
> Nearby, on the stairs, the skeletal remains of a young woman were
> discovered. . . . The third skeleton was that of a child. . . . Could it be
> that we had discovered the bones of . . . [the last] fighter [on Masada]
> and of his family? (p. 54)

In the *Encyclopedia Judaica* (1971, vol. 11, p. 1007) Yadin writes about
that find in locus 8: "The skeletons undoubtedly represent the remains of
an important commander of Masada and his family."

But the most intriguing interpretation of the finding in locus 8 was
presented on April 11, 1973. On that date, Yadin made a speech at the
top of Masada to members of two professional associations—the Society
for the Study of Eretz Israel and its Antiquities and the Society for the
Protection of Nature: "I shall mention the remains of the three fighters
that we found in the northern palace: a very important commander, his
wife, and their child, just like in the description of Josephus Flavius"
(Yadin 1973). The gap between the November 26, 1963, factual discussion and the April 11, 1973, interpretation speaks for itself.

Part II

The Masada
Mythical Narrative

Chapter Four

Shmaria Guttman

IN THE NEXT chapter I will discuss how the issue of Masada was dealt with in the various youth movements. However, before doing so, I must delve a bit deeper into the particular contribution of one individual—Shmaria Guttman.[1] As we shall see, two moral entrepreneurs (Becker 1963) had a decisive influence on the development and transmission of the Masada myth—Guttman and Yigael Yadin. Both had their influence in different periods and in different areas. Shmaria's influence on the youth movements was decisive, especially in the formative years of the 1930s. More than anything else, it was his personal motivation, conviction, and zeal that helped the Masada myth into being at that early stage.

Shmaria Guttman[2] was born in 1909 in Glasgow, Scotland, into a Jewish family that had immigrated from Russia. He was one of five brothers and sisters. In 1912 the family immigrated to Palestine and settled in Merchavia (where today the moshav of the same name is located). Shmaria's father was a baker and a member of the group that organized Po'alei Zion, together with David Ben-Gurion, Berl Katznelson, Yitzhak Tabenkin, and others. These figures became the main leaders of the Yishuv. Thus, Shmaria Guttman grew up in an ideological and political ambience that was very sympathetic to socialist ideas and to secular Zionism. He remained in Merchavia till the age of seventeen and was among the activists and organizers of new branches of the Noar Oved (a central socialist youth movement) in the Jezreel Valley. Shmaria's involvement with the Noar Oved was to have a profound influence on the development of the Masada mythical narrative. At seventeen Shmaria went to study in the agricultural school Mikve Israel (near Tel Aviv), where he spent two years before returning to his parents' farm. However, since he was so deeply involved in the Noar Oved, he found himself working as a guide in that movement in different cities in Palestine. From there he arrived to Kibbutz Naan, in 1934, where he was to spend the rest of his life.

Shmaria has told Michael Shashar (1987) that the atmosphere at his home emphasized not only socialist Zionism but also Judaism, as symbolic Jewish traditions (e.g., lighting Sabbath candles) were followed. Among Shmaria's teachers were Breslavi, who wrote some of the most influential popular books and papers about Masada, and Yael Gordon, the daughter of A. D. Gordon, one of the most famous and influential ideologists of the Yishuv.

Naan was the locus of one of the first groups of the Noar Oved. Shmaria's prominent position in that youth movement enabled him to disseminate his ideas, but the questions of what ideas and why still remain.

According to Shmaria, his teachers in school instilled in him a love for the land. In 1933 he went with two friends for a walking trip around the Dead Sea and arrived at Masada. Shmaria mentioned specifically, in my interview with him in January 1987, that he went on that trip with a copy of some summaries of Josephus Flavius's book in his hand. He and his friends were not aware of the "snake path" leading to the top and climbed up another, extremely difficult way. Masada as a site left a tremendous impression on young Shmaria. There can hardly be any question that that trip convinced him that Masada deserved special attention.

Before embarking on the 1933 trip, Shmaria had asked Yitzhak Ben-Tzvi, then the head of the Jewish national committee, for advice and help. Upon returning from the trek, he requested a meeting with Ben-Tzvi to share his experiences. According to Shmaria, Ben-Tzvi said to him: "Tell me, Shmaria, why are you so excited? Nine hundred Jewish robbers ran from Jerusalem to Masada and committed suicide. So what? What is this excitement all about?" (Shashar 1987:24 and my interview). At that time, Shmaria told Ben-Tzvi that he was an emotional young Jew and that Masada as a site was exciting. Shmaria was not deterred by Ben-Tvzi's response and continued to develop his interest in Masada.

Shmaria realized two things at this point. First, he knew from personal experience the tremendous psychological impact of the physical environment of Masada. Second, he had read and knew well the Masada poem that was published in 1927 by Yitzhak Lamdan (to be discussed in a later chapter; see also Schwartz, Zerubavel, and Barnett 1986). That poem was very influential, but Shmaria realized instinctively that the poem itself was not enough. So there he was with the makings of a terrific story of heroism and a powerfully dramatic location.

What Shmaria had in the palm of his hand was a "suasive image" à la

Geertz (1964), that is, an ideological construct that could provide, with the proper social construction, authoritative concepts capable of rendering a situation meaningful. Geertz's "suasive image" concept implies that this aforementioned meaning could be sensibly grasped, in a way that could arouse emotions and direct mass action toward objectives that promised to resolve a mental and cultural strain. The physical site of Masada itself was an ideal means of providing authenticity and authority for this social construction. The two factors—story and environment—had to be combined. Shmaria clearly understood that and acted toward that end. Getting people to trek through the Judean desert, to climb Masada, and to be exposed at the top to a well-orchestrated and stunning ideological narrative was the perfect combination to achieve a most potent and long-lasting effect.

Shmaria's developing interest in Masada reached a successful culmination when he asked and was allowed to organize a seminar for guides from Hanoar Haoved Vehalomed and Mahanot Haolim (two youth movements to be discussed in the next chapter) about Masada, on Masada. This one-week seminar took place in January 1942, and about forty-six guides took part in it. Most of the participants were from Hanoar Haoved Vehalomed, a few were from Mahanot Haolim, and one member was from Hashomer Hatzair (*Bamaale*, February 27, 1942). The most significant fact about this seminar is that these forty-six members were the elite future leadership in the youth movements and, later on, in the state of Israel. For example, Shimon Peres and Meir Amit were participants in this seminar. These guides were exposed for one week to the awe-inspiring environment of Masada, to the myth as it was being developed by Shmaria, and to the integrating force behind it all—the energetic, dramatic, and very self-assured Shmaria Guttman. The seminar took place, it should be mentioned, against the dramatic background of Rommel's Afrika Korps' advances in the western desert. It is difficult to imagine anyone coming away from that seminar indifferent. This kernel of forty-six participants went forward convinced of its validity and of its educational and moral lesson to spread and exploit the Masada narrative as it was provided to them by Shmaria Guttman. Additional seminars followed in later years.

Bamaale of February 27, 1942, reported Shmaria's Masada seminar as follows:

> Before our eyes, the world is on fire. We see nations disintegrate
> when they confront the diabolic Nazi power. And we see a heroic

stand by other nations whose will for freedom and life is strong, that
stand unmoved in the war. . . . The Jewish people is participating in
all the world's battles. . . . We must strengthen ourselves and stand on
guard for our land and freedom with all our might. Toward this role
the Noar Oved is being socialized. For this readiness, we must
intensify and amplify the mental connection with the chain of
Hebraic heroism in the past. Before us we must imagine Masada—
fortress of Israel that stood in the battle for the freedom of the people
and the land against the legions of Rome. . . .

The people who fight today at the front lines and behind the
lines, on every mountain . . . against the cruel invader—the sons of
Soviet Russia, Yugoslavia, etc—rely for their power on the heroes of
their people in the distant and recent past. When the young Hebraic
generation defends its homeland, it will rely on the heroes of its
people, the fighters of Masada and the defenders of Tel Chai. (issue
261, p. 4)

Many years later Shmaria would comment: "Well, is there any need to
state why we came to Masada in the early 1940s? . . . In my Masada seminar . . . I saw an opportunity to prepare the young ones for what might
come. We discussed there, among ourselves, the possibility of standing
against the enemy." (1986:31).

Shmaria Guttman mentions that before conducting the 1942 seminar
he spoke with David Ben-Gurion, who questioned the wisdom of educat-
ing people with a narrative that ends in suicide. Silberman too points out
that originally Ben-Gurion was not an admirer of Masada (1933:272–
73). The answers Shmaria Guttman developed for both Ben-Gurion and
Ben-Tzvi were to become part of his ideology and the Masada mythical
narrative.

A number of factors make up the general background for the development of the myth by Shmaria Guttman: first, his own upbringing, which
was based on socialist Zionism and some traditional Jewish values; second, his personal fascination and infatuation with the physical site of Masada; Third, Josephus Flavius's narrative; fourth, a naturally energetic
and emotional personality that simply required an outlet. Moreover,
Shmaria was in the right social and political position and at the proper
junction in time to make his ideological dream about Masada come true.

In Shmaria's own words:

As an educator I realized that there was an interest in bringing the
story of Masada to the attention of the youth. These were difficult
years (1941–1943). There were fears that Rommel would arrive [to

Palestine] through Egypt. I was in the Hagana and I [knew] what was
planned[3]. . . . I thought, What would the young adolescents do? I
thought that they had to be socialized into being prepared for
anything, [particularly] for freedom and liberty. Then I said, There is
nothing like Masada for this purpose. So I prepared the seminar . . .
so the guides would take the young adolescents there. . . . Since then I
saw myself committed to study the war of the Jews against the
Romans. (Shashar 1987:22)

Shmaria was puzzled by the Roman imperial army's interest in a
remote and desolate fortress that had about 960 "robbers" on its top.
His main conclusion was that they were not really "robbers" but genuine freedom fighters—rebels. According to Shmaria, the Romans perceived the existence of this fortress, with the rebels on top, as a threat to
continued Roman hegemony in the land and to their military victory
(eventually won with great difficulty). Masada could well have served as
the locus for a new revolt against the Romans. Thus, according to
Shmaria Guttman, the military effort of the Roman imperial army
against Masada was unprecedented.

Shmaria says that Josephus Flavius is perceived as a questionable and
enigmatic figure. His point is that this perception of Josephus (mostly as a
traitor) gave birth to some serious doubts concerning the validity of his
account. However, Shmaria is quick to add that without Josephus Flavius, there is not much we know about the Great Revolt and Masada.
Moreover, he also insists that Josephus Flavius is quite reliable and accurate. This last statement will, however, become problematic for him.

It is Shmaria's interpretation that Jewish orthodoxy in the Diaspora
(*gola* in Hebrew) has thrived on the *longings* for the holy land and has
thereby justified the continued exile of the Jewish people. The story of
Masada and the Jewish wars for national independence in Eretz Israel have
been repressed because they implied that instead of being left to the mes-
siah, salvation had to be sought by concrete heroic Jewish efforts to live,
fight, and die for a *real* country, not limited simply to a vision or to mystical
"longings." This alternative, to actually reach the holy land, to fight for it
and perhaps to die for it, was totally repressed in favor of what appeared to
be a safe existence with a fantasy about fulfilling an old dream accompany-
ing it (till the ascendance of national socialism in Europe).

For Shmaria, *knowing* the land and fighting for it were basic elements
of his Zionist consciousness. For him, it was essential to forget the comfortable surrender of Jews outside of Palestine and Israel to the pleasures
of European and American material existence and instead to create a new

type of hard-working and determined Jews. This new Jew *had* to seek personal freedom and national liberty and, above all, to be connected to his or her land, ready to fight for it and—if necessary—to die for it. To construct Masada as a national symbol for this type of socialization seemed to Shmaria Guttman to be the natural thing to do.

Thus, the myth was born. In effect, it was Shmaria Guttman who *created* much of the mythical narrative. How was this done? Simply, by emphasizing some aspects of the original Masada narrative, by repressing others, and by giving the whole new mythical construction an interpretation of heroism. It was Shmaria that helped develop the belief that Jewish fighters, remnants of the Great Revolt, fought the last battle on Masada. In his view, these were proud Zealots who hoped to kindle the fire of resistance once again. The messages of rebellion, a proud stand, and a fight to the end for one's country are the main lessons of Shmaria's interpretation.

Now that we are aware of the birth process of the myth, we should take a look at how Shmaria dealt with some of the more problematic issues involved.

The first issue, concerning the reliability of Josephus Flavius, was quickly solved. Josephus Flavius is the *only* source we have about the period. Thus, whenever his validity and accuracy were placed in doubt, the doubt was dismissed. Shmaria even gave examples. One such example was his reliance on Josephus Flavius for the true location of Gamla. He does state that Josephus Flavius was a complicated figure, but he insists on his reliability.

The second issue concerns the act of suicide itself, as reflected in Ben-Gurion's doubts as to the wisdom of education young people "to suicide." Shmaria's reply was "This is too simplistic. What is it? Did these people look for a nice place to commit suicide? Did they look for a . . . tower to jump from? Was this their goal?" (my interview with Guttman. See also Guttman 1986:10).

By this, Shmaria implies that the decision to commit suicide was not a matter of a preplanned and meditated choice but, rather, a brutal decision dictated by the circumstances. Moreover, Shmaria tended to underplay the suicide:

> At Masada I never read Elazar Ben-Yair's speeches where he called
> his people to commit suicide. That was not the subject I saw as the
> most important one. I faced it, and I would say that this was a heroic
> thing, it was a deed that I could not touch, terrible and
> wonderful. . . . I did not see myself as capable or ready to cope with

that deed . . . but we could use Masada for other purposes.
(Interview)

Furthermore, Shmaria repeatedly points out (my interview with him;
Guttman 1986:10) that suicide is not totally forbidden by Jewish Halacha.
The concept of Kiddush Hashem, he says, did exist in Spain, York, and
other places, where Jews did in fact commit suicide so as either not to
convert or to avoid demeaning and degrading situations as Jews. Masada,
says Shmaria, can be very easily grasped as another example of Kiddush
Hashem:

> I wanted to bring ourselves, the young adolescents, to the point
> where they would have the willingness to fight to the end. Not to die,
> but to fight to the end. We already stood in such difficult moments
> when Rommel was approaching the country, and then we turned
> Masada into a symbol for standing to the end. Not for a search for
> the end. The question is, is fight needed? Is it worth it? Why is fight
> necessary? Maybe it is better to surrender?
>
> Why did the Jews *have* to fight the Nazis? Did they *have* to go to
> the death camps, the gas, and [by doing so] maybe a few could have
> been saved. I did not accept this way. And I understand the people on
> Masada that hoped and *fought*.
>
> At some periods we wanted to turn this into a symbol—not to
> die, not to commit suicide, but to be ready for whatever is required
> for the goal in which you believe—if indeed you believe in a goal. If
> you do not believe in a goal, you have to put your neck forward and
> give it to the yoke. (Guttman 1986:11)

Shmaria also questioned how Josephus Flavius really could have
known the specific contents of Elazar Ben-Yair's two speeches when he
was not actually there. However, in the end he dismisses the significance
of this fact. The important thing was that Ben-Yair was able to persuade
this group of ideologically homogeneous people to commit suicide.

The third issue regards the Sicarii:

> Now, I'll ask you, what are 'Sicarii'? It can be a derogatory name
> Josephus Flavius used to call part of the Zealots and no more. . . . I
> ask myself, "What is a Sicarii?" First of all, there were different types
> of Sicarii. . . . Their common denominator was the war against the
> Roman empire. Of course, different opinions and world views
> characterized the different groups, but the war united them. . . . I do
> not have to accept [the assassinations]. . . . Maybe after the
> destruction, because he [Josephus Flavius] was a pretty sensitive Jew,
> his heart was bitter about what happened, so he felt he had to

attribute responsibility for that to someone. He did not attribute the
responsibility for the destruction to himself, so he attributed it to
others. . . . So, on the one hand, he describes the Sicarii as wonderful
and, on the other hand, he says [negative things]. . . . I cannot draw
conclusions from a man who talks like this. So on this subject I do
not want to be totally committed to the Sicarii type. I am not sure
that Elazar Ben-Yair was a Sicarii. What does he [Josephus Flavius]
write? "Elazar Ben-Yair and the Sicarii that were with him in
Jerusalem",[4] so I can interpret that that was Elazar Ben-Yair but that
those that were on Masada were Sicarii [Shmaria implies here that
perhaps Ben-Yair was not a Sicarii.] There were many types of
people . . . and in this case charlatans, murderers, and robbers join to
do things like this, and the movement is not always responsible for
the acts of this or that individual. We know that in every revolution,
in our generation too, even in a positive revolution, robbers and
murderers join in and use the context [for their own purposes]. So
there is no doubt that at that time it was true too. (my interview with
Guttman).

It is obvious from the confused manner of the above statements that
Shmaria has difficulty in dealing with this issue. What does he actually
imply? That we should not be too impressed with the labels Josephus Flavius uses, that it is more important to look at the unifying factors, that
what the Sicarii really were is not entirely clear. He tends to blur the issue
of the Sicarii and muddle it in such a confusing way that one needs to go
back to read Josephus Flavius just to be sure that in fact the Sicarii *were*
on Masada. "For now it was that the Roman general came, and led his
army against Elazar and those Sicarii who held the fortress Masada together with him" (*Wars of the Jews,* book 7, chapter 7, p. 599).

The fourth issue relates to the massacre at Ein Gedi.

Now let us take Ein Gedi. Since I am a big admirer of Ein Gedi, look,
I am not sure that his [Josephus Flavius'] statement about what
exactly they [the Masada people] did in Ein Gedi is the most
accurate. But what is entirely clear to me is that they came to Ein
Gedi and took food by force; this I am sure about.

So on top of Masada sits a group of people that is isolated from
the world, does not suspect that the war with the Romans is finished,
and believes that there still may be a chance to beat them, the
empire. . . . Such a group sits up there on Masada. They are lucky,
they have water, but additional food is needed too . . . and they come
to Ein Gedi and tell the people there: 'We ask you to give.' And then
they [the people of Ein Gedi] showed them their finger, so they took

it by force. Look, guys, this is not a nice thing to do. But in order to live people do things that are not nice. But the people of Ein Gedi could show more courtesy and give them something of their own. So they took it by force. So he [Josephus Flavius] turns it into 'butchered and burnt,' et cetera. I do not have to take it as an absolute truth [note how suddenly Josephus Flavius's reliability becomes questionable]. And it is possible that they did a few things that . . . were not moral. So I want, on this basis, to build a picture of the people who were in Ein Gedi. Who was there? Who were they? They were land tenants of the Roman regime. In fact, the people of Ein Gedi almost did not have private land. It was the state's property. The state then was the ruling Roman empire. So they [the people of Masada] had the feeling that they were taking something that the Roman empire was robbing from them, and they wanted to take that back. So there was a deed in Ein Gedi. Do we have to build on this act mountains of arguments about types of people? . . . I do not accept this. They had to reach an agreement that they [the people of Ein Gedi] would give something. They did not reach an agreement, so the problem had to be solved. But these people [from Masada] still believed that there was hope. (Interview with Guttman)

This is a fascinating yet rather shocking argument. What does Shmaria say here? First, we do not have to trust Josephus Flavius too much about the Ein Gedi massacre. Second, the people of Ein Gedi almost "deserved" their victimization by "refusing" to provide the Sicarii from Masada with food. But where he gets his information about the Sicarii "request" and the people of Ein Gedi's "refusal" is totally unclear.

Let me quote directly from Josephus Flavius:

There was a fortress . . . called Masada. Those that were called Sicarii had taken possession of it formerly; but at this time they overran the neighboring countries, aiming only to procure to themselves necessaries; for the fear they were then in prevented their future ravages; but when once they were informed that the Roman army lay still, and that the Jews were divided between sedition and tyranny, they boldly undertook greater matters; and at the feast of unleavened bread, which the Jews celebrate in memory of their deliverance from their Egyptian bondage, when they were sent back into the country of their forefathers, they came down by night, without being discovered by those that could have prevented them, and overran a certain small city called Engaddi:—in which expedition they prevented those citizens that could have stopped them, before they could arm themselves and fight them. They also dispersed them, and cast them out of the city. As for such as could not run away, being women and children, they slew of them above seven hundred. Afterward, when they had carried everything out of their houses and had seized upon all the fruits that were in a flourishing condition, they brought them into Masada. And indeed these men laid all the villages that were about the fortress waste, and made the whole country desolate.[5]

Despite these problematic issues, the Masada mythical narrative caught on. The 1942 seminar was followed by others and by continuous treks and climbs to Masada. Those young guides that had attended the 1942 seminar, as well as later "Masada experiencers," acted as powerful agents of socialization. They spread the word about Masada and were very effective in disseminating the powerful Masada mythical narrative into the various social and political movements of the Yishuv and, later on, of the state of Israel.

Shmaria Guttman certainly played an active role in all these developments. He was very accessible and typically willing to participate in the many treks and climbs, as well as to make speeches concerning Masada. Moreover, Shmaria Guttman actively participated in the two major archaeological expeditions to Masada, the first one in the 1950s and the second, much more famous, excavation headed by Yigael Yadin in the early 1960s. Shmaria Guttman made himself available, whenever asked, to help with anything related to Masada, whether it was the Israeli Army (more about this later) or the Israeli Ministry of Education doing the asking.

According to Shmaria, "History should not be studied in order to find analogies for today" (Guttman 1986:6), but he also stated: "It is true that I am influenced by those things that bother me now. I want to draw conclusions from . . . possible mistakes, lest we may be doing the same thing" (my interview with Guttman). This apparent contradiction characterizes his position. Josephus Flavius, he says, is accurate, but when the description Josephus provided does not "fit" a heroic tale, Shmaria becomes argumentative and develops his own interpretation, always careful not to denounce Josephus Flavius completely.

There can hardly be any doubt that Shmaria was searching for a genuine Jewish heroic narrative to use in socializing young adolescents. Masada offered him a golden opportunity. The biggest advantage of the Masada story is the site itself. The narrative was problematic. So it was overhauled and constructed in such a way as to "fit" a heroic narrative. The technique was simple: emphasize and magnify the heroic elements; add if necessary; ignore and discount the more problematic aspects. For example: disguise the Sicarii as "Zealots"; either don't emphasize the suicide or explain it away as a matter of "no choice"; do not mention the Ein Gedi massacre, or else revise its context. This technique was precedent-setting. As we shall see in the next few chapters, the creation of the Masada myth was *based* on its effective manipulation.

Finally, and before concluding this chapter, let me add a few items. My interview with Shmaria Guttman took place in January of 1987. Shmaria was then seventy-eight years old. I found him an energetic, powerful, charismatic, and very persuasive man. Shmaria clearly expressed distaste for the expression "myth" because it implied, in his view, something untrue. He felt that the values presented by the Masada narrative, as he believed in it, were as valid in 1987 as they were in 1942. Shmaria was very well versed in Josephus Flavius. I asked him why he picked Masada. Surely, there must have been other narratives in which the heroic tale was less problematic. Shmaria's response was that the very treks in the desert itself were valuable. On this issue, he and David Ben-Gurion seemed to agree. Power and strength can be generated from experiencing the desert's ancient majesty and unique wilderness; the desert experience can be easily constructed as one of cleansing. The effort of trekking in the desert and making the difficult climb to Masada directly illustrates the meaning of sacrifice.

Shmaria insisted that studying the ecology and geography of the land was not enough. One had to combine archaeology with actual knowledge of the landscapes. He told us in the interview that the first reactions to his efforts regarding Masada, political and social, were negative. Moreover, he pointed out "the lack of knowledge of the land. . . . They did not know where Masada was for years. They did not relate to it. What? It is there, in a far away desert. Yadin did not want to go dig there. Yadin did not think much of it. During one of the conferences Yadin treated . . . [Masada] like some fortress to which Herod sent criminals" (interview).

In any event, Shmaria Guttman knew that in order for Masada to be excavated, Yadin had to be convinced. Yadin had the power, the connections, the means, and the reputation that Shmaria did not have. Persuading Yadin was the key. Shmaria indeed directed a great deal of his time and effort toward this goal. He was eventually successful, and in 1963 Yadin headed the excavations of Masada.

Shmaria states that about four years before Yadin's excavations (around 1959), light diggings were carried out at Masada. The goal of these diggings was to examine the feasibility of a full-scale excavation. Shortly thereafter, Shmaria had a discussion with Nachman Avigad, Yochanan Aharoni, and Avi-Yonah, all famous archaeologists, in Avigad's home. Avraham Shalit, an expert on the Herodian period, was also invited to this gathering. Shmaria talked about his interpretation of the Jewish war against the Romans, elaborating on Masada. Shalit disagreed with him. He felt that Herod built the fortress as refuge for himself in time of need. Shmaria, on the other hand, believed that Masada was one of the most important fortresses in the land at the time, a place that was strategically located so as to enable forces from it to threaten a hostile enemy. So, as one can imagine, the debate became quite heated. Shmaria understood after a while that Shalit simply had never visited Masada. He repeated his explanation and also explained about the specific location of Masada in relation to the other two fortresses (Macherus and Herodium). And in response to the question of how he knew, Shmaria's answer was "You see, I *was* there." In the technical context of the conversation the statement could be taken to mean simply that Shmaria had visited Masada, but the statement had another implicit meaning too. It could also be taken to mean "I was there, in spirit, during the 66–73 A.D. Great Revolt." Shalit, however, was not persuaded.

At my first interview with Shmaria Guttman I was accompanied by my two research assistants at that time: Ms. Vered Vinitzky and Ms. Einat Usant. We all drove to Naan in my old, beat-up VW "bug," looking forward to an interesting interview. What we got instead were about four hours of socialization. Shmaria clearly made an effort to be nice but also spent the entire time trying to persuade us of the validity of his views. He knew very well why we had come since I had explained the purpose of the visit and interview. As we left his home in the early afternoon hours, he put his arm around my shoulder and asked, "You are not going to do bad, Dr. Ben-Yehuda, are you?" "No," I answered, "that is not my intention." As we got into my car, there was silence. We dropped Vered off at the central bus station in Ramla, and Einat and myself continued on to Jerusalem. Along the way, we came to a railroad crossing just as a train was roaring by on the tracks. I stopped the car, and as the roar of the passing train was receding Einat suggested: "Why don't we drop the research?" I told her that I did not think that should be done. However, I returned home in a very thoughtful frame of mind. Whether directly because of the interview or not, I did put the study low on my list of priorities for almost a year and a half. In the end, the study was completed long after both Einat and Vered had left Hebrew University. I think and hope that in publishing this book I am not doing something "bad."

Chapter Five

Masada and Youth Movements

AN INTERESTING AND important question concerns the presentation of Masada in Jewish youth movements. Its significance lies in the crucial role that these movements played in the socialization of young Jewish Israelis into the newly emerging state. Furthermore, many members of the political, social, and intellectual elite of the country participated in the activities of these youth movements. Some of these movements served as socialization institutes abroad, where young Jewish women and men, potential Israelis, were ideologically and practically trained for life in the new country. Their young minds were ripe for the Masada myth, and it helped to prepare them for the ultimate sacrifice, martyrdom and "a fight to the end." Moreover, the Masada myth is based on a very powerful social construction of an ideological connection to and identification with Jewish rebels, across an abyss of nearly two thousand years.[1] This connection is of an ethnic, religious, and national-historical nature. The Masada myth, which enhances this connection, was meant to provide a firm heroic base for a new type of national Jewish identity.

Much general literature has been written about youth movements, and it is impossible, indeed counterproductive, to devote too much space to a survey of all that within the framework of this book. However, a few general statements are required.

Most researchers of youth movements in Israel seem to agree that Jewish youth movements developed by modeling themselves after youth movements in Europe (German scouts had a definite influence). Although to some extent the Jewish youth movements copied their European counterparts, they also reacted to aspects in those movements that were not to their liking.

Different researchers tried to develop typologies for youth movements, viewing them as partly reflecting youth culture, pioneering, entertainment, and the like. Moreover, functionalist analyses of youth movements typi-

cally have emphasized the way in which these movements connect adolescents to society and help to prepare an easier and smoother passage from
childhood to adulthood. To some extent, within a functionalist analysis,
membership in these movements can be viewed as a preparation for leadership roles. Indeed, some researchers (e.g., Rivka Bar-Yosef in Naor
1989:17) explicitly state that these Jewish youth movements were schools
for leadership training. As such, adolescent members of these movements
typically received a considerable amount of political and ideological socialization and indoctrination.

There have been quite a number of Jewish youth movements in Palestine and, later on, in Israel. A publication by the Israeli Ministry of Education from 1992 lists twelve such movements in the country. Three of
the largest movements are Hatzofim (the Scouts), Hanoar Haoved
Vehalomed ("Youth Who Work and Study"), and Bnei Akiva ("The
Sons of Akiva"). Many local youth movements find their roots in already established and similarly functioning movements in Europe and
North America. The European and North American movements combined elements of youth culture, scouting, and entertainment to emphasize values such as rebellion, innovation, and a readiness to contribute
significantly towards national goals. The major Jewish youth movements in Palestine were established between 1919 and 1929. All these
movements attracted youth from the middle class, and their symbolic
societal value was very prominent: almost all of them accepted the ideals of the Zionist movement and designed a socialization program structured to fit the experience of the emerging Jewish Israeli society, the Zionist ethos, its symbols, and its myths. These movements provided an
almost ideal environment where national mythologies could be constructed and transmitted in an atmosphere of zeal, credibility, and readiness. This was made possible, in part, as a result of the suspension of
disbelief of the adolescents whose susceptible young minds were exposed to these heroic tales against the background of the cataclysmic
events from which the new Jewish state was developing. The peak period for these pioneering youth movements was, no doubt, between
1930 and 1948, when thousands of adolescents joined them. Most of
the movements had an ideological political organization that sponsored
their existence, in most cases one of the various kibbutz movements.
However, the overwhelming majority of adolescents who participated in
these youth movements did not later join the political organizations
which had sponsored them. While this reveals a major failure on the

part of these movements in acquiring new recruits for their sponsors, their success lay elsewhere. For a nation in birth pangs having to absorb thousands of immigrants from varied backgrounds in a very short period, the socialization role played by these youth movements in helping to create a national culture and ethos and in initiating thousands of youth into it was crucial. To do that, a variety of didactic devices were employed, including mythologies. Clearly, the Masada myth was a major building block of the aforementioned ethos. Thus, Naor's (1989) volume about youth movements in Palestine and Israel does not fail to mention Masada and discusses trips to Masada.[2]

As noted above, there have been quite a number of important youth movements, and it is not possible to discuss the way in which the Masada myth was handled in each and every one of them. Such a task cannot be accomplished with the limited resources available. Moreover, it is really not necessary. An examination of the major secular and religious movements will surely provide a fairly good overview of the issue. Those youth movements that we shall take a look at are Hanoar Haoved Vehalomed, Mahanot Haolim ("The Camps of the Immigrants"), Hatzofim, Hashomer Hatzair ("The Young Guard"), Bnei Akiva, Ezra, and Beitar.

Looking at the way the Masada mythical narrative was transmitted in youth movements is thus important from a few points of view. First, many of the future leaders (and elite) of Israel spent much time in these youth movements during their formative years. Second, these movements provided the locus where the Masada mythical narrative was translated from a mere story into a dramatic reality, frequently with a trek to Masada itself. Third, examining these youth movements will give us a more accurate and complete historical picture about the way in which the myth was revived, with the different nuances in the different youth movements, strictly in accordance with the natural history approach.

As we delve into the way in which the Masada narrative was handled in the various youth movements, we are brought back to the early years of the Masada myth. There is no question that the myth began its "tour of duty" with these youth movements. It was there that it was crystallized, transmitted, and adhered to. These young people, participating in the various activities of the different movements, absorbed the myth, and then, when they moved on to assume major leadership roles—military, political, social, and educational—in the Yishuv and later on in Israel, they carried the Masada legacy with them. Therefore, we shall examine this period with a good deal of care.

HANOAR HAOVED VEHALOMED ("Youth Who Work and Study")[3]

Hanoar Haoved Vehalomed was originally formed in 1959 by the merging of two other youth movements, Hanoar Haoved and Hatenua Hameuchedet. Hanoar Haoved was originally established in 1923–1924 as a movement of working youth. Hatenua Hameuchedet (affiliated with the Mapai political party) had split away from another youth movement, Mahanot Haolim, in 1945. Hanoar Haoved Vehalomed basically accepts the principles of Zionism, democracy, and socialism and has been affiliated with the Israeli socialist labor union, the Histadrut.

We examined just how the Masada narrative was dealt with in this youth movement by checking its monthly newspaper, *Bamaale,* and by conducting a number of interviews. The manner and frequency with which Masada is mentioned in *Bamaale* and in other documents of Hanoar Haoved Vehalomed is not uniform and changes with time. It is useful to distinguish between three periods in this regard: from 1940 until 1948; from 1948 until 1967; and from 1967 until 1989–1990.

1940–1948

In October 1941, Shmaria Guttman led a group of ten hikers to Masada. This was his first trip to the mountain since 1933. Like himself, most members of the group were affiliated with Hanoar Haoved and were from Kibbutz Naan. This trip yielded one of the very first documents concerning trips to Masada. This was a letter from Shmaria Guttman and the other members of the trip to the director of the youth department of the management of the Zionist administration, dated October 1941. This letter claims that the road to Masada should be improved and made safer, that a budget should be allocated for research on Masada, and that the area should be settled (see also D. Bitan 1990:227). Another letter from Shmaria Guttman requests funding for educational seminars about the Masada area and also includes a suggestion to improve the route to the site. Pictures and reports describing the many trips to Masada at that time, in the company of Shmaria Guttman, are abundant. Issue 6 of *Bamaale,* from March 31, 1942, focuses on Masada and compares it to the exodus of the Jewish people from Egypt. The central educational message of the report is the emphasis on the freedom of the Jewish people. Between 1942 and 1948, *Bamaale* ran at least one report per year concerning Masada. The contents are more or less identical, the emphasis being on freedom.

The year 1942 witnessed a number of important events. As I already mentioned, the threat from Rommel's Afrika Korps was very strongly felt. At that time Shmaria Guttman was one of the instructors in Hanoar Haoved Vehalomed. It was his feeling that "we had to develop within the members the knowledge to walk in the paths of the land . . . and to provide the younger generation with the knowledge and ability to use weapons, which would be useful to any movement that needs to protect itself. . . . I thought that we could use Masada to help develop these characteristics."[4] As we have said, Guttman was an impressive and persuasive fellow. His convictions led to the formation of a seminar for guides on Masada during that same year. This proved to be a turning point. Shmaria Guttman, extremely knowledgeable about Masada, dramatic, authoritative, and very eloquent, left quite an impression on the young guides ("Madrichim") who participated in the seminar. Following the January seminar, Hanoar Haoved Vehalomed organized a camp on top of Masada during Passover of 1942. *Bamaale* of March 31, 1942, opens with a big picture of Masada, and its headline is "Put Guards, Masada, on Your Walls." As Ofra Elad (1989) states (p. 8), the impression one gets from all this is one of urgency, that a grave danger exists and that "the entire country is for us one Masada." Moreover, targeting these guides for an intense indoctrination concerning Masada was a clever idea: they left Masada committed to the mythical narrative Shmaria Guttman exposed them to. Already in 1943, groups from Hanoar Haoved Vehalomed began to climb Masada. The tradition created in 1942–1943 by Shmaria Guttman has been continued in Hanoar Haoved Vehalomed till this very day.

A glance at *Bamaale* from this period reveals that while there was apparently much concern for Eretz Israel (including Masada), there was no less concern for the European fight against fascism.

In 1943, Breslavski's *most* influential books about Masada (1941 and 1943) received a very enthusiastic review in *Bamaale*. In 1944 (vols. 6–7), it was suggested that the story of Masada should be commemorated as the most significant event in the life of the Jewish people, and the pioneering youth were commended for their efforts in memorializing the Masada legacy. One simply cannot fail to notice how the tremendous influence and drive of Shmaria Guttman was so clearly echoed here. In 1945 (vols. 6–7), *Bemaale* compared the heroism of the heroes of Masada to that of the Jewish rebels in the ghettos of Nazi-occupied Europe and stated that "from the top of Masada the call and oath must be made to avenge the spilled blood of Israel, to establish the Jewish homeland, and to erect Masada—a symbol of the heroism of Israel for all generations." In the years 1944 and 1948, *Bamaale*'s references to Masada appear during Pesach, the Jewish holiday that symbolizes, among other things, freedom and liberty. Indeed, in the aforementioned 1945 issue, *Bamaale* published an anonymously written poem about Masada emphasizing that it was better to die free than to become slaves to the enemy. The hallmark of Masada in this period in Hanoar Haoved Vehalomed was thus characterized by several foci. First, these were formative years, as Shmaria Guttman was developing his successful drive to turn Masada into a national symbol by twisting Josephus Flavius's original narrative and by pushing this youth movement to embrace the newly constructed myth. Second, the emphasis was placed on Masada as a symbol for national freedom and liberty. Trips to Masada during this period were made with the explicit goal of *making* Masada the symbol of these important values. It was at this time that the Masada mythical narrative began to crystallize.

1948–1967

After independence, Masada continued to play an important role for Hanoar Haoved Vehalomed, and it took on an added dimension: as a preferred site for trips. With the establishment of the state, Hanoar Haoved Vehalomed found itself with a new homeland. One of its primary goals was defined as touring and becoming familiar with this new homeland. Many of the youth were new to the land, immigrants from different countries, and acquainting them with the new landscapes, sites, geography, and climate became a key goal. Strangely, although during this period the issue of Masada appeared in a much higher frequency and in more contexts than previously, its appearance was more neutral. It seems almost as if the very mentioning of Masada became the (compulsory) issue. Masada appeared to be losing its earlier status of a vehicle for an ideological statement. Instead, Masada was now the message itself: a message of a common past, of heroism, of liberty, and of independence. The unavoidable impression one gets is that the multiple use of Masada was geared toward amplifying a feeling of national unity and solidarity for all these young newcomers. The events of the past, Masada included, were thus socially constructed in such a fashion as to form a shared cultural core for a nation being reborn. For example, in issue 11 of *Bamaale* (1949), Masada appears in a column of recommended sites for trips. This could not have happened before 1948. The description of Masada is very "technical"— how to get there, necessary preparations, what is to be seen, and a report of a trip. The next issue of that same year contains a report about a new book on Masada and states that the book once again helps to recreate the linkage with "ancient brothers."

Hence, we still find simultaneous references in *Bamaale* to Masada and the revolts in Jewish ghettos (1950, issue 7, and again in 1953); references to Masada as an ideological symbol for freedom (e.g., 1952, 1966); and many additional references to trips made there (two of which, in 1952 and 1953, were guided by Shmaria Guttman). The research expeditions and archaeological excavations to Masada, first in 1953 (with Shmaria Guttman, between December 14 and December 27) and again in the early 1960s (led by Yadin), received much coverage. In 1953, *Bamaale* (no. 8, p. 122) states that Josephus Flavius was one of "the greatest traitors in Jewish History for daring to call Elazar Ben-Yair a 'robber.'" In *Bamaale*'s preferred version, Elazar Ben-Yair is presented as a hero, "the ideal expression of a free and liberated person" [the text uses a male form of conjugation]. As we move through the years from the 1950s onward, more and more reports concerning Masada as a tourist attraction and referring to its climate, geography, and environment can be found. Eventually, these reports dominate the way in which Masada is presented. By the mid-1960s, Masada was a very well established site for trips of Hanoar Haoved Vehalomed; however, it was only one site among many being visited by the movement.

An interesting angle to the references made to Masada is found in 1964, when *Bamaale* (vol. 5) discusses the inability of Jews from the Soviet Union to immigrate to Israel and suggests that when they finally do arrive, "we shall climb to Masada."

Another most fascinating and significant report, titled, "Masada—History or Existence?" is also found in *Bamaale* in the year 1964 (vol. 23). In this report, explicit concern is expressed in regard to the archaeological excavations being carried out at Masada. The reason for this concern is the possibility that these excavations might uncover findings that are incongruent with the accepted beliefs held by the Hanoar Haoved Vehalomed youth movement. In the event that this does occur, the report suggests, amazingly, that one should not surrender to archaeological authority and should, instead, continue to believe in what was accepted as absolute truth up until that point: "The important thing is not to lose a sense of proportion and not to become enslaved to . . . authority. With all due respect, there are things larger than archaeology. For the human truth we create, archaeology is but one ingredient" (p. 112). At the very least, such an incredible statement indicates that this youth movement created a

Masada of its own, in complete disregard as to whether or not its social construction fit objective, external findings.

However, those in Hanoar Haoved Vehalomed had nothing to fear. The archaeological excavations did nothing to alter the mythical narrative of Masada. If anything, their findings were used to amplify and magnify the myth. Moreover, as we shall see shortly, the "threat" to the mythical narrative of Masada was hidden elsewhere, in a totally unexpected event—the 1967 war. There was nothing Hanoar Haoved Vehalomed could do to prevent the demise of the Masada myth following that war. Furthermore, as we have seen, the mythical narrative was already in decline, ideologically—Masada was being transformed, slowly but surely, into a tourist attraction.

1967–1989

The year 1967 marks a very clear change of attitude toward Masada. A seminal event for Israel, the Six-Day War, occurred during June of that year. Israel emerged completely victorious from this war and, as a result, acquired a considerable amount of new territory. This development allowed Israelis to reach previously inaccessible sites, such as the Western Wall and Gamla.

It is *quite* obvious that although Masada was a star in *Bamaale* till 1967, it most definitely lost that cherished position in that year. Since then, Masada has appeared from time to time, but infrequently. Moreover, no further reports concerning the annual trips to Masada are to be found in *Bamaale* (as they were prior to 1967).

It is easy to attribute the decline in the space devoted to Masada in *Bamaale* to the opening up of new territories after the Six-Day War. However, this is not the only reason; there is another ideological explanation. In the wake of the 1967 war, the "no choice" and "last stand" ideological concepts were difficult, if not impossible, to swallow. Moreover, the political cleavage between "right" and "left" among Jewish Israelis deepened following this war. Nationalism and the symbols associated with it gradually shifted into the domain of the right, whereas Hanoar Haoved Vehalomed is a left-oriented movement.

It is interesting to note that in 1967 a new group of members from Hanoar Haoved Vehalomed formed a Garin[5] that called itself Masada. The report in *Bamaale* (vol. 4) is short and is only about the Garin. Not a word is mentioned about Masada or why that particular name was chosen. A pre-1967 issue of *Bamaale* would certainly not have passed up the opportunity to use the occasion to expand on Masada. However, circumstances were different now.

Between 1967 and 1972 there was not even one report in *Bamaale* mentioning Masada. In 1972 (vol. 10), we find one short report about a traditional trek to Masada. In 1973, Masada is mentioned again in the context of the death of David Ben-Gurion. Under the title "Farewell to the Old Man," two passages concerning Hanoar Haoved Vehalomed are quoted from an old speech of Ben-Gurion's, titled "Masada of our Forefathers" ("*Metzada shel harishonim*" in Hebrew). The main theme of the report is the "real war of the Jews for their liberty and homeland."

During the 1970s and 1980s, hardly any mention of Masada is made. The few places where it is mentioned are usually reports concerning trips to Masada. It is thus obvious that, from the early 1970s on, Masada not only lost its "starring" position but was also no longer *the* preferred site for trips of Hanoar Haoved Vehalomed. Moreover, whereas until 1979 the stereotypical narrative given in *Bamaale* about Masada was the mythical one, that year witnessed a very significant change. In a 1979 booklet published by Hanoar Haoved Vehalomed as a guidebook for trips to Masada,[6] one can find, for the first time, the original narrative as provided by Josephus Flavius—an unpleasant narrative, but it is there. Another surprise may be found in 1985, in another booklet about touring Masada. There, Menachem is described as, lo and behold, a "robber."[7] This booklet was even reprinted in 1988. No more mythical tales for Hanoar Haoved Vehalomed. The newly adopted perspective was, first, to provide the *full* original narrative and, second, to be much more critical. Thus, the reader is exposed to both the positive and the negative aspects of the narrative. This is a clear sign of maturity. However, Masada is still included in the program of trips organized by Hanoar Haoved Vehalomed, and the basic orientation to Masada is positive, although not exclusively so. Criticism is now allowed.

These developments took place at a time when the size of Hanoar Haoved Vehalomed was unprecedented. In the late 1980s, this youth movement had more then 130 centers and over a hundred thousand members: Jews, Arabs, and Druze. Its primary ideological message was identical to that of the Israeli workers' union, the Histadrut.

In more modern times, the head of education and training in Hanoar Haoved Vehalomed, Mr. Ovadia Tzur, was interviewed.[8] His opinion was that it was necessary to teach the youth about Masada, especially about what he termed as "the negotiations" (?) between Flavius Silva and

Elazar Ben-Yair. The suicide, in his view, should not be presented as an educational lesson. He stated that "today, in our view, we have to go against the suicide. There is nothing more sacred than life. We should not teach something positive about death because there is nothing after death. What we must emphasize is negotiation, which can lead to something positive." Mr. Tzur claimed that treks and climbs to Masada must continue because "Masada is a national asset, for us too. The slogan 'Masada shall not fall again' is our slogan too. . . . Masada is not a myth but rather a historical reality that needs to be judged by today's criteria, while facing the good and the bad aspects of it." Other instructors and guides from Hanoar Haoved Vehalomed who were interviewed expressed similar positions. However, some guides went even further and claimed that the subject of Masada should not be presented at all in Hanoar Haoved Vehalomed. One guide, who asked to remain anonymous, stated explicitly that "dealing with Masada contradicts the ideology of the movement because Masada symbolizes fanaticism and destruction." However, other guides stated that although this criticism is valid, there was heroism on Masada and it needs to be taught. Some guides still adhered to the mythical narrative: that of Jewish heroes who were successful in standing up to the enemy, by no less than a proud suicide. Thus, the attitudes toward Masada vary—another sign of maturity.

In summary, it is clear that the treatment of Masada in Hanoar Haoved Vehalomed underwent a dramatic transformation. In the 1930s, Masada was a heroic, almost sacred narrative whose accuracy was certainly not to be questioned. Josephus Flavius, calling Elazar Ben-Yair a "robber," was severely criticized. The Masada narrative during this period was mythical and was much influenced by Shmaria Guttman's unquestioning interpretation. That is, Masada was presented with a serious omission of some of the more problematic aspects (e.g., Ein Gedi, the escape from Jerusalem, the Sicarii). The murderous nature of the Sicarii and their cruelty are not mentioned. A heroic tale is constructed by emphasizing the last Jewish warriors, fighting to the end for freedom and liberty. This manner of presentation continued, although in a much attenuated form, into the 1960s, with one major difference: gradually, Masada was transformed from a sacred place into a tourist attraction. When the archaeological excavations in the early 1960s caused some concern about a possible incongruity between "scientific" truth and myth, the suggestion was made to ignore science in favor of myth. This development represents an interesting phenomenon. On the one hand, Hanoar Haoved Vehalomed had found in the Masada myth the roots and the source for the values of nationality, freedom, and liberty. On the other hand, it was constantly trying to create this myth and reinforce it and was concerned about its "truth." This was achieved through a variety of methods, from the publication of the "proper" interpretation of the Masada story in *Bamaale* to the annual ritual of trekking and climbing to Masada.

The Masada myth in Hanoar Haoved Vehalomed in the first two periods discussed above was very intimately associated with the Zionist emphasis in this youth movement. It is interesting to note that this focus on Masada and Zionism was characteristic of Hanoar Haoved Vehalomed only in the post-1942 years. Prior to that, the major emphasis was placed on socialism. *Bamaale* and other publications of Hanoar Haoved Vehalomed devoted much space to explaining socialism and to discussing universal—not Zionist—socialism. Up to 1942, a clear Marxist influence can be discerned in Hanoar Haoved Vehalomed, and no particular emphasis is to be found concerning uniquely national Jewish subjects. In reflection of this ideological commitment, no reference to Masada can be observed there till 1942. In the early 1940s, with the new knowledge about the fate of European Jews filtering in, there was more and more interest and involvement in Zionism, combined with the continuing interest in socialism. The 1940s mark a period when the most salient interest was the drive to establish a Jewish homeland. The tradition of the treks to Masada began, and Shmaria Guttman's moral entrepreneurship and mythologization fell on willing ears. Following the establishment of the state of Israel in 1948, the ideology of a "homeland in the process of becoming" was transformed into the national ideology of an already existing state, with Masada becoming one of its first national symbols. For Hanoar Haoved Vehalomed, the narrative behind the Masada myth was the type of nationalism that it wanted to bestow on its apprentices.

The year 1967 marked another major shift. Following the Six-Day War, national symbols appear to have become the property of the Israeli right, to which Hanoar Haoved Vehalomed was not affiliated. Hence, an emphasis was no longer placed on Masada. The symbol was still there, and it continued to play an important role. Treks and climbs to Masada were still carried on, but the myth had become much weaker.

The final development is that since the late 1970s, Masada has been presented "as is"—that is, faithful to Josephus Flavius's account. The word *robber* is used to describe a Sicarii, and some very serious questions and criticisms have also been raised. Masada is still a place to visit, but it has lost its sacredness. If anything, this must be taken as a sign of maturity. Socially constructed and fabricated mythical narratives are no longer "needed" as before. The historical truth can be fully faced. Moreover, the playing down of the suicide and the new emphasis on negotiation seem to strike a chord in relation to the key issue facing Israel and Hanoar Haoved Vehalomed in the early 1980s—negotiating a peace with Israel's Arab neighbors. It is also reflective of the disappearance of the "No choice" slogan and a youth movement clearly located on the left side of Israel's political spectrum.

MAHANOT HAOLIM ("The Camps of the Immigrants")[9]

In early 1926 a small group of pupils from the eleventh grade in the Gymnasia Hertzlia in Tel Aviv began to work together without a clear goal. Their main concern and interest was the conviction that there was a need to change the lifestyle of adolescents educated in the Gymnasia Hertzlia. Most of all, they felt a need to challenge the emphasis placed on personal career, which, in their eyes, led the graduates to ignore the needs of the land. In other words, they wanted to close the gap between Zionism as an ideology and Zionism as an act—the development of the land. In the same year, additional groups were formed in other high schools in Tel Aviv. The main activity of these groups was focused on meetings and discussions concerning Zionism. Their number grew rapidly, and many adolescents who felt dissatisfied with the other alternatives also joined. Some even decided to go and help in developing the kibbutzim.

By the end of 1927, many of the participants began to understand the implication of these developments. A large number of these adolescents were drawn together by a common cultural background. They were bonded by an emphasis on freedom, independence, sociability, sing-alongs, trips, and rebellion against contemporary conventions. The original Tel Aviv group was joined by others from Jerusalem, Haifa, and other places. However, the dominant social kernel was the Tel Aviv group. The various groups that were forming this new movement underwent a rather long process of crystallization. In 1930, a major unification camp was held in the Herzl forest in Ben-Shemen. At Hanukkah in 1932, this collection of groups ran a national convention in Kibbutz Naan and decided that "the kibbutz is the only way to achieve the actualization of the values we teach" (Bachar 1989:53). Thus, the years 1926–1932 witnessed the emergence of this new youth movement, which grew from grass-roots pressure and needs. The movement placed a clear emphasis on socialism, personal actualization, and active Zionism, and it viewed the kibbutz as the proper way of life, through which people could—indeed should—achieve cherished personal and social goals. A decision was made in the 1930s to join the Kibbutz Hameuchad movement (rather than Hashomer Hatzair), an affiliation that helped the group in its ideological identification. Basically, the orientation was to the left.[10] As Bitan points out, the goal was to guide adolescents, who were perceived to be spending their lives in an empty and career-oriented manner, toward a life-style of work and creativity in the service of socialist Zionism. The different groups decided to call themselves Mahanot Haolim, meaning in Hebrew "the camps of the immigrants" (to Palestine/Israel) (see also Kafkafi 1975a, 1975b).

Although, as Uri Bitan points out,[11] much of the decision-making process in Mahanot Haolim during 1938–1945 can be understood as a reflection of larger political conflicts within the political party Mapai, with which Mahanot Haolim was affiliated, I shall limit the discussion here solely to the Masada issue.

Masada was not the central focus of interest or attention of Mahanot Haolim until 1942. Much like Hanoar Haoved Vehalomed, Mahanot Haolim was immersed in ideological debates about universalism, socialism, and related topics. The year 1942 witnessed two important and relevant developments. More and more information about the fate of European Jews under Nazi occupation was filtering into the Yishuv, and the threat posed by Rommel's Afrika Korps in the south (by June 30, 1942, Rommel had reached the El Alamein line) was becoming very real. Moreover, the Hagana/Palmach was involved in the debates and preparations for the "Plan for the North" (to be discussed in the next chapter), and the drive to recruit young people for future defense purposes was also being debated and already being put into operation. There was a demand to recruit pupils from the twelfth grade to the Palmach.

One of the very first references can be found in a report on a convention of graduates of Mahanot Haolim held on top of Masada, in October of 1942, in which a call was made for the recruitment of twelfth-grade graduates to the Palmach. The fact that this call was made on top of Masada, obviously, was meant to endow it with a dramatic moral and symbolic validity.

Mahanot Haolim was not the only or even the first youth movement to use Masada as a symbol. The movement was crystallizing during a period in which the issue of Masada was very much up in the air. Members of Hanoar Haoved Vehalomed were in the initial process of getting involved in Masada; Simchoni's Hebrew translation of Josephus Flavius's narrative was published in 1923, and Lamdan's poem was published in 1927.

Student trips to the Masada area were already taking place in the 1920s. These consisted mostly of groups from the Gymnasia Hertzlia (Tel Aviv) and from Jerusalem (Hug Hameshotetim, meaning a group of people who travel). The Gymnasia Hertzlia made boat trips around the Dead Sea. During these trips, attempts to climb Masada were made. For example, groups from the Gymnasia Hertzlia and the school for teachers in Jerusalem reached Masada during their trips between 1925 and 1927. In a trip to Masada in 1927, a group, including pupils that helped to establish Mahanot Haolim, climbed to Masada even though their tour guide could not find the right path to the top (Kafkafi 1975a:76).

In 1927, a tragedy occurred during one of the trips to Masada when a girl fell from a cliff and died. Consequently, the trips were stopped for a while. The Arab-Jewish clashes of 1929 put a complete stop to trips to the area (Alon 1969:90). Azaria Alon's report (1969) makes it quite clear that in the 1930s Masada was a destination only for a small number of die-hards, as well as for groups of people who lived and worked in the Dead Sea region.

In the first fifteen years of Mahanot Haolim, not even one national trip to Masada took place. One of the main reasons was the relative inaccessibility of the place. The major explanations given for this fact are that a 1927 earthquake had dropped the top of the Roman siege ramp below the level of the entry to the upper plateau and that the "snake path" from the other side was not well known or easy to climb.

Only in 1942 did Shmaria Guttman renew the mass climbing to Masada. This occurred only after he and a seminar of Hanoar Haoved Vehalomed put a path in place with strings and wedges at the problematic spots. The lack of visits could also be attributed to the absence of adequate organizational and infrastructural support in Mahanot Haolim at that time, to the Arab revolt of 1936, and perhaps to a lack of strong enough ideological support for such trips.

The reports from the few tours to Masada by Mahanot Haolim's groups in the pre-1942 years clearly project an image of Masada as a place that symbolized the heroic fight of Jews for their land and their liberty. Moreover, the identification of Masada as a fight "to the bitter end," for freedom, is characteristic of this period, despite the absence of trips. For example, a play about the "chain of defense in Israel," presented in Haifa in February or March of 1938 as a joint venture of Hanoar Haoved

A close look at the natural spur on which the Roman 10th army built its siege ramp. The picture was taken during the 1955–56 survey. It is easy to see that this structure almost reaches the top of Masada. Using this structure is the easiest and fastest way to reach the top of Masada even today; one can reach the top of Masada within a few minutes.

Vehalomed and Mahanot Haolim, used Masada as its focus. These are also years in which an increasing interest in Masada can be detected. The reasons for this are not entirely clear, but it is more than plausible that a few factors contributed to this. One was the Arab revolt of 1936–1939 and the need felt by many Jews for an active as well as a symbolic response. Another was the continuing evolution of Mahanot Haolim, on both the organizational and ideological levels. Thus, the "Freedom Hagada," published by Mahanot Haolim for the Passover of 1939, included passages about Masada and excerpts from Elazar Ben-Yair's speeches.

The above processes must have picked up speed and vigor because the 1940s witnessed a rather radical change in the attitude toward Masada. Mahanot Haolim moved from a hesitant position to a decisive and definite attitude. During these years, Masada became a very central and important symbol in this youth movement. Members of Mahanot Haolim climbed to Masada every year, and their most important annual convention took place on top of Masada. During this period, the main conceptual debates in Mahanot Haolim shifted their focus from socialism to issues of defense, rebellion, and heroism. Members of Mahanot Haolim took an active part in the 1942 seminar that Shmaria Guttman organized on Masada. Moreover, from 1943 on, the Palmach–Mahanot Haolim connection was strengthened and institutionalized as more and more members of the movement joined the Palmach. As we shall see in the next chapter, Masada occupied a very central role in the symbolism of the Palmach.

Additional factors contributed to these developments. First, at least since 1940 there was a feeling in the Yishuv that European Jewry was being destroyed. However, this feeling became a reality in 1943 when reliable information about the actual extermination of European Jews arrived. Together with the threat from Rommel, this information created much anxiety and a feeling of isolation and siege. The "Plan for the North" was worked out by the Palmach to, in effect, create a new Masada-type situation around Haifa (the plan will be discussed in the next chapter). Thus, the members of Mahanot Haolim must have been searching for symbolic narratives concerning the heroism of the desperate. Remember that Lamdan's 1927 poem about Masada (see, e.g., Schwartz, Zerubavel, and Barnett 1986) uses Masada as a metaphor and asks whether the Zionist enterprise also represents a "last stand" for the Jewish people.[12] During 1943–1945, the danger to the Yishuv passed and the dimensions of the Holocaust in Europe became clearer and clearer. The question of how much and to what extent European Jewry actually "fought to the end" tormented the Yishuv, along with some very strong feelings of guilt about not having done enough for European Jews. Thus, the 1943 revolt in the Warsaw Ghetto became a positive symbol.[13] Masada, as well, was a very comforting and conducive symbol for the heroism of a desperate people. As the British Mandate regime limited trips within Palestine, the trek to Masada became more and more of a protest activity.[14]

Hence, from 1940 on, we can find references to Masada in different contexts of the movement. The first book brought to the Beit Haarava's[15] library was Josephus Flavius's, and it was clearly viewed as a representation of the heroism of those fighting for their land. Beit Haarava also served as a base for the trips around the Dead Sea region, including Masada. *Bamivchan,* the journal of Mahanot Haolim, reports in its December 5, 1940, issue (p. 12) how the difficult trip in the Dead Sea region serves as a test of sacrifice, and it therefore recommends that those traveling to Masada should do so only on foot. Another issue of *Bamivchan,* from January 1941, features Masada extensively in an editorial aimed at increasing the motivation of young people to enlist in the military effort against the Nazis. In 1945, a member of Mahanot Haolim stated simply that "a trip to Masada is a trip to [our] roots" (*Bamivchan,* January 1945, p. 9).

What was it that members of Mahanot Haolim heard about Masada? Clearly, not the full version of Josephus Flavius. They did read Breslavski's dramatic book, *When Masada Fell,* which is an imaginary mythical tale. The major lesson presented there is that the people of Masada faced two choices: either to fall into the hands of the Romans and suffer the horrendous fate of demeaning slavery or to commit suicide and die in a heroic, clean, and pure way. To surrender, negotiate, or actually fight to the end were not mentioned as alternatives to suicide. Members of Mahanot Haolim therefore were consistently exposed to the mythical narrative of Masada and not to the full original narrative. Mahanot Haolim tended to mix Lamdan's fiction with Josephus Flavius's version. Masada, in Mahanot Haolim, was used, clearly, consciously, and explicitly, for the social purpose of creating a symbol of Jewish heroism and "a fight to the end."

As Uri Bitan points out,[16] Masada symbolized a number of things in Mahanot Haolim. First, Masada was perceived as the *last* fortress of the Jewish rebels in the Great Revolt. In the early 1940s, this perception was very meaningful because Israel was then perceived as the *last* fortress of the Jewish people following the extermination of European Jewry. Second, Masada represented a symbol for the heroism of a desperate people. In this framework, the suicide itself was viewed as an act of heroism in the face of an assured defeat. Third, Masada was taken as an example of "activism," of putting up a fight instead of surrendering, and of frustrating the enemy's wish for prisoners and the spoils of war. This "activism" was held in contrast to what was perceived as the "passivity" of Jews in the Diaspora, or Galut. In a way, Masada symbolized the negation of what was viewed as the passive Jew of the Galut ("Yehudi Galuti"). Fourth, Masada was utilized as a symbol of sacrifice. Suicide was thus redefined as an act of preference for freedom over wretched slavery. That is, the value of freedom and liberty was placed above life itself.

In this mythic symbolism, the Sicarii are never mentioned. "Zealots" is the term of choice, or "the heroes/defenders of Masada." The massacre at Ein Gedi is not to be found anywhere. Elazar Ben-Yair's speeches are censored, and quoted from them are only passages about how bad slavery is and how good freedom is. From interviews Uri Bitan conducted in 1989 with two important figures in Mahanot Haolim, Azaria Alon and Shabtai Beeri, it is clear that the movement simply neutralized (read "repressed") all of the problematic elements in Josephus Flavius's narrative to create a consistently heroic tale. This heroic tale and the harsh real environment of Masada are the key elements of Mahanot Haolim's fascination with the site. The Zionist ideological link with Masada was almost unavoidable.

One more aspect about Mahanot Haolim added fuel to the burning furnace of its "need" for Masada. This is the dominant ideological zeal in Mahanot Haolim in those years for a maximalist territorial solution, that is, for a *large* Jewish state; it was strongly felt that the homeland could not be divided. If Mahanot Haolim had a secular belief system, a sacred element in that belief system was the land of Israel. Trips were therefore the main ritual for its expression. Trips, especially those to the Judean desert, had the character of a pilgrimage to a lofty and exalted place.

Members of Mahanot Haolim went through a ritual that was also adopted by other movements. This was to put Josephus Flavius on "trial" for treason. Typically, the Masada affair was used by the defense to show that Josephus was not a traitor.

Thus, the main activity of Mahanot Haolim in the 1940s in regard to Masada found its expression in two ways: massive trips to Masada and the repeated exposure of members to the mythical narrative. This was especially reinforced among those members of Mahanot Haolim who joined the Palmach and vice versa.

With the exception of one report (*Bamivchan*, December 1944, pp. 7–8), which discussed the attitude of Mahanot Haolim to Masada (and perhaps reflected some second thoughts about the uncritical admiration of Masada), no record is to be found of any deliberations (or hesitation) in Mahanot Haolim concerning the adoption of Masada as a symbol during those early years. Even in this report, the main debate was over the problematic symbol of the suicide. Here, again, the point is made that the real issue was not suicide but, rather, freedom, independence, and the people's commitment to their land. In a January 1945 debate over Yavneh and Masada (see chapter two), it seemed that Masada was the consensual symbol while Yavneh was questioned (*Bamivchan*, February 1945, pp. 5–24).

One could, perhaps, posit that the establishment of the State of Israel in 1948[17] should have marked an ideological and physical change of such a nature that Mahanot Haolim would alter its attitude toward Masada. Not so. Until 1971, there was really not much change. With the precision of a well-tuned clock, Mahanot Haolim climbed each year to Masada. For example, the May 1950 issue of *Bamivchan* (no. 41) includes a report by Mori David (p. 15) about a trip to and convention on top of Masada. This is what she has to say:

> Alone stands the rock; dark and dreary is the fortress of the heroes. Masada, here your sons visit you again; [they] come to commune with the memory of your heroes. Vibrations move us as we see you so terrible and dark. Why should you be silent? Why should you keep most of the rebellion and pain? Make a horrendous roar and the wind will come and whistle within your ruins, and the universe will come out, the desert and your sons—in a dance of freedom. . . . Don't be silent. . . .
>
> Masada was a refuge for every rebel and refugee. . . . during the days of the Great Revolt the Sicarii (the extreme Zealots) fortified themselves on Masada, headed by Elazar Ben-Yair, against the Romans. . . . The siege lasted for nine months, and when the defenders saw that their hope for survival was gone, they killed themselves so as not to fall into the hands of the enemy[18]. . . . Masada, which became a symbol for heroism and rebellion, attracts many young adolescents who climb [it] to commune with the memory of its heroes and draw from it their own heroism.

It is easy to see that though some of the elements of the myth are softened (the Sicarii are mentioned; the length of the Roman siege is not exaggerated), the essence of the myth is still found here. This is made clear by

the disregard of the more problematic issues (for example, *who* exactly
the Sicarii were; the Ein Gedi massacre; the lack of battle(s) around Masada), by the type of language used, and by the basically noncritical acceptance of the mythical narrative. As if to counterbalance this, on page 14
of the same issue one can read that

> the fortress of Masada was the largest among the fortresses in which
> Jews fortified themselves in the Great Revolt against the Romans. For
> three years, from the day that the [Second] Temple was destroyed, the
> Jews held their position. Their zeal for their people, their hatred of
> the enemy, and their belief in the lack of choice facing them aided
> them. Water reservoirs chiseled in rock and stocks of food saved them
> from starvation during the siege. The Romans closed in on them with
> a chain of camps manned by garrisons of disciplined and movable
> soldiers. When all hope was lost, the people of Masada killed one
> another so that the enemy would not capture them alive.

The February 1954 issue of *Bamivchan* (no. 57) repeats the basic
form of the mythical narrative. Its huge headline reads: "Masada—An
Unconquerable Fortress."[19] This report includes the main elements of the
mythical narrative with the addition of some interesting fabrications. The
author, one H. Dan, states (p. 19) that the Zealots and Bar Giora escaped
to the desert after the destruction of the temple and from there continued
to fight for another three years. This war, according to Dan, included
bold battles and raids on the Roman army and the organization of a fighting Jewish force. Where exactly Dan gets this "information" from is most
unclear. Dan also says that those sitting on top carried out raids on the
Roman soldiers surrounding Masada—again, a fabrication not mentioned by Josephus Flavius. And, lo and behold, at the very end of his
report Dan states that "the time was two o'clock in the morning. The
group hears the final words of Shmaria and rediscusses all that it heard
and saw in the last ten days." Since the source of this "information" is
none other than Shmaria Guttman, it is quite easy for us to understand
how such a "speculative history" was formulated here.

The mythical narrative keeps appearing till the early 1970s. However,
a change is evident: there is less of an emphasis on Masada, in general,
and when it is mentioned, it is less often in an ideological context and
more in the context of trips, the environment, the sights, and the experience itself.

In the report on the 1971 Hanukkah trip to the Judean desert,
Masada is no longer even mentioned. Masada is referred to again only

in 1978 in the context of a trip to the area. Only 50 percent of the potential participants joined the trip. Actually, from 1967 on, Masada as an ideological site disappears from Mahanot Haolim's publications. If it is mentioned at all, it is only in reference to the environment of the region.

The January 1986 issue of *Bamivchan* does report about a trip to the Judean desert. The emphasis in this report is placed on the desert, the enchanted landscapes, the isolation from civilization and the communion with life itself. In this issue we also find, for the first time, a satire of Masada! It is worth mentioning that thirty to forty years earlier no one would have even dared to think about such a blasphemy. Here is a translation of the feuilleton that Yuval and Etai, two adolescents from the Tel Aviv commune, wrote:

> Findings from the trip to the Judean desert.
> Subject: The impact of the cable car to Masada.
> As is known, there is a global phenomenon of plate tectonics. The different land masses move. One of the results of these movements is the Syrian-African rift and its expression in our area, the Jordan Valley and the Dead Sea. The two sides of the rift (that is, Israel and Jordan) are drifting apart from each other.
> A few years ago the cable car to Masada was built. These are the facts.
> We asked ourselves, What is the effect of connecting the top of Masada to the base of the mountain with a cable?
> Having examined this issue, we reached a few conclusions.
> (a) Already today the cable is too tight and therefore will cause a declination of the mountain till it will be like Pisa[20]-Masada. The cable will pull Masada to the east till it falls. The answer for this is that 'Masada Shall Not Fall Again.' The Romans took care of this problem and took measures against it: —They threw catapult stones from the top of Masada and piled them on the west side of Masada to counterbalance the pull eastward. —They built a siege ramp that connects Masada to the mountains west of it. This ramp would not allow Masada to incline eastward.
> So an absurdity was created. The Romans, who caused the fall of Masada the first time, are preventing its fall a second time. It is possible that had the Romans known this, their whole approach to the conquest of Masada would have been entirely different.
> (b) Another possibility is that the cable will stop the Syrian-African rift from widening. Simple but amazing! This could have far-reaching geopolitical ramifications. The Jordanians will claim that

this is part of the Zionist Imperialist policy, which does not allow
separation from the territories. (*Bamivchan*, January 1986, 156:8–10)

An interview with Miriam Glazer, who was in charge of education in
Mahanot Haolim,[21] confirmed that members of the movement do make a
trip to the Judean desert once a year (during either Hanukkah or Sukkot);
however, the main focus of this trip is the ecology and landscapes of the
desert, not what she called "historical sites." Sometimes they climb Masada, but if they do so, it is because of the majestic landscape and not
because of the history of Masada.

The it is easy to see how Masada has been dramatically transformed
from a place that was almost considered sacred into a tourist attraction
and even into something people feel comfortable laughing about. This
dramatic contrast is made most vivid by comparing the earlier issues of
Bamivchan (e.g., May 1950, no. 41) with the satirical passage quoted
above (January 1986).

HATZOFIM (Israeli Scouts)

The Hatzofim youth movement in Palestine and later in Israel was based
on the British scouting tradition and on ideas from the Free Youth movement in Germany. British scouting crystallized in the early decade of the
twentieth century with the aid of Lord Baden-Powell. It complements formal education with trips and activities in nature, as well as training in
various areas. Scouting, in this context, encourages identification with
the regime and the values of the mainstream culture in which it functions,
such as love of the homeland (nationalism). The German youth movement, which preceded British scouting, began at the end of the nineteenth
century. It coincided with the crumbling of the hierarchical structure of
family and society in Germany following the industrial revolution. The
basic attitude was one of rebellion—against arbitrary family discipline
and phony societal and cultural norms—combined with the espousal of a
return to truth, to simplicity, and to nature. Both German and British
youth movements thus emphasized nature treks, romanticism, and the experience of sitting around a lighted camp fire in the wilderness. Added to
this was a vague demand for personal fulfillment, which would bring a
change in values, improved individual development, and a better society
(Hemda Alon 1989:19–20).

The Histadrut Hatzofim Beeretz Israel (Organization of Scouts in Israel) was established in the spring of 1919. The Hertzlia and Young

Maccabi associations for gymnastics, from Jaffo, together with the Hikers Association from Haifa, joined to create the national Scouts (Hatzofim).[22] From the very beginning there was a split between Jewish and Arab Scouts. The Scouts did solicit aid and support from formal institutions (including the British regime in 1919). However, the decision of the Jewish Scouts to remain independent (separate from the Arabs)[23] forced them to make do with their own resources. In 1921, when Lord Baden-Powell visited Palestine, the Jewish Scouts were kept away from most of the ceremonies in his honor.

In 1924, the first national convention of Hatzofim took place in Jerusalem. This convention ended with the election of a leader (Aviezer Yellin), the further adoption of Baden-Powell's principles, and a request for support from the department of education of the Zionist administration. Although the administration did agree to sponsor the movement, this agreement did not translate into real and tangible support for another ten years. The lack of institutional support created a series of severe problems, in the ideological content of the movement, in the development of leadership, and in resource management. During 1932–1933, many efforts were made to combine the different groups of Scouts into one unified movement. During 1935–1936, this effort was crystallized, and a unified movement began to emerge. From this time onward, Hatzofim rapidly expanded. Thus, whereas in 1935 there were 878 Scouts in the various units of Hatzofim, the census taken in 1938 revealed a membership of 3,000 Scouts in twenty-nine units (called "tribes"). During the period of the 1936–1939 Arab revolt, members of Hatzofim provided the Hagana with a variety of services, such as first aid, signaling, camping, knowledge of the geography of the land, messengers, communications, and volunteer work in hospitals and fire departments. These activities obviously increased the appreciation for Hatzofim. In addition, Hatzofim worked to develop its contacts with similar groups abroad, particularly those in the U.S.A. Because of some bitter internal ideological conflicts, between October 1950 and May 1951, Hatzofim was split into two groups. One of these groups affiliated itself with the united kibbutz movement and later joined another youth movement, Mahanot Haolim.

Hatzofim has been a big movement. In 1947, one year before the establishment of Israel as a Jewish state, Hatzofim had about 5,500 members. Before the 1950–1951 split, there were 7,000 members in the movement. In 1959, the number increased to 11,500. Because it is not affiliated with any specific political party, Hatzofim is the only youth movement in Israel that has free access to schools and whose activities are allowed within schools (this situation has existed since 1959) (Hemda Alon 1989).

To check the involvement of Hatzofim with Masada, we examined references to Masada in the different publications of the organization, including its newsletter *Heye Nachon*.[24]

Although information concerning trips by Hatzofim to Masada exists from 1947 on, it is sporadic and unreliable. Beginning in 1953, reference to such trips is found a bit more frequently; however, it still does not provide a complete picture. Since Hatzofim is a well-established organization, it was relatively easy to find the information that does exist. When we tried to collect similar information about other youth movements, what we found was even more sparse.

Between the years 1959 and 1984, it appears that Hatzofim made a trip to Masada almost every year. At first, the trip usually took place during the Passover vacation, and later on it was held during Hanukkah (both holidays are associated with freedom and national liberty). It generally lasted for a period of three to eight days, with an average of approximately 680 participants. The timing of the trips was most probably changed in favor of much more comfortable and cooler climate in the region during the Hanukkah season. The Passover holiday takes place during a much hotter period, usually around April, when the danger of dehydration is increased.

It is important to note that the archives are full of information testifying to the strong institutional support provided by various organizations for Hatzofim's trips to Masada—for example, the Ministry of Culture and Education (monitoring the trips, providing subsidies), the Israeli Army (providing security escorts for the trips), kibbutzim (providing manpower for instruction, scouting, security, and first aid).

Hundreds of booklets and instruction manuals of Hatzofim were checked, but they contained very little, if any, information concerning Masada. This is a fascinating observation: on the one hand, Hatzofim takes its members to Masada almost every year; on the other hand, it provides very little information about Masada in its formal educational literature.

Basically, the official instruction manuals of Hatzofim simply ignore Masada. No admiration for the myth is expressed, but neither is any criticism. For example, manuals for tour guides from 1945, 1949, 1956, 1968, and 1976, which deal explicitly with Jewish heroism, do not even discuss Masada. The examples of heroism they do discuss include the Maccabees, the Hasmoneans, Rabbi Akiva, Bar-Kochva, Tel Hai, and the rebels in the

Table 5.1. Hatzofim's trips to Masada

Year	Length of trips in days	Time of year (vacation)	Number of participants and grade	
1947	7–8	Passover	Unknown	
1953	Unknown	Passover	Unknown	(tenth and eleventh grades)
1955	5	Passover	Unknown	(eleventh grade and others)
1956	Unknown	Passover	Unknown	(eleventh grade)
1959	4	Passover	600	(tenth grade)
1960	3	Passover	Unknown	(tenth grade)
1961	5	Hanukkah	780	(tenth grade)
1962	7	Hanukkah	800	(tenth grade)
1963	5	Hanukkah	600	(tenth grade)
1964	4	Hanukkah	1000	(tenth grade)
1965	No information			
1966	5	Hanukkah	800	(tenth grade)
1967	Unknown	Hanukkah	650	(tenth grade)
1968	5	Hanukkah	720–800	(tenth grade)
1969	4	Hanukkah	450–550	—
1970	Unknown	Hanukkah	530	(tenth grade)
1971	5	Hanukkah	Unknown	(tenth grade)
1972	No information			
1973	No trips due to the Yom Kippur War			
1974	Unknown	Hanukkah	600–650	(tenth grade)
1975	No information			
1976	No information			
1977	5	Hanukkah	1200	(tenth grade)
1978	No information			
1979	No information			
1980	No information			
1981	4	Hanukkah	Unknown	(tenth grade)
1982	4	Hanukkah	500	(tenth grade)
1983	4	Hanukkah	1100	(tenth grade)
1984	The yearly trip did not include the Judean Desert			

Jewish ghettos in Nazi-occupied Europe. Even when, in 1949, the topics of Kiddush Hashem (giving one's life for the sanctification of God) and suicide as a heroic act are discussed, Masada is ignored. This must have been deliberate. It is a very different situation than that existing in other youth movements such as Mahanot Haolim or Hanoar Haoved Vehalomed, in which the Masada myth was very central and influential. The formal instruction manuals of Hatzofim clearly demonstrate that to pass on the value of heroism one need not rely on Masada. For example, in 1944, Hatzofim's booklet, *Lamadrich,* discusses Tel Hai, where one of the pre-

1948 Israeli mythical heroes—Joseph Trumpeldor—fell in its defense. The slogan "Masada shall not fall again" was replaced by "The legacy of Tel Hai shall not Fade."

Despite the glaring absence of Masada from the formal instructional manuals of this movement, one can still find quite a number of references to it in letters and in the newsletter of Hatzofim. In many of these references, neutral language that does not reveal much detail is used. For example, a "trip to Masada" or a "tour to Masada" is mentioned. There are a few references to unsuccessful trips to Masada. For example, the 1968 trip was considered a bore. Hatzofim's guides had nothing to say when the group visited Masada, and the entire affair was defined as "shameful."

However, a few references to Masada as a site of heroism can be found. These mostly concern its place in Israel's struggle for independence and its potential educational power and value. A report in Hatzofim[25] about the 1967 trek to Masada states:

> Masada has remained until this day a symbol of Jewish heroism without compromise or retreat; and to this day we proclaim, as a symbol for our hopes for the stability and continued existence of our State, that 'Masada shall not fall again. . . .' Masada is one of the most interesting remnants of a glorious period in our past. Try to look at it through the eyes of those who lived and fought there, and you will see that the remnants spring to life, and there is no doubt that the interest and pleasure you find in your tour of Masada will be increased.

A 1969 speech, made on Masada before a group of adolescents who had just climbed it, perhaps best expresses the ambivalence of Hatzofim toward the site. In this speech, the speaker told his listeners that the heroic stand was the aspect of Masada that had to be remembered. However, it was also stated that there were things better off not known about Masada, such as the suicide. Later, the speech touched on the dilemma of spiritual compromise versus physical defeat. The solution offered was that the slogan "Masada shall not fall again" should not be taken to mean a spiritual compromise or a physical defeat but, rather, a vow that what happened then shall never happen again. Clearly, this is a very original and painful speech, full of contradictory messages. This 1969 trip was also accompanied by many complaints. We can read, again and again, that Masada was not attractive to the youth, that they felt lazy and did not want to climb up, and that Masada had lost its meaning. Moreover, the leader of this trip suggested canceling trips to Masada during Hanuk-kah altogether. In this same vein, a letter from the Ein Gedi field school suggested that Masada should be restudied, indicating some second thoughts about its moral value.

In 1974, following the Yom Kippur War, a convention of Hatzofim's tenth graders took place at the bottom of the mountain. The impact of that war can clearly be seen in the speeches made at that time. There was a return to the old rhetoric of Masada as a symbol for Jewish heroism. However, in that very same year, Hatzofim also published a debate on the issue, titled, "Masada: Yes or No?"

It is interesting to note that only ten years later, in 1984, the annual trip of Hatzofim did not include Masada. However, that very year, Shmaria Guttman also wrote a report to Hatzofim about the educational value of Masada.

Since the Masada narrative was not discussed much in Hatzofim, it is difficult to identify the deviations from Josephus Flavius's original narra-tive. Yet we can still ask ourselves whether or not there are any significant deviations in the few places where it *is* mentioned. The examination of this issue yielded very interesting results.

We first took a look at guidebooks published and used by Hatzofim. In a 1961 "Page to the Traveler," published by the Israeli Labor Union (Histadrut), we are told on the front page that "after the destruction of the temple in Jerusalem, the last fighters found refuge in Masada." Only one speech is attributed to Elazar Ben-Yair, and according to this source, the Roman siege of Masada began in 73 A.D.

In another stenciled document (not dated, but probably from 1965–1966 or 1967), distributed by the national headquarters of Hatzofim in Tel Aviv, the following information is provided to the traveler to Masada and Ein Gedi (p. 8):

> At the beginning of the Great Revolt (66 A.D.) Masada was
> conquered by the deceit of Menachem Ben Yehuda from the Galilee.
> This conquest was, de facto, the signal for the general uprising. After
> the conquest the victors left to Jerusalem, where they became
> involved in inner feuds, in which Menachem was killed, and his
> relative, Elazar Ben-Yair, took command of Masada. In 70 A.D.,
> Jerusalem fell, and the rebels now had only three fortresses
> remaining—Herodion, southeast of Jerusalem; Macherus, in Moav;
> and Masada. After two years, the first two fell, and the Romans went
> to Masada. They did not charge the fortress but, rather,
> systematically isolated it from the external world and in this way

starved its defenders. Within four months the Romans built eight military camps from all sides of Masada. They built a siege ramp on the western side . . . and placed siege machines on top, with which they finally broke through the wall. And so a regular army of 8000 men [took over] a fortress that was held by 960 starving men, women, and children. . . . Legend has it that after all hope was lost, Elazar Ben-Yair made a momentous speech, after which they all committed suicide, the last one setting fire to all the buildings. Masada has remained until this day a symbol of Jewish heroism without compromise or retreat; and to this day we proclaim, as a symbol for our hopes for the stability and continued existence of our state, that 'Masada shall not fall again!' "

This passage contains some interesting fabrications, two of which are glaring. The first concerns the "starvation" of the rebels on top of Masada. This is simply contrary to what Josephus Flavius tells us. The second is the transformation of Elazar Ben-Yair's two speeches into one. Furthermore, reference to the suicide as a "legend" is an interesting way to escape the facts as we know them. A page earlier the anonymous author tells the reader that the only source for what occurred on Masada is Josephus Flavius. However, it appears that the use of this source is a matter of convenience. When this use is problematic, then what Josephus has to say is defined as a "legend." The usual omission of the massacre at Ein Gedi and a failure to admit the lack of a "Masada battle" is also found here, along with a total disregard of the fact that the Sicarii were on Masada.

Two additional authorless and dateless documents (probably from the early 1970s) that discuss Ein Gedi and Masada were used by Hatzofim. These documents were printed by the Ministry of Culture and Education and by the field school at Ein Gedi. Clearly, they were used to provide tour guides and travelers with information about these sites. The document about Ein Gedi describes its historical development, and on page 2 it tells us: "Josephus Flavius states that in a raid made on Ein Gedi by the Zealots from Masada to get supplies, seven hundred of the people [from Ein Gedi] were killed and many others escaped."

The second document only concerns Masada and does not mention the massacre. It states: "Masada for us is a memory of Jewish heroism. That is why it has become one of the sites of pilgrimage for Hebraic youth in the last decades. . . . In the year 66 A.D., the Great Revolt against the Romans began. Early in the revolt a group of fighters moved from Jerusalem to Masada. . . . The Zealots felt very secure on Masada." Next, we have a long passage about how the "Zealots" lived on Masada while maintaining a Jewish life-style. The report goes on to state that

> seven years after the Zealots arrived to Masada, the Romans reached it. . . . After seven months of siege, involving an army of thousands of soldiers, they managed to destroy the outer wall. . . . When the besieged realized that there was no more hope, they destroyed as much of their property as they could. . . . Elazar Ben-Yair . . . in a moving speech asked them to commit collective suicide so as not to . . . become slaves. It took some time to persuade them, but eventually they all complied. . . . Only two women and five children survived.

Again, we find a total disregard of the Sicarii, the events in Jerusalem, Ein Gedi, and the lack of battles around Masada.

Another "innovation" that can be observed here, one we shall find elsewhere too, is the use of a technique of separation or compartmentalization of problematic issues. For example, the massacre at Ein Gedi is not discussed in the context of Masada but, rather, as a separate incident. An author might simply say that the Sicarii looted Ein Gedi and killed its people. Typically, the event is not elaborated on and the puzzled reader is left guessing who the Sicarii were and from where and why they came. Since in the discussion of Masada typically the world *Zealots* is used, an interesting separation is achieved between the Sicarii and the Zealots and between Ein Gedi and Masada. Confused? Of course you are. This confusion is exactly the goal of those making the compartmentalization. It is precisely this confusion that enables them to weave a heroic tale of Masada.

That these interpretations are biased is clear, but they are not as bad as those versions of Shmaria Guttman and others in the 1940s.

Next, we examined the newsletter of Hatzofim, *Heye Nachon.* Again, not much was found here. In 1937, in Jerusalem, a new tribe of Hatzofim called Metzada was established in association with the Gymnasia Ivrit school.[26] Explaining the establishment of the new tribe, it stated that from the fall of Masada in 73 A.D. until 1937 the chain of heroism was not severed.[27] However, nothing else is mentioned in that context about Masada. Another reference can be found in the April 1947 issue of *Heye Nachon.* There, a report about a trip to Masada states: "The heart trembles in remembrance of the monumental tragedy that occurred here 1874 years ago, when a handful of Zealots stood alone against the armies of a huge empire and fought for their right to freedom and liberty. In our generation, Masada has gained a reputation as a symbol of heroism. It makes every Jewish heart tremble" (7:8). A 1966 report by two youths from Hatzofim contains a sarcastic remark concerning a trip they made to Masada: "An instructor with eyeglasses told us about the history of Masada. . . . It was interesting to see and hear the bluffs."[28]

In summary, the hallmark of Hatzofim's attitude toward Masada has been its ambivalence. On the one hand, Hatzofim has made trips to Masada and presented it as a symbol of heroism. On the other hand, Hatzofim did not place a special emphasis on Masada. It appears, therefore, that Masada was not a major issue for Hatzofim. There is no doubt that, as time passed, the Masada myth became considerably weaker for this movement.

From the mid- to the late 1960s, Masada's place in the Israeli symbolic dialogue became weakened even further. The heroism of the Six-Day War and the resulting newly accessible tourist sites pushed Masada into a corner. Although it appears that some members of the older generation of guides in Hatzofim may have wanted to continue some of the Masada tradition, the new members were clearly not too impressed or interested. Although, after the 1973 war, there was a renewed interest in Masada, it did not last. More and more emphasis was being placed on other values within the context of Masada—ecology, trips, nature.

HASHOMER HATZAIR ("The Young Guard")[29]

Hashomer Hatzair was established in Galicia (an area located between the Ukraine and Poland) in 1913. Despite a problematic beginning for its branch in Eretz Israel (then Palestine) between 1925 and 1930, the first youth groups associated with the movement were established in 1929. Hashomer Hatzair was a youth movement very close, ideologically, to the Soviet Union and to the Kibbutz Artzi movement.

The first national convention of Hashomer Hatzair in Eretz Israel took place on April 20, 1938, and was an impressive indication of the vitality and growth of this youth movement. The nuclei of many kibbutzim grew out of this movement. The members of Hashomer Hatzair were socialized with a deep love and appreciation of the land, and from 1944 on, Hashomer Hatzair also became active in urban centers (Ben-Nachum 1989).[30]

As with the other youth movements, a survey of the newsletter of Hashomer Hatzair, *Al Hachoma,* [31] was a good method for examining how Masada was handled in Hashomer Hatzair. We began our survey with the July 1938 issue of *Al Hachoma,* and it lasted until the December 1986 issue. The first reference to Masada, however, is only found in 1942, when a member from Hashomer Hatzair took part in the famous seminar organized by Shmaria Guttman.[32]

The April/May 1942 issue of *Al Hachoma* is devoted to Masada and to the first trip there by Hashomer Hatzair. The historical report about Masada is brief. It states that Sicarii were there (but no explanation is provided as to exactly who they were), that Elazar Ben-Yair made one speech, that the rebels committed suicide, and that there were seven survivors. No mention is made of the Ein Gedi massacre or of the length of the siege.

However, this trek to Masada ended in tragedy. Having finished the climb to Masada, the young hikers descended to Ein Gedi. On April 9, 1942, at around two o'clock in the morning, a hand grenade exploded near a camp fire and killed eight members of the group. This tragic accident left a very deep impression among the members of Hashomer Hatzair. An investigation of the incident revealed that while the group was cutting wood for the camp fire, a hand grenade accidentally fell and rolled into the fire, where it exploded. *Al Hachoma* continued to report, through 1943, attempts to remember and commemorate those eight members of Hashomer Hatzair who had died so tragically. The April/May 1943 issue reports a decision to hold an annual pilgrimage to the memorial erected at Ein Gedi in their honor and, indeed, documents the first annual pilgrimage (p. 6).

It is clear that members of Hashomer Hatzair continued to trek to Masada throughout the 1940s. One can find many positive references to these trips in *Al Hachoma.* The Masada experience is described in almost religious terms:

> We could not give expression to the emotions awakened in us. . . .
> About Masada itself one cannot talk. . . . Masada is not like any
> other antiquity. It is free, proud, greater than any imagination. No
> picture, no writing, no description, no story can create within you the
> exalted feeling that this ancient and lonesome rock named Masada
> [creates]. . . . Masada is not something about which one should talk.
> It is not worth it. Every person must see Masada, however, not as a
> tourist but, rather, with one's actual feet, when the whole body is
> part of the experience.[33]

For security reasons, the annual commemoration in 1944 was not held on Masada. Instead, Hashomer Hatzair held trips to the Galilee.

In 1945, Hashomer Hatzair organized an educational program, titled "The Sons of Masada," which focused on the nourishment of a strong identification with the Zionist cause. The program emphasized that Jewish Israelis were pioneers and that, as the true successors of the heroes of Masada, they had to settle the land. This program was directly connected to the tragic accident. As Elad points out, the attitude of members of Hashomer Hatzair to Masada in the 1940s was complicated. The Masada mythical narrative in itself was an intricate and emotional issue, and when the 1942 accident was added to it, the emotional complexity of the whole affair was, obviously, magnified (1989:13–14).[34]

The fact that members of Hashomer Hatzair visited Masada in the late 1940s and early 1950s is corroborated by an uncomplimentary source. The April 20, 1950, issue of *Haaretz* contains a complaint by one Zeev Schweig. He states that during a Passover tour to Masada he climbed the mountain, experiencing the awesome feelings induced by its atmosphere and its history. However, he also says that the experience was badly marred by a big red sign left on one of the arches by members of the Hashomer Hatzair youth movement. Schweig demanded that the culprits be punished.

Hashomer Hatzair made another exciting trek to Masada in 1954. On that trip, the Masada mythical narrative was emphasized over all else.[35] Additional treks in 1956[36] and 1957[37] elicited similar responses of reverence. The trip in 1958 was also used to commemorate the victims of the 1942 trek.[38] In that year, members of the youth movement helped Shmaria Guttman carry out some reconstruction and renovation work on Masada. Among other things, they helped to renovate the eastern snake path leading to the top.[39] In 1960, members of Hashomer Hatzair trekked again to Masada and held their annual commemorative ceremony.[40] The feeling about Masada was then still one of great respect:

> There are high mountains in the world. . . . There are high mountains
> in Israel, but there is a mountain that is the king of the mountains.
> This is the mountain to which most people in this country have
> climbed. Masada is the mountain. When the top is reached and one
> stands there, mouths suddenly drop, and the feeling of how big,
> beautiful and immense this mountain is, is overwhelming. Precisely its
> human size. . . . in the feeling that we too are capable of big deeds,
> like those that made history here.

Beginning in the early 1960s, the reports about Masada in *Al Hachoma* tend to become much shorter, and the main gist is a brief report about the trip and, occasionally, the number of people that took part. Some reports concerning trips do not even make it clear whether or not Masada was included. Between 1961 and 1966, even the tragedy of 1942 is not mentioned. It is brought back to memory once again in 1967, when *Al Hachoma* reports that all members of the youth movement have joined forces to plant a forest commemorating the memory of those eight victims of the 1942 trip to Masada.[41] However, the sparse reporting and lack of pathos continue until January 1969. The two issues of *Al Hachoma* from January 1983 and January 1985 report trips, but again Masada is not mentioned.

During the 1980s, *Al Hachoma* changed shape and style continuously. Trips are referred to very rarely, and when such a reference is found, Masada is not mentioned. This development does not mean that there were no more trips there but, rather, that the interest in Masada had declined. Moreover, issues of *Al Hachoma* from the 1980s, in comparison to those of previous decades, look more "serious." They feature debates about politics, ideology, and other more varied topics, and the newspaper is significantly less "experience-oriented" than before. It is not just that *Masada* is not mentioned; one can hardly find reports about experiences from trips in general or other events of Hashomer Hatzair.

Interestingly enough, *Yediot Ahronot*[42] from December 5, 1991, carried a large article about the 1942 tragedy. Shlomit Tene, the journalist, interviewed Nathan Yonathan—a famous Israeli poet—who claimed that he was one of the guides of that trip. The report opens with the observation that the 1942 trip itself has become a myth. Yonathan, who was sixty-eight years old at the time of the interview, admitted that "Masada . . . was perceived as a very heroic and charged symbol. . . . The myth of the Ein Gedi disaster was combined with the myth of Masada. . . . The trip was characterized by excessive adventurism. . . . In such trips young men, who later established the Palmach, were strengthened" (p. 27).

Additional information was garnered from an interview in July 1992 with Mr. Roni Giter, chief of education in Hashomer Hatzair. Mr. Giter stated very clearly that the importance of Masada for—and hence the interest of—Hashomer Hatzair in Masada began to decline in the 1960s. However, despite this, the movement does make an effort to climb Masada every year during Hanukkah. Thus, Masada, for Hashomer Hatzair, has turned into just another site to visit, one of many that exist in Israel. Mr. Giter's view was that the decline of Masada as an ideological site was part of a more general process of decline in the significance of symbols and myths in Jewish Israeli society. Of course, the 1942 tragedy has linked Hashomer Hatzair to Masada in a peculiarly intimate way. According to Mr. Giter, trips to Masada are accompanied now by educational and historical (not ideological) classes, like the ones held before trips to other significant archaeological or historical sites.

In summary, it can be said that Hashomer Hatzair did embrace the Masada mythical narrative in its early and formative years. This included a processing of the myth and a promotion of the actual experience of trekking to Masada. Unfortunately, the first trip of Hashomer Hatzair to Masada, in 1942, was accompanied by a horrendously tragic accident. This tragedy colored the attitude of Hashomer Hatzair, since it became a major part of the movement's collective memory about Masada. Moreover, that particular memory has become an integral part of the treks to Masada, as well as the main emphasis for a commemorative ceremony.

However, the importance of Masada for Hashomer Hatzair, both as an ideological site and as a symbol, has continuously declined since the 1960s, and Masada is now just one site among many others to visit in Israel. Of course, Masada will always remain unique for Hashomer Hatzair, not so much because of the myth but, rather, because of the tragedy that claimed the lives of eight members of the movement.

A few Jewish religious youth movements exist in Israel; however, unfortunately, there is very little documentation concerning them. Therefore, it was necessary to rely mostly on interviews for our information.

Three Jewish youth movements in Palestine and Israel have emphasized the religious identity of their members: Bnei Akiva, Ezra, and Brit Hasmoneans. Brit Hasmoneans existed between 1937 and 1949 only, mostly in Jerusalem, and was affiliated with Lehi (see the appendix). The members of Brit Hasmoneans made fewer trips than those of other youth movements and were more involved in paramilitary training (Tzameret 1989). Consequently, we shall focus our attention on Bnei Akiva and Ezra.

I wish to point out at the outset that we found that Masada played *no* significant role in the religious youth movements. Consequently, the main question we asked was, Why not?

BNEI AKIVA ("The Sons of Akiva")

The Bnei Akiva youth movement was established in Jerusalem in 1929 as a submovement of Hapoel Hamizrahi (a religious political party). At first, Hapoel Hamizrahi did not support Bnei Akiva and even avoided providing it with any form of aid. This was due to a fear of the possible "rebellion" of the younger generation and of potential competition with the parent organization and to a plethora of other explicit and implicit self-serving reasons. Most of these considerations were related to issues of political power and control. Nevertheless, Bnei Akiva set out to accomplish its goal of establishing a unique Jewish religious youth movement. The young movement found itself very quickly in a series of crises: personal, ideological, and organizational. During the 1930s, there was a split in the movement, but it continued to exist. By 1948, the movement was in a much more crystallized state. Members of Bnei Akiva took part in the War of Independence, and afterwards, Bnei Akiva continued its activities, establishing yeshivot whose students served in the Israeli army (Bar-Lev 1989). Eventually, Bnei Akiva became affiliated with Mafdal (the National Religious Party) and became increasingly identified with Gush Emunim (a national religious movement whose main goal is to settle [mostly] what they refer to as Judea and Samaria[43]).

It is very clear that there was total disregard of Masada, in the 1980s, by Bnei Akiva.[44] It is also a fact that Bnei Akiva used to climb Masada in the 1950s and 1960s, mostly during Hanukkah, just as the secular youth movements made trips there. As far as we know,[45] these climbs to Masada were not accompanied by any major educational activities. The trips, much like those made by Hatzofim, were defined as experiential and aimed at getting to know the landscape. Following the Six-Day War, trips to Masada were terminated altogether. In September of 1989, Yochanan Ben-Yaacov (from Gush Etzion—a renewed post-1967 Jewish settlement near Hebron, south of Jerusalem) was asked to prepare some materials to help make use of the Masada story in Bnei Akiva; however, this plan has not yet been put into effect.

In an interview in December 1989, Ben-Yaacov stated his view that the educational messages from the Masada narrative were inappropriate and expressed his amazement at the fact that Masada became a national myth at all. Bnei Akiva, one must add, created its own mythical tales about the defense of Gush Etzion and Biria (February 1946. Biria was a Jewish settlement in northern Palestine) (in both cases religious fighters were involved). It appears that the tendency of Bnei Akiva was not to adopt myths that did not imply a religious commitment. According to Ben-Yaacov, Masada could not have been used as an example for *religious* Jews because it has no religious lesson or message. Despite this strong opinion, Ben-Yaacov did express his wish that religious children would learn the Masada narrative because of its message concerning willingness to fight to the end. Although in many people's minds the aversion of religious Jews to the Masada narrative is due to the suicide issue (a problematic act according to Jewish faith), what emerges from Bnei Akiva is that their main concern had more to do with the image of the rebels and their negative acts. It appears that already in the 1950s, Rabbi Neria, the rabbi of Bnei Akiva, had rejected Rabbi Goren's positive attitude toward Masada. It was felt that since 66–73 A.D. was a difficult period for the Jews and since, with the exception of Josephus Flavius, there are virtually no Jewish sources concerning the period, one needs to view his account with suspicion.

Ben-Yaacov was quick to point out that the message "Masada shall not fall again" is not derived from the historical story of Masada. He stated that the perception of the Masada narrative as heroic hinges on how we view the alternative.[46] Thus, Bnei Akiva developed a very passive stance toward Masada.

EZRA

Ezra is an ultra-orthodox youth movement whose origins are in post–World War I Germany. There, young ultra-orthodox Jews reached the conclusion that a different way had to be found by which to attract the new generation to a deep belief in the Torah. In 1919, these young German Jews established Ezra. They added to the explicit religious-ideological content some external flavor of trips, simplicity, debates, and parties so as to increase the appeal and attractiveness of the new movement. In the beginning, Ezra was affiliated with Agudat Israel (or Aguda, an ultra-orthodox Jewish political party). However, it later detached itself from Aguda because it was felt that an organization whose goal was primarily educational should not be associated with a political party. From 1933 on, members of Ezra began to immigrate to Palestine. Some of them established the first kibbutzim of Poalei Agudat Israel in Eretz Israel. The first national convention of Ezra was convened in 1937. Ezra still sees itself, to this day, as a complement to ultra-orthodox Jewish education (Shneler 1989).

In an interview in the winter of 1989, Shmuel Shneler made it clear that the major emphasis of Ezra is that all actions must be conceptualized within the framework of the Torah. Thus, settling the land is not perceived as a secular and national act but, rather, as a decree from God as expressed in the Torah. In this fashion, all national goals are suffused with religious meaning. No contemporary problem is viewed as "new," and any "current" reality observed is defined as a continuation of older realities, which have already been interpreted by Jewish wisdom. Within this framework, it became possible to interpret the actions of the rebels in the Masada narrative as being in opposition to the wishes of God. In contrast, the wars of Israel may be conceptualized as permissible and thus a fulfillment of the wish of God.

The Bnei Akiva and Ezra youth movements have shared a discomfort with Masada, and both have tended to shy away from it. However, there are significant differences between the two. Bnei Akiva has found some use for the Masada narrative and has held climbs to the mountain. Ezra has no use for the narrative and has never organized a trip to Masada. The attitude of Bnei Akiva, therefore, can best be described as ambivalent; for Ezra, on the other hand, there is no ambivalence concerning the issue of Masada.

Still, there are many factors that set both of these religious youth movements apart from the secular movements. For the latter, there was a need to create a new type of Jew: proud, strong, capable of fighting to the end. This was almost intended as an answer to the traditional anti-semitic stereotype of the Jew. Therefore, these movements not only emphasized the discontinuity between the Jewish existence and experience in Europe and that in Israel; they also capitalized and thrived on it. The creation of a sharp and clear boundary between the Jew of the Diaspora and the Sabra became a major goal. This was not the case with the religious youth movements. Their emphasis was much more on continuity. They too wanted to create a new type of Jew, but not such a radically different type. Their aim was for an "overhauled" type—that is, a type that preserved the past and also added a few new refreshing elements. For them, the Masada narrative was aimed at creating a very significant difference. While Masada, constructed as a heroic tale, was crucial for secular Jews, it was not at all necessary for religious Jews. As a unification ritual, helping to create a new identity and instilling in people from different backgrounds a sense of belonging and solidarity, the Masada myth was a powerful tool in the hands of secular Zionism. Religious Zionism had no need for it. It *possessed* an identity it wanted only to improve, not to re-create. Furthermore, in the debate between those emphasizing a spiritual Judaism and those advocating a powerful, national Zionist Judaism, the religious movements were definitely more sympathetic to the former (see, for example, the story about Rabbi Yochanan Ben-Zakai[47]).

Strange as it may sound, it is more than likely that the Sicarii on top of Masada were much closer (in terms of their religiosity and adherence to

Jewish religious laws) to the religious movements, in spirit and in faith. And yet, those that were far from them ideologically were the ones that revered them, while those ideologically close to them repressed their memory. History indeed can play some interesting tricks.

BEITAR

Beitar began its existence in 1923 in Riga, Latvia, with a rather small group, forty-three young boys. From its very beginning, Beitar was part of a worldwide movement and affiliated with the revisionist faction in the Zionist movement, which also began to crystallize as an independent political force in 1923. It defined itself as an activist organization whose goal was to establish a state with a Jewish majority on both sides of the Jordan River. Militarization was a major element of the movement. This expressed itself both in the structure and in the contents of its activities. Beitar was close to both Brit Habirionim ("Alliance of the Hoodlums") and to Etzel (see appendix). The movement was active in both Palestine and, after 1948, Israel (see Peled 1989).

It is not easy to document the development of Beitar or its attitude on various issues (e.g., Masada), because written material concerning the movement is scarce. In fact, of all the secular youth movements we examined, Beitar was one of the most difficult to research.

That Masada must have occupied an important place in Beitar is easily deduced from Beitar's hymn, which explicitly mentions Masada and makes use of it as a heroic symbol. It also appears that members of the movement have traditionally visited Masada every year during their trip to the Judean desert. Although Beitar was not too happy about the suicide, it did make use of Masada as a symbol of sacrifice and of a proud stand.

One can find references to Masada in some of Beitar's written documents in the 1930s. A booklet published in April 1930, titled: *Festival in Beitar*,[48] discusses Masada as a national disaster that occurred during Passover (p. 5). Another booklet, from 1933, is titled *Beitar: A Journal for Questions of Life, Science, and Literature* and was edited by Professor Yosef Klosner. It includes a play by Avigdor Hameiri about Masada.[49] A few more reports appear in the 1950s in various documents produced by Beitar, most of which concern the annual trips to Masada and are focused on what can be described as "technical" matters (i.e., dates for the trips, cancellations, organizational details, etc.). It is also clear that during this period Beitar had a subgroup[50] named "Masada." The only report concerning the *experience* of a trip to Masada can be found in the April-May 1959 issue of *Kidma*. Written by David Avos (p. 34), the article "The Trip to Masada," is quite reflective:

> After twenty-nine minutes [of climbing] I was among the first to be on top of Masada. I withdrew into myself and thought:
> "Masada, the fortress of pride and symbol of heroism. I am here, breathing here, feeling every stone. Maybe some besieged soldier sat here too? Did he sit like me, in quiet and tranquillity, secure? Maybe without food? This fortress of heroes, how wonderful it is. What majestic sights can be seen from it, in all directions. I tried to imagine how the Hebraic heroes who were here and who fought for their freedom lived, fought, and died. . . . Finally, I was in the fortress of Masada too."

It is interesting to note that the terms Avos chooses to express his experience include words and phrases such as *soldier, heroes, fortress of pride, symbol of heroism,* and *wonderful*. Avos reveals absolutely no hesitation about what really took place on that rock. That is quite the stereotypical reaction of those trekking to Masada during that period.

From 1961, we found the first issue of a journal published by Beitar, called *Masada*. This issue contains a piece about a "big" trip planned to Masada. It is not clear whether this "big" trip ever took place or how and why this journal was launched and faded. (We were able to find only one issue.) A 1964 issue of *Kidma*[51] has a short piece by Moshe Ben-Shachar concerning the excavations of Masada led by Yigael Yadin. This piece states that it was Zeev Jabotinski, the founder and head of Beitar, who was responsible for the reference to Masada in Beitar's hymn. Ben-Shachar also states that 960 Jewish fighters fought heroically and valiantly at Masada against 10,000 Roman soldiers.[52]

It is very clear that the Masada mythical narrative was well ingrained among members of Beitar. Like the members of other youth movements, the members of Beitar were involved in an annual pilgrimage to Masada, in which an experience imbued with heroism was constructed. Until the early 1960s, all descriptions of the "Masada experience" use the familiar stereotypical expressions that relay a socially constructed experience full of awe and heroism.

We examined about seventeen different journals and publications related to Beitar; most contained no mention of Masada whatsoever. One journal provided an exception: *Maoz*.

An examination of *Maoz*, journal of Beitar for the period between the

1960s and the 1980s, reveals some interesting findings. That young members of Beitar visited Masada regularly is quite clear. These trips are described in *Maoz* in the usual heroic terms. A change, however, can already be discerned in the February 5, 1967, issue, when Hanan Reich, a participant in the annual trek to Masada, wrote that

> a strong slap woke me from my sleep.... It was 5:30 A.M.... Let us
> sleep! Even during basic training I did not wake up so early....
>   During the trek, we saw all sorts of caves and rocks near Ein
> Gedi; the devil only knows why we had to see them at all....
>   During the entire climb to Masada, I cursed Elazar Ben-Yair and
> his friends, who, for some reason, could not find a more normal
> place to fortify in their war with the Romans than this huge rock to
> which one's soul can almost fly away from the sheer effort needed to
> get there. I said in my heart, 'If they had fortified themselves in
> Dizengoff Street in Tel Aviv [one of the central streets in Tel Aviv,
> known for its entertainment centers], we could now eat some good
> steak, [go to] the swimming pool, and hear all the explanations about
> Masada on a full belly. [Instead] here we are, on a rock, in the
> middle of the desert, hungry....
>   Whoever goes on the next trip must be crazy. What is wrong with
> [staying at] home? (p. 9)

In the very same issue of *Maoz,* Haim Avni, one of the guides of that trek, provides his version of the trip (p. 12), in which the reader is exposed to the standard mythical narrative. According to Avni, the main goal of the trek was to examine the heroism of the Zealots. All in all, this issue of *Maoz* contained three reports about Masada, only one of which repeated the old clichés about the site. The two others were quite critical.

From December 1970 until the 1980s, there is no more mention of Masada in *Maoz* except in the April-May 1974 issue, where it is reported that a trip to the Judean desert included a noisy visit to Masada.

Although finding information about Masada in Beitar proved to be a difficult task, it seems safe to conclude that Masada was incorporated into Beitar's culture in a number of ways: the word Masada appears in Beitar's hymn; a journal named *Masada* was published by Beitar; and a subgroup within Beitar called itself "Masada." Of course, there was also the annual pilgrimage to the site. It does appear, however, that, as with the other youth movements, the importance of Masada began to decline for Beitar sometime during the early part of the 1970s.

One may also conclude from all the above that there *was* some ambivalence in Beitar concerning Masada. Perhaps a telltale indicator for this ambivalence can be found in a short piece published in *Moledet* of 1947 by K. Echad (probably a pseudonym, since *kol echad* means "anyone"). The author presents an extremely strong position against what he or she refers to as the "Masada ritual." For the author, Masada is a too-ancient event, one that involved a "no choice" situation. A major criticism is that what the author calls the "Masada ritual" is not meant to symbolize a struggle against annihilation but, rather, a struggle to "save face." Masada, according to this interpretation, represents defeatism and a "battle of despair," not a "battle of rescue." This, Echad maintains, makes the image of the Jewish Israeli activist equal to that of a desperate fighter. The major conclusion of Echad is that the modern activist Zionist should not limit his ideological world to a fight for honor, like the ones on Masada and Warsaw Ghetto, but expand his view to a struggle of rescue and thus save the body of the nation, not its honor.

JEWISH YOUTH MOVEMENTS OUTSIDE OF PALESTINE AND ISRAEL

We wondered whether or not Jewish youth movements outside Palestine-Israel utilized the Masada mythical narrative and, if so, what role it played for them. Despite some preliminary efforts, it became clear very quickly that carrying out research from such a distance was futile, so we gave up on that idea. However, in the end, we were able to locate some documentation here in Israel.

One series of papers that we found documents a youth movement called MASADA, which published a newsletter named, at first, *Masada*, and later on, *Masada News*. We were able to track down this publication from 1938 to 1948.

"MASADA was formed, in December, 1933, as the result of the amalgamation of several Zionist youth groups in the vicinity of New York with groups in Cleveland and Minneapolis. The former were then known as the Youth Zionist Organization of America. . . . The latter as MASADA, the Young Men's Zionist Organization of America" (*Masada*, February 1940:7). MASADA was a federation of societies affiliated with the Zionist Organization of America (p. 17). Eligible members were between the ages of 18 and 30. Why did they choose to call themselves MASADA?

> The name "MASADA" derives from the Hebrew word meaning "Foundation" and was the name of an ancient fortress in the hill country of southern Palestine.*

* The MASADA emblem which adorns all material used by the organization is a facsimile of the fortress. It appears on the back page of the cover. (*Masada* February 1940:18–19)

Built upon a towering rock, . . . impregnable in its strength,
MASADA remained in Jewish hands throughout the War against
Rome, a symbol of Jewish independence when the entire world was
engulfed in the Roman sea. It was the rallying point from which the
Jewish patriots struck out at the Romans again and again in defense
of land and liberty.
At MASADA the last struggle against Rome began, and here it
came to its bloody end. After the armies of the emperor Vespasian
destroyed Jerusalem in 60 A.D. and over-ran all of Palestine, a
thousand Jewish heroes at MASADA stubbornly held out for three
years longer, refusing to yield.
It was a hopeless resistance. At last the Romans broke through
MASADA'S walls. Inside they met the stillness of death. The
defenders of the fortress had destroyed each other, choosing to die by
their own hands as freemen rather than live as the slaves of Rome.
The real victory was with the Jews. MASADA was not destroyed. It
became the symbol of the Jewish will to live as a nation, of refusal to
surrender to the forces threatening its extinction.

Thus, thousands of kilometers from Palestine, in the U.S.A., an organization that called itself MASADA was already, in the 1930s, disseminating the Masada mythical narrative. That the historical narrative
provided there contains some factual mistakes is clear. For example,
Jerusalem fell in 70 A.D.; MASADA was not the basis for raids against
the Romans (but probably was a base for raids against other Jewish
settlements); the "heroes" were actually Sicarii; there is no mention of
Ein Gedi. So the American version of the Masada mythical narrative
was no different, basically, from the local Jewish version in Palestine;
both presented a mythical narrative.

The second document we found, titled: *A Practical Thematic Approach to Jewish Youth Group Education,* was based on the historical
period of the Second Temple and written by Baruch Fischoff. This document was produced and edited by the Information and Training section of
the Youth and Hechalutz Department, World Zionist Organization, in Jerusalem 1974. It was intended for those training to become guides for
groups of Zionist-affiliated youth abroad. What does this booklet tell the
guides about Masada?

It states (p. 18) that after the fall of Jerusalem in 70 A.D.,

pockets of resistance remained in each of Herod's three fortresses,
Herodion . . . Macherus . . . and Masada. . . . Masada held out the
longest. To isolate its thousand defenders, the Romans invested an

army of fifteen thousand under Titus, Vespasian's son and future Emperor of Rome and built a wall around the entire mountain. For the final assault, the Romans built an enormous ramp climbing up the citadel's sheer western wall. Seeing themselves doomed, the defenders defiantly committed suicide *en masse,* rather than be taken prisoners, on the night before the inevitable Roman conquest.

The Masada mythical narrative is very clearly presented here. The innovations added by this particular interpretation include Titus as the head of the Roman army that took Masada (a simple fabrication) and a reference to the "final assault," implying that there were previous "assaults."

A third series of documents we found was a file of Bnei Metzada ("the sons of Masada"): a dateless and elaborate program for the preparation of a long didactic seminar about Masada. The file was prepared by the World Zionist Organization (where we found it), in Hebrew, for what must have been a local audience (and visitors whose Hebrew was fluent). One document in the file dates to 1986, although the rest are probably from the late 1970s. This document says the following about Masada:

> In 70 A.D. Jerusalem fell. . . . The remaining Zealots gathered together in the Judean desert. These bands hid themselves in caves and valleys, and their center was Masada. . . .
> [A short description of Masada follows.]
> Here the warriors and their families gathered—960 people headed by Elazar Ben-Yair. They used the fortress as a last refuge— the final place in the land to be held by Jews.
> The Romans knew that they had to destroy the last rebels in order that their victory would be complete. The tenth legion of the Roman army, consisting of eight thousand fighters, descended from Jerusalem with its vehicles and equipment to conquer Masada. . . .
> The Romans had experience in conquering fortresses, and they tried the usual method—siege. . . . They built a wall around Masada. . . . All the roads to Masada were blocked. The number of Roman camps rose to eight. But all the efforts were in vain. . . .
> The siege lasted three years, as the Romans suffered from the desert's heat, from the difficulty in securing supplies, and from the lack of water. When the Romans realized that Masada was not going to fall in this way, they changed their strategy. In the most convenient place, south of the rock, hundreds of slaves and workers began to pour sand and soil till a huge siege ramp was erected. It formed a gradual slope enabling a comfortable climb to the top of the mountain. The war machines—iron rams and catapults—were

brought to the ramp and began to hit the wall of Masada. The first
wall fell, and a second wall from wood and stones was erected
quickly. During the day the Romans rammed, and at night the
Zealots went out and set the battle machines on fire. But, eventually,
the fire spread and burnt the wooden wall too. When the Zealots saw
that all hope was lost, they convened during the night before the
Romans broke [into the fortress], and inspired by Elazar Ben-Yair
they decided that it was better to die free than to become prisoners of
the Romans (pp. 1–2)

The narrative is heroic, continuous, and impressive. However, it constitutes a nice illustration of the Masada mythical narrative. The usual
omissions are found here (e. g., Zealots instead of Sicarii; no Ein Gedi
massacre). However, there are also a number of new fabrications in this
account: for example, the convening of bands, whose center was Masada,
in the Judean desert *after* the fall of Jerusalem; the three-year siege; the
change of strategy by the Romans; and the raids by the people of Masada
on the "war machines."

Hence, we can easily see how the Masada mythical narrative was dis-
seminated to non-Israeli Jews as well.

The way in which the Masada mythical narrative has been handled by the
different youth movements reflects its complexity in relation to Israeli society in general. The religious youth movements have basically down-
played or ignored it altogether. Among the secular youth movements,
Hatzofim never made a big issue out of it. Clearly, Hanoar Haoved
Vehalomed placed the most value on Masada. It is not surprising, therefore, that Shmaria Guttman was associated with this particular youth
movement. Hashomer Hatzair also valued Masada; however, it had a special interest in the site following the tragic 1942 accident. Mahanot
Haolim and Beitar also saw an important value in Masada. All of these
youth movements began losing interest in Masada as an ideological symbol in the 1960s and 1970s. As a microcosm, the rise and decline of the
Masada mythical narrative among the secular youth movements parallels
that which occurred in the Israeli army, as well as the general interest of
Israeli society in Masada.

Chapter Six

Masada and the Pre-State Jewish Underground Groups

WITH THE FORMAL ESTABLISHMENT of the State of Israel, in 1948, the Israeli army (IDF) came into existence. However, since the early days of the Jewish resettlement of Palestine, beginning in the 1880s, various Jewish groups that chose to describe themselves as "defense groups" were established. The early groups, such as Bar Giora, Hashomer, and Hakibbutz, were not very large. However, from the 1920s, three particular groups, in fact underground armed organizations with an ideology of direct action, were formed. These groups, in descending order of size, were the Hagana, Etzel, and Lehi (for more about these groups see the appendix). We shall next examine the way Masada was perceived in each of these groups. The importance of this detailed examination lies in the fact that many members of these groups became key political and military leaders of Israel following the establishment of the state of Israel. Two examples will suffice: Menachem Begin, who was the last commander of Etzel, and Yitzhak Shamir, who was one of the commanders of Lehi, became prime ministers of Israel. In the context of the Israeli experience, it is essential that we understand how Masada was viewed in these groups and what its role was in shaping the consciousness of members in the groups.

HAGANA-PALMACH (Pelugot Machatz)[1]

There can be no doubt that the Hagana, particularly its military elite force, the Palmach, made extensive use of the Masada myth.

Already in August 1937, speaking at a commemoration ceremony in Ein Harod, Yitzhak Tabenkin—a prominent Yishuv leader—made an explicit reference to the Great Revolt, stating that it was the "war heroism" and the memory of the Jewish Zealots that helped to perpetuate the Jewish national existence. Thanks to the Zealots, according to Tabenkin, some very important Jewish values, language and culture—as well as the Torah—were preserved.[2] In 1938, another prominent leader of this period, Berl Katznelson, stated that the "value of Masada for us lies ... in its power of renewal. This Masada, which ended as it did, and which everyone is aware of, its power of renewal and education, is for all the generations that grow up in the land." This statement was made in response to the possibility that under one of the alternative compromises suggested at the time to divide Palestine between Jews and Arabs, Masada would not remain under Jewish sovereignty. Katznelson objected to that emphatically.[3] On this matter, Tabenkin also added: "It is not only Jerusalem that we cannot relinquish but Masada too. And this [not giving up Masada] is not a mystical value but a very realistic one."[4]

There are two aspects to Masada in the Palmach. One is the plain record of the actual treks and climbs to Masada. The other is the phenomenology of the Masada experience itself.

Treks to Masada

Captain M. Yaakubovitz states in his book: "It was a tradition in the Palmach to climb, every year, in the Month of Adar (March), to the top of Masada. We had the privilege of participating in the last trek that the Palmach made to Masada in 1947" (1953:65). Yaakubovitz vividly describes that trip: the long walk, the glorious landscapes, the excitement of the climb to the fortress and the ceremonies there, the overnight sleep on top, and the continuation of the field trip to Sodom the next day. Zerubavel Gilad (1955, book 2, pp. 368–69) also reports on the Palmach's treks to Masada. *Sefer Toldot Hahagana* (S.T.H.), the monumental eight-volume history of the Hagana, also provides a picture of Palmach fighters on their way to Masada (vol. 3, p. 417). This, in the context of a chapter that describes the very creation of the Palmach. Apparently, the historical description of that creation needed framing within the Masada context.

One of the more detailed reports about trips to Masada has been provided by Meir Pail in a chapter titled, "On the Treks of the Palmach to Masada" (in Hillman and Magen 1986:32–37). Pail states that he loved to climb Masada and read Josephus Flavius. He also refers to the people at Masada as Zealots. According to Pail, until 1943, the Palmach's treks to Masada were carried out mostly by Palmach scouts who explored (and charted) the Judean desert and the Negev in a more or less systematic fashion. In 1943, the trek to Masada became much more organized and institutionalized, and from the winter of 1944 on, Masada was a regular part of a two-week trek in the Palmach. These treks were quite standard: the climb, ceremonies, and sometimes an overnight sleep on top of the mountain. These treks (of which Masada was only a portion; the treks continued on to Sodom) were certainly difficult and frequently dangerous. The terrain itself was hazardous, and the travelers were occasionally attacked by gangs of Arab bandits. Between 1941 and 1947, according to Pail, probably *all* recruits to the Palmach took part in the trips and therefore participated in the Masada experience. This view is clearly supported by S.T.H. (vol. 1, part 3, p. 270), where it is explicitly stated that compulsory trips in the Palmach included Masada and were an indispensable part of training.

It is interesting to note that Pail expresses no doubt that Masada represents an important site and value, something to be discussed and debated: "I still prefer swearing-ins on Masada to those at the Western Wall" (p. 37). Pail adds, however, that the Warsaw Ghetto revolt is easier for him to identify with than Masada.

The actual experience is also interesting to take a look at. For the sake of illustration, I shall provide two examples. The basic approaches of the persons writing these reports are different, yet they describe very similar experiences. The first report is by a female member of the Palmach:[5]

> And I walked in the same path—and Masada!!—the road to it was
> difficult. Members who more than once felt weak now felt very
> strong and walked the long path without failure. It must have been
> the magic of Masada. It reinforced and excited. Masada! We were
> marching, young thoughtful fighters from Israel, on its sacred soil.
> The eyes were covered with fog. Through that fog the vision of the
> last Zealots arose. We were breathing the same air those Hebraic
> heroes breathed: working people, farmers, against Roman legions—
> Hebrews whose honor was not desecrated.

Another report expresses more ambivalence but still represents a deep identification with the people of Masada:

> Precisely in these days, days of siege and loss, from within and from
> without, in the face of our deep anxiety for the fate of the land,
> which shall be decided upon when the war ends. . . . How deep is the
> unification experience when we commune with the great past that
> hides from generations within the walls of Masada! The feeling of the
> last on the wall, not to die but to live a constructive life.[6]

The influence of the myth, particularly what was perceived as the heroism of the people of Masada, was not confined to experiential rituals involving trekking and climbing in a harsh terrain. It could also be found in a number of other contexts, of which three deserve special mention: the area of operations, the Warsaw Ghetto, and what has become known as the "Plan for the North."

Gush Etzion

Both prior to and during the 1948 War of Independence, Jewish forces were caught in a number of desperate situations. On more than one occasion, the comparison to Masada arose. One good example is the battle around Gush Etzion. Gush Etzion was composed of four Jewish settlements near the Jerusalem-Bethlehem-Hebron road, about twenty-four kilometers south of Jerusalem, and was defended by Palmach forces. The Gush became increasingly isolated, and the last supply convoy,[7] on March 27, 1948, was unable to reach the settlements. The settlers in the Gush were under constant attack by Arab military and paramilitary forces. The final attack took place on May 13, 1948, at which time the defenders of one settlement (Kfar Etzion) were all killed. The remaining three settlements surrendered. In the chronicle of these events,[8] it is stated that "for forty-seven days the battles around the Gush did not abate. . . . The number of killed and wounded was high, and the 'Masada question' stood before the battle-ready, remaining, fighters."

Warsaw Ghetto

A second context in which the influence of the myth was particularly felt was the Warsaw Ghetto. In quite a few places, Masada is mentioned in the same breath as the April 19–May 16, 1943, Warsaw Ghetto revolt (e.g., Litai 1963 and Shapira 1992:453–55). The idea, of course, is to make a comparison to the mythical narrative, not to the original. Thus, the association is to a "last stand," to "fighting heroically against all odds to the end" with "no choice." Josephus Flavius's original narrative, as given, may even make the comparison to the 1943 Warsaw Ghetto revolt offensive. Indeed, Kedar (1982:58) points out that there is no reason to compare the two. However, as Shapira (1992:453–58) observes, the ideology prevalent in the Yishuv, which emphasized the need to *fight*, created an ideological kinship with the survivors of the revolt. Some *very* difficult questions regarding the amount of support and actual help that members of the Yishuv could provide to the Jews in Poland, as well as the unease among the elite of the Yishuv (certainly the Hagana) that European Jews *did not fight* and were slaughtered "like lambs," were repressed. This perception made it very difficult for them to identify with Holocaust survivors.

Hence, the association of Masada to the 1943 Warsaw Ghetto revolt must be viewed within the broader historical and analytical framework of Jewish-Israeli attitudes towards the Holocaust. Both Dina Porat (1991) and Tom Segev (1991) have studied this complicated issue. One nagging question for many of the Yishuv's leaders, was, as Gonen put it, "Why didn't the Jews fight?" (1975:217). The Masada mythical narrative presents an image of Jews "fighting to the end," whereas the Holocaust implied the slaughter of most Jews without even the semblance of a fight. How is such a contradiction reconciled? Against this background, the rhetoric was transformed into an emphasizing of the few occasions when Jews *did* fight (e.g., the 1943 Warsaw Ghetto revolt) to deny the very legitimacy of the question (e.g., Gonen 1975:217) and to provide a suitable "answer." The connection between Masada and the Warsaw Ghetto is a social construction that is definitely *not* grounded in historical fact but, rather, emphasizes the heroic light in which the ghetto revolt is presented. Only in due time and with a significant change in Jewish Israelis' perception of the Holocaust (mostly by a redefinition of the "role" of the victims in a way that makes their deaths more respectable and honorable) will Israel begin the painful process of coping with the terrible meaning of the Holocaust (e.g., see Segev 1991).

The Masada Plan

However, the most publicized connection of Masada to the Palmach (that is, with the exception of the continuous 1941–1947 treks to the desert fortress) is what has become known as the "Masada Plan" or the "Plan for the North" (in Hebrew, *Tochnit hatzafon*). This plan was a direct result of the fear instilled in the Hagana by the successes of Rommel's Afrikan Korps in North Africa in 1941. The danger of a German invasion of Palestine seemed a very real threat in early 1942. One must remember, too, that the fear of a German invasion went through different phases during 1940–1942. In the early stages, the fear was of an invasion from the north (after the fall of France, the French forces in Syria, commanded by General Mittelhauser, became loyal to Philippe Pétain's Vichy government [1940–1944]). Later on, the fear was transferred to Rommel's forces in the south.

Although the invasion never occurred, the debates about the *Masada Plan* between 1940 and 1942 occupy an extremely important place in the history of Israel. This was the time and the occasion when the significance of Masada as a myth was crystallized and amplified. It is therefore important to use this opportunity to understand the nature and dynamics of the Nazi threat, as well as the reactions to it.

The first discussions concerning the evacuation of the Middle-East were held by the British in June of 1940. Between April 1941 and November 1942 (Rommel's defeat at El Alamein), various plans of evacuation were discussed in London, Cairo, and Jerusalem. British plans crystallized in May 1941. In principle, only British citizens were to be evacuated; Arabs and Jews would not be allowed to leave. Since the danger of being a Jew under a Nazi occupation was obvious, the discussions concerning evacuation plans were suspended. The military situation improved during July-August 1941, and the urgency of the evacuation plans decreased. By January 1942, British planning for evacuation was no longer taking place, a position approved by London in April 1942 (Brener 1981:20–21; Gelber 1990).

In response to this situation and to the partial information arriving from Europe regarding the fate of the Jews there, anxieties in the Yishuv were high. The basic question was what to do should the Nazis invade Palestine.

There were many discussions, and the range of opinions was broad. Some thought that surrender was the answer, while others wanted to fight "to the end." The "Plan for the North" was considered one of the alternative solutions to the above dilemma. Yitzhak Tabenkin spoke at least twice in public about the fear of a German invasion and possible reactions to it.[9] He stated:

> Is there any point to fighting? Maybe a fatalistic surrender is called
> for. This is what happened to Poland, Norway, Holland, and
> Belgium. What else can we do? . . . No one can escape from a
> cemetery. But this sickness associated with preparalysis is damaging.
> It diminishes the power of life and quickens the reign of death—the
> enemy of life. Also sick is the belief in the fatal power of Nazism. . . .
> Life should be given for life, not for defeat. The end will not come
> tomorrow, and victory will not come the day after. . . . Nazism builds
> on treason. . . . But . . . there is no way to coexist with Nazism. It
> began with the extermination of the Jews, but a fate of slavery and
> suppression awaits anyone conquered by it. They too have no
> peaceful solution. There is no escape in surrender. The future will be
> bought by war and struggle. . . . The Jewish settlement in Eretz Israel
> must become today the center for the [Jewish] people, it must be in

charge of saving the people and guiding its daily life. . . . We have no choice . . . but to fight this war with all the power we have. . . . If we have the spirit, we shall fight this war with all our strength, or we will fall in it with all our strength—ready to stand and sacrifice. . . . We shall not beat the enemy power with fatalism but, rather, with great responsibility, because there is no choice, because this is the edict of life.

The British defense plan for Palestine was crystallized in early 1942 and was called "Palestine Final Fortress" (Gelber 1990:40). The British based their plan on the Carmel mountain as a natural place for command and control of British forces trying to block the advance of Axis forces.

The Jewish leadership in Palestine was apparently becoming more and more concerned in 1942 about the danger of a pro-Nazi revolution in Syria or in other Arab countries and of a combined Axis invasion of Palestine (first from the north, later on from the west by a paratrooper/amphibian attack, and in the spring and beginning of summer from the south) (Gelber 1990:44–62). Talk of increasing the military power of the Jews was common among Jewish leaders—both to aid the British and possible Arab allies in the fight against the Germans and for carrying on guerrilla warfare in the event of a German invasion and occupation. In the spring of 1942, it was clear to the leaders of the Yishuv that the Jews would not be evacuated from Palestine by the British and the leaders were not sure that they wanted to be. What has become known as the "Plan for the North" (or "Haifa-Tobruk," or "Haifa-Masada-Musa-Dagh"), was a product of the fear prevalent during this period.

The basic idea was to concentrate the Yishuv (the evacuation of women and children—perhaps to Cyprus—was considered) into a huge fortified locality around Mount Carmel and Haifa. The plan assumed an area of about two hundred square kilometers from where, so it was believed, the fight against the Germans could be continued for as long as possible. Since the scenario of a German invasion was uncertain and unclear, various scripts for such an invasion and alternative responses were envisioned, discussed, and debated. In one of the discussions, David Shealtiel, Palmach commander of Haifa, stated that "it was easier to die on Masada than it would be to live under the regime of the Gestapo. . . . It is better that we take three thousand men who are ready for everything (whom we'll find) and go to the mountains, prepared for guerrilla warfare" (in Gelber 1990:56). On June 30, 1942, Yitzhak Greenboim stated in a meeting of the leadership of the Jewish Agency that "if . . . we find ourselves in a state of invasion [and occupation], we must make sure that, at the very least, we will leave a 'Masada' legend after us. We should not be like the Jews of Germany and Poland, because if such were the case there would be no revival of Zionism" (in Gelber 1990:65).[10]

A dissenting view was expressed by Yigael Alon, who was later the commander of the Palmach:

> It was clear that the organized Yishuv and the Hagana were prepared
> for a loss of life and property in this battle. We had no illusions
> about it. However, the readiness to sacrifice for the salvation of the
> people and the readiness to sacrifice for the sake of "making" history
> are not the same. There was no justification for a total, Don Quixote
> type of war, lacking any real chance, or for a Masada-type war—a
> war that is beyond all hope. The defenders of ancient Masada
> reached their conclusion only after all other options were exhausted.
> And, indeed, only because of that we admire their terrible glorious
> act. (Alon 1985:23)

Historical researchers of the "Plan for the North" were also involved in an academic debate about that plan. It is easy to see that in the face of a possible German invasion, opinion among the Yishuv leadership was divided. The "Plan for the North," better known as "Masada on the Carmel," was worked out by Yochanan Ratner and Yitzhak Sadeh and was seriously debated, since quite a few commanders in the Hagana seem to have doubted its practicality. Moreover, Gelber points out (1990:56) that the "plan" never garnered much enthusiasm: "*Tochnit hatzafon* never progressed beyond ideas and wishful thinking; it is certain that there was no operational plan for a stand [against the invasion] by the Yishuv in those days." Hence, there exists a difference of opinion on this subject. Gelber (1990, clearly supported by Tom Segev), on the one hand, basically says that the "Plan for the North" never went beyond the drawing-board stage. In other words, he maintains that there was no real military "plan" but, rather, an idea loosely based on a number of discussions and debates. On the other hand, Uri Brener (1984), among others, maintains that there actually *was* a plan. When asked about this matter, Shmaria Guttman, who was one of those let in on the secret of the "plan," told me:

> If there are no documents, does that mean there was no plan? Thus,
> there is no document that says at a specific period a group of leaders
> of the Hagana decided to concentrate all the Jews on Mount Carmel
> against the Nazis that were supposed to be approaching Eretz
> Israel . . . that were believed to be approaching. No documents, so

historians say, "It never was," because no documents exist, because nothing was written then about it. It was so secret that people did not discuss it. So today, historians can say, "It never was." So it is good that there are still a few people that can say, "But I was [present] in these discussions," so they tell me that I may be imagining things, so [they say,] "we have either to believe you or not to believe you." Difficult things. (Interview, January 29, 1987)

The debate found its way, as did many others, into the daily newspapers. Yaacov Haelion, in a long report in *Maariv*'s weekly supplement (July 10, 1981), titled "Masada That Never Was," surveyed the debate and interviewed the various participants. Tom Segev, in *Haaretz* of August 24, 1979, referred to Gelber's work as "The Legend of the 'Plan for the North.' " The implication was, of course, that no such plan ever existed. The reason for the "legend," supposedly, was that the leaders of the Yishuv, feeling guilty in the face of events taking place in Europe, wanted to create a symbol that would demonstrate how far they were willing to go in resisting the Germans. This theory places the creation of the "legend" sometime *after* the conclusion of World War II. Responses in *Haaretz* from September 1979 testify to the anger raised by this claim. Moreover, while Tal merely reported the controversy, without expressing a clear position one way or another (1990), Porat, a reputable and solid historian, does not accept Gelber's interpretation (1990). It is not easy to resolve this debate. However, as pointed out in Haelion's *Maariv* report, there probably *was* a plan, accompanied by *some* preparations. This plan was not fully developed militarily, however. Using the term "legend" to describe the plan is, most probably, an exaggeration.[11] Professor Yehuda Bauer may have hit on the right interpretation when he commented on the debate in the following manner:

> There were probably no real, detailed military plans, like those prepared today by the Israeli army. Therefore, Dr. Gelber is correct when he claims that this was not a detailed plan with clear logistics. However, and, contrary to his [Gelber's] view, I think that this plan was taken very seriously and that the plan to base the defense of the northern region on forces from the Hagana, the settlements police, and the Jewish soldiers in the British army was quite practical. (In Haelion 1981:24)

In short, it was no mere coincidence that the trek and climb to Masada became integral parts of the training program and ambience of the Palmach. The Masada experience in the Palmach was an important building block in the process of socialization for heroism and sacrifice. A look at the newspapers of the period and at Palmach literature reveals not only the fact that these treks and climbs took place but also that they left a deep impression on the members of the Palmach ("Palmachniks") who had had the experience. It is evident that the Palmachniks felt total identification with the myth.

Hence, members of the Hagana and of the Palmach made it their business to visit Masada regularly. Hagana and Palmach socialization agents emphasized that the reconquest of a land involved many trips through the land and a knowledge of its geography.[12] Most of these trips involved a great deal of walking, in harsh terrain and sometimes under very difficult and dangerous conditions. Masada became a preferred site, difficult to reach, in the midst of the small but dangerous Judean desert. In fact, one of the more famous scouts of the Hagana, Rechavam Zeevi ("Gandhi"), named his daughter Masada. Thus, some very prominent commanders in the Hagana and Palmach were exposed to the Masada myth in such a way that they embraced it wholeheartedly and turned it into a key element of their newly emerging national identity. Many of these people later became important figures in the State of Israel and its army and carried their Masada heritage and legacy along the way. Through the Palmach, the political, educational, and social elite of Israel in the early years of the state adopted Masada as a prominent symbol in their newborn national identity.

ETZEL (IRGUN TZVAI LEUMI)

It is difficult to find references to Masada and to the Great Revolt in the publications of Etzel, unlike those of the Hagana. This lack is even stranger considering the fact that Masada is mentioned specifically in Beitar's hymn. That particular reference must be taken to imply an attitude of admiration toward Masada.

Occasional reference to Masada can be found in interviews. For example, Moshe Bar-Kochva, who was a member of Etzel and later a high-ranking officer in the IDF, stated in an interview (to be mentioned again in the next chapter) that Masada was discussed in Etzel.

A second reference is a small booklet titled *Masada,* published, in 1933, by a group which identified itself as "the organization of revisionist students in Jerusalem." The booklet attacks, on the front page, the "pacifists" and contains a paper by Klosner about Masada, with another piece

by M. Dar about anti-Semitism concerning the period from the fall of Masada until 1933.

A third, explicit reference was made during the period when the
"Plan of the North" was being developed. In describing the preparations of the Palmach for a possible German invasion, Niv, the "official"
historian of Etzel, states that the high command of Etzel had also
worked out a plan

> in the case that it would be clear, without a doubt, that the fate of the
> Yishuv were sealed for doom. Here too the exemplary model of Masada
> from the war of Judea with Rome was before the eyes of planners.
> However, the heads of the organization wanted to produce from this
> desperate stand a similar historical value by creating a political fact,
> even if it were only symbolic. The heart of the plan was to concentrate
> close to a thousand Etzel fighters from all branches in the Old City of
> Jerusalem. There they would fortify their position and declare the
> establishment of a Hebrew state and, as the army of this state, would
> fight and defend the city to the last fighter. As activists in the
> organization, who were also involved in the discussions, testified, the
> plan did not take into consideration any possibility of a Jewish victory,
> except the slight chance that the siege would take a few months—on the
> assumption that the Germans would not dare bomb the Christian holy
> places so easily. For the preparations, a special headquarters was created
> in Jerusalem. It began to accumulate water, cigarettes, etcetera, for war
> and for life under siege. Proper instructions were given to the
> commanders of the branches, and recruitment of manpower for the plan
> began; with it intensive requisitions of materials and equipment also
> began. The high command immersed itself totally in planning the
> operation. (vol. 3: 104)

Aryeh Naor (1990:263–64) adds that this plan was originally suggested to David Raziel by Eliahu Lankin. Interestingly enough, according
to Naor, Lankin believed that Etzel in the Old City would have to fight
the British, not the Nazis, and estimated that its fighters could hold out
for no more than twenty or thirty days, "but at least it will be a symbolic
example for future generations and will keep the idea of a Jewish state
alive in the hearts of the young." According to Naor, Raziel answered
Lankin as follows:

> You suggest a new Masada. What is the rush? The opportunity for a
> desperate act will not be lost to us. It is possible that at the end of
> this war, if it ends unsuccessfully, there will be no escape from
> Masada. But we must remember that only very few will be ready to

go to Masada, and if our generation will not make the necessary preparations during the big war, will not accumulate weapons, and will not get ready for the revolt at the war's end, then all that will remain from the heroism of the new Masada is a tragic episode.

Naor states that in the spring of 1941, as the fear of a German invasion increased, Raziel mentioned the Old City plan once more. Naor adds that there was no doubt that if the Germans had invaded and conquered Palestine, Etzel would have executed the plan.[13] That such a plan was serious and that it was based on the "lesson" of Masada is obvious. The symbolic importance of Masada is once again implied here, as in Beitar's hymn.

In 1946, Menachem Begin, then commander of Etzel, responded to an accusation made earlier by David Ben-Gurion that the activities of Etzel would lead to a modern-day Masada. He published a response in the newspaper of Etzel that also demonstrates an ambivalent attitude towards Masada: "Masada—to make a distinction—is a chapter of heroism that came after a military defeat. But we have not yet been militarily defeated. The fighting Hebraic force has not been broken yet. . . . There is no objective reason therefore to raise our hands; there is also no reason to commit suicide."[14]

Some support for the accusations of Ben-Gurion can be found in the debate that took place at the time in the British House of Lords. There, Herbert Samuel made a historical analogy between the rebel Zealots who fought Rome and the Etzel in its fight against Britain. In making the comparison, Samuel was sending an implicit warning to Etzel that its fate would be similar to the fate of the Zealots. In response, Etzel expressed pride for the very comparison to the Zealots and criticized Herbert Samuel for not making what they felt was the true analogy:

The Zealots indeed all fell in the battle, but their war, sacrifice, love, and death planted eternal life in the Hebraic nation, and it still exists; and look at the miracle: it is fighting again—after two thousand years of [dispersion in the] Galut—to free its holy land. . . . Where is the people whose heroes destroyed Masada? . . . Read well the writing on the wall.[15]

Begin's response reveals once again an ambivalence toward identification with Masada, particularly because of the suicide, which is referred to sometimes as a heroic act (the previous quote) and sometimes just as falling in battle (second quote).

BRIT HABIRIONIM ("Alliance of the Hoodlums")

The Zionist movement in the 1930s was sharply divided between two polar groups: one large group, socialist in orientation, with leaders such as Ben-Gurion, Yitzhak Ben-Zvi, and Dr. Haim Arlosoroff, and a much smaller group, the "revisionist" movement, with a right-wing, nationalistic orientation, headed by Zeev Jabotinski. In the 1930s, the debate between the two groups over social, political, and economic issues was very strong and bitter, and accusations were frequently made.

Within the revisionist camp, Abba Achimeir, together with the poet Uri Zvi Greenberg and Yehoshua Yavin, found that their ideological needs were not adequately satisfied. Therefore, they established, in October 1931, a militant activist group with fascist tendencies calling itself Brit Habirionim.[16] Their historical model was the Sicarii movement mentioned earlier and, to a much lesser extent, contemporary European fascist movements—especially that of Italy. Brit Habirionim began its operations in 1930 (with a public demonstration on October 9) and was formally established sometime in October of 1931. Although small, this particular group presented a more or less coherent ideological symbolic-moral universe (e.g., see Ben-Yehuda 1990; 1993:104–105, 140–141), and some of its publications could be interpreted as granting legitimacy to political assassination.

Members of the group defined their main role as carrying out activity against the British and others they defined as enemies of Zionism. The name they chose for their group reflected their vision of themselves as a continuation of the legacy of national zeal, a legacy originally developed by the extremist factions of the Zealots of the Great Revolt against the Romans during 66–73 A.D. (Niv 3:179).

Much like the Sicarii, Brit Habirionim preached political terrorism. It is also important to note that many of the members of Brit Habirionim had previously been members of Etzel and, later on, of Lehi. The ideological background of these people contained a very strong element of identification with the Sicarii. They apparently knew quite well just who the Sicarii were and their true nature: "The Sicarii selects as a target the hero of the existing regime. The Sicarii who kills the representative of the existing regime is not just a plain murderer. The important thing is that the Sicarii atmosphere will not fade away from the society" (Ben-Zakai 1946:16).

The attitude of Brit Habirionim toward Jews at the leadership level of the Yishuv was quite clear. They commonly viewed these Jews as collaborators of the British and felt that "they should be cut to pieces and be given as food for the mouth. We have to really fight with blood and war against the government of Hebron, against a narrow alliance with the Arabs and with the agents who sit with honor in the Zionist Leadership" (Ben-Zakai 1946:17). Members of this group, particularly its leadership, were people with a historical awareness who decided consciously to rely on what they viewed as the legacy of the Sicarii. Thus, one of the books of Brit Habirionim is titled *We the Sicarii* and opens with a poem by Uri Zvi Greenberg glorifying the Sicarii. It is interesting to note that in no place does the book explain who exactly the Sicarii were or what they did (Achimeir and Shatzky 1978). Abba Achimeir, founder of the group, in his total admiration and devotion to the Sicarii, attributes to them exalted heroic acts: most of all, the sacrifice of life in place of an undesirable existence. In his opinion, the Sicarii held an ideal view of life and felt that its sacrifice was a direct result of the wish to actualize a different and better existence. Consequently, Achimeir arrived at the conclusion that the Sicarii adherent was a unique person—that is, someone willing to kill and be killed (A. Achimeir 1972:218).

Abba Achimeir did not try to circumvent the Biblical commandment "Thou shalt not kill." His attempt to cope with it appears to be a direct result of the harsh criticism directed at him and his group by the Yishuv establishment. His answer to the question seems to have been based, in the main, on a distinction he made between what he defined as different types of murder:

> [A person] who kills for robbery is a murderer, but the Sicarii, who kills the representative of the existing regime, is not a murderer, even in the view . . . of the existing regime. From the moral point of view, it is permissible to kill for public aims, which is not the case in regard to private goals, and neither is it so for private revenge. It is not the murder itself that determines its nature and verdict but the reason for which that murder was committed. (Achimeir 1972:219)

Ben-Zakai adds that

> according to the testimony of one of the witnesses, they were told, during a meeting that took place in Haifa during Shavuot 1933, "You do not have the national spirit that characterized the German students who assassinated [Walter] Rathenau.[17] You have no one capable of assassination like the German students, who killed Karl Liebknecht and Rosa Luxemburg.[18] (1946:18)

This distinction between various types and, consequently, the legitimization of particular acts of murder did create some harsh public reactions against Brit Habirionim.

Anita Shapira (1992:266–82) points out that Abba Achimeir and Brit Habirionim used not only the precedent of the Sicarii but also the Masada narrative itself to legitimize their call for Jews to use terroristic means, including violence and assassination aimed at other Jews, in what they viewed as their struggle to achieve a renewed national independence.

The main counterargument was that the justification of particular murders would not end there and would eventually be expanded, leading to an increased reliance on blood instinct rather than on rational thinking:

> The hand that will not shy away from murdering an Arab, who is personally innocent and only "symbolizes" the enemy, will definitely not shy away from murdering a Jew who is a political or ideological adversary. Being surrounded by people on the outside who hate us and undergoing a process of disintegration on the inside—the legitimization of "explainable" murder may spell our doom. Precisely, we should not forget the historical lesson. We were uprooted a few times from this land, and we cannot forget the role of those extremists among us before each and every destruction. (Asaf 1939)

Pua Rakovski (1939) offers a similar warning against violation of the commandment "Thou shalt not kill" and the consequent resort to indiscriminate terrorism. She warns that if this trend continues, an assured destruction will follow.

On June 16, 1933, Dr. Haim Arlosoroff, a very prominent Zionist politician identified with the left, was murdered by two unidentified men on the beach of Tel Aviv. The labor movement and Ben-Gurion used this murder/assassination against Jabotinski's revisionist group, in general, and, in particular, against Brit Habirionim (and vice versa). The police accused three members of Brit Habirionim—Abraham Stavsky, Abba Achimeir, and Tzvi Rosenblatt—of the act. Achimeir and Rosenblatt were found not guilty, and Stavsky was later cleared in a higher court (he died on the ship *Altalena*) (see Ben-Yehuda 1993:140–43). However, in the trial that took place in June 1934, documents produced by Brit Habirionim were read in court. One of the documents was titled *Megilat Hasicarikin* (meaning "the Sicarii Scroll"). There it was written that

> a public society is based on the bones of its enemies and of those who place it under siege. Only that person who is willing to be killed is

capable of killing. The Sicarii war of terror is fought by anonymous heroes. [Being a] Sicarii makes it possible for an anonymous person to become a hero. One needs only to get used to shooting at the target. (Ben-Zakai 1946:16)

Even today, more than fifty years after the act, it is still not known exactly who killed Arlosoroff or why. However, the public trial in 1934 and the arrest of its leaders (Achimeir was very badly affected by his arrest; it seemed as though a different person emerged from jail), which led to the severe stigmatization of Brit Habirionim, simply meant the end of the group as such.

LEHI (LOHAMEI HERUT ISRAEL)

"Etzel in Israel," later called Lehi, split from Etzel in 1940. The founder of Lehi was Abraham Stern. Stern, influenced by revisionist Zionism, felt that direct, violent action was the best means by which to achieve national salvation. Joseph Heller, who invested considerable effort in deciphering the ideology and politics of the Lehi, points out that "Stern took it upon himself to carry out and fulfill the messianic goal, which [Stern's] hero Elazar Ben-Yair, on the one hand, and his teacher Abba Achimeir, on the other hand, had both failed to achieve" (1989, 1:14). While in the process of forming the Lehi, he changed his name to AVI—Abraham Ben-Yair. He explained that his chosen name was a symbol by which to continue the tradition of the Sicarii. Stern very quickly became identified simply as "Yair." Thus, in Yair's own mind the connection to the Sicarii and Masada must have been very strong and vibrant.

However, Lehi's attitude toward Masada was not of a singular nature. In an article called "The Philosophy of Masada," published by the group, it was argued that Masada was the point from where, in fact, Lehi took off. The "grand finale" in Masada, according to this piece, disqualified Masada from being an educational symbol, because "Masada was the final chapter and we have not yet begun. This and more. We do not want at all to reach this (or such a) point" (p. 517).[19]

Yair, however, did not seem to have any doubts. Masada for him was a symbol. The war of the Zealots was one of the factors, in his mind, that kept the Jewish nation alive (Stern-Yair 1976, p. 145). Yair was apparently fascinated by messianic Judaic movements, particularly the Hasmoneans and the Zealots. The failure of these movements did not discourage him. He felt that, in the end, the messianic perception would prevail. Thus, he saw in Lehi another link in the chain of activist messianic movements in Israel (Heller 1989, 1:154). As Heller points out, this perception was very close, even identical, to the views of one of Stern's teachers at Hebrew University at the time—Professor Klosner.

This ideology led Yair to advocate the creation of the Lehi as an independent organization (in 1937) and as the foundation for a Jewish army whose goal should be the conquest of Eretz Israel and the establishment of the kingdom of Israel. In effect, this ideology left Lehi with no choice but a head-on collision with the British Mandate regime, even if this led to defeat; this was because Stern was convinced of the need to follow "only the road of force, sacrifice and blood. Victory could be achieved at the price of 'loss of the individual.' . . . If England would not make some moral stock-taking, he [Stern] was ready for a second Masada" (Heller 1989, 1:131). Moreover, Heller (1989, 1:144) points to Yair's deep conviction in the validity of the idea of "the [chosen] few" (against the "many"), even if this idea might lead to a doomed war whose end result would be failure and disaster. This reflected a total acceptance of Klosner's and Achimeir's belief that the determining factor in the future of a nation was war.

The sanctification of death as a legitimate means by which to achieve the goals of the organization, a la Masada, found expression in a number of ways. One obvious way was in the portrayal of the heroism of members of Lehi who were caught by the British and condemned to death. In one such case, Moshe Barazani (Lehi) and Meir Feinstein (Etzel) were waiting in their prison cell to be executed. A hand grenade was smuggled into their cell by agents of Lehi. The two used the grenade to blow themselves up on April 21, 1947. After this act, Lehi's newspaper published a report in which the following was written:

> So died Moshe Barazani and Meir Feinstein, as the first of the kings of Israel died, as the fighters of Jotapata and Masada died, as died all the heroes of Israel who imparted the longings for life, homeland, and liberty to the following generations. It is because of them that the chain of the generations was not disconnected . . . and because of them we shall have life and liberty.[20]

In another incident, Shabtai Drucker and Menachem Luntz were killed (on April 6, 1944) in what Heller (1989, 1:192) defined as a suicidal battle with the British police. Israel Eldad-Sheib (one of the triumvirate leadership of Lehi) explicitly compared this particular battle to Masada:

They are only two with two handguns in their possession, surrounded
by troops armed with the best weapons. They [the British] do not
need to build a [siege] ramp because the rock of Masada is not in
front of them. Just a simple house, but Masada in spirit. The blood
of Elazar Ben-Yair is on the doorstep of this house. They will not fall
to the enemy. (Eldad 1988:81)

Much like the original Sicarii, Lehi was deeply immersed in political
assassinations. As I have indicated in my 1993 study,

in the 1919–1948 period Lehi was the *most* active organization in
political assassination events. Out of eighty-one cases that took place
in those fateful twenty-nine years, forty-two cases were carried out by
Lehi—a hefty 52 percent. If one discounts the years 1919–August
1940, in which Lehi did not even exist, and the [twenty-one] cases in
those years . . . then Lehi's "share" becomes even more pronounced.
Out of fifty-nine cases, forty-two can be attributed to Lehi—an
astounding proportion of 71 percent. (p. 397)

Moreover, Lehi clearly had a greater tendency to kill Jews than non-Jews,
and this was typically rationalized by an accusation of "collaboration"
with the "enemy."

Lehi very obviously and repeatedly made efforts to justify what it
called "individual terrorism" (read "political assassinations"). The person who has given this particular expression the most legitimacy, within
the context of Lehi (post factum), is definitely Zeev Ivianski, an ex-
member of Lehi (see his 1977, 1981, 1982, and 1987 works). However,
Lehi itself was also trying to cope with the commandment "Thou shalt
not kill" and to justify its numerous acts of assassination. In one publication it stated that freedom fighters were not to be viewed as murderers.
That label, according to the publication, was to be saved for the oppressors of freedom. It further claimed that not every blood spiller is a murderer and not every law keeper is a saint. Moreover, every blood spiller of
murderers is a saint and every law keeper of murderers is a murderer.[21]
Lehi attempted to justify these assassinations by comparing them to political assassinations in history that were already perceived as legitimate.
Thus, the Hasmoneans and Maccabees were presented as adherents of
"individual terrorism." The Hebrew word *mityavnim* referred to those
who had collaborated with the Greek empire. It obviously had a deroga-
tory connotation, and the assassination of *mityavnim* was considered to
be justified. In Palestine of the 1940s, the term was used differently. A
mityaven was defined by Lehi as a non-Zionist or as a collaborator with

the British Mandate occupation forces. For Lehi, Britain was equated with Adrianus, Titus, and Rome (see Shatzberger 1984:104). In Lehi's terminology, the commandment "Thou shalt not kill" is not applicable in the context of a war for national independence. In such a situation, private morality must be overruled by what they referred to as national morality. Hence, in making a distinction between "private" and "national" morality Lehi was trying to use a moral language intended to socially construct differential acceptance of a variety of meanings of the term *murder*.

Finally, the violent death of Yair himself is a matter that attracts one's attention. In early 1942, Lehi was in an advanced state of disintegration. Many of Lehi's members were in British detention camps, and the rest were being hunted and living in fear of being caught. Yair was a prime target of the British. His capture was not a matter of "if" but, rather, of "when." Despite offers by the Hagana, he refused to accept its help. In the end, on February 12, 1942, his hiding place in Tel Aviv was discovered by British intelligence. He was caught, and, under the pretext that he had tried to escape, he was shot and killed by the British officer, Jeffrey Morton.

The way in which Yair met his death and his consistent refusal to accept the Hagana's offered shelter raise a number of questions. Heller (1989, 1:152) feels that Yair actually made a conscious sacrifice in allowing himself to be killed like a victim. This was so that he could "die in a war for liberty and not a saintly death, and by this create an example that others could follow."

That the major pre-1948 Israel Jewish underground groups in Palestine used the Masada narrative as a central motif is without doubt. The Palmach and especially the Lehi used parts of the Masada narrative with full force.

In all groups, Masada was an important ingredient in the socialization process. In this way, a two-thousand-year-old narrative became a vibrant and important element of everyday life and a significant point of reference. Members of the Hagana/Palmach trekked regularly to and climbed Masada. However, for this particular group, Masada was mythologized. Most members were not aware of or did not attempt to cope with the full implications of all of Josephus Flavius's narrative. The Etzel and the Lehi were too small and were so deep underground that regular organized trips to Masada were not possible. However, the leadership of both Brit Habirionim and Lehi seemed to have known fairly well the original narrative. Their method was to embrace the original narrative and continue with the tactics originally used by the Sicarii. Lehi's record testifies to this. Furthermore, all the groups—to varying degrees—certainly implied that their members "continued" in some way what they perceived as the heroic tradition of the Zealots (or the Sicarii, in the case of Brit Habirionim). Needles to say, there is an abyss separating the members of Hagana/Palmach and the Zealots, ideologically and pragmatically. This gap tends to shrink somewhat in relation to Brit Habirionim and the Lehi, but it still exists. On the one hand, we have a religiously fanatic Jewish sect that committed some very questionable acts, did not participate in the defense of Jerusalem against the main Roman siege on the city, and witnessed (and contributed to) the loss of the partial national sovereignty they had possessed. On the other hand, we have mostly secular Jews returning after thousands of years in the Diaspora to participate in a renewed struggle for national statehood, in the middle of a terrible world war, after having indirectly witnessed the extermination of six million Jews.

The Masada socialization process was one of personal sacrifice and devotion to the idea of a national state. The "Plan for the North" and the Etzel plan for the Old City of Jerusalem illustrate this.

All groups found the suicide issue problematic, and all repressed the Ein Gedi story, since it sharply conflicted with their constructed image of "heroic courage." In the main, the underground groups exploited Masada as a symbol for a fearless "fight to the end."

Chapter Seven

Masada and the Israeli Army (IDF)

BEYOND ITS NORMAL military roles and assignments, the Israeli Army acts as an important agent of socialization and education (see Lissak 1972; Azarya 1983). As such, the IDF has traditionally invested valuable resources into the symbolic education of its young soldiers.[1]

Hundreds of thousands of soldiers from different units of the IDF have trekked to and climbed up Masada. Over the years, the overwhelming majority of soldiers have gone to Masada as part of their training, on trips designed to acquaint them with the geography and symbolic history of Eretz Israel. For soldiers from the Israeli armored units, however, Masada has had a special meaning. On a more or less regular basis, until around 1991, these soldiers climbed to Masada after completion of their basic training, to swear allegiance to the State of Israel and to the IDF in a most dramatic and memorable ceremony.

Two initial questions that need to be asked here are, when did these military pilgrimages to Masada begin, and what was the nature of the decision-making process that led to their establishment?

THE PILGRIMAGE TO MASADA

Although it is difficult to pinpoint exactly when these pilgrimages began, it is clear that from the early 1950s on, units from the IDF's armored units were climbing Masada. The first testimony is that of Yitzhak Ben-Ari,[2] who has stated that the first military climbs to Masada were made by reconnaissance company 135 in 1950 and/or 1953. These units were commanded by Zeev Eshkolot and Shmuel Lalkin. Lalkin[3] confirmed that his unit tried to climb Masada in 1953 but failed because of inaccurate navigation and fatigue. Yitzhak Arad ("Tolka")[4] already received command of battalion 9 (which was part of brigade 7, the only armored brigade at that time in the IDF) in 1953, on top of Masada. According to

Arad, battalion 9 was a unit that joined the IDF directly from the Palmach. Moshe Bar-Kochva ("Bril")[5] climbed Masada in 1953 as a company commander. The first recorded ceremonies of armored units on Masada took place on September 14, December 10, and December 20 of 1956.[6] From that time on, on a more or less regular basis, new recruits to the IDF armored units were sworn in on top of Masada.

THE DECISION-MAKING PROCESS

How the decision was made is not an easy question to answer. What is very clear is that the decision to utilize Masada as a site for swearing in recruits was not the result of an organized process. No background discussions were held or position papers developed and followed by a weighed decision. What appears to have happened is that so many of the new commanders of the IDF, having come from the Palmach (and some from Etzel and Lehi), carried with them the legacy of the Masada mythical narrative with which they have been socialized that it must have been very natural for them to think of Masada, "the Zealots' last stand" (in Yadin's much later terminology), as *the* appropriate site for a swearing-in ceremony. In light of the mythical narrative, they could not have been more correct. The selection of Masada was not only symbolic of the continuity of the Jewish nation—"We are here again"—but also an act of almost megalomaniac historical challenge and defiance: "Indeed, we were NOT beaten." The ceremonies represented a call to Flavius Silva, commander of the Roman tenth legion, "You did not win."

So the decision to use Masada was simply the result of a grass-roots demand from many different agents who were absolutely convinced of the truth of the myth. This conclusion is supported by most of the interviews we conducted. Shaul Bevar[7] was a key figure in the process, according to almost all the interviewees. He maintains that he was the entrepreneur and the one who came up with the idea of a swearing-in on top of Masada. Bevar stated that it would be impossible to find much documentation for this fact, because most of the persuasion was accomplished verbally, and that he had had to devise his own role in this affair. Along with him, Avraham Adan ("Bren"),[8] Moshe Bar-Kochva, and Herzel Shaffir[9] were all mentioned as officers under whose command soldiers began to be sworn in on Masada. However, while they all agreed that during their command indeed soldiers were sworn in on top of Masada, they also maintained that when they assumed command, that ceremony was al-

ready considered a "tradition." David Elazar ("Dado"), then commander
of the armored units, clearly supported the custom.[10] In fact, Rechavam
Zeevi ("Gandhi") maintains that Elazar was searching for a place for the
swearing-in ceremonies of his units and that he, Zeevi, suggested Masada. Together—according to Zeevi—they decided on Masada. Arad
also maintains that he came up with the idea of turning Masada into a
location for the swearing-in of recruits.

When we checked with the relevant figures, they all pointed out that
the use of Masada was not a new idea. Yaacov Heichal, Arad, Zeevi, and
Yehoshua Levinson all claimed that they had climbed to Masada previously with the Palmach. Ben-Ari stated that the idea of trekking to Masada was "natural." Moshe Nativ maintained that Masada was an important value in the Palmach and that IDF treks there were a continuation of
the tradition. He added that "the majority of the commanders of the
IDF's armored units were from the Palmach, and for them it was a natural continuation." Bar-Kochva confirmed this and added that Masada
had something more to it—it ignited the imagination. He himself came
from Etzel and told us that Masada was cherished there, too.

In the cognitive map of these commanders, it was only natural
to continue the prestate underground tradition of admiration for Masada.
Thus, there was no need for organized preparations. Whoever suggested
Masada as a swearing-in site did not encounter any major or significant
opposition. However, this ideological connection was not the only reason.

A number of the interviewees did point out some geographical, physical considerations. Bar-Kochva and Shaffir claimed that because the
IDF's armored units were training in the south it was convenient to use
the area for swearing-in ceremonies. Rabbi Shlomo Goren added that until 1967 the Western Wall was not in Jewish hands and there was no other
historical holy site that could express the heroism of Israel: "The only
place was Masada, so they chose Masada." Zeevi added, "They searched
for a location that would combine both a national symbol and a site of
Jewish heroism and that would require an *effort* to reach."

Some interviewees pointed to what may be considered social and
moral reasons. Heichal summarized this most succinctly:

> After 1956 . . . the armored units were in a momentum of
> development. We began to look for subjects that "would boost the
> soldiers' morale." The armored units were based at the time in other
> units that had their own traditional sites for swearing in, and we
> looked for a location that would *unite* everyone and that was not

connected to Palmach/Givati. . . . When we took the soldiers for [some very difficult] training, we searched for something that *would give them the strength to continue.* Then they [the soldiers] said, "Masada! Heroes!" etcetera. It was like a light projector, a flag [that everyone can see and identify with].

Additional reasons have been given for the specific choice of Masada. Many of these reflect Rabbi Goren's earlier comment: "There is here [in Masada] a sign of heroism, of standing, of endless devotion" (Shaffir). Nativ adds: "[Masada] was accepted by the commanders because it symbolized that the connection was not severed, that new fighters came and the connection with the fighters [of that period] was not severed." Zeevi continues: "This was a heroic chapter in the history of our people, relatively covered by written documents. . . . It was located in an unknown area. [People] want to travel to the mysterious, the unknown, the virgin." In Ben-Ari's words, "It was a place full of splendor, glory, and majesty," and according to Bar-Kochva, "We all knew the place as *the national* site: Masada as an educational symbol, for reinforcement of the spirit, pride, and the connection to the homeland."

These comments indicate that for all the interviewees the construction of Masada as a heroic narrative was deeply internalized. It was accepted as such uncritically. The process by which this came into effect is also of interest to us.

THE MASADA SOCIALIZATION PROCESS

We have seen earlier that many of the key commanders were already socialized into the Masada myth before they joined the IDF. How do they recall this process? Listen to them tell it in their own words:

"I first climbed Masada as an apprentice in Hashomer Hatzair every Passover vacation during 1941–1942" (Avraham Adan). "These things accompanied us from the Etzel—education about the heritage of our fathers, wars that took place, Maccabees, Bar-Kochva, Masada" (Moshe Bar-Kochva). "The legend of Masada was prevalent in Mahanot Haolim as far back as I can remember. It was a desire, a goal. In addition, at school, a teacher named Dr. Nathan Shalem, a man of the desert, a member of the Jerusalemite 'walkers' association,' Breslavski's booklet about Masada, and of course Flavius and Lamdan's poem [influenced us regarding Masada], and all the rest is oral Torah" (Rechavam Zeevi). "In the framework of Aliyat Hanoar [an organization for youth] in 1947, I climbed to Masada for the first time. We studied Ben-Yair's speech in school during history classes" (Moshe Nativ). "I was already educated about the Masada story in the Diaspora, in 'Tarbut' school in Lita (Vilna). During the Holocaust, I was a partisan . . . and deep inside I had sentiments to this historical . . . Masada. . . . I knew it as a narrative of Jewish heroism against the Romans. The suicide, the famous speech of the commander of Masada. This at the ripe age of ten or eleven, at which the Jewish and personal consciousness [and identity] is crystallizing" (Yitzhak Arad). "I knew the subject from the Palmach. When I was in Beit Haarava [a Jewish settlement near the Dead Sea], I climbed to Masada a few times. . . . This was a part of the stories we learned in the military course we took to become platoon commanders. The brave stand of women, children, and men and how they killed each other so as not to surrender to the Romans. It was also touched on in the military courses officers took to become battalion commanders" (Shmuel Lalkin). "Shmaria [Guttman] and Mahanot Haolim brought this to the youth. It was the fruit of their creation. . . . So the first guide told of Masada during a guides' seminar, and that is how it was passed on, and no one investigated the subject" (Shaul Bevar). Bevar was a key moral entrepreneur in the establishment of the Masada narrative and of the site as a backdrop for the swearing-in ceremonies of new recruits. In his interview, he summarized some of the elements that combined to make Masada an attractive site for Israel's armored units: "It was important to have a *challenge,* and the site had to have a *historic meaning.* In the eyes of the Palmach's members, the most natural thing was that this challenge and historical meaning would be suggested on top of Masada. There were many Palmach members in the armored units. Everyone you said 'Masada' to remembered a ceremony from his days in the youth movement—the guy with the flute and Lamdan's poem. . . . Personal experiences are immediately brought to memory. . . . Masada [as opposed to Latrun, where a fierce Jewish-Arab battle took place in 1948 (see Shapira, 1994)] is *the real thing.* In Masada you *walk in history!"*. Moreover, these personal memories were positive and plugged the officers into an experience they were familiar and comfortable with.

A very atypical opinion was voiced by Avraham Adan: "I was not involved in the subject with enthusiasm. I could not find a connection between Masada and the armored units, and, therefore, this whole affair did not appeal to me too much. But I found that it received momentum from others."

COMMANDERS' PERCEPTION OF HOW SOLDIERS EXPERIENCED MASADA

Another topic that came up consistently in the interviews was how the commanders viewed Masada vis-à-vis the soldiers who were the real object of the ceremonies:

"During 1953–1954, most soldiers were new immigrants, and climbing Masada had an influence on them" (Moshe Nativ). "The new recruits were Sephardic new immigrants, and we saw in this [climbing Masada] an important educational activity" (Shmuel Lalkin). "We must remember that, in the past, not every soldier had been—before being recruited—to Masada. So the very experience was primordial" (Amnon Reshef[11]). "The new recruits were 'the people of Israel,' who, except for hanging out in the neighborhood, never went anywhere else. And [the Masada ceremony] made them very excited" (Shaul Bevar). "Most of the new recruits were new immigrants. They hardly knew Hebrew. There were Holocaust survivors and people from North Africa. Some of the treks were made within an educational framework, part of learning to know and love the land. We included everything together. For them it was also the first time they saw the place and heard the story. [We wanted] to connect them to Jewish history through the treks" (Yitzhak Arad).

Hence, the conclusion is obvious. The trek to Masada, the climb, and the ceremony there were also meant to acquaint a new generation of young and ignorant Jewish immigrants with Israel, with what was viewed as a major ingredient of the newly emerging Jewish Israeli identity and its connection to the past. Once this was accomplished, the construction of Masada as a fundamental and widely accepted myth was complete.

THE STRUCTURE AND CONTENT OF CEREMONIES ON MASADA

Most of the ceremonies on Masada were quite standard, with a certain degree of improvisation given to the discretion of the commanders in charge. This standardization was not very strong in the 1950s, but as time passed the ceremonies became more and more routinized. Eventually, there was a file in which all of the particulars and required logistics were detailed.[12] These included the following:

1. The trek to Masada and the climb up the mountain.
2. A parade in special formation on the mountain and later arrangement in a specific standing formation.
3. A loud reading of Elazar Ben-Yair's "speech." This "speech" was obvi-

ously edited from the two original speeches. Sometimes additional selected passages from Josephus Flavius were also read.
4. Fire inscriptions (typically stating, "Masada Shall Not Fall Again").
5. Swearing in.
6. A speech by the commander of the armored units, usually followed by
   a speech by a chief military rabbi (Rabbi Goren carried out this function in many ceremonies).
7. Receipt of personal arms (usually an automatic weapon).

Sometimes, additional passages were read from various sources (e.g.,
from Lamdan's poetry), and occasionally some entertainment (typically
singing) was provided after the ceremony. Often, the families of the soldiers (and other guests) were invited to the ceremony (the army typically
provided transportation). Some age cohorts of soldiers prepared special
dramatic plays for the event. On a few occasions, the soldiers remained
overnight on top of Masada and woke up early in the morning to watch
the spectacular sunrise over the foggy and massive mountains in the east.
Sometimes, the commander of the armored units was, with the necessary
dramatics, flown in by helicopter. On more than one occasion the soldiers
spend additional time on and around Masada, divided into small groups,
and received instruction on the Great Revolt and on Masada itself. Our
interviewees pointed out that most of the ceremony was copied from similar ceremonies that they and other commanders had participated in when
they climbed Masada as members of the youth movements.

COMMANDERS' PERCEPTION OF THE MASADA NARRATIVE

How did the commanders perceive the Masada narrative? Most of our interviewees placed the emphasis on those elements in the narrative that were
conducive to the crystallization of the armored units. It almost seemed as
though they consciously chose to repress and ignore the more problematic
aspects (Ein Gedi, the role of the Sicarii, the failure of the revolt, etc.). The
suicide was a very sour topic, something they all felt had to be "explained."
When we raised these issues, most interviewees tended to dismiss them as
unimportant. However, this dismissal was based on the false impression
that they really knew the details of the narrative. On further questioning, it
turned out that most of them did not actually repress or ignore these problematic aspects but that they were simply not aware of them. In other
words, these commanders had themselves been exposed to the myth and
not to the full story as given by Josephus Flavius. Thus, despite their claim
that they had "read" Josephus Flavius, they really had not. Hence, the gaps

in their version were filled with unsubstantiated assumptions and inappropriate and inaccurate elements. This inaccuracy, I must add, did not appear to be a deliberate lie but, rather, stemmed from simple ignorance. In the very few cases where some of the real unpleasant elements *were* known, they were dismissed as either unimportant or damaging. Let me give a few examples from some commanders whose names became legends for courage, determination, and strength:

Rechavam Zeevi: "The Judean desert was utilized—all throughout history—as a refuge for resisters to the regime. Not only the Sicarii. I do not remember if we knew that the Sicarii were [there] or not. I assumed that this was not an important fact, because we did not look for the divisive, the lunatic and the crazy, but rather for the uniting elements and for the symbol of the final stand on the wall." Yaacov Heichal: "In Masada there were some fighters and some people who lived in the neighborhood. Groups that decided to fight. I do not remember if some of the Sicarii were there." Rabbi Shlomo Goren: "The Sicarii were also Zealots. They were the remnants of the Great Revolt who found refuge in Masada and fought till they realized that they could not win, and therefore I justify their story. . . . When we talk about Masada we must understand about *which period* we talk. Masada was built by Herod as a fortress for himself. . . . Everything he [Josephus Flavius] tells was in the period of the big revolts, in the period of the Temple. I do not contradict what he says. After [the destruction of the Temple], Masada was used by groups that were quarreling with other groups, such as those that were in an inferior military situation. *This is not* the Masada about which we speak. . . . But Masada to where they escaped three years after the destruction and continued to fight there three years after the destruction [of the Second Temple]. The thing that 960 people did there (that they all committed suicide) never happened again in history! It is not the place that matters. It is the events that took place there three years after the destruction that counts." Moshe Bar-Kochva: "The question is what is more important. There is no perfection. Exactly who these people were [on top of Masada]—it is not important! Were they Jewish? That is what is important! Of course, it is possible to find things that would show that not everything was in order. But, overall, there are struggles for this land. And when we look at this struggle, it becomes a potentiating charge that reinforces our struggle today. A heritage and tradition that we can rely on. The experience is so strong that even if other things are found—archaeological, historical, et cetera—they will not change it." Yitzhak Ben-Ari: "The Sicarii were Zealots. I got it from Shmaria Guttman. . . . We did not read Josephus Flavius in the original. We received translations in booklets distributed by the [army's] chief education officer. We did not ourselves delve into history. There [in the booklets] were *quotations* from Josephus Flavius. There was a special booklet for Masada." Herzel Shaffir: "I did not myself delve into it. What a people does from time to time is to take those things that are convenient for it and changes them to suit its needs. From time to time, when you are removed from history, things are received, emphasized, and processed. Like in the case of Bar-Kochva and Rabbi Akiva. And the ultra-Orthodox Jews ignored it. It is placed in the headlines, and this is the way things are done. This *is not a historical process* that can be followed." Avraham Adan: "We only knew the part of the myth about 'liberty or death.' This is the myth that was transferred along in the armored units." Yitzhak Arad: "Meirke Pail already tried to destroy this myth. As a leader and as an army man. *It is not important at all* if this myth is true or not. As long as it helps to activate the people and its light can be used for educational purposes . . . We are all selective, as a people and as individuals. We remember what was done to us. Myths are myths. It is good that there are myths. But it is not good[13] for a people to live *only* on myth." Shaul Bevar: "We accepted things as they were. Like 'It is good to die for one's country.' This was an oral Torah. I am telling you these stories so that you can understand how [they] could catch us so easily in our naivete and build myths for us. . . . Today [they] are moving in totally the opposite direction. Trumpeldor was a pimp, Ben-Gurion a pickpocket. Everyone corrupted [laughing]. But then, [they] accepted things as they were. . . . This was a naive and romantic period, and part of it was this business of Masada."

THE "BATTLE" OF MASADA

It is interesting to look at the responses of our interviewees, as officers in the IDF, to the question of the "battle" on (or around) Masada. Interestingly enough, and as perhaps one may have expected, they all were convinced that there was a battle there.

"Of course there was a battle! Catapult stones, wood and siege. Of course there was. . . . Of course there was! . . . The concept of the battle is a little foggy, but of course there was a *defensive battle*" (Herzel Shaffir). "Not the element of suicide, but *war* to the end. Nonsurrender. These are the concepts I thought had to be instilled through Masada" (Yitzhak Arad). "[They] *fought* till they realized that they could not win" (Rabbi Shlomo Goren). "The battle . . . the siege . . . lasted for a long period. When they saw that they could not hold out any longer, they decided to commit suicide" (Yaacov Heichal). "The Romans put a siege around Masada for three years. And it was a difficult effort. They were also hit by the Jews! It angered them that there were 960 Jews sitting up there and they [the Romans] had to sit there in the heat and with rationed water" (Rechavam Zeevi). "Because the Zealots who arrived there said, 'Here we shall fight to our last drop of blood' " (Shaul Bevar).

THE SUICIDE

The suicide theme is a difficult matter, handled by each one of the officers in his own way.

"We did not deal with the suicide issue. In the armored units, we said, 'Wait a minute! Should we educate people to commit suicide?' So we found an explanation for it, that we now have a state. We shall never again reach a situation like that in Masada" (Shaul Bevar). According to Amnon Reshef, the chief of staff at that time (Rafael Eitan ["Raful"]) objected, stating that Masada symbolized something negative, not heroic.[14] Reshef, however, chose to continue the tradition he found when he was appointed as commander of the armored units. He felt that even the chief of staff had no right to alter tradition.

One of the more interesting statements here was made by Yitzhak Ben-Ari,[15] one of the most famous tank-unit commanders in the Israeli Army:

> Don't forget that there was a Holocaust. And we wanted to make sure that "Masada shall not return," that we should not reach a situation of Masada. We are here in a place where people committed suicide, took their lives (they drew a lottery with ostracons with numbers on them, or names . . . I don't remember), and it was clear to people that we have returned to [our] homeland and that this is the role of each fighter in the IDF to help this idea into being, that we shall not have to fortify ourselves again on Masada. . . .
>
> We did not delve into [the suicide]; it was a form of heroics we did not touch on. . . .
>
> This terrible question of losing the kingdom but keeping the Jewish spirit, [such as] going down to Yavneh, and the possibility that the sovereignty and the [political] framework would remain in the hands of the enemy and that we would maintain the spirit of Judaism—we did not talk about this philosophy. This philosophy was

not "in.". . . . When we studied history in the Gymnasia, we talked about this, but here [in the IDF] we did not raise this issue at all.

If you take [for example] Y. Harkabi and what he writes, then you see that this problem exists.[16] We must know what the limit of our power is. This exists even today. Our nationalists are *leading* us to *Masada*, in the sense that "all the world is against us," we shall fight, and if we have a nuclear bomb, we shall use it! And what will remain for us? Nothing. . . . So [the Masada myth] gave us the power to cope. But we have to know what the limit of our power is; even if we have a nuclear [bomb], that does not mean we have to use it. . . . [Use of a nuclear bomb] is a terrible thing for the state of Israel, for the environment; this is the way the state of Israel will be destroyed, and we only have one [state]. . . . Our nationalists don't understand the limits of power.

In Masada they could not apply 'Let me die with my enemy'[17] because the Romans had the superiority in numbers. This legacy [of Masada] also tells us, We do not want to lose [our] independence, but we may lose the state.

There are two interesting things about this particular interview: first, the association of Masada with contemporary Israel; second, the obvious mistake in the analogy to the story of Samson. In the Biblical narrative, Samson's enemies did have a numerical advantage, which *was* the very reason for his "Let me die with my enemies" strategy. Yadin, as we shall see later, made the same mistaken analogy.

"Readiness to commit suicide . . . A community of 1800—how many were there? . . . that were ready to commit suicide and not become slaves. When, as young adults, we participated in renewal Zionist youth movements, Masada was a symbol for the love of freedom. . . . [The suicide] did not bother us at all! It seemed natural to us. We knew what the fate of prisoners in the Roman army was: some were sold as slaves; some were sent to the arenas to fight lions. When you correctly read Elazar's speech, [you see how] it would have persuaded you too" (Rechavam Zeevi). "You create an identification with them as fighters who made the decision to commit suicide so that they would not fall into the enemy's hands alive . . . *to fight to the end,* to show the enemy that he will not succeed" (Ya'acov Heichal).

Rabbi Goren added:

I had lots of business then with the armored units, lots of problems. He ("Dado") saw the acts of the heroes of Masada as symbolic of Judaism. I told him: 'No!' We need to present in front of us symbols

of victories and life and not of death. This is not our symbol, that
they committed suicide. . . .

    I appeared there [during the ceremonies on top of Masada] and
made a speech directly after him and said the exact opposite of what
he had said. That for us Masada is a symbol of *failure*. The
Hasmoneans are for us a symbol of the heroism of Israel, not
Masada.[18] [The Hasmoneans] fought with inferior forces and
nevertheless won. . . . In the article I wrote about the subject . . . I
justify their [the people of Masada's] acts (at that time the Christians
in England attacked me on this issue) . . . and I prove that they had
to act in the way they did according to Jewish Halacha . . . so that
they would not fall into the hands of their enemies. . . . Under those
conditions, they did the right thing. And this was an act of heroism,
and only one woman remained there. But I objected [to the
statement] that *this* would symbolize the heroism of Israel. This was
good for the Diaspora. Not after the creation of the State of Israel.
Here we have to take as an example the heroism of the Hasmoneans.
Kiddush Hashem[19] must be achieved by life, not by death. The season
of Kiddush Hashem by death is finished!

One simply cannot fail to notice the complicated position taken by Rabbi
Goren—justifying and yet distancing himself from the Masada myth—
and the wrong "information" about "one surviving woman" (see also
Goren 1985).

    If the suicide issue, a very central element in the Masada narrative, is so
problematic, what then was the major message that the commanders
wanted their soldiers to receive? Various answers were given in the interviews, but they all converged on certain values: "The love of one's country,
appreciation of independence . . . being ready to sacrifice one's life (Moshe
Bar-Kochva). "We wanted to make sure that "Masada shall not return,"
that we shall not reach a situation of Masada . . . that we have returned to
[our] homeland and that it is the role of each fighter in the IDF to help this
idea into being, that we shall not have to fortify ourselves again on Masada. . . . This was a way of tying the twentieth-century man to his roots in
a form that emphasizes content, emotion, and historical truth" (Yitzhak
Ben-Ari). "The hard trek, the will of people to fight for their freedom"
(Shaul Bevar). "When, as young adults, we were in revitalizing Zionist
youth movements, this was a symbol of the love for freedom. . . . People
did not *walk* to Masada. People *climbed* Masada" (Rechavam Zeevi).
"Not the element of suicide but, rather, the war to the end. Nonsurrender.
These are concepts I thought had to be provided through Masada . . . to tie
[the new recruits] to Jewish history through the treks" (Yitzhak Arad).

Hence, the commanders wanted to use Masada as a vehicle by which to instill what they felt were important values in their new recruits: a willingness to fight to the end, nonsurrender, a renewed link to the past, an identification with ancient Jewish warriors, a love of freedom, a readiness to sacrifice.

CESSATION OF THE SWEARING-IN CEREMONIES ON MASADA

A final topic of interest here concerns the cessation of the armored units' involvement with Masada. Many factors combined here as well, leading to this outcome. To begin with, after the June 1967 Six-Day War, two consecutive age cohorts of new recruits were sworn in at the Western Wall; later on, recruits began to be sworn in at Latrun.[20] The Latrun site has gradually become the chosen site for the commemoration of the armored units. It is now the location where the swearing-in of these units takes place, and an impressive museum of armored vehicles is found there. The reasons for this change are interesting.

"The basic consideration was that there had to be a place for commemoration of the *armored units* that was not connected to the heroism of others" (Amnon Reshef). Moshe Bar-Kochva stated that Masada was taken away from the armored units because it had become a *national* site. He added that until 1956 the armored units had very few heroic stories of their own; this state of affairs changed later on. In fact, the 1948 battle of Latrun ended with an Israeli defeat, so there were arguments over whether or not it was an appropriate site—"nothing to be too proud about" (Bar-Kochva). However, for a number of reasons it was finally chosen as *the* site of the armored units. First, after 1967, many new, exciting sites became accessible to Israelis, one of which was Latrun. As the age cohorts of soldiers entering the armored units became larger and larger, the logistics of maintaining the ceremony on Masada became prohibitively expensive and impractical. Second, there was no way the armored units could get permission to build a museum and a commemoration site on Masada. Both Rechavam Zeevi and Shaul Bevar expressed dissatisfaction with the move. Zeevi believes that the ceremonies were removed from Masada because "today we educate people with fewer values. . . . And Masada is a value." Bevar feels that Latrun is not an appropriate place and that "Masada . . . is the real thing! They moved for technical reasons. It is impossible to compare the excitement."

In contrast, Tamary (1984; quoted by Blaushild 1985:26, 77, 123), a high-ranking military officer, argued that Israelis should not socialize anyone in the light of Masada, because swearing in new recruits in the spirit of a collective suicide is not such a good idea. Tamary attributed the exaltation of Masada to the search for a new identity—one that rejected the near past but glorified the distant one. In his view, Israelis should look for more positive identifications.

The most important figure in the decision to move was Yossi Ben-Hanan, the commander of the armored units at the time.[21] As a young officer, Ben-Hanan had climbed Masada several times. He admits that the ceremony there was very impressive. However, "when I became commander of the armored units in the summer of 1986, the reality was different. The main base for new recruits was moved far south. At that time, some swearing-in ceremonies were held on the base itself. Masada was no longer the site for all the swearings-in. . . . Logistically, the swearing-in on Masada became a very difficult procedure. . . . I wanted to renew the tradition, but at that time I also became involved in the creation of the voluntary association of the armored units.[22] We began to think of erecting a large memorial site in Latrun. It became clear very quickly that we could not collect money for a commemoration site in Latrun and continue with the swearings-in on Masada." So Ben-Hanan was effective in persuading all the relevant past and present commanders to agree to move everything to Latrun.

The ceremony in Latrun retains no hint of Masada. According to Ben-Hanan, the arguments concerning the Masada myth had absolutely nothing to do with the transfer of the ceremonies. The considerations were mostly technical. In fact, in a sizable article in the *Maariv* supplement of May 3, 1987 (89:21, 32), it is reported that the armored units would move the swear-in ceremonies from Masada to Latrun. The article confirms most of what has been written above, emphasizing that true heroism and sacrifice of Israeli soldiers from armored units took place in Latrun. The report states that this change of sites was not without problems and was accompanied by arguments and debates.

GADNA

Another military branch that had an involvement with Masada was the Gadna—Gdudei Noar ("battalions of youth").[23] In 1949, the Gadna had declared the adoption of Hanukkah as *their* holiday.[24] On that particular occasion, the commander of the Gadna at the time, Moshe Gilboa, wrote an article titled, "In Those Days—At This Time," in which he compared the heroism of the Maccabees (that is, of Hanukkah) to the heroism of the Israeli army. He even called the Maccabees the "ancient" Israeli army. And he ends a paper justifying why the Gadna had adopted Hanukkah as *its* holiday, in which he compares the Israeli army to the Maccabees, "Masada shall not fall again; the State of Israel will actualize the vision of its prophets and builders." It is interesting to note that years later, Yigael Yadin gave the Hebrew version of his most important book about Masada exactly the same title: "Masada: In Those Days—At This Time."

As part of the Gadna youth training in 1950, a rather famous trek to Masada took place. It became known as "The Trek of the Thousand."[25] One thousand adolescents climbed to Masada after a long and hard trek by foot.[26] The Masada mythical narrative was emphasized by the Gadna in its various socialization programs. There were a number of reasons for this, as explained by Elchanan Oren:

> We had an interest to prove that the Gadna could be a base for a national youth movement. . . . The motive of ancient heroism *was* there. . . . At the time, we did not know about the Sicarii. . . . Those who made a myth of Masada were not aware of the details of the Masada narrative. . . . I do not accept the differences between the Sicarii and the Zealots. . . . The important thing was that we came to this land . . . and we will fight for each necessary place, and so it was in the [1948] Independence War. Therefore, this is an ethos and not a myth."[27]

Elchanan Yishai, who was the commander of the Gadna forces in 1949 when the "Trek of the Thousand" took place, told us that

> the connection to Masada was made by Shmaria Guttman. During an earlier period, we helped him build stairs there. . . . My first encounter with Masada was when I read Lamdan's poem, in my school days. It made a tremendous impression on us. Later we became interested in how to get there (I took every one of my children to Masada for his Bar Mitzvah). . . . Masada created so much excitement that—as commander of the Gadna—I decided in 1949 to take the Gadna there in a big operation. [This is how the trek of the thousand took place.]. . . It aroused a great deal of excitement in so many adolescents for whom this was the first visit to the site. In my kibbutz, Masada had so much influence that we added both the revolt in the Warsaw Ghetto and Masada to the Passover Hagada. Masada fell on the seventh day of Passover and the Warsaw ghetto fell on the second day of Passover. . . . In the Hagada we used portions of Ben-Yair's speech. . . . On Masada, the ceremonies included a 'trial' for [Josephus] Flavius [as to whether or not he was

a traitor]. . . . Was suicide the right thing to do?. . . . Fire inscriptions,
reading from Lamdan . . . I have no doubt that [Masada] is a very
exciting topic. Without getting into the suicide, the very stand
[against the Romans] is very exciting.

When asked about the Sicarii and the Ein Gedi massacre, Yishai
responded:

> This is not what interested me. . . . My world view and perception
> made us closer to the other part [of the story]. What should I tell the
> youth, that they murdered or that they defended themselves? That
> they murdered at Ein Gedi or that they fought to the last man? . . .
> But of course they fought before [the Romans] reached them. It is
> written! They defended [themselves] with catapult stones, with
> everything they had. That is the story as we know it. Like in
> Gamla.[28]

Yishai admitted that his association with Shmaria Guttman was very
strong and that he helped him any time it was possible. Guttman, as we
have already shown in detail, was one of the main figures helping the Masada mythical narrative come into being.

In the early 1960s, when Yadin excavated Masada, the Gadna forces
supplied him with a continuous flow of young volunteers to help in the
excavations.

Chapter Eight

Masada in Textbooks

THE EXAMINATION OF history textbooks used in Israeli high schools is an important task. These books were accepted as "official" history by teachers and pupils alike. The manner in which the Masada affair is described in them is very significant. These textbooks were used in schools to socialize young adults into the newly emerging national Jewish Israeli identity. What was the message concerning Masada that these textbooks projected?

NINTH-GRADE TEXTBOOKS

The first level we examined was the initial period when children learn history and are first exposed to the story of Masada. This has varied over the years, but it has typically taken place around the ninth grade. We managed to locate twenty-one different texts that were used at this level from 1903 until 1988. Examining the texts of this rather long period can provide us with some interesting clues to the construction of a myth in an official manner. All of the books we examined were used, at one time or another, as part of the curriculum for the ninth grade (or sometime around that grade).[1]

We must remember that we are discussing the use of specific textbooks throughout an entire country. Obviously, not all schools used all the textbooks all the time. Moreover, it has not always been easy to determine whether a specific textbook was used exclusively by a particular grade in specific years. It may be that in some cases the very same textbook was used by lower and higher grades.

What can we conclude from table 8.1?

With absolutely no exception, none of the textbooks reflect Josephus Flavius's full account of the Masada narrative. Instead, they all present a biased and deviant account. With the exception of one textbook (Hecht,

Table 8.1. Elements of the Masada Historical Narrative in History Textbooks for Young Adults: Around Ninth Grade

Textbook	1 Escape from Jerusalem	2 Nature of Sicarii	3 Ein Gedi massacre	4 Sicarii on Masada	5 Elazar's two speeches	6 Describing suicide on Masada	7 Mention of seven survivors	8 Length of siege and war	9 Battles on and around Masada	10 Number of people on Masada
Grazovsky 1900	–	(Zealots)	–	–	–	+	+ (2 women + a few children)	3 years	fighting	1000
Hecht 1904	–	–	–	–	–	–	–	–	fighting	a few
Blank & Kutcher 1933	–	+	–	–	–	+	–	3 years	–	–
Zeldes 1935	–	+	–	–	–	+	–	2½ years	fighting	–
Weingarten & Teuber 1936	–	–	–	–	–	+	–	3 years	fighting	–
Hazan 1939	–	–	–	–	–	+	+	–	fight implied	–
Zuta & Spivak 1950	–	+	–	–	–	+	+	2½ years	fighting	960
Avivi & Perski 1951	+	+	–	–	+	+	+	3 years	fighting	960
Avivi & Perski 1955	–	–	–	–	+	+	+	2½ years	–	–
Shochat 1956	+	+	–	–	–	+	+	2½ years	fierce resistance	battalion
Dubnov 1958	+	–	–	–	–	+	+	4 months	fight implied	–
Ahia & Harpaz 1959	+	+	–	+	–	+	+	2½ years	fight implied	–
Zabludovski & Immanuel 1959	–	+	–	–	–	+	+	2½ years	fight implied	1000
Avidor & Spivak 1960	+	+	–	+	+	+	–	long time	fight hinted	–
Hendel 1961	–	–	–	–	–	+	+	3 years implied	–	960
Shmueli 1963	–	–	–	–	+	+	+	2½ years	fighting	–
Argov & Spivak 1963	–	–	–	+	–	+	–	3 years	fight hinted	battalion
Ahia & Harpaz 1968	–	–	–	–	+	+	+	–	heroic fight	–
Rapoport 1976	–	–	–	–	–	+	+	8 months	–	960
Shavit 1983	–	–	–	–	–	+	–	–	–	–
Shamir 1988	–	–	–	–	–	+	–	–	–	–
Summary										
% –	81	62	100	86	87	5	43	Only two sources (10%) use "months"	43	57
% +	19	38	0	14	14	95	53		57	29

Key: + means that the narrative is in accordance with Flavius.

– means that the issue is omitted altogether, or not according to Josephus.

1904), all discuss the suicide. Hecht states that those on Masada (no identification is provided) were "captured" by the Romans and were "destroyed." The rest of the details are reported very selectively. The Ein Gedi massacre is not discussed in any textbook. The fact that the Sicarii escaped from Jerusalem prior to the Roman siege on that city is reported in only four textbooks (19 percent). Moreover, even the fact that the Sicarii were on top of Masada is only mentioned in three textbooks (14 percent).

The fact that the Sicarii on Masada were reluctant to commit suicide and that Elazar Ben-Yair was required to make two speeches in order to move them in that direction was mentioned in only four textbooks (19 percent). Eight textbooks (38 percent) describe, in some way, the nature of the Sicarii. An interesting contrast may be found here. While some textbooks explain, albeit partially, the nature of the Sicarii, the Sicarii are typically not mentioned in the context of Masada. They are discussed as part of a general description of the Great Revolt or in relation to Jerusalem. If they are mentioned at all in the context of Masada, it is very briefly, perhaps only once, and then the author continues to describe the people on Masada as "rebels," "Jews," "Zealots," "defenders," "heroes," and so forth.

About half of the textbooks (twelve) do mention that there were survivors of the collective suicide at Masada. The siege around Masada is typically reported to have lasted either two and a half or three years (thirteen textbooks). One textbook refers to "a long period." Only two textbooks report what was probably the true length of the siege: one of them refers to four months, and the second reports an eight-month siege. Only seven textbooks (33 percent) state the true size, in actual numbers, of the Jewish population on top of Masada. Eleven texts (52 percent) report that there were fights during the siege on Masada (in one case, "fierce fighting").

The texts we surveyed clearly project a one-way biased interpretation of Josephus Flavius. Generally speaking, these texts use a variety of deceitful literary techniques to construct a narrative of heroism. The Masada myth, as described earlier, is easy to discern in these texts: heroic Jewish warriors, survivors of the fierce battle of Jerusalem, ended up on Masada. There, they fought—the few against the many—against the Roman imperial army for at least two and a half years. When they saw that there was no escape, they all, willingly, preferred death to surrender and slavery and decided to commit collective suicide.

To achieve the desired effect of heroic narrative, certain inconsistent and uncomfortable items of information provided by Josephus Flavius are either ignored or minimized. The nature of the Sicarii is not revealed. When it is discussed, there is a discontinuity between the description of the Sicarii and mention of the fact that they were on Masada. The Sicarii are typically mentioned in one context (usually in a section about contemporary Jewish factions), but they are not mentioned again in the context of Masada. The best and most effective use of this literary trick is made by Avivi and Perski (1955). They provide a fairly accurate description of the Sicarii in one section of their book; when they discuss Masada in another section, however, it is not made very clear that those same Sicarii were on Masada. The authors show a preference for the term *Zealots*. Hecht (1904) does not state who was on Masada; Blank and Kutcher (1933)) call them "the survivors of the heroes of Judea"; Zeldes (1935) uses the term *Zealots* (adopted by most authors) or *defenders*. Hazan (1939) calls them "Jews" and "besieged"; for Weingarten and Teuber (1936), they are "the heroes of Masada"; Shavit (1983) uses the terms *defenders* and *warriors*; and Shamir (1988) calls them "the last Zealots led by Elazar Ben-Yair." The story of a bunch of assassins who were chased out of Jerusalem before the Roman siege and who fled to Masada, looted nearby villages, and conducted a massacre at Ein Gedi is not exactly the stuff that heroic tales are made of.

Moreover, heroes do not hesitate, so Elazar Ben-Yair's two speeches are edited into one inspiring speech. Only four books mention that Ben-Yair had to make two speeches. The books that quote even part of the speeches typically quote the end of the *second* speech (Josephus Flavius, chapter 9, p. 1): "They all cut him [Ben-Yair] off short, and made haste to do the work, as full of an unconquerable ardour of mind, and moved with a demoniacal fury." This is a very clear expression of determination. What is forgotten is the fact that this "determination" was the result of two speeches and despite much hesitation (mentioned specifically by Josephus Flavius).

The fact that there were survivors is rarely mentioned. To refer to these "deviants" is inconsistent with the idea of a collective and unanimous decision. Furthermore, when we examine the books where there is mention of the survivors, we typically find a softened and distorted presentation of this fact. For example, we read that a few people survived "by chance" (e.g., Shmueli 1963; Dubnov 1958), or the number of survivors is reduced from seven (two women and five children) to "one old woman" (Weingarten and Teuber 1936), the implication being, of course, that this is an insignificant survivor.

The omissions here are not coincidental but, rather, deliberate; the technique used is that of selective reporting. Thus, most texts report the suicide and the amazement of the Romans when they entered Masada and discovered that almost all the people on top of the fortress had killed themselves. Moreover, the description is not neutral. The authors select and use specific words and idioms that typically convey exalted and glorified heroism. They also tend to add their own interpretations to explain why the Masada deed was so important for the honor of the Jewish people. Two of the texts illustrate this. The first is by Zabludovski and Immanuel (1959:137–38): "So died the last heroes of Judea.... The heroism, enthusiasm, and self-sacrifice that were revealed in Masada have not been matched in any other war of a small nation against a huge power.... Masada has become the symbol for national heroism across the generations." The second is by Avidor and Spivak (1960:190): "The bold affair of the heroes who cherished death more than slavery. The Masada affair remains till this day a symbol of heroic people who knew how to die fearlessly as they knew how to fight fearlessly and tirelessly." In only three texts is the description phrased in what could be described as a more or less factual manner, without any attempt to glorify.

The biased reporting in the texts did not change much over the years. What did change, however, was the space devoted to Masada. In textbooks dating to the early 1900s, we find mention of the Masada affair in one or two paragraphs; later textbooks devote one or two full pages to the affair. This most certainly reflects an increased interest in the narrative.

ELEVENTH- AND TWELFTH-GRADE TEXTBOOKS

The second level of textbooks we examined was that of the eleventh and twelfth grades. This was much more difficult. Finding which relevant texts were used exclusively in these grades in approximately the last forty years was not a simple undertaking. Apparently, in many cases the young adults in these grades simply used general history books. We were able, however, to locate about ten textbooks that were used in these grades since the early 1950s. Table 8.2 summarizes our findings.

Some interesting observations can be deduced from this last table. To begin with, *all* texts completely ignore the massacre at Ein Gedi. Only two texts (Lifshitz and Friedner) mention that the people on top of Masada came from Jerusalem, but neither tells whether the escape from Jerusalem was made before or after the Roman siege on the city. As noted before, the escape from Jerusalem is a very important issue. Only one text (Kirshenboim) mentions explicitly that the Sicarii were on top of Masada,

Table 8.2. Elements of the Masada Historical Narrative in History Textbooks for Young Adults: Eleventh and Twelfth Grades

Textbook	1 Escape from Jerusalem	2 Nature of Sicarii	3 Ein Gedi massacre	4 Sicarii on Masada	5 Elazar's two speeches	6 Describing suicide on Masada	7 Mention of seven survivors	8 Length of siege and war	9 Battles on and around Masada	10 Number of people on Masada
Hendel & Shochat 1954	–	–	–	–	–	–	–	–	–	–
Hendel 1961	–	–	–	–	–	–/+ (only mentions suicide)	–	"long time"	–	–
Rapoport 1976	–	–	–	Zealots & Sicarii	–	"	–	–	"the Sicarii . . . fought"	–
Fisher (ed.) 1985	–	–	–	"	–	"	+	–	–	about 1000
Kedem 1987	–	–	–	–	–	+	+	–	"fierce battle"	950+
Lifshitz 1987	+/–	–	–	+/–	+	+	+	–	–	about 1000
Shorek 1988	–	–	–	Zealots	–	(only mentions suicide)	–	–	fought the Romans	1000
Kedem 1988	–	–	–	–	–	"	+	"long siege"	–	950
Kirshenboim 1988	–	–	–	Sicarii	–	"	only one old woman	–	–	1000
Friedner 1989	+/–	–	–	–	–	"	–	–	–	a few hundred fighters with their families
Summary										
% –	80	100	100	60	90	10	60	No Sources used	70 (30% state "fights")	30
% +	20	0	0	40	10	90	40	"months"		70

Key: + means that the narrative is in accordance with Josephus Flavius.
+/– means that the narrative is partially in accordance with Josephus Flavius.
– means that the issue is omitted altogether, or not according to Josephus.

and three other texts (Rapoport, Fisher, and Lifshitz) mention Sicarii and Zealots, but the *nature* of the Sicarii is not elaborated on or explained. Lifshitz does state explicitly that the Sicarii were on Masada but mentions them only in a general context. Two texts (Rapoport and Fisher) report that the Zealots and the Sicarii were on Masada, and Shorek states that the people at Masada were Zealots. Only Lifshitz is specific about the fact that one speech was not sufficient to persuade the people to commit suicide and that another speech was necessary. The other texts either do not mention any speeches or refer to only one speech. Out of the ten textbooks we examined, six (60 percent) do not mention any survivors, three report the account as provided by Josephus Flavius, and one textbook (Kirshenboim) states that only one old woman survived. Most textbooks do mention that there was a suicide, but they elaborate very little on the matter. With two exceptions, no text mentions the length of the Roman siege. The two texts that do mention it (Kedem 1988 and Hendel) state that it was a "long" siege. Only three texts report that there were "battles" around Masada. Rapoport states that the Sicarii on Masada, commanded by Elazar Ben-Yair, fought the Romans heroically, and Shorek makes the same claim in reference to the Zealots. Kedem (1987) says that there are indications of a "fierce" battle between the opposing sides at Masada (he refers to the remnants of the fire that was discovered in Masada). Most textbooks mention that the number of rebels on Masada was around 950–1000 people. In addition, only two textbooks provide an estimate of the size of the Roman tenth legion. Lifshitz states that the legion was comprised of about ten thousand combat soldiers and auxiliary forces. Kirshenboim gives the same figure.

Again, what we see from these ten textbooks is the reformulation of a heroic narrative. The rhetorical devices used by the different authors to create this narrative of heroism are interesting. Some of them have been used by others (e.g., not mentioning Ein Gedi, reducing the two speeches of Elazar Ben-Yair into one speech, not mentioning survivors [or referring to "one old woman" survivor], etc.); however, we also find some innovations here. For the first time, we read of the escape from Jerusalem, but that account totally ignores the circumstances of this "escape," as well as its timing. Kedem (1987) uses one sentence from Elazar Ben-Yair's first speech and hastily adds that it is not clear whether Elazar in fact made the speech or any other speech.

Lifshitz uses an interesting device to bypass the problematic issue of the Sicarii. The technique he uses (and he is not the only one to do so) is to mention the Sicarii somewhere in the narrative, say a few words about them, and then continue on with the narrative. When the time to describe Masada arrives, the word *Sicarii* is somehow made to disappear in the text, and it is difficult for the reader to place the term in the proper context. A similar use of this technique can be found in Fisher. On page 269 of his book he says that the Sicarii were an extreme faction of the fourth philosophy (Josephus Flavius in fact equates the fourth philosophy with the Sicarii; he does not, however, state that the Sicarii were an "extreme" faction of the fourth philosophy). Moreover, Fisher does not explain what the fourth philosophy was. His description of the Great Revolt lasts until page 308, and the fall of Masada is described on pages 304–5 (more than thirty pages after he has provided a faulty "explanation" of just who the Sicarii may have been). At this point, the Sicarii are mentioned almost offhandedly; only one speech by Elazar is mentioned, and when it comes to the suicide, the text changes. Those committing suicide are referred to as "the Zealots" (not the Sicarii). The text emphasizes that the "Zealots" in the fortress remained faithful in the end to the conviction that they recognized the authority of God and nobody else. Clearly, this conviction is attributed by Josephus Flavius directly and exclusively to the fourth philosophy and to the Sicarii (and *not* to some "extreme" faction of the fourth philosophy). So, by making slight changes and by orchestrating the historical sequence in a given fashion, the author achieves a particular effect.

Finally, it is worth our while to look at how two very popular encyclopedias for young adults commonly used in Israel mythologize Masada. The first is *Encyclopedia Aviv* (1976–1978, vols. 11–12, pp. 2470–74):

> Following the fall of Jerusalem, in 70 A.D., the last rebels headed by Elazar Ben-Yair escaped to Masada. The Romans, commanded by Silva, turned from Jerusalem to Masada and tried to break into it but failed. They decided then to besiege [Masada] to prevent the besieged from having food and water. The number of the besieged was about a thousand. . . . The Roman army had about ten thousand men. . . . The siege lasted for a few months. Once the Jewish fighters realized that they had no hope, they decided to commit suicide and not fall alive into the hands of the Romans. . . .

Another very popular textbook for use by pupils between the fifth and tenth or even eleventh grades is the Hebrew version of the *Children's Encyclopedia Britannica* (published by Youth Encyclopedias in Tel Aviv). Based on the London edition, the Hebrew version retains many of the original entries but adds many more entries that are relevant for the needs of Israeli Hebrew-reading pupils. Here is what this encyclopedia has to say about Masada (1977, vol. 10, pp. 177–78):

> In the year 66 A.D. a group of Jewish resistance fighters with their families, led by Elazar Ben-Yair, escaped from the battles with the Romans in Jerusalem and hid in the fortress Masada. . . . For six years these Jews lived in relative peace in Masada. But in 72 A.D., two years after the fall of Jerusalem and the destruction of the temple, Flavius Silva, the Roman governor, led the Roman tenth legion to attack Masada. Silva besieged Masada [the text describes a "battle"]. . . . At the end, after seven months of siege, the Roman soldiers set the wooden walls on fire, and the besieged Jews decided to commit suicide. The Romans won, but it was a hollow victory. When they broke into the Jewish camp, they found there nobody to capture. . . .
>
> Today Masada is not only a tourist site accessible by cable car but an inspirational source and symbol of heroism and courage for the people of Israel. . . .

HISTORY BOOKS

Having delved into history textbooks written specifically for and used in schools, we are led to another important question: how the Masada narrative was presented in relevant reference history texts written not specifically for schools but for a wider, more general readership. We were able to locate twelve such major texts. Most people in need of historical information would probably turn to one or more of these books as authoritative references. How do these sources present the Masada narrative? To answer this question, we examined and focused on two types of texts: major texts and minor texts. For each we have constructed a table.

Major Texts

A look at table 8.3 reveals the typical pattern, the regular omissions and emphasis. To some extent, a large degree of mythmaking is presented in these books, and it is of a more sophisticated nature than in the texts we have previously examined. Since much of the bias is clear, let me add only a few words, again, about the more innovative aspects.

To begin with, out of the twelve texts we scrutinized, four did make a statement about the size of the Roman army. However, Avi-Yonah states only that one Roman legion (without stating its size) was involved in the siege. Dubnov says that the Romans were "many." Both encyclopedias

Table 8.3. Elements of the Masada Historical Narrative in Major Relevant History Books

History Texts	1 Escape from Jerusalem	2 Nature of Sicarii	3 Ein Gedi massacre	4 Sicarii on Masada	5 Elazar's two speeches	6 Describing suicide on Masada	7 Mention of seven survivors	8 Length of siege and war	9 Battles on and around Masada	10 Number of people on Masada
Graetz 1893	–	–	–	Sicarii & Zealots	–	mentions suicide	+	–	–	1000
Klosner 1952	+	–	–	+	+	+	+	–	–	690
Dubnov 1958	+	+	–	– (Zealots)	+	+	+	–	fierce resistance	battalion
Klosner 1958				Text identical to his 1952 text (see above)						960
Dubnov 1967	–	–	–	("valiant Zealot unit")	+	mentions suicide	+	–	–	–
Encyclopedia Judaica 1971	–	–	–	(Zealots)	+	"	+	long siege	–	960
Safrai 1970	–	–	–	(Zealots)	–	–	–	long siege	–	–
Ben-Sasson 1972	–	–	–	+	+	mentions suicide	+	–	–	–

	1	2	3	4	5	6	7	8	9	10
Encyclopedia Hebraica 1972	−	−	−	+	+	−	+	−	−	about 1000
Gretz 1972	− ("Jewish Rebels")	+/− (Sicarii & Zealots)	−	+	+/−	−	+	about one year (72–73 A.D.)	"fought with much power"	1000
Avi-Yonah 1974 (*Carta Atlas*)	−	−	+	− (Zealots)	(no speeches)	+	+	end of siege 74 A.D.	−	960
M. Stern 1983	+	+	+/−	+	+	mentions suicide	+	−	−	−
M. Stern 1984	+/−	+/−	+/−	+	+	"	+	−	−	−
Summary										
% −	67	75	75	50	25	17	33	75 months not mentioned	83 (17% state "fights")	42
% +	33	25	25	50	75	83	67	−	−	58

Key: + means that the narrative is in accordance with Flavius.

+/− means that the narrative is partially in accordance with Flavius.

− means that the issue is omitted altogether, or not according to Josephus.

173

(*Judaica* and *Hebraica*) report that the Roman tenth legion was re-inforced by auxiliary forces and thousands of Jewish prisoners. Also, the figure of 690 used in Klosner 1952 for the number of people on Masada is obviously a printer's mistake. The correct number, 960, appears in Klosner 1958. It may be more interesting and meaningful to look at some examples from the different texts with more care.

One interesting example is Klosner. In his 1952 book, when he feels the need to explain who exactly the Sicarii were, an unpleasant task, he states that the Sicarii and Zealots were young and enthusiastic patriots and communists, the real extreme revolutionaries. On exactly what factual basis he makes his wild statement is not at all clear. Dubnov, another important historian, simply uses the term *Zealots* as if the Sicarii had vanished into thin air. To bypass the question of from where the Sicarii arrived at Masada and when, he states that when the Great Revolt began, "refugees" from the area of Judea came to Masada. From where and just how these "Valiant Zealots," as he calls them, arrived is completely foggy in his account.

The *Encyclopedia Judaica* is another important source. There, the curious reader can learn that the people on Masada were Zealots who ran from Jerusalem during the time of the Roman siege.

The *Encyclopedia Hebraica*, a text in Hebrew that is considered a most authoritative source by many, does not tell the reader from where or how the people on Masada arrived. They are referred to as Zealots, and the reader is told that they were "Jewish Rebels." Moreover, according to this source, the siege around Masada lasted one year. The "Masada" piece in the encyclopedia (vol. 24) was written by Yigael Yadin; however, this is not the only reference to Masada found in this work. Volume 6 of the encyclopedia is devoted entirely to Eretz Israel, and it contains a large historical section. There, one can find a "description" of the Great Revolt on pages 378–88. This description is simply fascinating. On page 378 we are told that the "fourth philosophy" was focused on the Zealots (a *very* questionable assertion). No mention of the Sicarii is made. Although the description of the "fourth philosophy" is short and not completely inaccurate, it obviously refers (in Josephus Flavius) to the Sicarii and not the Zealots. On page 379 we are told that what the text refers to as the party of the Zealots received much support from the (Jewish) people and that the Romans fought against them fiercely. When it seemed that they were crushed, the Sicarii rose in their place (lines 8–10 from bottom of the page). It is not at all clear what was the factual basis for this incorrect account. It certainly was not Josephus Flavius. The text keeps referring to the *mitkomemim* (a neutral Hebrew rhetorical device meaning "rebels" or "insurgents"), without telling the reader just what the ideological-political composition of these *mitkomemim* was. The Sicarii are not mentioned again until page 388. There, it is stated that Silva was given the task of conquering Masada. According to the text, there were a "few hundred" Sicarii there, who, combined with their families, numbered about a thousand people. No mention is made of the length of the Roman siege, the size of the Roman military force, Elazar's two speeches, or the massacre at Ein Gedi. The encyclopedia states that when the Romans entered Masada "they looked in terror mixed with admiration on the heroic deed of the Sicarii." Thus, the *Encyclopedia Hebraica* not only rewrites the Masada story but creates a "new" set or sequence of events so that the brutal and murderous nature of the Sicarii somehow is made to disappear. The narrative in the encyclopedia contrasts the "Jewish heroes" against "the Romans." The true nature of some of these "heroes" is squelched. Perhaps it is no coincidence that one of the academics among the central editorial team of this particular volume was Professor Joseph Klosner. The tendency of this scholar toward theatrics and inaccuracies was already documented earlier and will be discussed again later on.

The final two items were written by Menachem Stern, a scholar from Hebrew University who is regarded by many as *the* expert on the Great Revolt. Overall, his descriptions are the most faithful to Josephus Flavius. However, a few "glitches" can be found in his writings, too. For example, when Stern mentions the Ein Gedi massacre, he does not specify what happened there. Instead, he refers to "the Sicarii's attack on Ein Gedi" or "the bloody attack on Ein Gedi," without informing the reader of the murderous nature of the "attack" and why it took place. In his 1983 text he states that the Sicarii on Masada held out for about four years after the fall of Jerusalem, without pointing out that this was *not* the length of the Roman siege. A careless reader who does not pay attention may very easily deduce that the Sicarii held out in their fortress against the Romans for four years. In this source, only one speech by Elazar Ben-Yair is mentioned. In his 1984 text, Stern tells the reader that the Sicarii carried out attacks on Jewish settlements "in the neighborhood" (Masada?). If, instead of reading these texts, which are obviously meant for a more general audience, we look at Stern's more professional works (e.g., 1989), we can find a fairly accurate (meaning faithful to Josephus Flavius) account.

One very important text that I have not included in table 8.3 is Yadin's 1966 book about Masada. Being such an excellent illustration of how the Masada mythical narrative was constructed, it has already been analyzed in chapters 1 and 3. Yadin's approach[2] is mentioned in many other places in this book as well. Generally speaking, his work implies that the rebels on Masada were Zealots (he typically does not explain why he prefers this identification over the term *Sicarii*) who came there after the destruction of Jerusalem. He also implies that they "held out" there for three years. All of the typical omissions may also be found there (e.g., no mention of the Ein Gedi massacre). The phrase "last stand" was pushed forward most strongly by Yadin, both as the subtitle for the English version of his book and as a concept particularly suited to Masada. As Zerubavel (1980) has pointed out, the very use of the rhetorical device "the last stand" in itself transforms "defeat" into "victory" (see also Rosenberg 1974).

Minor Texts

Other history and history-related texts, less available and accessible than the ones we have included in table 8.3, are also worth examining.

Generally speaking, the two books in table 8.4 nicely present the Masada mythical narrative. Batz and Lapid, for example, wrote their book for a readership whose command of Hebrew is not very good. The book is written in a very light, easy-to-understand language. The authors state explicitly (on the first page of the text) that Professor Yadin helped them greatly. The book says that *after* the destruction of Jerusalem, more fighters arrived to the fortress. The authors call these fighters "Zealots" and "heroes" and state that they fought there for three years. According to these two authors, the rebels on Masada were able to repel repeated Roman attacks; they raided the Romans and fought valiantly—a nice fact-free account.

Two other books, which we found difficult to classify, were written by Beno Rotenberg, a photographer who participated in various archaeological excavations, including the first 1955 and 1956 expeditions to Masada. His first book (1960) discussed Masada but mostly in technical terms. Rotenberg's second book was published in 1963 and is very interesting. This work is extraordinary from a number of aspects. It is very lavishly illustrated with pictures and drawings and was obviously produced as a luxurious (and expensive) edition. The book opens with a reprint of a speech Yadin made on Masada in June 1963 for a swearing-in ceremony for soldiers from the Israeli armored units. Yadin praises Elazar Ben-Yair's speeches and states that Israelis are no longer helpless against their enemies, because "we, the descendants of these heroes, stand here and reconstruct the ruins of our people. . . ." The book also contains two long quotes from Josephus Flavius. The first concerns what the book calls

Table 8.4. Elements of the Masada Historical Narrative in Relevant History Books

History Texts	1 Escape from Jerusalem	2 Nature of Sicarii	3 Ein Gedi massacre	4 Sicarii on Masada	5 Elazar's two speeches	6 Describing suicide on Masada	7 Mention of seven survivors	8 Length of siege and war	9 Battles on and around Masada	10 Number of people on Masada
Ben-Yehuda and Shochat 1974	–	–	–	– (Zealots)	–	+	+	1 year	–	about 1000
Batz and Lapid 1976	–	–	–		–	+	+	3 years	+	960

Key: + means that the narrative is in accordance with Flavius.
– means that the issue is omitted altogether, or not according to Josephus.

"hoodlums" (really the Sicarii, among others). The second is composed of selected portions from Josephus Flavius and the translation of Elazar Ben-Yair's speeches. The translation was made by Yonatan Ratosh, a famous Israeli social and political activist and poet.[3]

It is interesting how the Masada narrative is presented in this book. We are told that after the murder of Menachem his people were forced to escape to Masada. At this point in the text the word *Sicarii* is not used, although many pages earlier the connection between Menachem and the Sicarii was already made. However, these two places in the text are disconnected from each other. When the siege on Masada is described, the text states that those on top of it were "the Sicarii," "men of the dagger," but these factually descriptive words appear only once. For the rest of the text the people of Masada are referred to as "fighters," "defenders," and "Zealots." If one reads the book very carefully and remembers the text, then the unflattering description of the Sicarii and their nature does appear (mostly in the beginning of the book). However, in the section describing the siege and destruction of Masada many pages later, these qualities are not emphasized. Ein Gedi is not mentioned. A normal reader, in my view, will definitely *not* make the necessary connections. Rotenberg gives an accurate account of the two speeches, the number of rebels on Masada, and the seven survivors. He does not explicitly use the word *suicide* and writes that the "960 defenders of Masada chose death with freedom rather than slavery, humiliation, and strange deaths" (p. 52). He does not state the length of the Roman siege or say that there were fights around Masada.

Looking at the way the Masada story is given in a variety of textbooks and related books is important and instructive. These books constitute the foundation on which Israelis learn, in their formative years, about Masada.

In different degrees of sophistication, all the books we looked at do not reproduce an accurate report from Josephus. They all give biased, inaccurate, and misleading accounts. As we see in the different tables, these biased reports tell us how the Masada mythical narrative was actually constructed. The method of construction consists in omitting some important information, adding others, and presenting the account in specific ways. The overall product is a narrative that deviates considerably from Josephus and turns a problematic and complex historical sequence of events into a simple heroic narrative.

Chapter Nine

Masada, the Media, and Tourism

THE SIGNIFICANT ROLE played by the school textbooks and general historical texts, discussed in the previous chapter, in the formation and perpetration of the Masada mythical narrative cannot be underemphasized. However, two additional factors that have played no small part in the education of the populace in regard to the narrative deserve their fair share of attention. Therefore, in the present chapter we shall examine how the story of Masada has been presented in the media and in guidebooks, as well as by the tour guides who have provided numerous tourists with a firsthand exposure to the site.

MASADA AND THE MEDIA

The first question we shall entertain is how the Masada narrative has been portrayed in the media. From a methodological point of view, this is a difficult question to answer. One way of doing so is by carrying out a survey of dozens of newspapers and journals covering a period of about sixty years. This task in itself could exhaust the resources of a decent-sized team of researchers for an extended period of time. Hence, we decided to use a different strategy and, instead of spreading ourselves too thin, to focus on a particular period. In this way, we could better utilize our modest resources and have a more powerful and magnified glimpse at the media's coverage of the narrative and the entire issue.

The important decision here was, of course, *which* period to focus on. We needed a period when there were enough newspapers and journals and when Masada was pretty much in the public's attention. Luckily, these conditions existed during the archaeological excavations of Masada, under the guidance of Yigael Yadin, which took place during two separate periods: the first between October 1963 and May 1964 and the second between November 1964 and April 1965—all in all, eleven months of excavations, which constituted a major effort at that time. Thousands of volunteers from Israel and from all over the world came to help out in these excavations. The Israeli army also assisted by contributing means and volunteers.[1] Obviously, this project received some attention in the media.

The two newspapers we surveyed were *Maariv* and *Yediot Ahronot,* at that time the two major daily Hebrew newspapers available in Israel.[2] *Maariv* provides a more extensive coverage of the excavations because it had signed an agreement with *The Observer* of London, which helped to sponsor the excavations.[3] The reason we surveyed only the written media is because at that time Israel had no television and a retrospective examination of radio broadcasts would have been a very complicated—virtually impossible—task.

Since we were searching for the ways in which the Masada narrative was presented by the relevant newspapers, we were more interested in a qualitative analysis. We examined how the newspapers in question projected the Masada narrative in three broad areas: (a) how the identity of the Sicarii was described; (b) how the siege, battle, and suicide were described; and (c) which values and opinions concerning Masada were projected.

According to Josephus Flavius, the identity of the people in Masada is clear—they were Sicarii, morally a very questionable group of people. However, despite the hundreds of large and small reports carried in these newspapers during the period examined, in only two pieces was the word *Sicarii* used. The first was in *Maariv* of October 13, 1963 (pp. 3 and 8). In that report, it is stated that when the Great Revolt began, Masada was conquered in a surprise attack by Menachem Ben Yehuda of the Galilee, who headed the Sicarii. The second piece is in *Maariv* of November 11, 1963, which refers to "the leader of the Zealots, Elazar Ben-Yair the Sicarii," leading the reader to believe perhaps that Elazar was the only Sicarii on Masada, the rest being Zealots. In both places no explanation of the Sicarii is given. This is an interesting omission, for in almost *all* of the reports a clear choice has been made to use the term *Zealots,* and yet this alone was not considered sufficient: additional rhetorical devices were required to explain just who the Zealots were and also who the non-Zealots were. Some of the expressions used for this purpose are "fighters," "Masada fighters," "Hebraic fighters," "last fighters of the rebellion," "freedom fighters," "defenders of Masada" (by far the preferred expression), "last defenders," "the besieged," "the besieged rebels," "the revolutionary Jews of the First Rebellion," "Hebraic Zealots," and "Zealots for the freedom of Judea." None of these are, of course, neutral terms. They all reflect a decidedly positive attitude toward the people of Masada and are intended to foster empathy and identification with them. These expressions were very meaningful in the Jewish Israeli reality of the early 1960s—a state under siege. The ethnic nationalistic element of the identification is quite obvious (e.g., the use of the word *Hebraic*). The expressed admiration for the people who were on Masada developed not only because of what they did (or did not) do but also in so small sense because they were of the Jewish people, fighting for its national independence. The addition of the words *freedom* and *revolution* enhanced the account by implying that these people were in the midst of an active ideological struggle to achieve a revolutionary state of freedom. The social construction of heroism is supplemented by the term *last,* which portrays the determination of these fighters who, in the end, were pushed into reaching such a fateful decision.

The social construction of the Sicarii in this fashion achieves two goals. First, it hides their very problematic identity and the questionable reputation given to them by Josephus Flavius's original account. Second, it *presents* the Sicarii as a positively heroic group of people who may have functioned in circumstances similar (at least in some respects) to those of the State of Israel in the early 1960s. This particular reconstruction of reality must have made it easy and comfortable, in the Jewish Israeli mind-set of those years, to bridge a gap of close to two thousand years and create a mystical identification with this group of "last Jewish freedom fighters."

The next area we examined was the description of the siege, the battle(s), and the suicide. Most of the reports we found described the archaeological findings and/or the complicated logistics required for the excavations in such a remote site to be feasible. Only a fraction of the articles discussed the historical narrative of the 66–73 A.D. events at any decent length. The few reports that did so typically appeared at the beginning of the excavations and were basic attempts to acquaint the reader with the narrative. This type of coverage seems to be characteristic of the period, but it reflects the Yadin touch even more. Although Yadin was strongly associated with the Masada excavations, he did not write very much about them, and most of what he did write contained *very* little concerning the historical narrative and, instead, a good deal of rather uninteresting (and mostly irrelevant) information about the environment, architecture, archaeology, and geography of the place.

When the newspapers did report the historical sequence of events, however, an interesting and curious picture emerged. In *Maariv* of October 13, 1963, it was reported that

> after the fall of Herodium and Michvar [Macherus], Masada was the last fortress of the Zealots. A few of the fighters from Judea, who fled to the desert, went there, and among them was Elazar Ben-Yair, who became the commander of the place. Believing that this rock provided adequate protection from the Romans, the defenders of the fortress continued to fortify it and made all the necessary preparations for battles and siege. (p. 3)

That this description is almost totally inconsistent with Josephus Flavius is clear. Its implication is interesting nevertheless. This inaccurate account clearly states that the "defenders" of Masada arrived there *after* the fortresses of Michvar and Herodum had fallen. In this way, the idea of the "last stand of the last heroes" is reinforced. Totally ignored are such facts as the exact nature of the "defenders" of Masada, the questionable circumstances of their arrival to the place, and the time of their arrival. The report thus creates a crucial fabrication. Later on in the same article, *Maariv* tells its readers that "in 72 A.D. Silva, the Roman commander, convened a large contingent of Roman military forces in the province at the time and began to move toward the last Jewish fortress—Masada. Among his soldiers was the famous Roman tenth legion. However, his first attempts to conquer the mountain failed." As we recall, it was the Roman tenth legion that besieged Masada. The phrasing of the above passage is deceptive and meant to imply that the military force against Masada was huge indeed and just happened to include the tenth legion— clear support for the "few against the many" theme. Similarly false is the statement that the "first attempts to conquer the mountain failed." Josephus Flavius does not mention *any* first and failed attempts to conquer Masada, and there is no logical reason to assume that an experienced commander would send his troops to conquer a mountain without the proper preparations (in this case, a siege ramp). There is no basis for the view that Flavius Silva was the kind of impatient commander that the report seems to imply he was.

In addition, the reader is told (p. 3) that the reason the Romans built the wall around Masada was to prevent any supplies or reinforcements from reaching the besieged. This is *not* what Josephus Flavius says. According to him, the wall "around the entire fortress" was built so "that none of the besieged might easily escape."[4] The Romans clearly wanted to eliminate the last remnants of the Jewish revolt. Moreover, judging from Josephus Flavius's description, it is very doubtful that there was anyone who wanted to—or was *able* to—resupply or reinforce the Sicarii. However, such a portrayal certainly helped to create an association between the siege of Masada and the bitter and brutal 1948 Israeli War of Independence fifteen years earlier, so much alive in the memory of so many Israelis. The emphasis on the siege as preventing help from arriving (rather than preventing those trapped on the mountain from escape) played directly into this historical analogy because the resupply of food, ammunition, water, and reinforcements were among the hallmarks of the 1948 war, when Jewish settlements found themselves under siege by Arab military and paramilitary forces. In fact, one of the most heroic symbols of the 1948 war was the Jewish supply caravan to such besieged locations as Jerusalem and Gush Etzion. So the idea of a besieged group of people prevented from receiving help was a construction that, again, helped to create a mystical identification.

The length of the siege on Masada is mentioned in four reports. The first reference is in *Maariv* of October 13, 1963, on p. 8: "On the first day of Passover, April 15, in the year 73 A.D., Masada fell, after months of heavy siege and desperate heroic battles." "Months" obviously means less than a year, and "heavy siege" is not a very clear expression; what would be the opposite, "light siege"? And, of course, there is no mention in Josephus Flavius of any "desperate heroic battles." In reality, what seems to have occurred is four to eight months of a standard Roman army siege (see, e.g., Shatzman 1993) accompanied by no battles and followed by a collective suicide. The second reference is in *Maariv* of November 11, 1963, where it is stated that the siege of Masada took three years. The third reference, found in *Maariv* of November 24, 1963, states that the "defenders" of Masada "lived and fought" there for three years. Finally, *Yediot Ahronot* of October 20, 1963, reports that the siege on Masada took two and a half years. Thus, these reports portray a long siege accompanied by heroic battles or fights. The protracted length of the siege magnifies the elements of heroism, hardship, and stresses the characteristics of the defenders of Masada. Moreover, in a few reports it is stated that the size of the Roman military force was in excess of ten thousand soldiers plus thousands of slaves—such a large force against only 960 defenders.

The suicide is mentioned in almost all of the relevant reports. However, none of them mentions that Elazar Ben-Yair had to make two speeches to persuade his reluctant followers to agree to such a death. This complicated and painful drama is typically telescoped into a short account that states that when Elazar Ben-Yair realized that there was no

more hope of standing up against the Romans, he spoke to his people
and encouraged them to commit suicide, with the argument that death
was preferable to humiliation and slavery at the hands of the Romans.
These accounts generally do not make mention of any hesitation on the
part of the people. The act of the killing itself is typically underplayed.
The expressions usually used are "tragic heroic death," "dying," "committed suicide," "fell on their swords," and the like. The narrative given
by Josephus Flavius that "so great was the zeal they were in to slay their
wives and children, and themselves also!" and the long, passionate description he provides[5] are simply ignored. Some of the reports do not
even mention that there were women and children involved in the death
scene or that those making the decisions most probably did not include
the women and children. Those making the decisions are typically referred to as the "defenders," "fighters," "Jews,"—always in the mascu-
line plural form. Moreover, the decision and act of suicide are generally
mentioned in combination with what is considered to be the opposite,
negative alternative: surrender and enslavement. In this way, suicide is
presented in a positive light. That is, the act of collective suicide is mentioned in a way that compromises the dissonance of the act and attempts to present it positively, as if there was no other alternative, and
consequently as an act of true heroism.

The final area we examined focused on the projected values and
stands concerning Masada. We will divide the discussion here into three
subtopics: (1) the link between the people on Masada and Israelis/Jews,
(2) Masada as a heroic tale, and (3) the Masada narrative as a symbol and
a positive value for Israelis/Jews.

The Link between the People on Masada and Israelis/Jews

It is quite obvious that in most reports a conscious attempt was made,
both implicitly and explicitly, to associate the "defenders" of Masada
with contemporary Jews in Israel, as well as with contemporary non-
Israeli Jews. This connection may be found in quite a number of references and idioms.

For example, Eliezer Livne writes in his January 3, 1964, piece in
Yediot Ahronot that in the death scene, Elazar Ben-Yair "ordered us life."
That is, the lesson of Ben-Yair's act in 73 A.D. is meant for us in 1964.
Moreover, Livne states explicitly that the "message" from Elazar is not
only for religious Jews but for secular Jews as well.[6] This moral lesson
provided to us so generously by Livne follows his (rather pointless, I must
add) question "Why did Masada fall?" He apparently sees no military

reason for the fall of Masada and instead attributes it to "spiritual weakness." Livne ends his report with a quote from Lamdan's poem "Masada Shall Not Fall Again" and tells us that this quote was placed on a sign at the bottom of the mountain. Livne's warning is that if we remember and guard, Masada shall indeed not fall again.

In *Maariv* of April 12, 1964, it is stated that young Israeli adults have turned Masada into *the* main site for their pilgrimages. In the May 3 issue of the same year (p. 18), we are told that Masada "is now considered the most cherished national asset." On May 16, 1964, it is reported that Masada is "the mausoleum of the saints of the nation." Further examples are plentiful. The link between the years 66–73 A.D. and the 1960s is implicitly made by the use of rhetorical devices emphasizing the connection between "them" and "us." Furthermore, explicit associations are made between "them" and Israeli youth.

These connections are made even more powerful in the descriptions of the swearing-in of new recruits to the Israeli army on top of Masada. The headline of *Yediot Ahronot* of September 24, 1963, reads: "The Soldiers of Elazar Were Sworn In on Masada." The Elazar mentioned was Brigadier David Elazar.[7] However, it is clear that by leaving the word "Elazar" in the headline as is, an implicit connection is made to the other Elazar (Ben-Yair), as if these were still the soldiers of Elazar Ben-Yair. The report describes the difficult climb to Masada and the burning of large letters forming the sentence MASADA SHALL NOT FALL AGAIN—an impressive display of light and smoke. The ceremony was long and complicated, and the soldiers listened to the speech that had been made by Elazar Ben-Yair, received their personal arms, and swore allegiance to the state of Israel and its people. This description makes the connection between the original "defenders" of Masada and the young soldiers of 1963 very explicit. It is even stated that the organizers of the ceremony brought an artist-entertainer to Masada for a postceremony program, the reporter apparently complaining that this was inappropriate. Perhaps it was a sign that the organizers felt the historical burden of Masada was too great and that an entertainer was required to counterbalance such a terrible legacy.

A much more common link is made between the people of Masada and the archaeologists and volunteers who participated in the excavations there. *Maariv* told its readers on October 13, 1963: "Today, 1890 years after the sounds of battle died and the smoke of destruction dissipated, the distant descendants of the fighters come to the mountain to dig up its remnants." *Yediot Ahronot* on October 17, 1963, adds that "1890 years ago the singing of the Roman troopers who destroyed Masada was heard here [on Masada]. . . . But at night [now] the singing of the descendants of the heroes and foreign volunteers who have come to save the mountain can be heard. . . ." And in *Maariv* of November 22, 1963, Yadin told Yehoshua A. Gilboa explicitly that "it can be determined that archaeology is used as a concrete and real factor in [making] the historical connection of the nation to the land."

In all these illustrations, as well as in other examples, the "defenders" of Masada are explicitly and positively linked to the 1963 diggers of Masada. The use of the expression "the archaeologists assaulted [attacked?] Masada" is quite common, especially in *Maariv*. The term *assaulted* (or *attacked*) conveys, of course, a sense of a fight or a battle. This helps to construct a mystical association between the "fighters" of Masada in 73 A.D. "battling" for freedom and the modern-day archaeologists "battling" to uncover Masada's secrets. This association was typically highlighted by the fact that Yadin had previously been the chief of staff of the Israeli army and by the significant help provided to the diggers by the Israeli army.

Another symbolically powerful connecting element is the repeated emphasis on the religiosity and Judaism of the "defenders" of Masada. Some of the references to Masada explicitly refer to the fact that the defenders of Masada were observant Jews. In truth, this element is not very central to the various reports, but it exists nevertheless, creating another link between the past and the present. The association of the religious Masada rebels to secular Israeli Jews is certainly a historical irony. On the one hand, it was secular Jews who freed themselves from the choking yoke of Orthodox Judaism, established the Zionist movement, and revived the memory of Masada by creating the Masada mythical narrative. On the other hand, if indeed the Sicarii were observant Jews, then the irony lies in the fact that these very same secular Zionist Jews who rejected, by and large, the Orthodox yoke found themselves creating a secular ritual of admiration for people whom they would have rejected had they been contemporaries. Thus, the secular Jewish Zionist rebels against Orthodox Judaism of the nineteenth and twentieth centuries found a comfortable identification with Orthodox Jews who had rebelled (partly, no doubt, for religious reasons) against the Roman empire. Indeed, a delightful historical irony.

Masada as a Heroic Tale

As we noted earlier, the Masada narrative had been practically dormant for nearly two thousand years. The heroism contained in it was not just given automatically in the original narrative but was constructed as such.

This was partially accomplished in the media by the repeated explicit reference to "heroism" within the narrative itself: for example, "the story of the heroism and death of 960 last defenders of Masada" (*Yediot Ahronot,* September 24, 1963), or "The women told the deed of heroism . . . a national symbol of heroism . . . the suicide of the bold defenders . . . this mountain of heroism" (*Maariv,* October 13, 1963), or "a shocking operation of heroism" (*Yediot Ahronot,* October 20, 1963). Often, the suicide and the heroics have been tied together as if suicide is the epitome of heroism (the alternative of fighting to the end is not mentioned). Moreover, in many of the reports the collective suicide was presented as a legitimate act. The motif of heroism appears in the different articles without any reservations, qualifications, hesitations, or second thoughts. However, it is not entirely clear on exactly what this claim of heroism is founded. If it is based on the suicide, then one must admit that there *is* a sense of awe and respect for the power of collective suicide. Josephus Flavius clearly conveys a strong sense of respect for the act. However, the systematic uncritical presentation of this collective suicide as an act of heroism ignores other difficult questions (that of the fighting, of other alternatives, of the nature of the defenders, etc.) and helps to perpetuate this socially constructed myth.

The Masada Narrative as a Symbol and a Positive Value for Israelis/Jews

There can be no doubt that the major Israeli newspapers of 1963–1964 helped in a most significant way to create and propagate the myth. The "information" they provided concerning the original narrative was not only biased, inaccurate, and fabricated but also full of rhetorical devices that magnified the mythological dimension. The deviation from Josephus Flavius's narrative is very significant. The newspaper reports helped to turn a rather problematic historical narrative into a heroic tale while questioning neither the myth nor the necessity (scientific or political) for the excavations. Not a single voice of dissent or criticism regarding the excavations can be found in the secular newspapers we examined.

One must be reminded here that most of the written (and state-controlled electronic) media at that time basically supported the government in what appears to be a joint effort at a nation-building process. The newspapers were rarely critical, and investigative journalism hardly existed. Within this general context, the written media cooperated in the social construction of the Masada mythical narrative as a positive symbol and value.

Out of curiosity and a sociological desire to compare, we also examined two daily religious newspapers: *Hamodea,* an ultra-Orthodox organ, and *Hatzophe,* a national religious outlet. Both had at that time a much smaller circulation than the major (secular) newspapers we examined. The major differences between the religious and secular newspapers emerged: (1) there is *much* less coverage in the religious newspapers of Masada, and (2) the religious newspapers' reports focused on the religiosity of the Masada rebels. Again and again we read in the religious newspapers about findings that indicate (or support the hypothesis) that the rebels were very observant Jews.

In summary, one can very easily observe that the two major daily Hebrew newspapers in Israel during the period of the excavations did not "reflect" Josephus Flavius's account. Nor were they in any way critical of the enterprise; rather, they took a very supportive role in distributing and amplifying a questionable tale that deviated quite significantly from the original narrative. If one of the major purposes of journalism is the duty to report the truth, then the fulfillment of this role, in this instance, was problematic, to say the least. In this case, the newspapers gave sustenance to—indeed, helped to construct, amplify, and distribute—a questionable and rather distorted tale and lent strong and unquestionable support to the excavations themselves, primarily for what seem to have been national political reasons.

MASADA AND TOURISM[8]

As Gurevitz and Aran (1991) point out so well, touring and trekking across the country has become a national obsession for Jewish Israelis. It was certainly perceived as one of the best ways of "getting to know" the new land. The quantity of available manuals and tour guides, as well as background information for potential tourists and guides, is overwhelming. This basic craving seems well placed in a country one of whose major industries is tourism.

How do we conceptualize tourism in Israel? Pilgrimage is typically seen in a religious context, as a trek to a place that is perceived to be unique from a religious point of view.

It is quite obvious that the Masada mythical narrative is very intimately associated with Zionism and the revival of national Jewish life in the Holy Land. In this respect, it is interesting to take a look at Liebman and Don-Yehiya's 1983 book *Civil Religion in Israel.* The claim made there is that Zionism can be viewed as a "civil religion." In other words, the Zionist experience may be seen as the equivalent of a religious experience. Thus, the concept of a "civil religion" proposes that agents of the state view themselves and are viewed by others as the priests of this religion. In this context, it is interesting to note that Zionism originally preached that the modern Jew should ignore the not-so-glorious past of living in the Diaspora and concentrate instead on the new national secular life in Israel. This meant a clash with Judaism as a religion or, at the very least, with its Orthodox version. Such an ideology implied that almost 1800 years of rich Jewish cultural life have become irrelevant for the new secular Zionists, excluding of course the persecutions and pogroms that were considered to be among the reasons for establishing a new Jewish homeland. The secular Zionists required a new past. This created a very strong motivation among the Zionist moral entrepreneurs to look for periods in Jewish history that were characterized by national independence. The biblical period and that of the Second Commonwealth were naturally attractive to them. These periods were characterized not only by that sought-after national independence but by Jews living, working, and fighting—sometimes heroically—in *their* own homeland. In fact, Liebman and Don-Yehiya discuss the Masada myth in exactly this context (1983:98–100). As so many authors (e.g., Gurevitz and Aran 1991; Katz 1985) have pointed out, the experience of a *tiyul,* that is, of a trip or trek in the Holy Land, has become a central one for most Israelis. It was certainly given an almost sacred status by the new Zionist movement.

Knowledge of the land, gained intimately, directly, and in detail by walking through it, has become a central Zionist experience. The trips have been described as a means by which the trekkers are forced to go back in time, to become reacquainted with their Jewish roots and to strengthen their connection with the land. Thus, these *tiyulim,* particularly on foot, have become a central and key element of the newly emerging secular and national—Zionist-oriented—Israeli culture. In fact, Shaul Tchernichovski, one of Israel's most interesting and admired (certainly by this author) poets, in a poem titled "A Man is Nothing But . . . ," states: "A man is nothing but an image of his homeland's landscape."[9] From this ideological point of view, trips and treks organized by schools and youth movements are seen as goals in themselves. Choice of the route, its level of difficulty in terms of walking, the sites and their educational importance—all these have become part and parcel of a long-range plan for the education of the youth into a new type of secular national Jew consistent with the new Jewish Zionist consciousness. The concept of *Yediat Haaretz,* meaning "knowledge of the land," so commonly used in Israel in reference to trips, trekking, and geographical classes, can be very easily interpreted as having a symbolic sexual connotation, that of knowing (and conquering) in the biblical sense.[10] That is, those who *know* the land also *own* it. Interpreted in this way, the concept of Israel has been socially constructed as a huge sacred locality in which trips and treks acquire an atmosphere and aura of pilgrimage. In this national secular conception, the centers of worship were those sites that were charged with national symbolic meaning and constructed to represent the various myths on which the Zionist movement wished to crystallize and shape its new people and its new consciousness. Obviously, a major concept in this new consciousness was that of "Jewish heroism." The central moral and political Zionist entrepreneurs nourished the cult of Jewish heroism as an element of the highest priority required to change the self-image of the new Israeli Jew. They wanted to mold a new Jew: dynamic, hard-working, young, with deep roots and commitment to his or her homeland. This was the new pioneer—the daring, conquering, brave, fighting type. I am tempted to say, the macho John Wayne type.

Although such important social, political, and scientific personages as Yitzhak Ben-Tzvi, David Ben-Gurion, and Yigael Yadin originally objected to the selection of Masada as a preferred site for a center of the new secular Zionist ritual, the reality of 1940–1942 and the 1950s, plus Shmaria Guttman's relentless campaigns of persuasion, had their impact.[11] Masada was gradually in the process of being socially constructed as a shrine for Jewish martyrdom and heroism. The "defenders" (or "Zealots") of Masada (not the "Sicarii") were portrayed as the last ones to hold out against the Romans, the last ones to give their life for the political independence of Israel. They could not be viewed as a questionable group of fanatics who were chased out of Jerusalem, who did not come to the aid of its defenders, who robbed and killed other Jewish settlements, and, when faced with a choice, who chose to "die in the end" rather than "fight to the end."

The years in which the Masada mythical narrative was created and crystallized were also characterized by external events that somehow added to the need for Jewish symbols of heroism: the Arab revolts, actions, and pogroms against the Jews during 1920–1921, 1929, and 1936–1939; the fear of a German invasion during 1940–1942. Moreover, the 1948 war and the years following it, until 1967, created a feeling among many Israelis that they were living in a "state under siege." Such symbols as the Masada mythical narrative were needed to crystallize the consciousness of the young generation around national themes, strengthen and solidify their loyalty, and increase their conviction and determination concerning the Zionist cause. No less important, these symbols, placed in the proper historical context, most certainly provided a feeling of belonging to an ancient chain of heroic Jewish warriors in the struggle for their land. In this context, to paraphrase an old saying, if Masada would not have existed, there would have been a need to invent it. The fact is, however, that Masada *was* there—an impressive story and an even more impressive site. The story and the site enabled the development of the two facets of the Masada mythical narrative. One was the *cognitive* side. The other was the *emotional,* experiential side of an actual visit to Masada. Thus, the combination of the cognitive with the emotional created a very powerful concoction.

With some modifications, omissions, and fabrications, the Masada mythical narrative came into life. This narrative was significantly reinforced by the trips and treks to the area and by the difficult and challenging climb to the top of the fortress. Moreover, the periods of the secular pilgrimage to Masada tended to coincide with two other significant Jewish holidays: Passover and Hanukkah. Both holidays are also religious celebrations of liberty and freedom.

This point is easy to examine in four of the most early and influential books about Masada. These books were not guidebooks proper but were used in courses for tour guides, as well as by the guides as a necessary background for preparing both guidebooks and tours. The books are by Klosner, Bar-Droma, Breslavski, and Yadin. What do these texts have to say about Masada as a symbol?

Yoseph Klosner, in his 1937 publication, wrote (p. 33) that "the heroes of Masada did not die; their names and memory will forever live and will be a symbol for their physical and mental heroism and for their national sacrifice for generations to come." In the same year, Bar-Droma, also writing about Masada, stated:

> For us, the Jews, Masada is a history and a symbol . . . [of] past and future and hope. We shall see in Masada and its defenders—our defenders, huge in spirit—that all generations will refuse to deny their . . . holy assets. . . . We, the Jews, listen to the voices in the ruins of Masada. Voices of a nation in the ashes of destruction in all places and in all times. A nation yearning for resurrection, bewildered in its birth pangs, trampled in its blood on the verge of salvation.
>
> We shall listen to these voices and our hearts will expand, our

soul will know—the day of salvation will come for the whole nation, and then we will recall the memory of the heroes of Masada—the last of a war of freedom, of a nation that is rooted in its land. (p. 82)

Yoseph Breslavski (or Breslavi), in his 1944 book, wrote that "Masada for us is a symbol for a heroic spirit and for an unprecedented self-sacrifice" (p. 397) and that "those climbing to Masada tell that those, last of the Great Revolt, who fell there for the cause of political and spiritual freedom did not do so in vain. There is a reward to their deed because the sons are back in their homeland" (p. 448). Finally, Yadin in his 1966 work states that "Masada represents for all of us in Israel and for many elsewhere, archaeologists and laymen, a symbol of courage, a monument to our great national figures, heroes who chose death over a life of physical and moral serfdom" (p. 13) and that "it is thanks to Ben Ya'ir and his comrades, to their heroic stand, to their choice of death over slavery, and to the burning of their humble chattels as a final act of defiance to the enemy that they elevated Masada to an undying symbol of desperate courage, a symbol that has stirred hearts throughout the last nineteen centuries" (p. 197). Three elements are salient in the above four books: the element of *heroism,* the element of *belief and sacrifice,* and the element of *historical justice.* The heroes of Masada did not fall in vain. Clearly, it is difficult to imagine that this "heroism" is directly linked to the suicide. The "heroism" mentioned so frequently by the social constructionists refers to what they chose to see and define as the unconditional commitment and loyalty of the Masada rebels—even at the price of murder and suicide—to their ideology of national liberty and personal freedom. This was interpreted as a heroism *for* such values as freedom, homeland, and religion and *in opposition to* torture, wretched slavery, loss of liberty, and humiliation. In retrospect, it was this very interpretation that helped to socially construct the justification of the suicide.

Guidebooks

We have tried to locate as many guidebooks as possible to examine how Masada was portrayed by them. The table below, constructed in the format used in other chapters, includes books and pamphlets easily identifiable as guidebooks. However, we decided to include in the table a number of additional books that may not seem to most to be guidebooks. This is because we know from our interviews either that these were used directly as guidebooks or that they were used in courses for tour guides as "manuals of Masada" and for all practical purposes can be viewed as guidebooks.

Table 9.1. Elements of the Masada Historical Narrative in Guidebooks

Guidebooks	1 Escape from Jerusalem	2 Sicarii on Masada	3 Nature of Sicarii	4 Ein Gedi massacre	5 Elazar's two speeches	6 Describing suicide on Masada	7 Mention of seven survivors	8 Length of siege and war	9 Battles on and around Masada	10 Number of people on Masada
Yeshayahu Peres 1921	–	–	–	–	–	+	–	2½ years	fought valiantly	–
Zeev Vilnai 1935	+	+/–	–	–	–	+	–	–	–	–
Joseph Klosner 1937	+	+/–	+	–	+	+	+	–	–	967
Pinhas Cohen and David Benvenisti 1938	–	Zealots	–	–	–	died as heroes	fortress held 3 years		fought valiantly	–
Zeev Vilnai 1942	–	–	–	–	–	+	–	–	–	–
Yoseph Breslavski 1944	–	+/–	–	–	–	+	+	3 years	–	960
In Masada and the Negev 1944	–	+	–	–	–	+	–	3 years	–	960
Yoseph Breslavski 1955	+	+	+/–	+	–	+	+	3 years	–	960
Yochanan Aharoni 1958	+	+	+	+	–	+	+	8–9 months	–	960
David & Meron Benvenisti 1959	–	–	+	–	–	+	+	few months	–	960
Menashe Harel 1960	–	(Zealots)	–	–	–	+	+	4–8 months	–	967
Ephraim & Menachem Talmy 1960	–	+/–	–	–	–	+	+	3 years	–	960
Micha Livne 1961	–	+	+/–	+	–	+	+	4 months	–	967
Yosef Weitz 1963	–	–	–	–	–	–	–	–	–	–
Zeev Vilnai 1964	–	+/–	–	–	–	+	+	3 years	–	967
Shmaria Guttman 1964	–	+/–	+/–	–	+	+	+	–	+	–
Yediot Ahronot Vacation Guide, 1965	–	–	–	–	–	+	–	–	–	1000 people
Micha Livne 1965	–	Zealots	–	–	–	–	–	–	–	–
Ephraim & Menachem Talmi 1966	–	+/–	–	–	–	+	+	3 years/ a few months	–	960

(table continued on following page)

Table 9.1. Elements of the Masada Historical Narrative in Guidebooks (*continued*)

Guidebooks	1 Escape from Jerusalem	2 Sicarii on Masada	3 Nature of Sicarii	4 Ein Gedi massacre	5 Elazar's two speeches	6 Describing suicide on Masada	7 Mention of seven survivors	8 Length of siege and war	9 Battles on and around Masada	10 Number of people on Masada
Uri Yaffe 1967	–	–	–	+	–	+	–	a few months	–	960
Avinoam Haimi 1967	–/+	+/–	+	+	+	+	+	–	–	967
Nathan Shalem 1968	–	–	–	–	–	+	–	–	–	–
Tzvi Illan 1968	–	(Zealots) +/–	–	–	+	+	+	1 year	–	about 1000
Azaria Alon 1969	–	–	–	–	–	+	(one woman) –	–	–	–
Yitzhak Zaks & Mordechai Gavrieli 1969	–	(Zealots) –	–	–	–	+	–	–	–	960
Aharon Bir 1969	–	–	–	–	–	+	+	2½ years	–	967
Micha Livne & Zeev Meshel 1969	–	+	–	–	–	+	+	a few months	fights implied	967
Dov Nir 1970	–	(Zealots) –/+	–	–	–	death by choice	–	–	–	about 1000
Menashe Harel 1971	–	–/+	–	–	–	+	+	4–8 months	–	967
Yigael Butrimovitch 1972	–	+/–	–	–	–	+	+	–	–	–
Society for the Protection of Nature (edited by Tzvi Illan 1972)	+/–	+/–	–	+	–	+	+	–	–	967
Avraham Negev & Yehuda Ziv 1975	–	–	–	–	–	–	–	–	–	–
Aharon Bir 1976	–	–	–	–	+	–	–	–	–	–
Masada, by Scouting (Israeli Government) 1976	–	–	–	–	+	+	+	many months	+	967

Publication								Duration		Year
Zeev Meshel 1977	+	+/–	+/–	+	–	+	+	a few months	+	967
Kol Makom Veatar 1978 edition (Zealots)	–	–	–	–	–	+	–	3 years	–	960
Zeev Vilnai 1978	–	+/–	–	–	+	+	+	3 years	–	967
Madrich Israel*	+	+/–	–	–	+	+	+	long siege	–	967
Tamar Miller 1984	–	+/–	+	–	–	+	+	–	–	967
Yaacov Aloni 1984	–	+/–	–	–	+	+	+	–	–	–
Facts about Israel 1985	–	+/–	+	–	–	+	+	3 years	–	close to 1000
Micha Livne with Irit Zaharoni 1986	–	+/–	–	+	–	+	+	–	+	960
Micha Livne 1986	+	+/–	+	+	–	+	+	–	–	967
Kol Makom Veatar 1989 edition (rebels)	–	–	–	–	–	+	–	3 years	+/–	960
Micha Livne and Zeev Meshel 1966	–	–	–	–	–	+	–	–	+	967
Bob Baseman (no date) (Zealots)	–	–	–	–	–	+	–	implies a few months	–	960
Summary										
% –	83	52	85	85	81	11	46	46 — 20% "months" / 34% "years"	78 — (22%)	24
% +	17	48	15	15	19	89	54		46 — state "fights"	76

Key: * This is the *Guide For Israel: A Practical Encyclopedia For the Knowledge of the Country*, by Aryeh Yitzhaki. The volume about the Judea desert and the Jordan valley is by Safi Ben-Yoseph, and the chapter on Masada is by Yigael Yadin.
+ means that the narrative is in accordance with Josephus Flavius.
– means that the issue is omitted altogether, or not according to Josephus.
+/– means that the account is partially in accordance with Josephus Flavius.

195

This table is, of course, exceptional in its size, and this reflects the great interest in guidebooks and *Yediat Haaretz* found in Israel.

One item that appears almost unbiased is that of the suicide. Another is the number of rebels on Masada. The other elements of Josephus Flavius's narrative are reported quite selectively. Seventeen texts (38 percent) explicitly state that the rebels arrived at Masada *after* Jerusalem was conquered by the Romans. This is factually untrue. Sixteen texts (36 percent) simply ignore the issue. Thus, 74 percent of the texts do not provide the reader with the true story of how and when the Sicarii arrived at Masada.

The overwhelming majority of texts do not tell the reader that the rebels on Masada were Sicarii. Needless to add, very few texts indeed reveal the *true* nature of the Sicarii. However, we did discover a few innovations here. These found expression in a number of ways. First, when the author of a book discusses the rebels on Masada the words *heroes,* and *defenders* and the *much* more common word *Zealots* are used. This is not new. However, when the very same author needs to quote from Josephus Flavius, suddenly the word *Sicarii* appears. Second, while Elazar Ben-Yair is described as a "Sicarii," the rest of the rebels are called "Zealots." Third, a new original formulation is used when the rebels on Masada are referred to as "Zealots-Sicarii."

However, the best innovation I discovered—and perhaps the fairest—was by Livne (1986). Note the linguistic acrobatics Livne performs:

> The proper expression for the people of Masada, according to Yosef Ben-Matityahu [Josephus Flavius], would be "Sicarii" (or "robbers"). Moreover, the expression used today, "Zealots," was used by Yosef Ben-Matityahu to [describe] a clearly different unit than the Sicarii. . . . Despite this, we shall use the term "Zealots" to refer to the people of Masada. Why? First, there is no doubt that they showed much zeal for their political-religious views and fought for them with literal zeal. Second, this term is already attached to them in our literature and in the consciousness of the nation; third, this use [of the word] expresses doubts as to whether all the inhabitants of Masada were Sicarii, and if there was still any meaning left to the term at the end of the revolt. But after all this, I feel obliged to emphasize again that the use of the term "Zealots" for the people of Masada stands in an explicit and conscious contradiction to the terminology used by Yosef Ben-Matityahu. (p. 14)

Only seven books (16 percent) mention the massacre at Ein Gedi. Here, too, some interesting rhetorical devices are found. For example, one book mentions the raid and "killings" without providing details. Another example can be found in Zeev Vilnai (1964). His book describes the Dead Sea and its Israeli beach (the other side is under Jordanian control). The book contains separate chapters on Masada and Ein Gedi. In the chapter on Ein Gedi there is a fairly accurate description of the Sicarii's raid there. However, in the chapter on Masada, it is not mentioned at all.

The overwhelming majority of texts (37, or 80 percent) do not mention that Elazar Ben-Yair had to make *two* speeches to an initially reluctant following.

Twenty-four (52 percent) of the texts do provide an accurate account of the survivors of Masada—a commendable achievement.

The reports in the texts concerning the length of the siege vary. About eleven texts (24 percent) report months and fourteen texts (30 percent) report years of siege.

The next issue is that of battles during the siege. In about eight books (17 percent) we can find fairly detailed (but *totally* imaginary) descriptions of the actual fights between the Jewish rebels on Masada and the soldiers of the Roman tenth legion (e.g., raids by the Sicarii on the Romans. No doubt, Zeev Meshel's 1977 book is the "richest" in this regard). Other texts use general or broad phrases, such as "the heroes of Masada fought," that imply that there were battles around Masada. These texts do not provide any details, however.

One interesting aspect of these texts, one that was typically lacking in other sources, was a direct reference to the estimated size of the Roman tenth legion and its auxiliary forces (including slaves) (found in twenty-two of the books, or 48 percent). The numbers run from a conservative six thousand or eight thousand to fifteen thousand. Although not mentioned by Josephus Flavius, these figures are certainly consistent with the relevant literature. The typical context in which the size of the Roman tenth legion is made is a discussion about the siege on Masada emphasizing that "the many" (Romans) were against "the few" (Jews).

Many of the books found in table 9.1 are clearly "manuals" for tour guides or at least have the appearance of a "guidebook." As Katz (1985) has noted, the role of the Israeli teacher-guide (of tourists) is also ideological. His uniqueness lies

> in his role as an eager creator of new knowledge. The 'cultural brokering' activities of the common guide are based—as in the case of the ordinary schoolteacher—on content and interpretations that have been learned and digested from the available sources of information produced by others. What typifies the Israeli teacher-

guides [for tourists], or at least those who belong to the "elite" of the occupation, is the fact that in addition to their usual function as carriers and dispensers of certified or accepted knowledge, they intentionally produce new knowledge. This new knowledge, which often sees light in special publications, is used for the edification of the guides themselves and their colleagues. (p. 51)

With some slight variations, the basic Masada mythical narrative can be rather easily found in the overwhelming majority of the books we examined.

It is quite interesting to look at one of the most popular tour guides in Israel, the *Kol Makom Veatar* manual. This is a compact and condensed 543-page text, accompanied by a map, in a plastic travel bag. The tenth edition was published in 1989. This manual is *designed* for travelers. Here is how it presents the Masada mythical narrative:

> During the days of the Great Revolt . . . [Masada] was captured by the rebels, and after the fall of Jerusalem the last Zealots convened there, headed by Elazar Ben-Yair. Three years they held their position [and] stood against the Roman army commanded by Flavius Silva, which placed [Masada] under siege. When the defenders realized that all hope was lost, they set the fortress on fire and committed suicide—960 men, women, and children (on the first day of Passover, 73 A.D.). (p. 338)

Visitors

Since we are dealing with tourism and *Yediat Haaretz*, we should ask ourselves just how many people actually visit Masada each year. To answer this question, we examined the literature and requested the relevant figures from the Israeli Authority for National Parks. The statistics we gathered are summarized in table 9.2.

Until 1987–1988 we can see a clear general increase in the number of visitors to Masada, with occasional fluctuations. Significant drops seem to have occurred during years in which the Middle East conflict erupted into actual war, which took its toll on tourism to Israel in general: in 1967, the Six-Day War; in 1973, the Yom Kippur War; in 1978, the first Israeli invasion of Lebanon; and in 1982, the second and considerably more involved Israeli invasion of Lebanon. A notable increase in the number of visitors to Masada is found in 1971, the year in which the cable car to the top became operational. From 1987–1988 to 1991 we observe a steady decline in the figures, with a very sharp drop in 1991, most probably attributable to the Persian Gulf War, which was quite damaging to the

Table 9.2. Number of Visitors to Masada

Year	Number of Visitors	Israeli Visitors	Notes
1958	27,000		*Haaretz*, January 20, 1960
1959	34,000		*Haaretz*, January 20, 1960
1960–1965	no data		
1965–1966	42,000*		
1966–1967	118,090		
1967–1968	79,670		
1968–1969	90,160		
1969–1970	113,970		
1970–1971	186,190		
1971–1972	357,690		
1972–1973	384,150		
1973–1974	293,170		
1974–1975	273,980		
1975–1976	330,640		
1976–1977	457,470		
1977–1978	532,650		
1978–1979	470,560		
1979–1980	482,990		
1980–1981	467,160		
1981–1982	471,480		
1982–1983	368,320		
1983–1984	426,800		
1984–1985	479,330		
1985–1986	517,640		
1986–1987	477,830		
1987–1988	532,250		
1989	417,620	146,160	
1990	377,430	132,120	
1991	279,830	97,920	
1992	549,870	192,460	
1993	582,806	203,993	
1994	646,000	77,351	

*All data from 1965–1966 on is provided by the Israeli National Parks Authority.

tourist industry of the entire region. The trend for Israeli visitors, for which we have only figures since 1989, also appears to show a decline until 1991. No consistent patterns can be discerned for other tourist sites in Israel that we examined, except for similar drops in the number of visitors during periods of tension. However, since 1991, for both categories (Israeli visitors and overall visitors) there is a marked increase in the number of visitors, and 1993 shows the highest number of visitors in one year.

Overall, the figures indicate that almost eight million people have visited Masada since 1965. This number does not include unregistered visitors, so it is a minimal estimate.

The reversal of the trend, from 1987 until 1991, has received some unexpected reinforcement from a surprising source. Upon examining the tour guides, we came across a fascinating finding: the disregard of Masada in some recent guidebooks. This phenomenon deserves some special attention.

The first tour book in which Masada simply does not appear as a recommended site was published in 1977 by Uri Dvir, a *very* famous and respected tour guide in Israel. No other guidebooks around that period neglected Masada. However, three new guidebooks from 1983, 1984, and 1985 also made no mention of Masada. The first of these books, by Yehuda Ziv (1983), was published by none other than the Israeli Ministry of Defense. The second book (*Views and Landscapes,* 1984) was also published by the Ministry of Defense and the Israeli Army and surveys recommended places to visit, again without reference to Masada (but Ein Gedi is mentioned). Finally, in Paz's guide for tours in Israel (1985 edition), Masada appears in two maps, but it is not included in the list of places recommended for a visit. This is in contrast to the 1972 edition of the same Paz guide, which specifically discussed Masada (see Butrimovich 1972). Another more recent guidebook, two volumes of which are filled with tour suggestions by Dafna Meroz, does not mention Masada at all in the second (1992) volume, and in the first volume (1991) Masada is mentioned only in passing, as five lines in a table (p. 220) that suggests other sites as well (e.g., Ein Gedi). A detailed description of the site is not provided, and what is given is just a general statement that there are a cable car, a palace, water holes, and sight-and-sound show that tells "the story of the besieged."

Does this surprising find indicate a trend? Possibly, but if so, it is most likely only a weakening of the central position of Masada as a major tourist attraction for Israelis. That is, Masada may slowly lose its special meaning and importance for Israeli tourists and become just another tourist site among many in Israel for non-Israelis (table 9.2 seems to reinforce this hypothesis). It is difficult to imagine that Masada will simply disappear from the tourist map. As a site, it is most certainly worth a visit. In fact, *Yediot Ahronot*'s special edition for Passover (April 2, 1993) contained, as usual, a small pamphlet suggesting different tours. Among the many tours it suggested, Masada was mentioned in a *very* nonmythical, nonspecial, and technical way. The significant increase in the number of non-Israeli visitors to Masada during 1992, 1993, and 1994 seems to re-inforce this conclusion.

That Masada will probably continue to be a central focus for non-Israeli tourism is evident by the amount of investments planned for it by the Israeli Authority for National Parks. The Authority and the Administration for the Development of the Negev together plan to invest forty million U.S. dollars (in 1994 prices) in Masada for a period of five to ten years, beginning in 1995. The money will be invested in building an additional cable car, constructing a new open museum, reconstructing mosaic floors, extending visiting hours, making the sight-and-sound show longer, and building a big visitors' center (*Yediot Ahronot,* July 20, 1994, p. 10 in the monetary supplement). So we can most certainly expect Masada to be less and less of the ritualistic place it used to be and more and more of a tourist attraction. The investors obviously will do their best to maximize the re-turn on their investment.

Tour Guides

During the period of this research, I made a number of trips to Masada, some with students, some without. I was curious to hear just how tour guides "explain" Masada. So I attached myself to their groups and lis-tened to the explanations they gave to the tourists whom they were ac-companying. Generally, the guides spent a great deal of time describing the site itself (architecture, excavations, etc.), devoting very little time to the most fascinating thing about Masada, that is, the narrative. When the narrative is related, it is the Masada mythical narrative that unfolds, with the emphasis placed on the suicide. The method by which these guides attempt to grapple with this issue is fascinating. The best "undoing" of the suicide I heard was by a tour guide in 1989 explaining it to a group of English-speaking tourists.

The guide described the site, recited a more or less standard version of the Masada mythical narrative, and then arrived at the suicide. "You know," he told his eager listeners, "that the Jewish faith does not allow suicide. Those that commit suicide cannot even be buried in a Jewish cemetery." Well, then, how to explain what the "Zealots" did? Elemen-tary, my dear Watson, elementary. There *was* no suicide on Masada. What *really* took place was murder. They murdered each other. A terrible thing to do; Judaism certainly does not allow it. One of the Ten Com-mandments specifically forbids it. *But* murder is not suicide. If one com-mits murder, one can still be buried properly. So now that the suicide has been turned into murder and basically "undone," there is one problem left. What does the last person do? Well, the version that those attentive English-speaking tourists heard was the following: The last Zealot took his sword, ran out toward the Roman soldiers who were pouring into Masada through the breach in the wall, and yelled, "Follow me." The Roman soldiers thought that he was the commander of the Zealots calling his warriors to follow him. So they killed him. Again, no suicide. There are a few interesting things about this fairy tale. First, any Israeli will recognize the command of "Follow me" ("Acharay" in Hebrew) as that given by Israeli officers to their soldiers. Israeli officers lead the way in battle. The connection to modern Israel is thus made. Second, how could the Roman soldiers understand what the last "Zealot" was yelling? Did he speak their language? Third—and *this* is the reason I call this "ending" a fairy tale—is what Josephus Flavius has to say about this, and here he is *very* explicit: "He who was the last of all . . . with the great force of his hand ran his sword entirely through himself and fell down dead near to his own relations."[12]

I watched different tour guides, from different backgrounds, "explaining" Masada to similarly different tourists, and concluded that although there are certainly differences in style and in emphasis among them, these differences are not very significant. Tour guides tend to devote most of their explanations to the ecology of the desert and to Masada within that ecology. This is a safe route to follow. It is based on immediately observable, impressive, noncontroversial facts. The archaeology and architecture of Masada falls into this very same category. The Masada narrative is a different issue. It is a long, complicated, and questionable tale. With no exception (at least that I could observe), tourists to Masada receive the Masada mythical narrative. True, different guides would give the myth in different ways, but they all basically convey the myth. Moreover, the myth is typically told very briefly, and within this short account, the suicide assumes a central position. On one of the visits the Israeli guide was asked what the source of the narrative was; his response was Yadin, not Josephus Flavius. When I asked a few tour guides the same question, I received the same answer: Yadin.

Finally, let us have a glimpse at one interesting document that is not a textbook but has wide distribution: a very impressive, high-quality brochure (in either Hebrew or English) about Masada, given to every visitor who purchases a ticket to visit the ruins of the ancient fortress. The brochure I have must have been produced sometime between 1991 and 1993. The brochure was researched by Ehud Netzer and edited by Leah

Karni. The brochure is published by the Israeli National Parks Authority and is composed of six double-sided 10.5-by-22.5-centimeter pages printed on glossy paper, with text, maps, charts, and pictures. Here is what is written there (in the English version) about "Masada under the Zealots" (my own comments are inserted in brackets):

In the year 66 CE, at the beginning of the Great Revolt against Rome, a group of Sicarii commanded by Menahem Ben-Yehuda of Galilee captured Masada from the garrison stationed here. (The Sicarii were a group of Zealot extremists determined to fight against the Romans till death, and were named after the "Sica"—a dagger which they carried [no mention of the main feature of the Sicarii—assassinations; deliberate confusion of them with the Zealots]). During the years of the revolt, Masada became a refuge for more Zealots who fled with their families, as well as for other desperate elements such as the Essenes [no mention of any of this by Josephus]. Following the murder of Menahem [no explanation why he was murdered; no use of the word *murder* in connection with the Sicarii] by his [Jewish] opponents in Jerusalem, his surviving followers, among them his nephew Elazar Ben-Yair, who later became the commander of the fortress, fled to Masada. After the destruction of the Temple in 70 CE, the last rebellious members reached Masada [no mention of this by Josephus]. Designed as a stronghold for a king, the fortress now became a refuge for the masses ["masses"? No mention of this by Josephus. The text implies that very many people were on Masada], who used various parts of the palaces as well as thin walled rooms in the casemate wall as their dwellings. . . . In 72 CE, three years after Titus captured Jerusalem and destroyed the Temple, the Roman army, under the leadership of . . . Flavius Silva, turned to Masada in an attempt to conquer the fortress. At first they hoped that the besieged people would surrender due to hunger and thirst [no mention of this "hope" by Josephus]. Silva's camp numbered some ten to fifteen thousand men, while the entire besieged population on Masada numbered 967 people, including men, women and children [still remember the "masses" mentioned earlier? The text now projects an impression of a small number of people]. The siege lasted several months [elsewhere in the brochure it is stated that the siege lasted seven months], during which time the Romans continued with their efforts to prepare an embankment on the western slope. Once the wall was breached, the besieged Zealots [Sicarii] improvised a wood-and-soil wall. But when the Romans set fire to the earthen wall, the Jewish warriors [Sicarii; whether they were warriors is an open question, but assassins they were for sure], realizing that there was no hope left, decided to take their own lives rather than be captured by the Romans.

Needless to say, the raid on Ein Gedi is ignored. Throughout the brochure the people on Masada are referred to as "Sicarii," "Zealots," "the besieged," "Jewish warriors," "Masada's defenders." Most of the time they are called "Zealots." Thus, by carefully carving the narrative and selecting words and expressions to add and subtract morally loaded issues, a heroic story emerges.

Other Tourist-Attractive Ceremonies

As Masada became more and more accessible, its commercialization was developed further and further. At the bottom of the mountain one can today purchase a variety of souvenirs. Moreover, a sort of custom developed to celebrate individual and collective bar mitzvahs and bat mitzvahs on top of that doomed fortress,[13] with specific tour agencies specializing in the organization of these ceremonies.[14] Another group even decided to have a Passover seder on top of Masada (for a short review, see Zerubavel 1980:47, 51–52).

There are other illustrations. For example, on December 22, 1989, the Ministry of Absorption, together with the Jewish Agency and the Student Union of Hebrew University, organized a mass ceremony for students (new immigrants and Israelis) to light the first candle of Hanukkah on top of Masada.

On the west side of the mountain, some distance from its base, there is an amphitheater in which audiovisual shows and concerts (even rock concerts) take place.

A particularly grandiose tourist event was held on October 13, 1988. On that date, the Israeli Philharmonic Orchestra, conducted by Zubin Mehta (with Yves Montand, Gregory Peck, and Martin Grey as guests of honor), played Mahler's Symphony no. 2 on top of Masada. This concert was the last in a series of events commemorating the fortieth anniversary of the State of Israel. Prime Minister Yitzhak Shamir, President Chaim Herzog, and other dignitaries (including Maurice Chevalier) also attended the concert. The cost was between 150 and 550 U.S. dollars per ticket. However, some invited guests paid thousands of dollars, including flight tickets and other contributions. El Al, Israel's national airline, offered special deals. The concert was attended by about three thousand guests from outside Israel and about one thousand Israelis. The reports all concluded that the concert was a most impressive production. Young attractive waitresses, in Roman classical dress, distributed food, and fireworks were displayed—the show must have been absolutely incredible. In fact, one of the reports (*Yediot Ahronot*) carried pictures of the ceremony and of the food and contained a large article about the attire of the various guests attending.[15] A 120-minute video cassette recording of the event is also available now for interested parties. There probably can be no more distinct contrast than that between this hedonistic, decadent event and the gloomy, bitter, and doomed Sicarii and the determined Roman tenth legion locked in a tragic siege. One is simply left to wonder how the Sicarii and the Roman soldiers would have responded had they been given a chance (courtesy of an imaginary time machine) to watch the October 13, 1988, Masada festival—perhaps just one more historical irony connected to the entire issue of Masada and its portrayal.[16]

Chapter Ten

Masada in Children's Literature and in Art

IN THIS CHAPTER we shall try to document and analyze different art forms through which the Masada historical narrative has been projected to a wider audience. Because of its unique quality, we have chosen here to place children's literature into a separate category of its own. Due to its educational nature, its simple language, and the fact that it is aimed at a less sophisticated audience, it seems that this written form may contain much sharper and more unicolored messages.

CHILDREN'S LITERATURE[1]

It is perhaps surprising, but not many children's fiction books have been written about Masada. Despite the search for such books, we found only a few.[2] We did succeed, however, in finding five children's stories on the subject.[3] Let me point out that the search we conducted was quite intensive and covered the entire period of 1940–1989. I highly doubt that additional books and stories exist, but it is possible that they are hidden somewhere.

All of the children's stories discussed are, by definition, fictional narratives. However, even though they are fiction, it is interesting to observe just how much they deviate—and in which aspects—from Josephus Flavius's original narrative. We examined these stories to see if and how seven key issues of the original narrative were presented. The examination yielded table 10.1.

It is quite obvious from the table that the overwhelming majority of the more problematic aspects of Josephus's narrative either are not mentioned or are presented quite differently. The manner in which the Sicarii are portrayed is a good illustration; however, it is not the only one. All of the fictional narratives deliberately disregard the fact that the Sicarii were

Table 10.1. Elements of the Masada Historical Narrative in Children's Literature

Literature	1 Escape from Jerusalem	2 Truth about the Sicarii	3 Ein Gedi massacre	4 Elazar's two speeches	5 Protesting collective suicide	6 Survivors	7 Length of siege and war
Breslavski 1941	–	–	–	–	+	–	–
To Masada (Meizel 1941–1942)*	–	–	–	–	–	–	–
Gospel of Masada (Asmuel 1941–1942)*	–	–	–	–	–	+	–
To Masada (Shirei 1947–1948)*	–	–	–	–	–	–	–
Trek to Fortress (Beno 1949–1950)*	–	–	–	–	–	–	–
Walk with Gadna (Tzabar 1949–1950)*	–	–	–	–	–	–	–
Tzoref 1960	–	–/+	–	–	–	–	–
Freilich 1962	–	–/+	–	+/–	–	+	–
Habron 1962	–	–	–	–	–	–	–
Hertzberg 1964	–	–/+	–	+/–	–	+	–
Gafni 1970	–	–	–	+	–	+	–
Hailan 1973	–	–	–	–	+	+	–
Ron-Feder 1982	–	–	–	–	–	+	–
Summary							
% –	100	77	100	77	85	54	100
% +		23		23	15	46	100

Key: * denotes stories.

+ means that the narrative is in accordance with Josephus Flavius.

– means that the issue is omitted altogether, or not according to Josephus.

–/+ is used when the description includes some true elements (according to Josephus Flavius) but also either includes fictional elements or is presented in a way that changes the original meaning in a significant way (usually, making it appear less problematic, more positive).

For full references of books and stories, see notes 2 and 3.

chased out of Jerusalem before the Roman siege and later destruction of the city. Moreover, in one book (Hertzberg), Elazar Ben-Yair tells his brother that his strategy was for his people (that is, the Sicarii) to leave Jerusalem so as to take the war outside the city. Not even one story mentions the nature of the Sicarii as terrorists or the massacre of the people in the Ein Gedi settlement.

Only one of the fictional stories states that to persuade his people to commit suicide, Elazar had to make *two* speeches. Thus, Galila Ron-Feder describes the enthusiastic willingness to commit suicide immediately after the (according to her story) only one speech. In both "The Legend of Masada" and "The Gospel of Masada," the suicide also immediately follows Elazar's one speech; no hesitation requiring a second speech is even mentioned. Determined and strong-willed freedom fighters do not, after all, need so much persuasion in order to choose death over slavery, or do they?

The idea of suicide is not any easy one to digest, especially for Jews, whose faith holds it in disdain, and particularly for children. In all of the stories the suicide is presented as a choice preferred to slavery. However, the suicide issue is a tough one, and undoing it is not a simple task. As we saw earlier, many tour guides to Masada had to develop an elegant resolution for this issue.

The category of protesting suicide was put in the table in this way because the suicide seems to be negotiated in the books. It is rarely, if ever, described in the same harsh and dreary colors that Josephus Flavius used. Contrary to other tables, the problem of mentioning the suicide in this context of fictional accounts concerned not only whether it was mentioned or not but also how.

More children stories (four altogether) than books do indeed state that there were a few survivors. There is an obvious moral problem in mentioning them. How, after all, could these survivors choose bondage and slavery over a liberating death? Their choice of life places the choice of suicide in serious question.

Finally, not even one story states the true length of the war and the Roman siege of Masada. Thus, although we already know that it is most likely that the war and siege of Masada lasted for about four to eight months, almost *all* of the fictional stories choose a length of three years.

Heroic terms are used unsparingly. For example, Shraga Gafni (1970) states that Masada was a glaring illustration of the courageous fight of the last remaining Zealots. Y. Freilich wonders whether Flavius Silva *really* won. All books relate more or less fierce fighting by the "Zealots" on top of Masada against the Romans—the battle of the "few against the many" and the heroic and awe-inspiring death of the rebels on Masada. The "Zealots" of Masada are typically described as survivors (or remnants) of the siege of Jerusalem. The Roman army is generally not portrayed in very positive terms. Thus, Gafni contrasts a Roman army composed of mercenaries with the voluntaristic and willing Jewish freedom fighters ("Zealots"). Gafni is also one of the few who actually describes the suicide, but he is quick to point out that this suicide was an example of supreme heroism and honor.

What all these stories do is to contribute to a process of socially constructing a narrative of heroism. This is accomplished in a number of ways.

One obvious strategy is to ignore the more problematic aspects of Josephus Flavius's narrative—"problematic" in the sense that these aspects are inconsistent with a heroic narrative. Another technique is to use the narrative given by Josephus Flavius as only a baseline, to be molded in a manner aimed at impressing on the reader that a heroic story is about to unfold.

An additional technique is to use the original names and heavily biblical jargon, in combination with heroic superlatives. Thus, the people on top of Masada are presented as the "heroes of Masada," their heroism being offered as a fact, not as something to be questioned. On the rare occasions when the Sicarii are mentioned, the murderous nature of the group is omitted, and extra emphasis is placed on their heroism. They are portrayed as lovers of freedom and fighters against the Roman oppressors, and the word *Sicarii* is often replaced by the word *Zealots*. Thus, when Herzberg mentions the Sicarii, he talks about their self-sacrifice and weapons of revenge (remember that Josephus Flavius does not mention any fight between the Sicarii and Roman soldiers from the tenth legion during the Masada siege). In Rina Habron's story there is even a direct accusation that Josephus Flavius distorted his own writings. In a few stories the nature of the Masada dwellers is shrouded altogether under the term *heroes*.

Another very important ingredient is the plot. The original narrative of Josephus Flavius waxes into an imaginary, animated story that forms the basic script of a children's tale. One method of weaving such a plot is a presentation of the Masada narrative as seen through the eyes and mind of a child who lives through the cataclysmic events. Elazar Ben-Yair appears in all the children's stories as a towering hero. Thus, an imaginary plot becomes a central literary device through which a heroic narrative is woven. This plot allows for the willing suspension of disbelief by means of identification with the literary figures and with the heroic tale itself. Moreover, the presentation of some real facts and information adds credibility to the imaginary story.

As I stated earlier, the social construction of the Masada narrative as a heroic tale necessitates the use of language in a particular manner: not an objective, cold verbal account but, rather, the application of emotionally loaded and powerful rhetorical devices; a heavy use of images and metaphors and a tendency to repeat idioms that portray heroism in sharp contrast to its antithesis. These stories are written in almost a stereotypical fashion.

In this context, it is interesting to compare two such creations. The literary narrative written by Breslavski in 1941 uses biblical language, as well as the consistent repetition of numerous idioms, to create an abundance of sharp contrasts. Reading this narrative now, one is left with a very strange impression (mostly of a distant, almost irrelevant legend); however, in the context of the renewed Hebrew language of the 1940s, this book was a big hit. In contrast, Galila Ron-Feder's 1982 book uses a modern, simple, colloquial Hebrew. Her book reifies the heroism not through the use of poetical, heavily biblical jargon but, rather, through an immediate, direct identification with personalized heroes who speak the everyday language of contemporary sabras.[4]

Two more elements seem to characterize all the children's stories. One element that repeats itself is the emphasis on the theme of a few Jewish heroes against the many Roman soldiers. "The few against the many" is one of the central themes of the Masada myth (it is, perhaps, worth mentioning that 960 people on top of Masada cannot exactly be described as "few"). The other element is the use of historical figures such as Elazar Ben-Yair in the most intimate and direct way. Figures like Elazar become personalized, familiarized, humanized, and understood over almost two thousand years. Moreover, these figures are idealized and described positively as having acted with the best moral, political, and social intentions. This literary device is used to create a strong identification with the relevant figures, their motivations, and their acts.

These children's books and stories basically provide an imaginary narrative about a few proud Jewish freedom fighters who, against tremendous odds, fought the Imperial Roman Army and, when faced with what they felt was a certain life of slavery, chose death. These Jews did not just go to the slaughter passively; they fought to the end in what Yadin has called "the Last Stand."

Not very many books or stories about Masada exist in Hebrew for children. We are tempted to conclude that, although this statement may be inaccurate and based on an indirect index, whatever Israeli children and adults know about Masada, children's literature probably did not play a major role in its determination.

In an interview with Galila Ron-Feder,[5] she insisted that a very clear distinction *must* be made between history and literature. According to Galila, an author can do as he or she pleases with historical materials. She believes that children cannot possibly be interested in the complexities of the 66–73 A.D. period. To our great surprise, Galila told us that her book about Masada was very unpopular in comparison to other books she wrote. The reason she gave for this was the difficulty in writing a story about such an ancient period and still create and maintain an authentic and credible literary atmosphere. It is very obvious that Galila had read Josephus Flavius, as well as other sources. She was well aware of the complexities of the Great Revolt, the Sicarii, and Masada. And yet, despite all these complexities, she chose to socially construct a heroic tale about the Sicarii of Masada. She was not forced to. One could just as well describe the Sicarii as the "bad guys," much in the spirit in which Josephus Flavius describes them. That would not be too difficult.

One is left pondering why so few children books and stories have been written about Masada. After all, there is a terrific potential there for some incredibly heroic stories. Going beyond the specific answer given by Galila Ron-Feder, Tali Geiger[6] suggests three reasons: One, the historical narrative of Masada is somewhat foggy and controversial. Two, most children's stories have a "happy ending," which Masada does not. Not only is the end of the story tragic, but it involves a massive collective suicide. How is one to explain *that* to a child? Third, Masada is not a "fresh" story. It happened almost two thousand years ago. Such a remote occurrence is very difficult to construct as a relevant, reliable, believable and credible story. In other words, the suspension of disbelief is not easy to achieve with such raw materials as provided by the Masada historical narrative.

In summary, although it seems that the children's books and stories about Masada reflect rather nicely the myth and its deviance from the original historical narrative, not very many children's stories and books concerning the topic actually exist.

FICTION, SCIENCE FICTION, PLAYS, POETRY, MOVIES

Examining the manner in which the Masada narrative appears in other art forms is a much more complex task than examining how it appeared, say, in children's literature. In part, this is a result of the way in which we conceptualize art, and there are objective difficulties involved in searching for the relevant references. On the face of it, the Masada narrative has not inspired any major artist (e.g., author, musician, painter, sculptor) to compose a significant or important artistic creation. Likewise, no *major* Israeli author has made the Masada narrative a very central theme in his or her work. For example, Haim Nachman Bialik, Shaul Tchernichovsky, Rachel (Blovshtein)—three of Israel's most prominent poets—have never even mentioned Masada. The artistic creation most people tend to remember is the 1980–1981 TV miniseries "Masada" and the subsequent movie *Masada*. I myself underwent the punishment of watching this 131-minute inaccurate, overlong, and boring movie. I do not recommend the experience to anyone else. It is interesting to note that the film also reinforces some of the major elements of the myth (e.g., the few against the many; the "escape" from Jerusalem, supposedly after the Roman siege; a disregard of the involvement and true nature of the Sicarii).

It is important that we ask ourselves what we have in mind when we use the term *art*. It is a basic assumption of ours that many artistic creations have different cultural myths at their foundation. In fact, there should not be any real expectation of an artist to reproduce a faithful historical sequence. Thus, historical reality and myth can "serve" in various artistic forms as teasers, as basic building blocks, or as a general frame on and within which an imaginary, fantastic, and creative art is manufactured. Artists, by definition, seem to want to be remembered for the uniquely creative way through which they treat and interpret a topic. The premise that artists need have no intention of being faithful to the original narrative, only makes it more important and interesting to take a look at artistic creations relating to Masada. It is in this context that we examine how different authors and artists have treated the Masada historical narrative. What did they choose to emphasize and focus on, and what did they choose to ignore? For obvious practical reasons, we concentrated mainly on written forms of art: books, plays, and poetry. However, the few musical and visual forms of art we found in our research gave us no reason to believe that our general conclusions had to be altered.

We located a number of artistic creations of different forms that are in one way or another related to Masada, some of them directly, some indirectly. Again, we looked at these art forms through the eyes of Josephus Flavius and tried to see how many of the more problematic aspects of his historical narrative are mentioned there and how.

I shall mention those artistic creations we found,[7] but in this case, the more mature and complex nature of the creations makes the presentation of the findings much more complicated than that for the children's literature. I shall discuss the way Masada was processed by different artists. The presentation will be arranged according to the different and unique artistic expressions and categories in which they appeared.

Fiction

Josephon. The book of Josephon (also spelled Josippon) dates back to the tenth century A.D.[8] and is a work of fiction that must have been based primarily on Josephus Flavius in its description of a Masada-like story. The book of Josephon was one of the most famous—and most widely read among Jews—to be found in medieval Hebrew literature. In a strange sense, Jews who were not exposed directly to Josephus Flavius could read Josephon instead. The central narrative in the imaginary account of Josephon is focused on Elazar's presuicide speech, and the account of the suicide itself is altered. Josephon's version has it that the men first killed their offspring and wives and then went out to engage the Romans in a fight in which they all died—a somewhat better "heroic" finale than "plain" suicide. Josephon presents a less "hostile," perhaps more positive account of the period of the Second Temple than does Josephus Flavius. This is clearly an overhauled interpretation of Josephus Flavius, written for Jews and aimed at acquainting them with the period in question. The book of Josephon is a very clear indication that, from a very early time, Jewish scholars knew and read Josephus Flavius and that, hence, the Masada narrative was not alien to them. Judging from Josephon, the memory of Masada was not forgotten but, rather, repressed and altered.

Guttman. Guttman's book is quite interesting. It describes the Jewish revolt in the Warsaw Ghetto.[9] Guttman draws a clear parallel between the revolt and Masada and states that Masada stood as an example for the Jewish fighters of the Ghetto. It is important to note that the identification between Masada and the revolt in the Warsaw Ghetto was "one of the typical identity elements in a common mental reaction of the Yishuv during the 1940s and early 1950s. During those years a pattern emerged that drew associations between historical periods: the Holocaust and renewed national uprising, the Holocaust and revolt. This pattern gave these associations a mythical character" (Shaked 1993:30). Shaked added later that the Yom Kippur War "brought back into Hebrew literature the Jewish historical bill, the realization that it can happen here too. . . . There was a feeling that we have not finished our debate with

Table 10.2. Elements of the Masada Historical Narrative in the Arts

Art Forms	1 Escape from Jerusalem	2 Truth about Sicarii	3 Ein Gedi massacre	4 Elazar's two Speeches	5 Protesting collective suicide	6 Survivors	7 Length of siege and war	8 Additions to original historical narrative
Josephon Guttman (1963) *Rebellion of the Besieged*	−	−	−	+	−	−	−	+
Haim (1963)	+	+						
Hazaz: *In One Collar*								
Y. Ponner (1921)					−	−		+
Yehuda Ben-Hizkiahu								
Avigdor Hameiri (1955)	−	−	−	+	−	−	−	+
S. Shalom (1950)	−	−	−	−	+	−	−	+
Y. Leivick					+			
Yitzhak Lamdan (1923–1924)					+			
Pinhas Sadeh (1974)					+			
Yigael Tomarkin (1980)					+			
Amos Keinan (1975)					+			
Reuven Ben-Yoseph (1978)					+			
Esther Rab (1979)								
Levi Ben-Amitai (1979)								
Israel Eliraz (1973)	+	+	−	+	+	+	+	+
Avi-Tamar 1989	−	−/+	+	−	irrelevant	−	−	+
Milner 1989	−	−	−	+	−	−	3 years	+

Key: No mark means the issue is irrelevant in the context.

+ means that the narrative is in accordance with Flavius.

− means that the issue is omitted altogether, or not according to Josephus.

Owing to the nature of the information in the table, no summary percentages were computed.
For full references of books and stories, see notes 2 and 3.

Jewish history, that Zionism did not eliminate the dangers for the existence of the Jewish people. The *Kotel* [Wailing Wall] was always a symbol for destruction and salvation. Against this symbol, Zionism set up Masada as a national symbol" (in Sahish 1993:80).

It is difficult to know just how accurate Guttman's thesis really is. However, I must admit I was quite resentful of the analogy being made as I read this book. The Jewish fighters in the Warsaw Ghetto fought a true "last stand" against a lethal racist enemy. Instead of being slaughtered like lambs, they chose to die with their weapons in hand, in a hopeless and truly heroic fight, against all odds. In Masada? Not quite. The fighters of the Ghetto were not at all reminiscent of the Sicarii; they were not chased away in shame by their own people after having been involved in terrorist activities. The Jews before the Great Revolt *had* an alternative—not to revolt. The Jews in Nazi-occupied Europe between 1939 and 1945 had no alternative. There was really not much they could do to change the Nazis' minds about their fate. However, suicide was not the option chosen by the Jewish fighters in the Warsaw Ghetto. Although there is not a shred of evidence that the Sicarii on Masada actually fought the soldiers of the Roman tenth legion, we know that the Jewish fighters in the Ghetto fought the Nazis very ably.

The interesting thing, though, is not whether the analogy is correct or appropriate but that Guttman found it necessary to make this bizarre historical connection at all and to imply that the fighters themselves may have made the same analogy (we could not find further substantiation for this claim).

Litai. Warsaw's Masada, a documentary-historical book by Haim Lazar Litai (1963), clearly makes, by its very title, a connection between the Warsaw Ghetto uprising and the events at Masada. However, not once in the book does its author explain the connection—apparently because he believed it to be self-evident.

Hazaz. Hazaz's 1963 book (*In One Collar*), like Guttman's, is focused not on Masada but on an event that took place before the establishment of the State of Israel.

In October of 1946, Etzel (Irgun) planned an attack on—and the blowing up of—the Central Railway Station in Jerusalem. On October 30, 1946, the attack was indeed carried out (Niv, 5:47–49). However, the British captured four of the attackers, possibly thanks to an informant (*Maariv*, July 23, 1954, p. 4). Those arrested were put on trial before a British military court in Jerusalem on March 25, 1947. Moshe Horowitz and Masud Buton presented an alibi and were therefore acquitted. Meir

Feinstein and Daniel Azulai were found guilty and sentenced to death. Azulai's sentence was later commuted to life imprisonment. Feinstein was placed in a prison cell with Moshe Barazani, a member of Lehi (the Stern gang) also awaiting execution. Lehi managed to smuggle a hand grenade into their prison cell. The two used the grenade to blow themselves up on April 21, 1947.

Hazaz apparently uses this true event as the basis for a story about two members of Etzel, Menachem and Eliahu, who blew themselves up in a prison cell in Jerusalem during the days of the British mandate over Palestine. Hazaz describes the deliberations of his two heroes prior to this suicide and has one of them make a direct analogy to the period of 66–73 A.D., when the Jewish Great Revolt took place. He even has this character explicitly mention Elazar Ben-Yair and the Sicarii. In fact, Hazaz lets his heroes repeat part of the speech Elazar made to the Sicarii on Masada prior to the collective suicide. In the story, Menachem states that by blowing themselves up they'll be "closing the circle" with Masada. The analogy here with the suicide on Masada is both powerful and explicit. Both cases of suicide are apparently fully justified in the eyes of Hazaz.

Sadeh. Pinhas Sadeh, another famous Israeli author, wrote a book in 1974 in which he recalls a post–Six-Day War trek across Israel, during which he visited many places, with one glaring exception—Masada.

Sadeh describes the Beit Shean Valley (in the northeast part of Israel) and expresses his ecstatic amazement at the breathtaking landscape. He depicts the afternoon sun, the chain of mountains, and a small settlement on the top of one of these mountains. The name of the settlement is Masada, and Sadeh explicitly refuses to go and visit it. This highly symbolic account conveys a clear message about Sadeh's attitude toward Masada.

Keinan. Amos Keinan wrote a book in 1975 titled *Shoah 2.* There is no other way to interpret this book than as a very strong anti-Masada statement. It is about a person who has lost all faith in his previous ideals and repeatedly finds that whichever way is chosen, it always leads to destruction. The message of the book is that we should abandon the paths leading to destruction. In the context of Israel in 1975 and Keinan's known political views, it is not very difficult to interpret this book as the cry of a disillusioned man in lament over the political direction his country has chosen (to the conservative, religious right). Like that of Sadeh, Keinan's message is a potent artistic antidote to the Masada mythical narrative.

Avi-Tamar. Avi-Tamar is the pseudonym of Israeli archaeologist Yoram Tzafrir. The novel he wrote is loosely based on the Masada narrative. Basically, it is a story about incomplete (or unfulfilled) love. The novel uses the Great Revolt and the Masada narrative as the background for the unfolding of these interrupted love stories. The author even warns the reader that his book does not provide an accurate reflection of Josephus Flavius's work and refers the reader explicitly to that source. Nevertheless, the book does include some of the major elements of the original narrative (including the Ein Gedi massacre) and may reflect the original narrative better than some of the more historically oriented texts. However, it blurs the issue of when and whence the rebels of Masada came, it fails to make a distinction between Sicarii and Zealots, it ignores the two speeches made by Elazar Ben-Yair, and it is inconsistent about the fact that there were survivors (the author states in one place that *all* of the rebels committed suicide, and in another place he mentions seven survivors). Avi-Tamar also clearly describes battles and fierce fights around Masada. However, he has expressed, in an interview, his criticism of Menachem the Sicarii leader and of the Sicarii and their extremism in general (Admoni 1989).

Science Fiction

As a science fiction fan, I find it difficult to ignore Joel Rosenberg's 1988 book *Not for Glory*. In it, Rosenberg fantasizes that the survivors of the State of Israel have become galactic mercenaries of a sort who get involved in various disputes for a fee. He calls these mercenaries MASADA. This book uses an interesting idea to develop a science fiction fantasy in a credible atmosphere so that the suspension of disbelief is quick. The MASADA theme in this book has very little to do with the historical Masada narrative, except for the symbolism of what might be the horrifying apocalyptic result of a "no choice" situation: a nation of warriors involved for eternity in never-ending wars, battles, and fights. Since the book was originally written in English as a science fiction novel, it had virtually no impact on Israelis. It was translated into Hebrew in 1991; however, because its availability on the Hebrew-speaking market came many years after the major peak of the Masada mythical narrative had declined, I did not include this book in our table.

Plays

Ponner. Y. Ponner (Meir Ben-Yehuda) (1921) does not deal directly and explicitly with Masada. His play is focused on the revolt of the Zealots from the Galilee against the Romans. However, the play does address the issue of suicide. One of the characters, Hanania, murders his children and commits suicide so as not to become a Roman prisoner. The hero of the play, Yehuda Ben-Hizkiahu, acts similarly. Much like the Sicarii in Masada, Ponner's heroes prefer what they view as the value of national freedom above that of personal survival. The message, if any, is that when one is involved in what is viewed as a struggle for national freedom, at times one has no choice but to follow through to the bitter end—even if that end is murder and suicide. There can hardly be any doubt that this play is an expression of Masada hero worship, particularly for the idea of the collective suicide there.

Hameiri. Another play is by Avigdor Hameiri (1955). Here, a fictional narrative of the last hours of the Sicarii on Masada is presented. This narrative is quite accurate (that is, consistent with Josephus Flavius), with one exception. In the eleventh act Hameiri introduces a fantastic element. A Roman officer, acting as a delegate of Flavius Silva (commander of the Roman tenth legion), enters the scene. He offers Elazar peace in exchange for surrender. Elazar refuses. The Roman officer is so deeply impressed that he asks for permission to remain in Masada with the besieged, knowing quite well that by doing so he is sealing his fate to die with the Sicarii. To Elazar's puzzlement about the soldiers' request, the Roman officer responds that "Rome will win but will be lost. Judea, the winner, will rise for eternal resurrection." Elazar allows the Roman officer to stay. Hameiri's description of the central suicide scene is, basically, symbolic of the ritualistic sacrificial ceremony held during Passover. Clearly, Hameiri is completely supportive of the Masada mythical narrative and views it as a positive heroic myth.

Shalom. S. Shalom (Shalom Yoseph Shapira) (1950), in his fictional play/narrative, describes a gathering of the last remnants of the Great Revolt in the Galilee in a cave. The cave is completely surrounded by Roman soldiers, so there is no way out—anyone who leaves is captured. The people in the cave are desperate and decide to commit suicide. The act of suicide is seriously questioned in this play as Shalom contrasts, quite sharply, suicide and death against the desire to live. The sharpness of this dilemma is accentuated by an interesting dramatic device: a young woman is included among the young fighters found in the cave. This allows an erotic tension to develop that helps to emphasize the contradiction between life and death.

Leivick. Leivick is the literary name of L. Halperin (1888–1962), who is considered by many to be one of the most important Yiddish poets and playwriters (Horowitz 1988). Leivick's dramatic play is a clear statement against the sacrifice of human life for *any* idea. His Yiddish drama warns us, in its introduction, that this is indeed his goal. The play is focused on the biblical sacrifices of Isaac and Ishmael (and a fictional test sacrifice of Abraham). Although Leivick does not mention Masada specifically, he expresses as extreme a stand as one can imagine against human sacrifice in any shape or form. It is difficult not to arrive at the conclusion that Leivick's position about the Masada mythical narrative must have been extremely negative (see Biltzky 1976, 1979).

Sobol and Heitner. Adar reported in 1993 that the Israeli playwright Yehoshua Sobol and British playwright Nicholas Heitner were collaborating in an effort to create either a series of three plays or one large play focusing on the Great Revolt and Masada. The plot supposedly concerns three figures: Josephus Flavius, Yochanan Ben-Zakai, and Martha Bat-Beitos. In an interview, Heitner and Sobol told Adar that

> the general idea is to reveal the history of the period through these three dissenters. Each one of them survived, not only physically but spiritually: Josephus through history, "The War of the Jews"; Rabbi Yochanan Ben-Zakai, whose figure casts a shadow on all of his contemporaries because of the alternative he presented of a tolerant and universalistic Judaism, which was not actualized; and Martha as a symbol for physical survival. It is thanks to her that we know the story of Masada. This is a woman who passed through all the suffering of the revolt in Jerusalem, and with the destruction she leaves for the Judean desert with a group of refugees. She arrives at Masada. When they commit suicide, she saves herself, a few children, and one old woman. The next day, when the Romans climb and enter Masada, they meet her and tell Josephus about what happened. The last days on Masada . . .

Because at the time of the writing of this book the plan was that the play or plays would be put on stage in 1996, I did not put this potential production in the table.

Milner. We have no indication as to whether the plays mentioned above were actually ever shown on stage. Despite our searches, we could not find actual theater productions that focused on Masada. Finally, one such show, *Masada,* was brought to our attention.[10] This show was written in 1989 by Arthur Milner and presented in Canada only in 1990.[11] The play is a superb illustration for the Masada mythical narrative. In it, the myth is presented and justified completely. For example, the Sicarii are never mentioned; one presuicide speech is mentioned; there are factual mistakes, such as the description of the different Jewish factions and the name of Elazar Ben-Yair. The play uses, in a powerful and persuasive way, the Masada mythical narrative to justify Zionism and the right of

Jews to Eretz Israel, and it argues against contemporary compromises with Israel's Arab neighbors.

> Compromise with the Arabs? Live side-by-side in peace—a Jewish
> state, a Palestinian state? Compromise is for the weak as miracles are
> for the weak. . . .
>   But if the United States decides its interests are better served by
> Syria or Saudi Arabia, we will take care of ourselves. . . . Let the
> Arabs send their armies against us. If we are resolute, if we are ready
> to sacrifice, we shall not be defeated. We shall take strength from the
> land. . . .
>   Yes, we want peace and we shall have peace—on our terms. We
> shall choose a never-ending war over an Israel cut up and divided.
> We shall not shrink from the methods God used to rescue us from
> Egypt. If we fight with the courage and determination of the
> Zealots—and if we are willing to die a thousand deaths—we cannot
> be defeated. (p. 14, last page of the play)[12]

Clearly, this play was not written or meant for Jewish Israeli audiences.

Poetry

Lamdan. Yitzhak Lamdan is the one Israeli poet whose work about Masada has gained momentous fame—for a while. With the exception of Josephus Flavius's writings, Lamdan's *Masada* was a most influential literary work for a whole generation of Jewish Israelis (but is not any longer). Although Lamdan wrote many other poems, his Masada poem is the most remembered of his works. Lamdan, however, does not qualify as a major Israeli poet.

Lamdan (1899–1954) was born in Mlinov, in Wohlin, the Ukraine, where he received a traditional secular education. During World War I, he was separated from his family, and his beloved brother was killed in a pogrom. His formative years were thus shaped by a secular orientation, by the rise of communism, and by anti-Semitism.[13] If he was to remain in Eastern Europe, his choices at the age of twenty-one were limited to three: (a) revengeful violence, (b) commitment to communism, or (c) passive accommodation to existing conditions (Schwartz, Zerubavel, and Barnett 1986:153). The first choice would most probably have led to self-destruction, the second was very questionable because the promises of egalitarianism in communism were broken time and again, and the third seemed to lead to nowhere (ibid.) Lamdan thus rejected all three options and chose instead to immigrate to Palestine in 1920. He spent his first years here as a pioneer but soon drifted into poetry and literature and eventually left physical labor in favor of literary work, which he carried on with, exclusively, from 1934 until his death. Although Lamdan became an important and prolific poet at the time, his fame and reputation came, no doubt, from only one of his works, *Masada,* written in the years 1923–1924 in Ben-Shemen and published originally and fully in Hebrew in 1927: "Masada is a part-dramatic, part-epic poem, composed of six sections. . . . [The poem] describes the spiritual struggle of the poet in arriving at his decision to "ascend," that is, to emigrate to Masada (Palestine); his reactions to the new environment; and his adaptation to the new country" (Yudkin 1971:49). Masada was reprinted in eleven different editions since 1927 (Blaushield 1985:1) and has become an allegory for Jewish Palestine (Schwartz, Zerubavel, and Barnett, 1986: 153–58).

The name Masada existed before Lamdan used it. Blaushield points out that in 1906, Yoseph Haim Brenner established a new association that published a magazine called *Hameorer* ("the waker"). He named the association Masada. For Brenner, *Hameorer* was like a lone fortress of a few Hebraic people (1985:21).

For Lamdan, Masada symbolized Jewish immigration to and renewal of national life in Israel (then British-occupied Palestine and Transjordan). Moreover, it meant the short- and long-term hopes offered by the reestablishment of a Jewish homeland, in contrast to the places where either Jews could not go or where their life was under constant threat. The 1920s were for Lamdan a critical period in Jewish national life.

To ask about the degree of consistency between Lamdan's poem and Josephus Flavius's narrative is, to a large extent, irrelevant. Masada for Lamdan was a symbol, an allegory, not a "real" narrative whose accuracy was important. For him Masada was a remnant of a once-glorious past, of proud Jews who fought to the bitter end against tremendous odds (whether or not there actually was fighting at Masada). In a very real sense, the struggle to reestablish a Jewish state was for him a struggle against similar odds. Lamdan gives expression to this when he writes (contrary to the disaster in Masada), "God, save Masada!" (p. 78) and what has probably become the most famous quoted line from his poem, "Masada shall not fall again!" (p. 48). The poem conveys a sense of tremendous hope and optimism but also of concern, despair, anxiety, and anguish.

The sense of hope and optimism conveyed by Lamdan was expressed by Schwartz, Zerubavel, and Barnett (1986:158): "Lamdan's . . . use of military metaphors, his designation of Palestine's inhabitants as "fighters," his complimentary reference to Ben Yair, leader of the Jewish garrison on Masada . . . " The strong phrases found in his poem, including the last line (capitalized in the original) of the collection of the Masada poems, "BE STRONG, BE STRONG, AND WE SHALL BE STRENGTHENED" (p. 90), all seem to convey power, reinforcement, and faith but also weakness and fear. In other words, ambivalence.

Overall, there can hardly be any doubt that Lamdan provided a very powerful and hopeful yet gloomy allegory using Masada as a general base. Lamdan's poems were required readings in Israeli schools for many years. His hopes, anguish, and anxieties were thus acquired by—and consequently inspired—generations of young sabras. Moreover, Lamdan's reputation went far beyond the boundaries of Palestine and Israel, and his *Masada* also became well known abroad. For a while, it was the symbol for the emerging Jewish national identity.

In an interview (February 1989) with Lamdan's wife, Annie, a few interesting details were revealed. Clearly, Masada became *the* symbol for what has become known as the third wave of Jewish immigration to Palestine. However, Lamdan himself never visited Masada or even expressed a wish to do so. This is quite ironic, since thousands of youth climbed Masada, often after a long and difficult trek in the Judean desert, to hear Lamdan's poems read to them. To think that Lamdan himself never even bothered to visit the doomed fortress is instructive. Annie was very explicit in maintaining that for Lamdan Masada became bothersome. It was the fame from Masada that gained him a reputation as a poet, and as a result he became overly identified with Masada. However, he wanted to be recognized as a good poet in general and not just because of Masada. Unfortunately for Lamdan, the fact remains that it is *only Masada* that is still remembered from his poetry.

Historically, the importance of Lamdan's *Masada* cannot and should not be underestimated. Its impact on generations of Jewish Israelis has been tremendous (see, e.g., Blaushild 1985; Schwartz, Zerubavel, and Barnett 1986). However, it must be remembered that Lamdan was not operating in a vacuum. His poem was preceded by Simchoni's superb translation of Josephus Flavius into modern Hebrew in 1923, as well as by the Berdyczewski–Achad Haam debate in the 1920s in which Masada was used as an important and illustrative case of extreme Jewish heroism. The timing (and setting, in Palestine) of Lamdan's *Masada* was perfect. However, the manner in which secular Zionists utilized the poem, that is, as a major element for experiencing the Masada mythical narrative, deviated—very clearly—from Lamdan's original intent. Lamdan's ambivalence simply disappears. His genuine concern that Eretz Israel may become a trap (and not a refuge) for Jews (that is, a second Masada) was almost completely eliminated in favor of what was presented as a proud, heroic national interpretation.

Lamdan's poem became a compulsory part of the curriculum in Israeli schools. Following the rise and fall of the Masada mythical narrative means also following the entrance and exit of Lamdan's poem into and from the curriculum. Blaushild (1985:39–42) notes how Lamdan's *Masada* was adopted by the Yishuv and later by official institutes in Israel. The educational authorities in the 1940s viewed the poem as having a very high educational value. The poem became an integral part of Hebrew school curriculum in the late 1930s and early 1940s. It kept that position until the early 1960s. The Passover Haggadot put together by the kibbutzim (dating to the early 1930s) included large passages from the poem. The interest in Lamdan's poem peaked in the 1950s (Blaushild 1985:41).

The 1960s witnessed the demise of the interest in Lamdan's poem. There are less critical articles about it, and it loses gradually its position in the school curriculum until it is no longer compulsory reading. Blaushild (1985:49–53) provides a number of reasons for this demise. First, *Masada* was accepted by a generation who identified with its emotional and ideological messages. Later generations did not have that identification. The problems they faced were very different. Second, the literary taste changed from appreciating works characterized by an ideological content to appreciating works that emphasized individualism and humanity. The pathetic tone was transformed into a nonpathetic one. Third, collective values of the 1930s and 1940s were losing their validity. As an illustration, Blaushild quotes Moshe Steiner's sad words reflecting his experience in 1978 of trying to buy Lamdan's book *Masada*. Steiner could no longer find a copy of the book.

The demise of the interest in Lamdan's poem dates therefore to the 1960s and reflects a process of social change (in values, literary taste, problems, and solutions) that occurred at that time in Israel.

Ben-Yoseph. In 1978, Reuven Ben-Yoseph published a poem called "Masada," in which he expresses an admiration for Masada while attempting to ignore its negative aspects. This strange concoction is achieved by looking at Masada through the eyes of an Israeli soldier in the armored division, a sort of soldier-poet. His main message is that Masada shall not fall again.

Rab. Another poet, Esther Rab, published a series of poems in 1979 about Eretz Israel, one of which is focused on the Great Revolt and Masada. This was the first time that a female poet wrote anything about Masada.

Esther's poem describes herself as one of the Jewish women who goes to Masada during the Great Revolt. The poem combines an escape from the everyday life to the purification involved in living an ascetic Jewish life in the desert, together with the human sacrifice (suicide) in Masada. This combination is presented in a powerfully and delicately woven poem.

Ben-Amitai. Levi Ben-Amitai, like Pinhas Sadeh, travels in post–Six-Day War Israel and conveys his impressions to the reader. Part of his poetry is devoted to figures from the days of the Jewish Second Temple, and he expresses admiration for what he viewed as the ascetic and pure life of those who chose to dwell in the desert then (including the Masada dwellers). However, this positive attitude seems to be specific to a particular lifestyle and not to the Masada myth generally.

Art

Tomarkin. In 1980, Yigal Tomarkin, one of Israel's most famous artists (sculptors), created an exhibition about what he termed "the craziness of the sacred." In this exhibition, Tomarkin presented such items as an olive tree stem, parts of barbed wire, and soil, among others. The intention of the exhibition was to use art to project a political statement. The exhibition itself was named "Masada Shall Not Fall a Third Time—After a Renewed Reading of Josephus Flavius." The main message of the exhibition was a protest against political extremism.

Music

There is one known musical creation with Masada as its theme. It is the opera *Masada 967,* written in 1972–1973 by Israel Eliraz and Joseph Tal (Eliraz wrote the libretto and Tal the music).

Eliraz[14] has stated explicitly that it was clear to him and Tal that they were not obligated to remain faithful to the historical narrative of Masada as provided by Josephus Flavius. Instead, they were looking for the contemporary meaning of the narrative, bridging a temporal abyss of more than 1900 years. For Eliraz and Tal, a major puzzle was the fact that no reports or historical narratives from the Roman perspective remained. How, they asked themselves, could one explain the fact that no such narratives exist, despite what must have been an obviously enormous military (and logistic) effort? The Romans, after all, did have the habit of recording their military campaigns. Their answer was that despite the fact that it may be viewed as a decisive Roman *military* victory, this is not how the Romans saw it. The suicidal death of the people on top of Masada must have thus translated itself into a *moral* victory for the defeated. It is interesting to note that Eliraz's work for the presentation of the opera was a collaboration with non-Jewish choreographer Hans Krasnik and musician Gratziano Mandotzi. They all combined their talents for its presentation at the Vienna Festival for Modern Ballet (see Eliraz 1977). *Masada 967* was also performed in the 1973 Israel Festival in Jerusalem.

During that same festival, a similar ballet concerning five thousand Armenians who were besieged on the mountain Moussa Doug (or Musa Dagh) was presented. In the narrative, the Turkish siege brought those who were trapped to a Masada-like situation, in which they were close to a debate over the possibility of committing suicide. Fortunately, at the last minute a French warship approached the beach and shelled the Turkish coastal towns. Consequently, the Turks ceased the attack on Moussa Doug, and the Armenians were spared. Although this narrative is not a replay of Masada, it became a symbol. Eliraz has mentioned a similar incident related to him by Hans Krasnik. This story concerned a train with four hundred Partisans aboard (men, women, and children), which, in accordance with the Yalta agreement (February 1945), was returned to the Soviets, in violation of the agreement signed between the local British commander and the commander of the Partisans. When the Partisans realized that there was no escape and that they were being shipped to the Soviets, they closed the doors and windows of the train and killed themselves. According to Eliraz, Krasnik asked him if this was not a "Partisans' Masada."

Cinema

One famous movie has been made that popularized the Masada mythical narrative to a great extent.

In Israel, news items about a Masada movie began to appear in 1973.[15] In October of 1976, a semidocumentary TV production about Masada was apparently broadcast in the U.S. The movie, produced by a Christian missionary, created a bit of controversy in Israel, angering Yigael Yadin so much that he considered suing its producers.[16] During December 1978 and February 1979, the Israeli press reported that American Universal was about to begin production of a major movie called *Masada*.[17] During 1979, preparations for producing the movie, based on a novel by Ernest K. Gann, were made, and shooting was under way. The book and the movie both repeat many elements of the Masada mythical narrative while clothing it in a synthetic "love story." The movie itself was shot partly in Israel and was directed by Boris Segal, with actors such as Peter O'Toole (Flavius

Silva), Peter Strauss (Elazar Ben-Yair), and Barbara Carrera. It was broadcast by ABC as a miniseries on American television in 1981. The first episode aired on April 5, 1981. It was also broadcast on Canadian television. Its release was accompanied by an educational campaign of Jewish organizations in the U.S. and by an intensified marketing effort by El Al in North America.[18] The miniseries was converted into a 131-minute feature film in 1984.[19]

Reviews in the Israeli press were not too enthusiastic, aside from compliments on its technical quality; the movie seemed to have caused embarrassment. Here is what Gideon Samet, *Haaretz*'s U.S. correspondent at that time, wrote about it in 1981:

> "Masada" . . . was the Israeli answer to the Japanese *Shogun* and to the black *Roots*. . . . Suddenly on the screen [Masada] looked pathetic. It was better off not having been retold. . . .
>
> It was no coincidence that in two preview articles in the *New York Times* and the *Washington Post* the collective heroic suicide on Masada was compared to the massacre-suicide of the Jim Jones bunch. Despite its epic character, the Masada story is an intimate national experience that cannot be easily interpreted. Its presentation on television is inappropriate. . . .
>
> Indeed, for the contemporary Israeli viewer the miniseries seems to create threatening associations and troublesome thoughts about the wisdom of the heroics and the chances of the struggle with a superpower seeking to increase its influence. . . .
>
> A survey by ABC before the airing of the miniseries indicated that 92 percent of the viewers had no idea what Masada was. Many responded that it was a model of a new Japanese car. . . .
>
> . . . There was a genuine attempt to portray the besieged and their leader in the most complimentary way. They are [made to appear] brave and sensitive, devoted parents and husbands, Orthodox in their religion and striving for peace. But apparently there is no way to present the Masada story in the modern mass media except as an act of deviance that is difficult to accept. Although the producer of the series says that it describes an "epic struggle to live in freedom," the script also leads to another unavoidable impression: that this is also the story of religious fanaticism and of a pointless sacrifice.[20]

The movie repeats the elements of the mythical narrative, such as the lack of mention of the Ein Gedi massacre, the escape from Jerusalem after the city was destroyed, and the lack of mention of the Sicarii (the movie portrays the defenders of Masada as Zealots); the siege is shown to have lasted for three years against ferocious resistance, complete with fierce, pitched fightings. Moreover, the movie adds some elements, too, such as the contact between Flavius Silva and Elazar Ben-Yair. Basically, the movie uses Josephus's account as a basis for the myth.

The movie was not received very well in Israel and played a very small role, if any, in the crystallization of the Masada mythical narrative. It is interesting to note that the souvenir shop at the bottom of Masada has quite a number of items, including video cassettes. The video cassette of the movie *Masada,* however, is not available at this shop.

Overall, various artists, in different areas, have used the different themes in the original Masada narrative to construct their artistic creations. Although most have felt obligated to deal with the collective suicide and the major symbolic contradiction behind it (slavery vs. death and/or freedom), most have not touched on the other problematic aspects of the original narrative. Moreover, the attitude toward the suicide is not uniform. While some express admiration (e.g., Hameiri, Josephon, Guttman, Ponner, Hazaz), others voice clear doubts (e.g., Shalom) and reservations, some to the point of complete rejection (e.g., Leivick, Sadeh, Tomarkin, Keinan). It is evident that Masada has not become a major focus of inspiration for artists anywhere (except, that is, Lamdan). Moreover, as we move from the early decades of this century to contemporary times, more and more questions are raised about the morality of the narrative.

Chapter Eleven

The Masada Mythical
Narrative

A LOOK AT THE Masada mythical narrative up until the 1990s reveals an interesting picture.

Masada was destroyed in 73 A.D.—the last effort by the Roman imperial army against Jewish rebels of the 66–73 Great Revolt. Although Jewish resistance against Rome did not end in this revolt (the Bar-Kochva revolt erupted about sixty years later), the Roman victory against the rebels was decisive, and the second Jewish temple was reduced to ashes. However, out of this destruction, like a phoenix, rose a new form of Judaism, not nationalistic but spiritual, led by Rabbi Yochanan Ben-Zakai, who, like Josephus Flavius, had defected to the Roman camp. This form of Judaism was to prevail until 1948, when a new Jewish state was established.

Most of what we know about the Great Revolt comes from the writings of Josephus Flavius. We would not have known much at all about Masada without him as a source. It is a rather strange historical irony that such an important period in the history of the Jews is reported by a man who is probably considered by many to be one of the worst traitors in Jewish history.

JUDAISM AND MASADA

Orthodox Judaism has repressed the memory of Masada. In fact, Jewish traditional sources (e.g., the Talmud and the Midrash) simply do not mention Masada.[1] This has usually been taken to indicate dissatisfaction with the event. What exactly was it about Masada that was disliked? Was it the Sicarii, the collective suicide, or the goals of the revolt?

The Masada narrative was available to anyone who sought it in Josephus Flavius's writings. These writings were not hidden. Moreover, the books of Josippon do indeed give a positively overhauled version of Josephus, and these books were read by Jews since, at the very latest, the tenth century. Another mention of Masada can be found in a book written by Samuel Usque, a Portuguese Marrano, in the sixteenth century (translated and published in English in 1965). There, one can find a fairly accurate repetition of Josephus Flavius's version (pp. 137–51). Barry Schwartz (1991:221 n.1) states that the history of the Masada narrative provides a case of what he refers to as "collective amnesia" (see also Schwartz, Zerubavel, and Barnett 1986). However, there was no amnesia with regard to Masada. Amnesia is a passive situation that "happens," whereas Masada illustrates a powerful, active, deliberate, and forceful collective repression of a historical event, for a period of close to two thousand years, by a specific group: Orthodox Jews. A typical explanation for this repression is that the Masada narrative involved a choice of death over life. Indeed, Zerubavel (1980:110–11) feels that since the rabbinical model was Yavneh (see chapter 2, and notes 38 and 39 there), the alternative, Masada, was repressed. Moreover, she feels that the Masada narrative contradicts the value of *survival,* which plays an important role in Judaism. This spirit is truly negated in the Masada story.

The mass suicide itself is quite a troublesome issue. Jews, we are told, are not big admirers of death, especially not of suicide. Kamikaze pilots and others who behave in a similar fashion are not likely heroes of Judaism, which is basically a life-loving religion. And yet, despite the usual rhetoric, there *are* a few heroic narratives in Judaic history that do not negate suicide or death (for a review, see Stern 1989).

While rabbinical Judaism repressed the memory of Masada, another powerful Jewish group, secular Zionists, was able to revive the memory, despite active opposition.

Moreover, Shmaria Guttman states: "I'll tell you something in the name of one of the pupils of the Ga'on of Vilna. The Gaon [translates as "genius"] asked that Josephus Flavius be translated into Hebrew (at the time, the book was available only in Greek and Latin). He felt that there was a period in the history of the Jewish people about which we do not know much and that there was a need to uncover it" (Shashar 1987:24).

The Gaon, Eliahu Ben Shlomo Zalman (1720–1797), was an Orthodox Jewish rabbi who lived in Vilna. He is considered one of the most famous and respected religious figures in Jewish history. That he wanted the books of Josephus Flavius to be translated into Hebrew is a well-known fact. Simchoni, the translator of Josephus Flavius into Hebrew, confirms this in the introduction to his translation (p. 30). There he states that a man named Kalman Shulman translated Josephus into Hebrew. This translation, according to Simchoni, was pompous and inaccurate. However, it did appear in Vilna, in two separate editions, in 1862 and in 1884.

The issue of remembering Josephus, as well as the topic of "collective memory" in Judaism, has been commented on by Yerushalmi (1982), who contrasted memory against history. His general view is that, traditionally, Jews did not have official historians nor a systematic history. Jews relied on memory, not on history. Jewish memories were thus immersed in Jewish religious tradition, and that tradition, clearly, had no interest in remembering Masada (for more on this topic see Frankel 1994).

Why was this so? It is difficult to know. But, as both Zerubavel (1980) and Paine (1991) point out, the issue of the suicide was not an easy one to deal with. Moreover, as the Great Revolt was reaching its end, two cultural legacies remained: Masada and Yavneh. Masada meant death, whereas Yavneh represented life. The Yavneh survivors, therefore, had a vested interest in presenting their way as right and victorious and in repressing suicidal Masada. Also, it appears that the definition of the suicide on Masada as Kiddush Hashem was not accepted. This redefinition is, in fact, a rather new construction.

Clearly, knowledge of Josephus Flavius's account did exist. It was not too popular, and Orthodox Judaism was not too thrilled about it, but it was present. It was not forgotten but, rather, repressed. Had it been forgotten, it could never have been revived.

It is interesting to note here, too, how the development of the Masada mythical narrative influenced the very act of "remembering the remembering." This issue appears in quite a number of places, but to illustrate it, let me quote from just one source: "The legend and example of Masada were admired by Jews for centuries" (Gonen 1975:217). This is obviously a factually incorrect statement. However, it enhances the reverence and heroism of the event. It can easily be interpreted as follows: "If Jews throughout the ages admired the Masada rebels, then who are we to question this?"

An interesting glimpse at this issue can be found in a long article published by Y. Glis in 1964 in *Hamodea* (a daily Hebrew-language newspaper), a significant *shofar* ("ram's horn," or clarion) for the ultra-Orthodoxy in Israel. Glis states very clearly that what he terms "the wisdom of Israel" was against the Great Revolt and against the very essence of the Zealots. He states that Elazar Ben-Yair's speeches do not have a shred of Judaism in them and present an anti-Torah perception. So does the suicide. For him, Masada was a tragedy because of the suicide and because it reflected an ideology that was antithetical to Judaism:

> There is propaganda focused on the excavations of Masada. This propaganda aims to place Masada at the center of Israeli life during the period of the destruction of the Second Temple. The propaganda aims to present Masada . . . as a 'symbol for generations.'. . . . We must speak of Masada knowing that 'this is not the way' and not the tradition of Israel. . . . We must tell our children . . . that Masada is not a symbol, that it never was a symbol, and that it will never be a symbol. The only sense in which it can be a symbol is in what should not be, and for an ideology that must be kept away and never be accepted. (Glis 1964:2)

Indeed, Glis compares Masada to the deeds of Rabbi Yochanan Ben-Zakai and Yavneh and states explicitly that Yavneh and love of life should be the national symbols, not Masada, doomed Zealots, and death.

Finally, it is worth noting that Orthodox Jews to this day are not very keen on Masada. This is not just because their youth movements have deemphasized Masada but because most of them have actually repressed it. To check this particular point I conducted a small investigation during Sukkot, in September-October 1992. Sukkot is a holiday when most Jewish Israelis, including some non-Zionist ultra-Orthodox Jews, tend to travel throughout the country. I went to Mea Shearim, a *very* religious Jewish neighborhood in Jerusalem, and searched for posters advertising tours for ultra-Orthodox Jews. These wall advertisements (a common method in this neighborhood to pass on information), offering a variety of trips during the Sukkot holiday, were plentiful. However, not even *one* ad offered a visit to Masada. I further checked for trips offered to the Judean desert. Such trips indeed *were* offered, with a variety of interesting locations to visit—including Ein Gedi—but none to Masada (which is only about seventeen kilometers south of Ein Gedi).

An interesting response to the Masada affair was provided by Professor E. E. Urbach. Professor Urbach, a humanist and a religious person, was one of the most respected scholars in Israel. He was well published and was the president of the Israeli Academy of Sciences. During an Israeli television program about the Tisha Be'av fast (a day commemorating the destruction of the Temple), he stated that Masada contributed nothing real to nationhood and that it was a virtually unknown episode in history (*Haaretz*, August 9, 1976, in Heda Boshes's column).

ZIONISM AND MASADA

The Zionist movement, without a doubt, helped to develop and nourish the Masada mythical narrative as a central symbol of heroism. This development began hesitantly in Europe but picked up speed in the early decades of this century. The original narrative provided by Josephus does not contain a heroic story; therefore, the Masada narrative, if it were to become a national symbol, had to be transformed and molded into a heroic tale. This process was successfully achieved by two very prominent moral entrepreneurs: Shmaria Guttman and Yigael Yadin.

Although Shmaria Guttman was certainly a key figure in the early years of the myth's development, the interest in Masada preceded him. We have seen this expressed in at least three important developments. One was the debate between Achad Ha'am and Berdyczewski (see chapter 13), in which Berdyczewski used Masada as a symbol for Jewish heroism. This probably occurred at the outset of the 1920s. Then, in 1923, an excellent and readable translation of Josephus Flavius into modern Hebrew was published. Finally, in 1927, Lamdan's influential poem appeared. Shmaria Guttman was thus operating in a public atmosphere that offered little resistance and hungered for heroic Jewish tales.

Regarding the site itself, one must remember that non-Jewish travelers correctly identified and visited Masada since at least the nineteenth century and on into the early decades of the twentieth. The first trips to Masada by Jews date back to 1912. Furthermore, the Masada mythical narrative was used by both Hanoar Haoved Vehalomed and Mahanot Haolim in their various activities (especially after 1927). This interest in the Masada mythical narrative increased in the late 1930s.

As we have said, between the early 1920s and the late 1930s—the period in which Shmari Guttman, the most important figure for the development of the Masada mythical narrative, began to operate—a few important events related to Masada took place. The first was the publication of an excellent Hebrew translation of Josephus Flavius. Shmaria Guttman read this translation and later admitted that Josephus's book left a very strong impression on him and raised his interest in the Judean desert and the Dead Sea region. Lamdan's very powerful poem impressed not only Guttman but many others as well. Reading the poem today, even with a basically cynical attitude, is still an impressive and powerful experience. In 1928, a youth organization in Warsaw, affiliated with the Revisionist Zionist Organization, called itself "Masada." During 1922–1925, various Jewish groups and individuals climbed to Masada. Masada was thus in the air in the 1920s, and its effect continued to be strongly felt on into the 1930s.

In 1933, Shmaria Guttman climbed to Masada with two friends. As could be expected, the visit left another strong impression on him. In 1934, the Jewish National Fund attempted to purchase Masada (see Weitz 1962:7–12 and Zerubavel 1980:29–30 for a summary). In 1937, a new tribe of the Jewish Scouts called "Masada" was established in Jerusalem by the Gymnasia Ivrit school. In the same year, a new kibbutz named "Masada" was established in the Jordan Valley, about four kilometers south of the Sea of Galilee (the group that formed the new kibbutz was already established in 1930).

At least two additional books appeared during this period without any connection to Guttman. One was a booklet, published in 1937 by the Jewish National Fund, containing two pieces. One, by Bar Droma, concerned the environment of the Dead Sea. The second was by Yoseph Klosner, a right-wing yet respected academician. Klosner focused on the heroism of the Sicarii and did his best to justify the suicide. Moreover, he emphasized Masada as a national symbol and tried to cleanse the image of the Sicarii by, among other ways, describing them as heroic freedom fighters.[2] Furthermore, in 1925 Klosner had written that Elazar Ben-Yair was a national hero and that a nation capable of such a heroic act as Masada was invincible indeed (Klosner 1925:115–18, 240–41; Blaushild 1985:21).

Another book, published in 1941 and edited by Israel Halperin, was titled *The Book of Heroism: A Literary-Historical Anthology.* It originally comprised two volumes (a third was added in 1980) and provided a survey of Jewish heroism. Anita Shapira (1992:425) points out that this was the first book released by Am Oved, the publishing house of the Histadrut (the Israeli Workers' Union), whose chief editor then was Berl Katzenelson. According to Shapira, Berl's literary taste was usually better than that reflected in this book, but "this time his goal was didactic: he wanted to teach youth that Jews have already experienced, in the past, dead-end situations and knew how to die heroically." It is clear that the Hagana attributed much significance to this book, and passages from it were read during its meetings (Shapira 1992:425). As Bitan (1990:229) indicates, it is clear that the main goal of the book was to demonstrate to the Yishuv that Jewish heroism existed throughout the generations. The book ends in the twentieth century, but the interesting thing is where it begins. The first incidence of Jewish heroism described in the book is the story of Masada (using Simchoni's translation).

Hence, Guttman's initiative in the late 1930s and early 1940s did not develop in a vacuum. He acted as a much-needed moral entrepreneur and at the right historical moment, crystallizing his activities soon after the successive publication of the excellent translation of Josephus Flavius into modern Hebrew and the full version of Lamdan's poem. The need for a positive symbol of Jewish heroism existed even before the fateful years of 1940–1942. The idea of providing such a symbol would have fallen on receptive ears even without Rommel's threat of invasion. Zionist ideology was ripe for symbols that could convey not only heroism but also resolution, power, pride, and the will of determined Jews to live, fight, and even die for their homeland. The original narrative of Masada does not contain all of this. Although Guttman did not invent the Masada mythical narrative from scratch or initiate the trips to the site, he definitely was the one who helped to transform and crystallize it into its complete mythical form and to institutionalize the treks to the site.

Guttman guided the Masada mythical narrative into a few directions. To begin with, he realized the nature of this ecologically impressive site. Thus, the considerable physical effort involved in the trek to Masada and in climbing it became a goal in itself. This experience fit very well in a culture that emphasized trips and *Yediat Haaretz—knowledge* of the old-new land. The physical effort and challenge involved in getting to Masada to some extent illustrated and paralleled the difficulties involved in establishing a new Jewish homeland—very difficult indeed, but possible and achievable.

The consequence of this realization was that efforts had to be invested in the physical Masada—new roads, excavations, museums, and so forth. As the Masada mythical narrative developed, Guttman saw that there was a better, more powerful symbol than the place itself, and this was the psychological Masada. For Guttman, the more people who came to Masada the better. Hence, he made a very serious effort not only to persuade the right individuals to excavate Masada but also to enable as many people as possible to visit the fortress.

In emphasizing both the mythical narrative and the visit to Masada, Shmaria Guttman was developing two major elements: the narrative itself and the powerful experiential ritual attached to it. In this way, the Masada mythical narrative was not just left as a story to be told but was also presented as a narrative that fit a most impressive site. The credibility of the story of Masada was thus supported and magnified tremendously by means of the Masada experience.

It was not too difficult to develop the Masada mythical narrative. The original version of the event already contained the major ingredients, some of which were already laid out by Berdyczewski and much more by Klosner. Guttman did not publish many documents, but from the few available, as well as from the reports by participants in his seminars, it is clear what he did to Josephus Flavius's original narrative. The main ingredients of the narrative remain. Guttman did not undo the suicide. The siege and the fact that the rebels on Masada were part of the Jewish Great Revolt are still included. However, the massacre at Ein Gedi is missing. Guttman does not use the word *Sicarii*. Instead he uses "the besieged of Masada" (e.g., 1964) and "Zealots." He indicates that there "must" have been battles around Masada, as well as Jewish raids against the Romans, and he describes these "battles" and "raids" in detail. He also blurs the length of the Roman siege. His narrative, very carefully crafted, implies by its style, its selection of words, and its imagination that the super-strong, efficient, and disciplined Roman army was afraid of the fighters on Masada and was *compelled* to eliminate them at a great cost by fighting a siege-war in a hostile environment. He also blurs the part of the original narrative that tells whence the rebels on Masada came, why, and when. Also, there is a marked difference between Guttman's lectures to unsuspecting audiences (which were characterized by a powerful and persuasive dramatic style, with lots of pathos) and his writings (which are rare).

His 1964 Hebrew piece, titled *With Masada*, is an interesting illustration of his technique. First, he presents some original descriptions from Josephus Flavius. However, these are typically selective and brief. Then, as if Josephus either did not say a thing or said too much, Guttman moves on to *his* version. For example, he states that Josephus identified those on Masada as Sicarii. However, in the very next passage, without *any* explanation, he begins to use the terms "Zealots" and "the besieged of Masada" (e.g., 1964:144–45) interchangeably, totally ignoring Josephus's terminology. In the same place (1964:144–45), he admits that Josephus does not mention "battles" around Masada but still goes on to state that "it is certain that raids" took place and to describe those raids. The fabrication of these important details no doubt helped in creating the heroic story. We also know that when he spoke to audiences, Guttman allowed much more freedom to his imagination.

The presence of such a convinced, committed, and fairly knowledge-able moral entrepreneur during a period when there was real cultural hun-ger for a heroic narrative such as the Masada mythical narrative, coupled with the truly threatening crisis that existed during 1940–1942, provided a situation in which Guttman simply could not fail. However, Guttman had another edge on Klosner. He exploited the site to the limit, transform-ing Masada into *the* place where receptive young minds were exposed to the mythical narrative. The groups he accompanied to Masada, in particu-lar his 1942 seminar, represented turning points in the development of the mythical narrative. The fact that he was so influential must be also understood in terms of his audiences. Guttman's initiative could not have succeeded without the receptive youth who were willing to digest and em-brace the Masada mythical narrative. These audiences were available for more or less the same reasons that led Guttman to develop his moral ini-tiative to begin with: a desperate cultural need for a real and tangible his-tory of Jewish heroism. A newly emerging secular Zionist culture was be-ing born, and to prove its point it needed heroic stories and symbols. The Masada mythical narrative was one of the central stories and symbols of this new culture. Internal and external events and the intense nation-state-building process that the Yishuv was undergoing were the necessary background factors against which the mythical narrative made sense. As we saw earlier, as this symbol made less and less sense in the 1970s, it declined in importance.

The activities of Shmaria Guttman set the pattern. He constructed the selective historical sequence we call "the Masada mythical narrative," and he emphasized the idea that "telling the story was not enough." Peo-ple had to actually go and visit Masada. As the Masada mythical narra-tive became more and more attractive, acceptable, and powerful, the need for the physical challenge diminished. It was then more important to get as many people as possible to reach Masada and become exposed to the "Masada experience." This entailed a dramatic exposure to the mythical narrative in the natural environment of the site. Once there, the visitors were exposed to a most impressive sight-and-sound show (see Donevitz 1976, 1984) depicting the Masada story in a powerful and persuasive manner. Participation in excavations, a swearing-in ceremony, a concert, an opera, or a bar mitzvah on Masada heightened the experience. A pow-erful suspension of disbelief was thus achieved, and the message of an-cient, relentless, courageous, and gallant heroism, of "a fight to the end," unfolded before receptive minds.

With its popularity during the pre-1948 years among members of youth movements, including many of those who would later be the political, social, military, and educational elite of the country, a whole generation of Jewish Israelis were exposed to the Masada mythical narrative. This became an integral part of the socialization process during the formative years of the new state. This new generation was to carry the mythical narrative along with it as a basic ingredient of its national and personal identity.

The early years of the State of Israel most certainly witnessed the continuation of the Masada ritual: trekking and climbing to the fortress. The social activities surrounding the Masada mythical narrative reached a peak in the early 1940s and were reduced somewhat thereafter but still continued well into the 1950s, in particular the military swearing-in ceremonies (mostly held by the Israeli armored units).

A second peak was spurred by the archaeological excavations of Masada in the early 1960s, led by the second most important moral entrepreneur in the unfolding of the Masada story, Yigael Yadin. Although reluctant at first to become involved, Yadin became the most famous person associated with Masada in the modern period. If Guttman helped to initiate the creation of the Masada mythical narrative, Yadin crystallized it and gave it an official and scientific stamp of approval. Like Guttman, Yadin repressed the massacre at Ein Gedi and referred to the rebels at Masada—in a most systematic fashion—as "Zealots" (contrary to Josephus's narrative). On page 11 of his book about Masada he most certainly gives the impression that the rebels there arrived *after* the destruction of Jerusalem. Not a word about the Sicarii appears, and the index of his book does not have an entry for the Sicarii. Elazar Ben-Yair's two speeches are combined into one, and the reluctant agreement of those on top of Masada is transformed into a decision made by Elazar Ben-Yair. The terms he uses imply a three-year war between the Romans and the rebels on Masada. Certainly, one of the principles motivating forces behind the excavations was Yadin's wish to examine Josephus Flavius's narrative, as Yadin himself interpreted it. His attempt to confirm the narrative was not very successful. Nothing in the excavations really confirmed or contradicted Josephus Flavius's account. In the main, however, the excavations uncovered the Herodian palaces and confirmed the destruction of Masada. That the Romans had built a wall around Masada and a siege ramp was clear even before the excavations began. The results of the excavations were a mixed blessing, from Yadin's point of view. Some of Josephus Flavius's claims were certainly confirmed by findings: the Roman army camps, remnants of materials made and used by the besieged, the siege ramp and siege wall, and the destruction and signs of a fire on top of the fortress. However, most of these findings were known beforehand. Some more questionable and problematic discoveries are the ostraca and the remains of skeletons (twenty-five in one place, others in the lower terrace of the northern palace). Yadin also discovered scrolls, coins, and remnants of armaments. However, the excavations did not uncover the remains of 960 bodies, the identity of the rebels (Sicarii?), the suicide, the lots, the escape from Jerusalem, the length of the siege, or a number of other details. In some other areas, the narrative provided by Josephus Flavius was revealed to be somewhat inaccurate: he missed one palace (the western palace), and his description of the number of towers and the height of the wall are not quite accurate. If Gill's (1993) work is valid, he may have also missed the fact that the siege ramp was built on a natural spur (see note 3, chapter 2). Although Josephus states that the Sicarii started one big fire on the last night, the excavations revealed many fires (see also S. Cohen 1988).

It is important to note all of these points because on page 15 of his 1966 book Yadin writes: "It would be one of the tasks of our archaeological expedition to see what evidence we could find to support the Josephus record." In view of the myth creation, this sentence appears almost grotesque. Add to this Yadin's statement (p. 17) that "it is not my purpose to offer a dry scientific record; rather it is to enable the reader to share our remarkable experience" and the grotesque becomes even somewhat cynical.

Regardless of this disappointment, the excavations themselves became—through Yadin's efforts—a world-famous enterprise. Volunteers from Israel and abroad flocked to Masada to take part as the diggers of the ancient fortress, and the media in Israel and in England had a field day. It is beyond any doubt that those years in the early 1960s witnessed a peak in the diffusion of the Masada mythical narrative.

According to Tal Ben-Shatz and Yossi Bar-Nachum,[3] the Masada myth was amplified in the daily newspapers, during the early 1960s, for a number of reasons: 1. In a society in which one of the *main* symbols or cultural codes was the perceived external threat and what its leaders viewed as a struggle for survival, there was a need to educate the masses for heroics and sacrifice. This need most definitely required symbols and myths. The corrected Masada tale fit into this siege and war mentality: "the few against the many"; "Masada shall not fall again" (one can easily replace the word *Masada* with the word *Israel*). 2. Israeli society needed a heroic symbol of a fight for national freedom, one that would serve as an antithesis to the nonheroic, passive existence associated with living in the

Galut, as well as an antidote to the Holocaust and the view that Jews had been led by the Nazis to be "slaughtered like sheep."

Along the way, we have seen how the Masada mythical narrative was created, maintained, and nourished in different areas of Jewish Israeli culture: textbooks, arts, media, tourism, the Israeli Army, youth movements, prestate underground movements, and so on.

Two additional points are worth mentioning here. First, Masada provided a crucial historical element in helping to crystallize a new individual and national identity. Masada connected the distant past with the immediate present, bridging a gap of close to two thousand years. Second, in a period when the Jewish territorial and social claim to the land of Israel was constantly challenged, Masada provided a strong and clear supportive statement. Its message, in essence, was something like "We have always been here. We fought and died valiantly on this land, two thousand years ago and now. It is ours."

A number of issues related to Masada during this time period deserve some special attention. I will discuss them now one by one.

THE CABLE CAR

The first issue was the debate over the construction of the cable car at Masada. The first reference to this issue can be found in *Haaretz*, July 10, 1962 (p. 6). There appears there a short news item stating that a Swiss-based company will build a cable car to Masada. The motivation was obvious: to make Masada much more accessible, so that more people could be exposed to the "Masada experience." Zerubavel has already shown that the motivation to make Masada accessible to as many people as possible accompanied Yigael Yadin's attempts to internationalize Masada by recruiting volunteers for the 1960s diggings and by deciding to reconstruct Masada while carrying out the archaeological excavations (Zerubavel 1980:39–47).

However, the ease of accessibility the cable car promised very clearly contradicted a basic element of the Masada experience—the hardship and challenge involved in the actual trek there. So it didn't take long for Yochanan Peled to write to *Haaretz*, on July 15, 1962, that

> again there is an attempt to sell the beautiful landscapes of this land. Again quick businessmen try to destroy one of the most beautiful artifacts still left in the country. It is a bad thing to make this ancient landscape ugly by putting steel cables and cars in it. There will be

people who will claim that the Alps also have such cable cars . . . but, in comparison . . . there is only one Masada in the entire world. Building the cable car will constitute an act of disrespect and contempt for the heroes of Judea. What kind of an experience will there be for the thousands of climbers when above their heads will be stretched a thick steel cable on which tourists will glide? How will this rock symbolize the heroism of Israel if pictures will be shot and ironed shirts and even high-heeled shoes will visit it daily? (p. 2)

Apparently the debate over the cable car to Masada ended in the decision to go ahead with its construction. On January 5, 1967, *Haaretz* reports that the construction of the cable car would be completed by the following winter. This was six months before the Six-Day War, an event that was to change the importance of Masada as a site in a most significant way (since new sites now became accessible after the war, e.g., the Western Wall). Again, this last item was not left unanswered. Zeev Meshel in *Haaretz* of January 13, 1967 (p. 10), protests the construction of the cable car to Masada. His main argument is that the cable car will considerably damage the landscape. Aryeh Gottesman, in a letter to the editor, disagrees. He argues that Israel is a tourist country and should promote and develop tourism. In his view, many tourists should be brought to Masada so that they will be given the opportunity to learn about the heroism of Israel (January 27, 1967, p. 10). However, as a result of the debate (and perhaps budgetary problems too), the actual construction of the cable car did not begin until January 14, 1970,[4] and it was well under way by December 8, 1970.[5] On February 11, 1971, the cable car to Masada was operational. Masada was now easily accessible to thousands of people who could not have made the trip beforehand.

As was characteristic for Israel, the cable car created yet another clash between secular Zionist Jews and the non-Zionist ultra-Orthodox populace. The Israeli government was immediately faced with a demand from the ultra-Orthodox parties to stop the cable car from operating on the Sabbath. This demand caused quite a stir. The issue was discussed by the government.[6] Although the Orthodox parties in Israel were not too crazy about the Masada mythical narrative to begin with, this did not prevent them from trying to exercise their political muscle in relation to this secular symbol.[7] Yadin responded (perhaps with hidden sarcasm) by claiming that the last stop of the cable car was tens of meters below the top of the mountain and thus there was no violation of the sacredness of Masada.[8] The entire affair was raised in the Knesset (Israeli parliament) by an Orthodox member, Shlomo Lorentz (in his speech he used quotations from

Ben-Yair's speeches too), in March, but his initiative was rejected in a vote.[9] It apparently took more than Yadin's conciliatory statement to pacify the Jewish religious fanatics. The chances that any of these ultra-Orthodox people would reach Masada during the Sabbath was, in any event, virtually nil (they do not drive on Saturday). Yigael Allon, previously commander of the prestigious Palmach, one of Israel's most revered figures, and then the deputy prime minister, responded to Shlomo Lorentz's initiative in the Knesset. On March 26, 1971, an anonymous reader wrote in *Haaretz*:

> Allon's answer . . . will, hopefully, finish this strange and barren
> debate. Strange because Agudat Israel suddenly discovered the Zealots
> and hooligans, murderers of Hanania, the high priest, and it declared
> a war to prevent the violation of their sacredness. Barren because the
> government has no authority—and it is good that it does not—to
> instruct the National Parks Authority to violate a commercial
> agreement that it signed with the company that operates the cable car
> or to tell that company when to operate the cable car.
>
> The cable car is there to serve the public. More than 50 percent
> of those who climb Masada by means of the cable car do so on
> Saturday. This fact in itself demonstrates what the public wants. The
> deputy prime minister said it well yesterday in the Knesset when he
> noted that many citizens prefer to spend their Saturday in a different
> manner than member Lorentz. And it is their right. They are not
> ready for religious people to force a lifestyle on them. (p. 8)

The cable car became fully operational on February 11, 1971, and it was run on Saturdays too (*Hamodea,* February 12, 1971, p. 6). A news item in *Haaretz* from June 22, 1971, states that in the four-month period in which the cable car was operational (including Saturdays), about a hundred thousand people used it to climb Masada.

THE SKELETONS

The second issue was that of the burial of the remnant skeletons found on Masada. The affair began in October 1963,[10] when the skeletons of a number of people were discovered on Masada. Yadin (1966:193) reports about three skeletons that were found in the lower terrace of the northern palace-villa and about twenty-five additional skeletons that were found in one of the caves at the southern end of the Masada cliff. A few other skeletons and burial places were found too (see Livne 1986:47). Immediately, there were newspaper reports to the effect that the remains were probably of the fighters of Masada, and a state burial ceremony was called for.[11] This issue was raised in March 1967, once again, by the same Shlomo Lorentz of the ultra-Orthodox party Agudat Israel. In a blazing speech in the Knesset he demanded that the remains of the skeletons found on Masada should be given a Jewish burial. Mr. Aharon Yadlin, then the minister of culture and education, pointed out that the Jewish identity of the skeletons had not been established and suggested passing the whole issue on to one of the Knesset's committees.[12] His suggestion was accepted.[13] In fact, the Knesset's Committee on Culture and Education held a discussion with Yadin on this particular issue in February and March of 1968.[14] The manner in which to establish the identity of the skeletons was debated. The committee stated that it was a matter of historical and national importance to determine the identity of the skeletons. Agudat Israel demanded an immediate Jewish burial. The decision on what to do with the remains was delayed until March of 1969, when it was decided that the "bones of the heroes of Masada" would be buried in an official state ceremony.[15] A few days following that announcement, the public was told that the ceremony would be delayed.[16] On March 12, 1969, Yigael Yadin told *Haaretz* that he was opposed to a public burial ceremony. He stated that the evidence of the identity of the skeletons was not conclusive enough. He also stated that he believed that the bones were those of the people of Masada but that he lacked definitive proof. In response to this, the spokesman for the Ministry of Religious Affairs stated the next day, also in *Haaretz,* that "the heroes of Masada came there from Jerusalem and fought the war of the holy city; therefore, it is only natural that their bones would find their final resting place on the Mount of Olives, which was a Jewish cemetery during the days of the Second Temple."[17] However, the entire burial affair was not yet finished.

In March of 1969, several ministers in the Israeli government had second thoughts about burying the skeletons in Jerusalem, and Masada was suggested instead. Of course, a committee was asked to deal with this matter.[18] In July of 1969, the committee finished its deliberations and decided that the Israeli Military Rabbinate would be in charge of the burial and that the skeletons would be buried near Masada.[19] Indeed, on July 7, 1969, the skeletons that had been uncovered by Yadin's excavations about five years earlier were brought to burial in a full and formal military ceremony near Masada, at a place called "the hill of the defenders." By that point in time, Yadin cooperated with the authorities.[20] An impressive array of dignitaries (including Menachem Begin, Yigael Yadin, and Rabbi Shlomo Goren) were present at the burial ceremonies.

The debate over the skeletons also found its way into the professional literature as scholars attacked the identification of the remains with the rebels on Masada.[21]

THE "MASADA COMPLEX" AND THE "MASADA SYNDROME"

The third issue was that of the Masada complex. Aside from the phrase "Masada myth," "Masada complex" is probably the most popular expression regarding Masada. What is the meaning of this expression?

"Masada complex" may refer to any of a number of subjects: suicide, the "last stand," heroism, a siege mentality, and perhaps a few others. In essence, it refers to a desperate situation—to a worldview analogous to that of people on top of a remote fortress, besieged, haunted, with very few options left, realizing that their time may be running out. Such a world outlook may dictate policies, decisions, perception of options, and behavior. From this point of view, the "Masada complex" is a moral lesson. It is not a positive or flattering expression since it refers to a desperate and difficult mentality.

To discuss the "Masada complex" in a meaningful way, we need to look at the development of the concept from a historical perspective.

As Zerubavel (1980:122) points out, one of the earliest citations of the phrase "Masada complex" can be found in 1963.[22] Against the background of Yadin's excavations of Masada, the British *Jewish Observer and Middle East Review* published an anonymous one-page article titled "The Moral of Masada."[23] There, the author states that we may know *what* happened in Masada, but we also need to account for *why* it happened: "Ben-Gurion (and Weitzmann in his own way) understood that Jewish survival was decisively affected by the degree to which Jewish leaders could free themselves of the Masada complex: that glorious death in defeat was preferable to less dramatic victory and survival." The author adds that the "Masada complex" involves seeing "Israel forever on her own and alone. But that, fortunately, is not the belief of those who want finally to liquidate, not the magnificent spirit of the men and women of Masada, but the false and illusionary politics that led them to their tragic and, politically, futile end."

In essence, this 1963 piece, I think, very well captures the issue at the heart of the "Masada complex." This is a political issue concerning decisions that may lead to a new Masada—in other words, to a one-way street leading to doom. A glorious doom, perhaps one that the Klingons in "Star Trek" would appreciate, but doom nevertheless.

The real public notice and turmoil concerning the "Masada complex" was, no doubt, raised by *Newsweek*'s keen commentator Stewart Alsop. In his weekly column (July 12, 1971, p. 19), Mr. Alsop quoted a high official in Washington (later known to be Joseph Sisco) who accused Golda Meir, then Israeli prime minister, of having a "Masada complex."

According to Alsop, the main focus of the Masada narrative was "the mountain where the Jews, in the first century after Christ, died to the last man in their final stand against the Roman Legions." That event created the "Masada spirit," according to Alsop, a spirit not very open to political compromise. It appears that this accusation was leveled because of a significant compromise demanded of Israel that same year: what the Americans called an "extraordinary opportunity" for the reopening of the Suez Canal. Since the 1967 Six-Day War, the Suez Canal had been closed, with Israeli military units on one side and Egyptian military units on the other side. In 1971, the former Soviet Union had a logistical interest in reopening the canal. The Americans agreed that it could be opened, and the problem was to persuade the Israelis and Egyptians to cooperate on this issue.

The initiative to open the canal was not successful, however, and the Americans clearly placed the blame for the failure on Golda Meir, but not only on her: "Secretary of State Rogers, after his famous shouting match with Golda Meir, is said to have reached the conclusion that this remarkable woman's 'Masada complex' is a chief obstacle to any kind of settlement in the Middle East. The fact remains that her 'Masada complex' is shared by a great majority of her fellow citizens—and this is Israel's basic strength." Alsop concluded his article with a grim warning that as long as the canal remained closed, the danger of "a new outbreak of fighting will remain clear and present."[24]

Alsop's article must have spurred numerous discussions and debates among Israelis who read it. It did not take much to find out that the anonymous official mentioned in the article was Joseph Sisco. In the August 3, 1971, issue of the *Jerusalem Post*, Yaacov Reuel wrote a long piece titled "Sisco and the Masada Complex," in which Joseph Sisco was heavily criticized. To Alsop's article he responded:

> That master magician of American diplomacy, Doctor Joseph Sisco,
> also known as U.S. Assistant Secretary of State for Near Eastern and
> South Asian Affairs, was in town, and rumor has it that he conducted
> therapy sessions to try and cure Prime Minister Golda Meir of her

"Masada complex" which has reportedly hobbled efforts to secure an accord for the reopening of the Suez Canal. If that is so, he certainly had his work cut out: the alleged complex, if it exists, is not so much a personal affliction of Mrs. Meir but a national neurosis; and it is, in some measure at least, a fairly reasoned response to the observed facts of the outside world. (p. 9)

While the public development of the "Masada complex" was such that Golda Meir became most associated with it, it is quite clear that Moshe Dayan was also a true believer in the Masada mythical narrative (see, e.g., Shashar 1983 and Inbal 1991). Moreover, Moshe Dayan edited a 1983 book on Masada. (In fact, it was the last book he edited. The lavishly illustrated book was published a few months after his death.) He told Georges Israel, one of the publishers of that book, that "Eleazar Ben-Yair lives on in our hearts and in our actions, and I am ready to write a text which through the story of Masada will serve as a message for the generations to come" (Dayan 1983:47). The chapter Dayan wrote for that book (p. 14–22) is titled "The Victory of the Vanquished," which is really an oxymoron. In it, Dayan makes a revealing yet ridiculously inaccurate comparison: "A thousand years earlier than Eleazar ben Yair, King Saul led Israel. Like the defenders of Masada, when defeat faced him in war, he chose to fall on his sword rather than fall into the hands of his enemy" (1983:22). It is interesting that Rabbi Goren (1985) makes the same strange comparison. In the very same chapter, Dayan draws another direct (and just as inaccurate and aggravating) comparative line between Masada and the Holocaust (p. 21).

The "Masada complex" issue came up again in an interesting article by Boaz Evron, published in *Yediot Ahronot* on December 3, 1971. His piece was written against the background of Israel's attempts to purchase more Phantom-type jet fighters from the U.S. Golda Meir was supposed to go to Washington and persuade then-president Richard Nixon how necessary those fighters were for Israel's national security. Let us look at some of the issues Evron mentions:

We must, once and for all, free ourselves from the psychotic nightmare that the political-military game that we take part in poses a question of existence. That we are always on Masada . . .

   If someone speaks harshly about us, that person is not necessarily our enemy and may have some very legitimate arguments. . . .

   True, we carry a horrendous legacy . . . but we [should not] . . . act like the inhabitants of a ghetto in the middle of a pogrom. . . .

> The real question is not "existence or the destruction of the third commonwealth" but "Do we really want peace?" (p. 16)

The "Masada complex," according to Evron's article, implies both a "siege mentality" and a feeling that "everyone is against us."

On May 7, 1973, *Newsweek* published another long piece about Masada and its meaning. The article first describes the Great Revolt of 66–73 A.D. and Masada. It then explains that "the Masada complex that has grown out of that nightmare mixes fierce patriotism, a keen sense of beleaguerment, a stiff-necked refusal to compromise on serious issues and grim attraction for the Zealots' ancient choice of death over dishonor" (p. 27). The article, interestingly enough, combines the discussion of Masada and the "Masada complex" with contemporary Israeli-American issues.

Stewart Alsop again raised the "Masada complex" issue in a March 19, 1973, article in *Newsweek* titled "Again, the Masada Complex." In it, he reported about a visit of Golda Meir to the U.S. in which she addressed him directly and told him: "And you, Mr. Alsop . . . You say that we have a Masada complex. . . . It is true . . . we do have a Masada complex. We have a pogrom complex. We have a Hitler complex." Mr. Alsop went on to reiterate that with such a basic position, no progress for a peaceful settlement between Israel and its Arab neighbors was possible. That was in March 1973, seven months before the Yom Kippur War and about four years before Sadat's visit to Jerusalem.

The next contribution (in Hebrew) to the debate was made in April 1973 by Benyamin Kedar, a historian from Hebrew University.[25] Kedar claimed that the act of suicide on Masada was as far from Judaism as anything can be. He argued that the act was alien to the very spirit of Judaism and warned against the mixing of past and present in one political dish. Kedar urged Israelis to disconnect themselves from the Masada myth and forget the complex. In his 1982 paper (in English) he wrote explicitly that

> Masada becomes . . . an obfuscating obsession, a complex that could pervert moral criteria. For if in fact our situation is as desperate as Masada's, the lines of demarcation between forbidden and permitted begin to waver, and exceptional acts by subordinates are treated indulgently, no matter how distressing they may be. And when the policy of a leader ailing with the Masada complex is implemented by field commanders who adhere to the method of strike and get it over with the results are liable to be fatal.

> There is yet another danger. It is unavoidable that behavior influenced by identification with Masada will indeed resuscitate it. If the entire world is against us, then one begins to behave as if we are against the entire world, and such behavior is bound to lead to ever-increasing isolation (p. 61)

Kedar (1982:62) also reports that in April of 1973, at a ceremony on top of Masada, both Moshe Dayan and Yigael Yadin denied the existence of a Masada complex. In fact, the speech that Yigael Yadin made on top of Masada on April 11, 1973, was reprinted in full (*Maariv,* April 16, 1973, pp. 15, 33). Yadin said there, among other things, that

> foreigners call the psychology of the people in Israel, mistakenly, "the Masada Syndrome," and in this they mean that we are gripped with the consciousness of "Let us die with the Philistines." But there is nothing more distorted than this. . . . When [we] say "Masada shall not fall again," it means . . . our decision to be free and independent. But unlike Elazar Ben-Yair and his friends who swore to die free, we swear to live free. This is the new gospel of Masada today." (p. 33)

I can't help but make a comment here. What Yadin meant or did not mean is his business to explain. However, he was obviously mixed up here between the "Let us die with the Philistines" quote, associated with the biblical Samson, and the story of Masada. Masada *was not* a replay of Samson's desperate final act. It is difficult to imagine that Yadin was not aware of this. Unfortunately for Yadin, the Sicarii on Masada were *not* Samson types, neither in spirit nor in deed. Moreover, the quote he uses may apply to another different complex, a "Samson complex," but that is an entirely different issue. However, I find the fact that Yadin even needed to explain the issue—and, in his explanation, resorted to a quote from a totally different narrative—in itself very instructive.

Responding both to Alsop's second article and to Kedar, Alter (1973) argued that with the power of the Israeli military machine[26] "every day Masada seems less appropriate as an image of Israel" (p. 24). To this, Syrkin (1973) responded with an exploration of some of the complexities involved in using the Masada mythical narrative as a symbol, which, in his view, constitutes a paradox.

The 1973 Yom Kippur War was a total and bitter surprise for Israelis, and it wrecked havoc on the "macho" aspect of the Israeli mentality. Most observers agree that if the 1967 war created a new euphoric and boastful national feeling in Israel of a local superpower, the 1973 war shattered that feeling to pieces and created a long-lasting national trauma. On November 5, 1973, A. B. Yehoshua,[27] a famous Israeli author, asked in the wake of that terrible war if Israelis had done enough and the proper things to prevent another Masada. Indeed, Shaked (in Sahish 1993:80) pointed out that the Yom Kippur War created a feeling that Masada *could* fall again. In 1975, U.S. Secretary of State Henry Kissinger, was taken on a tour of Masada with Yigael Yadin as his guide. The main theme of that tour was that Masada was not a complex but a reminder.[28]

In a 1979 book by Yaakov Rabi, the author discusses the Masada complex and urges that "it is our obligation to free ourselves from this traumatic burden" because there "is much danger in sinking into the past" (p. 57).

It is interesting to note that in a different context, Agurski (1984) mentions the "Masada complex" in comparison to some recent national revolutions and states that Israel was built more on a "pogrom complex" than on the "Masada complex."

In a recent 1990 book about the Judean Desert and the Dead Sea (Naor 1990), we find two references to the "Masada complex" in two separate papers. Azaria Alon, a famous scout, guide, and educator, denies fiercely that youth in Israel were socialized with a myth of suicide. He states that the whole point of the Masada experience was to educate youth about a heroic tale. In his words, what was important was the "Masada spirit"—a heroic attitude—and not a Masada myth. An entire chapter in this book (pp. 236–44) is devoted to an open conversation between some important figures.[29] In this dialogue, Azaria Alon again denies, vehemently, that they (the educators and the scouts) had anything to do with the "Masada complex" (pp. 242–43).

The symbol of Masada was used, as we have seen, in quite a number of sociopolitical contexts, a peak of which was the "Plan for the North" (discussed in chapter 6) and the "Masada complex." There are even authors who have used the symbol of Masada to justify Israeli military actions against the Arabs. Let me illustrate this with two examples. In an anonymous editorial, in the November 25, 1966, issue of the *Jewish Observer and Middle East Review* (p. 2), the argument was made that an Israeli retaliatory military raid against Samu (in Jordan) was an "anti-Masada declaration" (that is, of active, not passive, defense). In another anonymous article, on April 27, 1973, in the same journal (p. 8), it was claimed that the April 10, 1973, Israeli raid against Black September in Beirut (see Ben-Yehuda 1993:309–10) was justified, and an association was made between the "Masada complex" and the raid, the implication being that retaliation was one of the lessons learned from Masada (see also Blaushild 1985:21–26, 101–4).

In case anyone believes that the "Masada complex" withered into nothingness in the 1970s, there is a nice reminder for its existence in the 1990s. The September 26, 1991, issue (vol. 34, no. 39) of the Washington-area-based newspaper *Washington Jewish Week* had on its front page a grand caricature of Yitzhak Shamir, then Israel's prime minister, fully dressed as a Roman soldier, against the background of what look like ancient ruins, with the following headline: "Shamir's Masada? West Bank settlements, Russian Jews, loan guarantees. Can Israel have it all?"

The concept of the "Masada complex" does exist in an abstract political sense. However, there *was* an attempt to operationalize it in psychological terms under the interesting name of "*the Masada Syndrome.*" In a book on the psychology of stress and ways of coping with it, Bar-Tal wrote a chapter on the Masada syndrome. There, he suggests that "the Masada syndrome is a state in which members of a group hold a central belief that the rest of the world has highly negative behavioral intentions toward that group" (1986:34).

Another relevant topic in which the association with the Masada complex keeps appearing is the ongoing debate between the Israeli right—in particular, settlers in the occupied territories—and the Israeli left, which opposes the settlements. There is a tendency among quite a few members of the "left" to relate to the settlement activity as "preparation for" a second Masada (see, for just one example, Kislev 1991).

The phrase "Masada complex" received its fullest attention in the early 1970s. Referring basically to a siege mentality, it has been raised in the political context of potential negotiations between Israel and her Arab neighbors and was used to criticize what has been viewed as Israel's hard-line position. The concept thus uses elements of the Masada mythical narrative to attack certain aspects of Israeli politics.

OBJECTIONS WITHIN ISRAEL

Although Zerubavel (1980) points out repeatedly that "most of the criticism of the symbol of Masada came from outside of Israel and is shared by a minority of Israelis" (e.g., p. 147), this is not exactly correct. It is true that much political and scholarly objection to the Masada mythical narrative was raised outside of Israel (by Stewart Alsop, Weiss-Rosmarin, Hoenig, Zeitlin, and others), but it is equally true that some major and consistent criticism of the myth has been raised in Israel as well.

To begin with, we know that Orthodox Judaism repressed the memory of Masada for centuries. Furthermore, as we could see in the section analyzing attitudes toward Masada among religious youth movements, it was very well repressed there too. This repression was not accomplished merely in a passive fashion. Effort was expended to keep Masada repressed or at least underemphasized. This task was not easy because the secular youth movements openly used Masada quite intensively.

Additionally, we know that both David Ben-Gurion and Yitzhak Ben-Tzvi were reluctant to promote the story of Masada. Shmaria Guttman himself admits their objections. Yigael Yadin too was very hesitant, at first, to develop the Masada mythical narrative. It took Guttman, by his own account, much effort to change their minds.

The ambivalent attitude toward Masada was expressed by Ben-Gurion in 1946. On August 23, 1946, he sent a letter from Paris to Mapai's conference in Palestine. He could not take part in that conference because he suspected that if he came to Palestine, the British might arrest him. The main question that was to be debated in that conference was whether to renew the struggle against the British occupation of Palestine and, if so, what form it was to assume. Ben-Gurion's position was "Not Masada and not Vichy" (Ben-Gurion 1993). By this he meant that he did not want to get into a Masada type of struggle, where the physical body of the nation could be destroyed in a desperate and hopeless battle. But he also meant that he did not want a Vichy (the Nazi-controlled French Vichy regime) type of solution because it meant resigning oneself to a very corrupt and destructive form of complacency, one that could destroy one's soul. Ben-Gurion stated specifically that Masada and Vichy presented a mortal danger for both the Yishuv and Zionism. It is thus clear that even in 1946 he was not a great or enthusiastic fan of Masada.

Obviously, the debate about the "Masada complex" revealed also that there was some strong objection to the use of Masada as a symbol within Israel.

There were other, more modern objections as well. Neri Erelli, a member of Kibbutz Ein Gedi, has expressed a negative opinion many times regarding the Masada mythical narrative (see, e.g., his 1983 and 1986 articles and Fishbane 1992). Erelli bases his objection on a strict reading of Josephus Flavius and states that the Zealots were, in fact, murderers—that they murdered the people of Ein Gedi. He also points out that they did not fight and explicitly adds that there is no comparison between the rebels of Masada and the heroes of the revolt in the Warsaw ghetto. In his later criticism (see Fishbane 1992), he directly accuses the Israeli Ministry of Education of deliberately preventing history teachers from teaching the original Masada narrative as Josephus wrote it and of preferring, instead, the Masada mythical narrative. According to Fishbane, thirty history teachers signed a petition protesting a directive by the Israeli Ministry of Education to teach the history of the Second Jewish Temple. According to Erelli, the reason for the protest was that the textbooks contained a clear attempt to mythologize and present this particular period in a heroic manner: "In most cases, [the period] is not taught in a critical way but as a basis for nourishing national values" (p. 9).[30] We have already noted that within the debate over the "Masada complex," quite a number of opinions were voiced against the Masada mythical narrative. Those of Kedar (1973, 1982), Evron (1971), and Rabi (1979:56–57) serve as three illustrations.

However, one of the most interesting debates surrounding the Masada mythical narrative has developed since 1985 and came to a sort of explosion in 1992. This debate involved Safi Ben-Yosef, a rather famous tour guide in Israel. In 1985, Danny Rabinowitz published a lengthy article in *Haaretz* in which Ben-Yosef was quoted as having denied the validity of Josephus Flavius's narrative. In that interview Ben-Yosef told Rabinowitz that what happened in Masada was

> very simple. The crazy Sicarii, who were vomited out of the mostly moderate Jewish community (the people were disgusted with them and their deeds, such as the massacre of seven hundred Jews at Ein Gedi), went up to Masada after the fall of Jerusalem. The Romans knew that the probability that they [the Sicarii] would attract most of the people [for continuing the revolt] was zero, and so they were not too worried. The siege was nothing but a big Roman [military] exercise. [It was] a way to employ [and train] the legions whose presence in the land was required because of the Empire's [eastern] border. [This exercise was necessary because] the legions were undeployed since the suppression of the Jewish revolt. This explains the huge siege apparatus, much of which was simply unnecessary. . . . The defenders? They escaped at night. . . . There was no suicide. (p. 21).

Ben-Yosef repeated his claims in February 1992 in an interview on Israeli television (Friday, February 7) and in reports in the daily newspapers (see Dubkin 1992). Although the 1985 piece did not draw reaction, the Israeli nerves of 1992 must have been a bit more strained, for a number of criticisms appeared following that broadcast.[31]

It is interesting to examine these reactions. The first one came from Shmaria Guttman. In an interview he gave Ailon (1992), Guttman admitted publicly that he was the one who transformed Masada into what he termed "an educational center." He accused Ben-Yosef of taking out of Josephus what he found useful while omitting those parts that were inconvenient. It is Guttman's claim that the identity of the Sicarii is not at all clear. However, he did admit, perhaps for the first time in public, that there was no battle at Masada (p. 29). The general point of the interview, however, was to challenge Ben-Yosef's argument and deny his claims. Meshel (1992) published another critique in which he, like Guttman, argues with every point Ben-Yosef raises and attempts to show that he was wrong. However, Meshel goes one step further and tries to delegitimize Ben-Yosef. At the end of his article, he brags about his effectiveness in persuading the head of the Eretz Israel Studies Department at Beit Berl (a college) not to allow Ben-Yosef to take on students for instruction about Masada. Talk about academic freedom! It is interesting to note that within Meshel's article there are two boxed opinions, one by Israel Shahak supporting Ben-Yosef and one by Aryeh Alkalay criticizing him (really trying to derogate Ben-Yosef). In another small article, Yaacov Shavit (1992) also states that Ben-Yosef's ideas are not credible because, among other reasons, "Josephus wrote for the educated Romans, part of whom knew what happened in Judea, and it was not possible to sell them stories that came out of the blue [lit. 'were sucked from the finger.'] " So Shavit challenges Ben-Yosef but, significantly, also adds that "the Masada myth has long since melted and been transformed into an empty ritual. More texts were written in the last decade criticizing the 'Masada Syndrome' than heroic texts. But even in the 1940s, there were those who saw in Masada an unfit lesson for responsible political behavior. Why then criticize the Masada story with so much noise? Why 'discover' that which was discovered a long time ago?"

Much as Meshel did, Shavit tries to imply that the very interest and study of Masada itself is not legitimate because everything is already known. Again talk about academic freedom.

Ehud Netzer, an archaeologist from Hebrew University and one of the main figures involved in the publishing of the final report from Yadin's archaeological excavations at Masada, also released a critique of Ben-Yosef's ideas. This critique is much closer in spirit to Guttman's interview in that both try to limit themselves to the facts without stigmatizing Ben-Yosef (as Meshel did) or censuring the very interest in Masada (as Shavit did). Netzer (1992), on the basis of the archaeological findings, argues that Ben-Yosef's views are simply untrue. What I found interesting in Netzer's response was not so much his debate with Ben-Yosef but some of his assertions. He mentions that (a) the rebels on Masada were "Zealots" (they were, according to Josephus, Sicarii); (b) Elazar Ben-Yair made one speech (he made two); (c) the name of Elazar Ben-Yair appeared on one ostraca (the name was "Ben Yair," not Elazar Ben-Yair); (d) Ben-Yair was the last person alive on Masada, and he was the one who burnt the palace (there is simply no mention of this in Josephus Flavius and no proof whatsoever to support it).[32] Apparently, the myth is still stronger than science.[33]

Finally, so as not to let myself off the hook here, let me state that Ben-Yosef's view just does not seem credible to me. However, it is one that is well worth debating.

A more recent confirmation of the realization within Israel that a Masada mythical narrative *exists* is the June 16, 1994, issue of the *Jerusalem Report* (in English; see also the December 31, 1993, issue of the *Jerusalem Post Magazine,* pp. 16–18, with many similar points), where four full pages are devoted to Masada without much hiding of the mythical dimension of the myth. Moreover, the phrase "Masada myth" has become quite common in Israel.

In summary, then, it is very obvious that debates over Masada, some rather bitter, have raged in Israel.

THE DECLINE OF THE MASADA MYTHICAL NARRATIVE

The Masada mythical narrative had already begun its clear ascent to becoming a major symbol of secular Zionism in the early 1920s. However, the peak influential period of the symbol lasted from the 1940s to the 1960s. There was a real need during those years, among some secular Jewish Zionist groups and elites, for heroic narratives. The Masada mythical narrative answered that need. It was the right narrative at the right time. However, the Masada mythical narrative's power and seductiveness began to decline in the late 1960s; during the 1970s, this decline became quite obvious and significant.

The decline of the myth did not occur in just one day but was instead part of a gradual process. It was expressed in a combination of a decline in the number of individual and group symbolic pilgrimages to the site, less citation in tour guide books, a more critical view of the Masada mythical narrative, more accurate reporting of Josephus's account,[34] and a significant decline in the Israeli army's use of the site as a place for swearing-in ceremonies. Furthermore, a visit to Masada tends now to have the character of a stop at just one more archaeological and historical site, with a reduction in or a total elimination of the earlier ritual-experiential aspect. The combination of these factors indicates that Masada is less the focus of the ideological attention of Jewish Israelis and more considered a tourist attraction. Why did this happen?

One obvious explanation is that the physical reconstruction of Masada, the establishment of the cable car, and the improvement of roads to the site all helped to turn Masada into a tourist attraction. The site has a stunning wild beauty to it, the ancient ruins are interesting to walk through, and—most important—there is a fascinating story attached to them. As a tourist attraction Masada offers an unforgettable experience. This experience is amplified by the guides, who relate to their groups some of the most dramatic narratives concerning the place, usually with the proper blend of theatrics, tone of voice, and fabrication. This combination explains why hundreds of thousands of tourists visit Masada every year. However, the fact that Masada can be so easily sold to tourists does not yet answer the question.

There are four main reasons, in my view, why Masada's value as a major national symbol declined: erosion in the support for the Masada mythical narrative by major figures in the Israeli intelligentsia, the three major wars between 1967 and 1973, changes in Israeli society, and a generational effect.

The first reason is the support given to the Masada mythical narrative by the Israeli elite. We have already seen that, contrary to Zerubavel's claim, the Jewish-Israeli secular intelligentsia has become quite critical of myths. That in itself provides a good basis for the beginning of the erosion of some major myths. It is very obvious that the Masada mythical narrative from the very start was not an easy symbol to digest. The most obvious problematic part was the suicide, but Josephus Flavius's original narrative has a few other unpleasant elements. There can hardly be any doubt that the value of the Masada mythical narrative was debated quite intensively among political, social, and educational elites. There are a few written accounts of that debate; however, not everything has been documented. It is my guess that much unrest and discontent were hidden behind the public facade of the Masada mythical narrative. Loss of the intelligentsia's support for the narrative was a major step in the erosion of the symbol. The debate about the "Masada complex" did not fall on deaf ears. Thus, the demythologizing of Masada was, in my view, in the making for a long time. What was required was a trigger, which provides the second reason.

That trigger was the June 1967 Six-Day War. This war enabled access to sites that were previously unreachable: the Western Wall, Gamla, the Tombs of Rachel and the biblical fathers, and more. Some of these places had real heroism attached to them, and there was no need to concoct any myth. Moreover, the Six-Day War was not the only war in the 1967–1973 period (only six years); the thousand-day war with the Egyptians along the Suez Canal (the "War of Attrition"—March 1969 to August 1970) and the Yom Kippur War in 1973 provided plenty of new and real heroic narratives. Also, the peace treaty with Egypt in the late 1970s has certainly acted against the siege mentality that has been an integral part of the Masada mythical narrative.

One may recall that even at its peak of popularity, there was much discontent with a symbol that contained such strong elements of death, suicide, and failure. Even Lamdan's poem, which was effective in nourishing the Masada mythical narrative, expresses a strong ambivalence toward Masada. It could be expected that with the availability of better, safer (culturally), and less controversial symbols of heroism, the value of the Masada mythical narrative would decline, and that is exactly what happened.

If there had been no doubts about Masada and it had qualified as a real, unquestionable site for a heroic tale, the trigger of the war would not have been necessary. Masada would then have been just one more heroic site and symbol, together with a new pantheon of similar sites and tales. Masada, however, did not remain in that heroic pantheon. It moved into the realm of commercial tourism.

One cannot fail to notice that the number of tourists visiting Masada was increasing very dramatically and that the commercialization of Masada was getting stronger and stronger. This may have taken some of Masada's magic away.

The third reason is that the cultural values of Israeli society changed. Up until the Six-Day War, Israel was a rather closed society, anxious, unsure, preoccupied with itself, and with a strong inward orientation toward absorbing immigrants, developing its economy, investing in infrastructure, and attempting to develop a democracy. It was also ideologically more cohesive. The post-1967 years witnessed a more sure society, with a better economy and more of an outward orientation, less claustrophobic, more tolerant of differences, more critical of itself—a society that had moved from an emphasis on building a nation toward questions of quality of life and peace. In such a critical climate, the maintenance of the Masada mythical narrative has become increasingly more difficult. Indeed, Clyde Haberman (1995) pointed out that the young generation in Israel (aged forty-five and below) has some ideological preferences very different from those of previous generations of Israelis. According to Haberman, the main goals for this new generation are meeting materialistic needs, achieving personal actualization, and improving the quality of life. The old collective ideals, such as sacrifice for one's country and the Zionist folklore, are just not that appealing to this generation. Haberman feels that this is a real revolution in the Israel mentality as the "I" and the "me" seem to replace the myths.

The Yishuv in Palestine was undergoing a powerful secular process of nation building. The Masada mythical narrative was most certainly an important element in the symbology of this newly emerging cultural entity. This nation-building process continued in Israel after 1948, but it was much more crystallized in the 1970s. As the process became more institutionalized, the need for such concocted heroic tales diminished.

Shargel's (1979:370) observation is interesting and relevant in this context. She points out that "by the middle of the 1970s, Masada had become, for many, a symbol of what Israel did *not* want to become." Her point is that during the 1970s the realization in Israel was that the nation must distance itself from the "Masada complex." Shargel adds that both Yadin and Dayan made that point explicitly. Both indicated that Israel should avoid the desperate choice faced by the rebels of Masada and that, contrary to the suicide on Masada, Israelis should—and would—continue to fight to live and survive, not to die.

Shargel's report found support when Israeli Television transmitted on Monday, October 5, 1992, a program about the heroic story of a physician—Dr. Avi Ouri—who was caught in a bunker on the Egyptian front in the 1973 Yom Kippur war. The physician described the situation in the bunker as extremely desperate: he remained alone there, without water, with a severely wounded soldier next to him. The interviewer asked him whether he did not consider a replay of the Masada affair. Dr. Ouri answered: "No. Suicide? No." This account is supported by a similar incident during the same war. During the first day of that war, Egyptian forces attacked all the strongholds (*maozim*) that Israel had built along the Suez Canal prior to the Yom Kippur War (the so-called Bar-Lev line). After three days of repeated attacks, all the Israeli soldiers in one of the strongholds, called Purkan, left the stronghold and escaped to Israeli-controlled territory: "Today, in retrospect, the decision to leave the stronghold looks like the only logical step that could be taken. But two decades ago when 'fighting to the last drop of blood' was the myth with which they were socialized, as in Masada . . . the decision was particularly hard" (Harnik, 1993:22) Avi Yaffe was the signalman in Purkan and described the decision to leave: "We remained in the stronghold for as long as we were useful. To be just killed is not dignified. I am against Masada and against becoming a prisoner" (in Harnik 1993:23).

Thus, it is clear that some very major and basic cultural changes were taking place in Jewish Israeli society during the 1970s. The transformation of Masada from an ideological site into a regular tourist attraction reflects these changes. The major change was the disintegration of the central legitimacy and authority of the older political elite and the emergence of new political elites. However, this was not the only change. These years also witnessed major changes and redefinitions of relations between different groups in Israeli society and the emergence of new political and social groups. Moreover, these years saw a differentiation of the older center of that society not only into diverse groups but also between Israeli intellectuals and the political centers. This process enabled Israeli intellectuals to develop both more independence and a better critical and distant stand from the political elite. The nation-state–building process that somehow integrated many different groups under its unified wings could no longer accomplish that in the 1970s. The interlocking and mutual support of youth movements, academia, and political and social elites began to break up, and their support in the Masada mythical narrative also began to crumble. The ideological and symbolic claims made by the Jewish Israeli political center were not unquestioningly accepted or supported anymore. These claims have increasingly become the focus of some extensive attacks by significant groups of Israeli intellectuals and professionals. In this sense, the transformation and decline of the Masada mythical narrative indeed reflects a major transformation in Jewish Israeli culture. The myth-wrecking activity mentioned earlier should most certainly be viewed within this context.

Fourth, the Masada mythical narrative may have had a strong generational effect. That is, the generation that was influenced the most by this narrative began to make way for a new generation of leadership that was not as influenced by or committed to the Masada mythical narrative.[35]

Although the combination of these four factors indeed caused the decline of the Masada mythical narrative, it did not alter the appeal of Masada as a tourist attraction.

Factoring in all of the empirical criteria we have discussed—number of visitors, publications, swearing-in ceremonies, interest, and so forth—it seems that the Masada mythical narrative began to pick up volume in the late 1930s and reached its peak before the 1970s. It then began to decline, first as an ideological symbol and more recently as a tourist attraction. As our analysis indicated, the decline in the empirical indicators in the 1970s was preceded by other changes in Israeli society. Overall, Masada was transformed from a quasi-sacred symbol of Jewish martyrdom and extreme heroism into a tourist attraction. It seems that this is, more or less, where Masada stands today.

To demonstrate just how much the Masada heroic narrative was eroded, another contemporary illustration can be made. Galei Tzahal, the official radio station of the Israeli army, transmitted on Friday, October 9, 1992, in its 3:00 P.M. news bulletin, a Masada-related item. The news item was that the Israeli police received information that a group composed of young upper-middle-class males and females between the ages of twenty and thirty were planning to have a drug party on Masada, including the use of various psychoactive drugs, loud rock music, and Buddhist-influenced dances. The police announced that it was taking all the necessary precautions to prevent this drug party from taking place. Such a party, *on Masada,* is, without doubt, quite a deviancy (not to mention illegal), even in permissive 1992 Israel. Such a news item could not even be dreamed up until the late 1960s.

Part III

Analysis, Discussion,
and Summary

Chapter Twelve

Methodological Framing

THE MAJOR QUESTION we need to answer in this chapter is a rather simple one: How was the Masada mythical narrative created? The answer will be based on Allport and Postman's (1945, 1947) model of leveling, sharpening and assimilation. Through the illustrations presented in this book, we have seen, again and again, how the mythical narrative of Masada was created. By contrasting it with Josephus Flavius's original account, we observed how far removed and biased the myth was from the original.

The interesting question is, how do we conceptualize, in terms of a theoretical model, this "mythmaking" process? The imagery I gave for the process was that of the duplication of an original picture. However, unlike the technical process of duplication, this one entails interpretation. This imagery approaches very closely the processes and problems of information dissemination in its various forms. One individual form of information dissemination that I found particularly relevant was that of rumor (see, e.g., Goode 1992:263–310; Kapferer 1990; Rosnow and Fine 1976). A close topic that may be relevant here is that of urban or contemporary legends (see, e.g., Goode 1992: 303–43). Goode defines a contemporary legend in this way: "Modern legends (some of which have ancient roots) supposedly happened recently or deal with newly-emerging threats, and they took place in the physical or social setting of the person telling the tale" (pp. 305–6). Thus, on the surface one may claim that the Masada mythical narrative (and possibly other myths as well) resembles an urban or contemporary legend. However, the very definition, characterization, and illustrations of such legends make it very obvious that comparing a myth generally and the Masada mythical narrative particularly to legends cannot pass the superficial level of a conceptual comparison. One extremely important element in myth is the symbolic, awe-inspiring dimension. That analytically distinctive dimension is lacking altogether in analyses of contemporary legends.

Thus, despite some superficial resemblance in a few elements, the Masada mythical narrative and myths in general are certainly not "rumors," "gossip," or "legends" in the way most of us, professionals and laypersons alike, understand these terms. Although it might be an interesting intellectual exercise to try to conceive the Masada myth as a form of gossip legend or rumor per se, this is definitely *not* my intention here. I will thus focus on the Allport and Postman model of rumors as a fruitful way to conceptualize only one element of the Masada mythical narrative—the process of its creation.

THE ALLPORT AND POSTMAN MODEL

There are, of course, many models that attempt to explain rumors, legends, and gossip. However, there is one model of rumors that *conceptually* is very useful for our purposes. I shall present this model shortly, but let me first say a few words about rumor. There are various definitions of this term, but, basically, a rumor is the dissemination of unverified information, in an ambiguous situation, characterized by the immediate need of the recipients of that information to alleviate the anxiety caused by uncertainty. The entire context of the development of the Masada mythical narrative simply does not fit this framework. Therefore, let me insist and reiterate that the choice of model has been made solely for analytical purposes. That is, my use of the model well exceeds its original goal.

The model I am referring to is a rather old one, developed originally by Allport and Postman (1945, 1947). It is one of the basic models in the study of rumor and gossip, yet it is also criticized within the field (see, e.g., Goode 1992:278–81). Because I intend to use the model for conceptual purposes and in a different context, almost all of the criticism simply becomes irrelevant.

To illustrate the point, let me use an example. Allport and Postman argue that rumors are created when the subject of the story is important to both the listener and the teller and the facts of the story are ambiguous. That fits the Masada myth only partially. That the basic facts of Josephus Flavius's original narrative are not all clear is obvious. However, in the main, the narrative is rather straightforward and understandable. There is no ambiguity in regard to the main points of the narrative concerning what took place at Masada. The ambiguity is found in some of the details (e.g., the length of the siege or the size of the Roman army). Furthermore, the interest of the dispensers and recipients of the mythical narrative was not a given. This interest was *socially constructed*. There was no "natural" interest in Masada. It had to be created and maintained. Shmaria Guttman mentioned that he encountered opposition to his attempts to "sell" the myth, and it took all his energy (and he had lots of it) to persuade the opposers, neutralize hostility to the idea, and move forward. Moreover, during the late 1960s and early 1970s, the attitude toward Masada changed quite radically, transforming it from an ideologically revered, almost sacred place into, basically, a tourist attraction. It is doubtful that this process can be reversed. Rumors, typically, do not emerge in such a context. Hence, there are some very major basic differences between the Masada narrative and a rumor.

The more interesting, relevant, and important aspect of the Allport and Postman model is its conceptualization of the *process* of rumor, that is, *how* a rumor is circulated. Here, on the conceptual level, the applicability to the Masada myth is striking.

Allport and Postman stipulate that three major processes are operating in the dissemination of rumors: leveling, sharpening, and assimilation.

Leveling refers to the fact that much of the detail in the original message gets lost. Rumors tend to be short, concise, simple, and easily grasped.

Sharpening refers to a cognitive process of selective perception, retention, and reporting of a limited number of details from the original narrative. Indirectly, the process of assimilation also indicates the important process of elaboration that also takes place in rumor making. Allport and Postman's model explains how certain themes in a (rumor) message tend to become sharper, crisper, and more salient. Sharpening, obviously, is the mirror image of leveling, and the processes complement each other in the creation of a shorter, more concise and focused narrative. As Allport and Postman have pointed out, both leveling and sharpening mean that rumors undergo a selective process that focuses attention on a few items.

What criteria are used in these processes? The answer to this question lies in the third process, that of assimilation. If leveling and sharpening are more technical processes of cognitive selection, assimilation is a process that explains how and why they occur. In other words, assimilation explains both the criteria used in leveling and sharpening and how the content of the messages is molded. Allport and Postman divide the process of assimilation into a number of subprocesses.

The first subprocess is assimilation to a principal theme. The second is assimilation to achieve a good effect of continuity. Much fabrication can occur here because of the conscious attempt to fill in missing information or gaps in the narrative. The third is assimilation by condensation, whereby several items are condensed into one element. The fourth is assimilation to expectation. In this process, which complements assimilation to a principal theme, events and processes are described as we wish them to be. The fifth is assimilation to linguistic habits. This simply means that the language we use to describe the narrative changes with the context. Finally, there is assimilation to interest. That is, the interests of the narrator help mold the narrative in particular ways. It is easy to see that assimilation implies the operation of a Gestalt type of mechanism. There is a wish to overcome an ambiguous situation and the availability of partial information by filling in the empty spaces, thereby creating one coherent and meaningful Gestalt. The different types of assimilation simply provide us with the components of this process.

APPLICATION OF THE MODEL TO THE MASADA MYTHICAL NARRATIVE

It is not too difficult to see how the creation of the Masada myth can be so easily conceptualized within Allport and Postman's model of leveling, sharpening, and assimilation. The Masada myth was created by emphasizing specific elements from Josephus Flavius's original narrative and by discarding others.

The original, complicated, and relatively long narrative provided by Josephus Flavius is leveled down—again and again—into a shorter, more concise, more easily related and grasped narrative. It is typically reduced to one paragraph or maybe three-quarters of a page. The number of elements retained from Josephus Flavius's original narrative is continually being reduced. The complementary process of sharpening can also be observed. The typical selective process associated with sharpening, that is, the retention and reporting of a limited number of details from Josephus Flavius's original narrative, is very obvious in the development of the Masada myth.

To observe the various aspects of assimilation taking place in the creation of the Masada myth was most fascinating. The assimilation process that the Masada mythical narrative has undergone has occurred with a specific goal in mind: the construction of a narrative that conveys a tremendous heroic tale. Those elements that fit this theme consistently become integrated and assimilated (indeed amplified) into the new narrative. Those that cannot be assimilated into the heroic theme (e.g., the massacre at Ein Gedi; the nature of those who were on top of Masada) are discarded. Alas, what can one do when most of the elements of the Masada narrative as provided by Joseph Flavius simply do not fit a consistently heroic theme? Simple, one fabricates new elements and changes Josephus Flavius's original account. Let us see how this occurred in relation to each of the elements of assimilation.

As discussed above, the principal theme of the Masada mythical narrative is that of Jewish heroism—of a valiant fight "to the end." This theme contains many undertones. For example, it concerns the *Jewish* warrior, courageous and willing to die for his land (in contrast to the anti-Semitic stereotype of the Jew). It also represents a statement that the forefathers of Zionism lived, worked, fought, and died in the land. Masada provided an enchanted, tangible, powerful, and strong link to this glorious past (as a force against the crystallizing Arab opposition to Zionism). This theme can be found in each and every manifestation of the myth.

The second aspect of assimilation is the achievement of a good effect of continuity in the presentation of the narrative. For example: "After the destruction of Jerusalem by the Romans, the Zealots escaped to Masada, where they valiantly fought the Romans for three years. When they saw that there was no longer any hope for them to win and that the choice was either death or slavery, they all chose to kill themselves." This passage very concisely summarizes the myth as we have observed it again and again in the previous chapters. This passage aptly conveys, I hope, the effect of consistency and continuity as constructed into the myth. It is simple, logical, short, and continuous. However, it is also highly inaccurate. In reality, the escape from Jerusalem occurred long before the siege on the city; the motives for the escape were not very honorable; it was not the Zealots who escaped but rather the Sicarii; there was no "fight" at Masada; with all probability the siege did not last three years but rather a few months; the Sicarii on Masada *could* have chosen to fight to the last, but they did not (they chose suicide instead); and the grave implications of mass suicide are simply ignored. Hence, while the narrative in its essence is somehow reminiscent of Josephus Flavius's version, the distortion of detail is so great that the reader gets an altogether different picture. So it is easy to see in the passage above, as well as in its various manifestations, how a good effect of continuity can help to achieve massive distortion. We have also witnessed, in this passage, the third process, assimilation by condensation, in that the reference to the "escape from Jerusalem" ignores the actual circumstances of the escape and its timing. These two items are crucial, but they have been combined in such a way that their importance and meaning are significantly changed.

Fourth is the process of assimilation into expectation. Clearly, the theme of heroism created many expectations. What does one expect of heroes? One most certainly does not expect them to commit atrocities. Thus, the Ein Gedi massacre is not mentioned. One does not expect them to commit acts of political terrorism and be shamefully driven away from Jerusalem. So the word *Sicarii* is replaced by "Jews," "defenders of Masada," or "Zealots." The true story about the events that took place in Jerusalem disappears. One does not expect heroes to shy away from a fight. Thus, a "battle" of Masada is added to the narrative. And in the end, the only choices presented are either suicide or slavery. A third possible alternative, that of "fighting to the death," is typically ignored. The suicide itself is typically "explained." Tragic heroes do not survive. So the fact that there were seven survivors is transformed into "no survivors" or "one old woman" or ignored altogether. Heroes are not meant to hesitate. So the deliberations of the Sicarii over whether or not to commit suicide and Elazar Ben-Yair's two speeches are processed into, respectively, "no hesitations" and one speech. Although it is *very* clear from Josephus Flavius that the Roman siege on Masada did not begin immediately after the fall of Jerusalem, most mythmakers ignore that. If, they argue, Jerusalem fell in 70 A.D. and Masada fell in 73 A.D., then "of course" those at Masada "stood against the Romans" (in the soft version of the myth) or "fought the Romans" (in the more heroic version) for three years. In fact, most researchers agree that the siege on Masada began in the winter of 72–73 A.D., and the fortress fell in the following spring, a matter of only a few months.

The fifth subprocess mentioned by Allport and Postman is that of assimilation to linguistic habits. That this occurred in regard to the Masada mythical narrative has been demonstrated on numerous occasions. For example, our description of children's literature illustrates this process in a very clear manner. The language chosen in those stories reflects both the period and the audience. We saw how at times a heavy, biblical-style language was used and at other times ultramodern Hebrew language was used.

The final process, assimilation to interest, can also be discerned. We have seen how Guttman molded the narrative to fit his own interests. Yadin followed along this route too, as did many other officers in the Israeli army.

APPLICATION OF THE MODEL TO JOSEPHUS FLAVIUS

One of the interesting ways in which the processes described above can be illustrated is the attitude toward Josephus Flavius himself. One cannot simply distort Josephus Flavius on such a massive scale and then say nothing about him personally. While the Masada myth was at its peak, Josephus Flavius was regarded as a questionable character. Many viewed him as a traitor who deserted his command at Yodfat (Jotapata), cheated his Jewish comrades, and "needed" to provide narratives that would satisfy his masters, the Romans, to whom he devoted himself. The common statement that one needs to take Josephus Flavius with a grain of salt is really a linguistic code that implies that his accounts are not to be trusted. That being the case, one has the legitimacy, indeed the obligation, to take "corrective action" (read "falsify" and/or "fabricate").

It is not too difficult to realize that Josephus Flavius could be defined as a defector and traitor. However, it is noteworthy how easily and to what purpose this label has been attached to him. In contrast, another rather famous defector during that very same period and war, Rabbi Yochanan Ben-Zakai, was not branded a "traitor" (see the relevant discussion in chapter 2). He too deserted his Jewish comrades in favor of the Romans. Thus, we see how the labeling of a person as a "traitor" achieves the effect of discrediting him.

It is true that Josephus Flavius was most likely not present during the siege of Masada, and one may doubt the literal depiction of the two speeches he attributes to Elazar Ben-Yair. However, why should we doubt the accuracy of his description of other facts? Moreover, if we discount Josephus Flavius, then there *is* no Masada. His account is really the only detailed source we have. In this respect we are fortunate. Josephus's account can easily serve as any of the original pictures used in Allport and Postman's classical experiments that examined how rumors are transmitted. Using it as a standard, it is very easy to measure the deviances from this account.

AN ADDITIONAL OVERVIEW

The model proposed by Allport and Postman was developed for the phenomenon of rumor. The Masada mythical narrative is not a case of the spontaneous transmission of a, relatively speaking, simple message. This narrative was created, invented, fabricated, and transferred in a conscious, carefully controlled manner. Thus, while leveling, sharpening, and assimilation seem to be very relevant here, a number of additional processes require mention.

First, the fabrication of certain items: the replacement of "Sicarii" by "Zealots" or other names; the "fighting" at Masada; the three-year siege;

the reduction of Elazar Ben-Yair's two speeches to one; playing with the number and type of survivors. It is true that these fabrications may be conceptualized within the processes of assimilation, but there is probably a stronger, more conscious intent here than is assumed in the original model of Allport and Postman.

Second, the choice of words. The Masada mythical narrative reveals that the mythmakers deliberately chose words that suited their intent. For example, the issue of suicide is managed by talking about a "choice of liberating death" rather than suicide. Those developing the myth found it difficult to squarely face this problematic issue. The choice of wording could be very straightforward, as illustrated above, or it could be achieved in a sophisticated manner, so that if and when the author is criticized, he or she can hide behind different possible interpretations.

Let me illustrate what can be the combined impact of a choice of words and fabrication. Yadin (1966:11) states that "in 70 A.D. the Roman general Titus conquered Jerusalem, sacked the city, destroyed the Temple, and expelled the bulk of the Jewish survivors from the country. One outpost alone held out till 73 A.D.—the fortress of Masada." A normal reader will assume that those expelled by Titus from Jerusalem escaped to Masada, where they "held out" for three years. Again, this same reader will assume that "held out" means "against repeated Roman attacks." These assumptions are incorrect. What Yadin implies here was simply never stated by Josephus Flavius. Yet the manner in which Yadin phrases his narrative may be very easily interpreted in such a way. Indeed, Yadin goes even further and states outright that "at the beginning of the 66 A.D. rebellion, a group of Jewish Zealots had destroyed the Roman garrison on Masada and held it throughout the war. They were now—after the fall of Jerusalem—joined by a few surviving patriots from the Jewish capital who had evaded capture and made the long arduous trek across the Judean wilderness, determined to continue their battle for freedom. With Masada as their base for raiding operations, they harried the Romans for two years" (p. 11). Again, and here the invention is apparent, almost nothing that Yadin says can be found in Josephus Flavius's account (or be supported by the excavations). Thus, it is not at all clear whether the Zealots took over Masada originally (a much better guess is that they were Sicarii). Nor is it clear whether they were joined, after the fall of Jerusalem, by others. Judging by their nature, they probably were not. The use of Masada as a base for raiding operations is probably accurate. However, contrary to what a normal reader may understand from this—that is, that these were raids against the Romans—the only raids

Josephus Flavius mentions are those made against other Jews (e.g., the murderous raid against Ein Gedi). The harassment of the Romans for two years, like the "raids," is pure unadulterated fiction. Another inaccuracy implied by Yadin, as well as others, is that the rebels on Masada arrived there *after* the destruction of Jerusalem.

Third is what may be called sequencing and isolation. What occurs here is that the historical sequence, as described by Josephus Flavius, is altered. Let me illustrate what I mean here so that we may evaluate the most obvious and effective impact of this technique.

The need to mention and explain the nature of the Sicarii on top of Masada is not so simple. An obvious technique is not to provide the unsuspecting reader with the true information. However, what then *should* the reader be told about the people on Masada? Who were they? Zealots? Rebels? Defenders? Jews? Heroes? Freedom fighters? To simply choose one of the above may appear too crude a solution. Another, more elegant alternative is to divide the discussion. In this way, some mythmakers describe who the Sicarii were within the context of a discussion concerning the different Jewish factions that took part in the Great Revolt. This typically appears early on in the text; thus, by the time the reader gets to the description of the Masada affair and encounters the word *Sicarii* again, he or she must make an effort to go back and search for an explanation of just who the Sicarii were. Sometimes, an author uses this technique of separation, adding to and amplifying it either by using a different name for the people on Masada (e.g., "Zealots") or by mention of the Sicarii in the context of Masada only once and then by going on to describe them by other names. A particularly clever manipulation is achieved when we are told that the people of Masada were *led* by Elazar Ben-Yair "the Sicarii," as if to imply that it was only Elazar Ben-Yair who was a Sicarii and that the rest were not. Clever!

Another illustration is the Ein Gedi massacre. This is something that most authors prefer to ignore. However, it is wrong to assume that they do it out of ignorance. For example, Vilnai's 1964 book contains separate chapters on Masada and Ein Gedi. In the chapter concerning Ein Gedi, there is a fairly accurate description of the Sicarii's raid on the settlement. However, in the chapter on Masada, it is not mentioned at all.

Another interesting illustration can be found in the reputable *Encyclopedia Hebraica* (6:375–89, on the topic of Israel). There, one can find a description of the Great Revolt, written by Avraham Shalit. Shalit does mention the fact that the Sicarii were on Masada (p. 388), but he does not explain just exactly who they were—not in the context of Masada or in any other context. The Sicarii are not even mentioned in the context of the discussion concerning the "Fourth Philosophy" (p. 378). Thus, an uninformed reader is not any wiser about the Sicarii after reading this account.

Hence, these separation and isolation techniques are related to how the authors sequence the events. These are very powerful and manipulative devices that help to further the social construction of the Masada mythical narrative.

Finally, there is the one advantage that Masada has over any rumor or legend: the environment of the site itself. As we saw in previous chapters, thousands of Israeli adolescents have made the difficult and dangerous trek through the Judean desert culminating in the effort to climb to Masada. This effort and the surrealistic atmosphere, almost unchanged since the year 73 A.D., are a natural setting for the suspension of disbelief. So the mythical narrative was hungrily swallowed by these large groups of adolescents as they reached the top of Masada, tired and impressed. It not only "explained" a component of their Jewish Israeli identity but also provided a neat justification for the hardships they were made to go through to reach the top. Standing there on top of that doomed fortress, listening to a coherent, consistent, and meaningful story about great Jewish heroism and of heroes who faced overwhelming odds—the myth is perfectly *constructed* to "make sense" in this particular situation and in this specific setting—and, moreover, witnessing firsthand the impressive remnants of Herod's majestic structures and the Roman siege camps, wall, and ramp reified and reinforced, in the most direct way, the mythical narrative they were exposed to. This orchestration, in what is defined as an authentic setting, helped to create in the minds of twentieth-century adolescents a sought-after mystical, emotional, and cognitive link bridging an abyss extending over a period of close to two thousand years. It helped into being a possible identification between two types of people, representing two very different cultures, who were so hopelessly separated by time. This was just possibly one of the best shows of the twentieth century. From my own personal experience, as well as that of many others whom we interviewed, it is not too difficult to understand the tremendous emotional and cognitive impact of undergoing this Masada experiential ritual (if done properly, of course). This experience most certainly leaves a significant and meaningful imprint on one's young, developing personal and national identity. The power of this imprint is clearly demonstrated by the angry responses elicited from those who are forced to confront the contrast between the myth and the original narrative.[1]

Chapter Thirteen

Theoretical Interpretation

IN THIS CHAPTER I am concerned with why and how we interpret the creation of the Masada mythical narrative. I will focus on the social construction of the Masada mythical narrative as a problem in the field of collective memory.

The sociological field of collective memory has split into two competing analytical perspectives. In 1991, Barry Schwartz suggested a theoretical integration for these two branches. In a very real sense, the usefulness and practicality of his proposal was tested in this research and received full empirical and analytical support. Nevertheless, to demonstrate just how this support was achieved, a discussion of the issues at hand is necessary. Therefore, I shall begin with a short presentation of the field of collective memory and will then focus on the analytical debate within it. To place Barry Schwartz's proposal into the proper context of this research, I will divide the discussion into a few subtopics. These subtopics will include a general discussion of collective memory; history and selection (including a discussion of the problem of selection in history, explanations in history, and historical sequencing); myth (including a discussion of the nature of myth, definitions of myth, political myth, definition of myth as based on this research, and myth and nation building and myth wrecking in Israel); moral entrepreneurship and the identity context.

Discussing the area of collective memory will provide some interesting and innovative insights into two other important issues: the "past" and "myth." Consequently, I shall discuss and try to develop an interpretation for the nature of the "past" and of "myth." This discussion will be followed by a discussion about moral entrepreneurship and personal and national identity.

With all this analytical apparatus in hand, I shall go back and integrate all of the findings and the analytical framework into one interpretation (the "Concluding Discussion" section) focused on collective memory in general and on Schwartz's proposal in particular.

COLLECTIVE MEMORY

The crystallization of the sociological interest in collective memory is, relatively speaking, recent. The main issue in collective memory is how human societies remember their past. The word *remember* needs to be understood, in this context, in a very broad manner. It can mean "recollect," as well as "commemorate."

Maurice Halbwachs's work (1980; Coser 1992) is considered by many to be the classical statement in the field. The term *collective memories*, as suggested by Halbwachs, describes memories of a shared past that are preserved by members of a specific group who experience them. The concept of collective memory is very seductive analytically but is difficult to operationalize into empirical terms. For example, collective memories may be interpreted to describe the societal level of analysis (assuming that that level can be operationalized), or it can mean the reflection and expression of those memories on the individual level.

Halbwachs points out that collective memory is socially constructed and that there are many different collective memories supported by the various groups that together form a society. He has also stated that collective memory is an act of "remembering together," much as Becker (1986) described culture as "doing things together." Following his "totemic father," Emile Durkheim, Halbwachs also emphasized the ritual aspect of collective memory. All this holds true in regard to the Masada mythical narrative. We see the dominance of one group, which repressed the memory of Masada for centuries, followed by that of another group, which both partly restored and constructed the collective memory of the Masada narrative *and* created the ritual of the Masada experience (the trek, climb, and ceremony to and on Masada).

An important matter here is the possible distinctions between collective memory, history, and myth. Later on in this chapter I shall delve into this issue. In any event, the subject of collective memory leads to a complex set of questions focused on the way in which we collectively remember the past. Different collectives will, of course, remember different pasts. Moreover, it is not too difficult to understand that within a pluralistic society, different groups may remember different, not necessarily overlapping pasts. The past is an important matter because many groups see in that past, or tradition, their roots and the basis for legitimizing different social, political, religious, and territorial issues, claims, and disputes. As O'Brien tells Winston Smith, in George Orwell's superb *1984*: "Whatever the Party holds to be truth *is* truth. . . . Who controls the past controls the future; who controls the present controls the past" (Orwell 1961:252–58).

Barry Schwartz has identified two major competing analytical trends within the field.[1] The first approach is rooted in social constructionism. Basically, it states that the needs, concerns, and interests of the present are the prime factor in remembering the past. That is, the past is socially constructed in such a way as to fit the needs of the present. Halbwachs himself advocated this approach when he stated that "collective memory is essentially a reconstruction of the past . . . if it adapts the image of ancient facts to the beliefs and spiritual needs of the present, then a knowledge of the origin of these facts must be secondary, if not altogether useless, for the reality of the past is no longer in the past" (quoted by Schwartz, Zerubavel, and Barnett 1986:149).

Obviously, such a social construction requires deception and fabrication, because the past typically does not exactly fit the needs of the present and "corrections" of that past will always be called for. The past as a social construction by different groups in the present seems to be the dominant view in the field and is shared by many scholars.[2]

This approach means that, as Schwartz argued, there is a fundamental *discontinuity* between the past and the present. The reason that this is so is that it implies that *there is no* "past." Accepting this approach is sort of like accepting Alice in Wonderland's Cheshire cat. The various groups in the "present" will construct different "pasts," which will appear and disappear as did that lovely Cheshire cat. Theoretically, this is not a very pleasant prospect—accurate, perhaps, but not pleasant.

The second approach in the field is diametrically opposed to the previous one. It stipulates that it *is* the past that enables, indeed shapes, our understanding of the present. The emphasis here is on a stable and solid past on which the present depends. This past gives meaning, a sense of continuity and purpose, to the present. The emphasis in this approach is on the *continuity* between the past and the present. A few scholars support this view.[3]

An awareness of the contradiction between these two approaches may be detected in Schwartz's earlier work, but not only there. Stanford W. Gregory and Jerry M. Lewis (1988) pointed out in their work that the erection of public memorials can be understood as a process of creating an "analogous linkage" between the past and the present. This process may indeed lie somewhere between the above two approaches. Gregory and Lewis do not explicitly recognize the two competing theoretical approaches, however, and therefore their solution is not very clear. In analyzing the Vietnam Veterans Memorial, Robin Wagner-Pacifici and Schwartz (1991) also place their own work between these two approaches, emphasizing the needs of the present in the memorial, as well as the difficult past that this memorial stands for and symbolizes.

In his landmark 1991 paper, Schwartz sharpened and focused the contradiction between the two approaches in relation to the study of collective (historical) memory and suggested that they "can be seen as special cases of a broader generalization that relates both change and continuity in the perception of the past to immediate human experience" (p. 234). That is, he alerts researchers of collective memory to the possibility that these two theoretical approaches are not necessarily contradictory and that they may be integrated into a coherent interpretation that emphasizes both continuity and discontinuity.[4] For Schwartz, the collective historical memory always demonstrates continuity but also reveals new elements as the "past" is made to better fit contemporary needs, concerns, and linguistic habits.

How does our study fare in light of Schwartz's proposal?

In the overall scheme, it fares very well. The Masada mythical narrative is an excellent illustration of the wisdom of Barry Schwartz's analysis. However, in its details, there are some minor problems in applying the conciliatory proposal.

To apply the approach Schwartz proposes, as well as advance it beyond its 1991 formulation, we need to examine several issues very carefully. Thus, the remainder of this chapter will focus on a discussion of those issues that are related to the topics he mentions in his presentation of the theoretical dispute in the field of collective memory, as well as his suggested solution. Such an analysis will, I hope, enable us not only to examine Schwartz's proposed solution but also to develop a more sophisticated analytical framework that will help us develop some new answers to the issues of collective memory, history, myth, and deviant belief systems.

Paul Connerton (1989:13) makes an interesting distinction between what he terms *social memory* and *historical reconstruction*. His main point is that whereas the latter is based on facts and traces, the former tends to rely more on rituals. Clearly, *historical reconstruction* need not depend on *social memory*. However, the reverse is more often true. We need, therefore, to clear up in our own minds a number of issues concerning what Connerton has called *historical reconstruction*. I will do this briefly and thus touch on what I feel is the most relevant issue for our purposes, without becoming completely immersed in a comparative discussion of collective memory and historical reconstruction.

The first issue that requires a closer examination is the use of the term *past*. What indeed *is* the nature of the past? How might we conceptualize it? Is there anything about the nature of the past that contributes to the dispute in the field of collective memory?

Once we clarify the nature of the "past," we shall examine the issue of "myth" as distinguished from "history," and we shall see that a myth is a particular construction of history.

The next issue to be discussed will be the Masada mythical narrative, a socially constructed historical myth, as a phenomenon of deviance and moral entrepreneurship. These discussions will be followed by a discussion about the national identity that the Masada mythical narrative was supposed to help bring into being.

Finally, the entire discussion will be integrated in an attempt to present one coherent interpretation of the Masada mythical narrative.

The following sections are thus intended to directly answer the questions posed above. The differentiated answers will give us a better conceptualization that we can utilize to understand and solve the controversy between the two approaches in the field of collective memory in the context of this study.

COLLECTIVE MEMORY

History and Selection[5]

Time. The dimension of time, its direction and its pace, has been determined by the "big bang," with which the known universe began (Ferris 1977; Silk 1980; Weinberg 1977). Einstein's (1968) conceptualization of time states clearly that it is a dimension in the cosmos that flows in only one direction: from the past to the future. Philosophically speaking, the present has no existence—one moment it is the future, the next moment it is the past. The one-directional flow of time (contrary to the speculations of a number of science fiction writers) cannot be reversed. Even if it were possible to invent a "time machine," once it had left the present, it would probably never be able to return to it.

Yet another feature of time is that, within a given system, it is a uniform, homogeneous process. Be this as it may, an endless number of events and processes nonetheless take place at the same time—which means that an accurate historical account (or narrative) of the past two thousand years should take the historian another two thousand years to record. Such a task may not be entirely impossible, but the scientific value of such a long project is, of course, doubtful. History is thus based on a selection of events that are then integrated into an historical narrative. *Selection of Events.* The selection of events presents the researcher with a number of problems. It is based on subjective criteria and may limit the scientific ability to describe a singular, consistent history, since alternative selections will in fact describe different histories—and thus invite different social interpretations.[6] Two good illustrations of this problem can be found in Beale's treatment of the American Civil War[7] and in the numerous "histories" that the former Soviet Communist Party had.

Another dilemma of the selection process is whether and to what extent it is at all useful (and for whom). It has already been indicated that it is impractical to describe and relate all of the past. Even if such a task were practicable, theoretically it is questionable.[8] Since it is my view that the selection process is the basis of the problems described above, it is crucial to examine this process more closely.

The selection of facts, actions, or processes from the past means that the "truth" as reported in historical accounts only includes a few aspects of reality. A historical explanation, therefore, is always an exercise in constructionism. It is evident that in a selection process, some items of information are emphasized and gain importance while others are discarded and ignored. Thus, a major question concerning such a process regards the selection criteria that are used. A theory, a hypothesis, or an interest can certainly serve as a criterion of selection (e.g., see Popper 1950). Obviously, establishing criteria for selection is an important but also a Sisyphean task.

Is it possible to think of objective, perhaps absolute criteria of selection? That certain historical events are highly significant is undeniable (the French and Russian revolutions, the two world wars, etc.). But if importance is the criterion, then the next questions are, importance for whom, when, and for what purposes? It is my contention that it is impossible to develop absolute criteria of selection in historical research, and therefore it is also impossible to establish absolute objectivity for historical explanations or interpretations. Therefore, to a large extent, history is subjective and is dependent on individual historians, but not entirely so. *Explanations in History.* The above discussion brings us to one of the most important aspects of the historical process: its "self-explanatory" nature. It is often claimed that "history is truth." Whether accepted or not, this claim can be neither substantiated nor refuted. Because of the mere fact that it "took place," any given historical process or event was, by definition, unavoidable; thus, historically speaking, hypothetical questions such as "What would have happened if X had not occurred?" are meaningless, merely because X did occur.[9] The fact that X did occur eliminates all other possibilities. Thus, while in other disciplines, postulates are derived from questions such as "Was A a necessary condition for B to occur?" such queries are irrelevant within the framework of history. The unique quality of social historical accounts lies in the fact that history is explained by the mere reality that is assumed to have taken place and is told (or written)—in other words, it is "explained by itself" or "self-explanatory."[10]

In this context, it is easy to see that research in history is a very problematic issue. Theoretically, the best tool for historical (and archaeological) research—a time machine—does not and probably will not exist. In such circumstances, the question of how we know about the past becomes a serious dilemma. Historical research is often based on secondary sources, since direct observation, as in the fields of chemistry, biology, astronomy, anthropology, and other disciplines, is impossible. Unfortunately, the past is not a place we can visit whenever we desire, and so our knowledge of it is problematic. It is necessary for us to rely on documents and artifacts whose authenticity and representativeness may be questionable. Contrary to research paradigms in the natural and social sciences, experiments in history are not feasible; therefore, it is very difficult to discuss the reconstruction or replication of "test conditions." There are no "historical laws" (except, perhaps, in the field that has been referred to as "speculative history"). The meaning of the term *prediction* as a result of historical research is entirely unclear. The research historian finds it difficult to discuss the "control" of historical processes. The result of all this is that the main contribution of research in history is not a reproduction, refinement, and/or improvement of historical "explanations" but, rather, an attempt to find additional information or a new configuration of "facts" so as to give rise to a new "historiography," the truth of which is likely to be the subject of debate, since its validity, reliability, and objectivity will be in doubt.[11]

Historical Sequencing. It is one thing for a dedicated historian to try to construct as meaningful a historical sequence as he or she can, one that is valid, "objective," and based on that historian's best professional judgment. It is obvious that honest mistakes and incorrect evaluations may occur in such a process. However, it is a totally different thing to construct a historical sequence, deliberately, systematically, and intentionally, that is based on a consciously biased selection, on the repression of important facts, on an emphasis on other facts, and on complete fabrications. As we shall see in the next section, a historical sequence that is constructed in such a manner is a perfect candidate for the label *myth*.

In summary, the "past," as we know it, is a selective construction of a particular sequence of events, structured along a time continuum, that "makes sense" within a distinctive culture. The reason that such a sequence is understandable and acceptable (in other words, that it "makes sense") in a given culture is that the discourse used in the sequence, the way it is constructed, and the symbols it uses are embedded within a particular cultural matrix (see, e.g., Portelli's 1991 work).

This peculiar quality of the past gives rise to another interesting question. If the past can best be conceptualized as a series of possible sequences, does that mean that there are endless "pasts"? If so, there is really no past. My impression is that this is not so. Yes, there are a very large number of pasts indeed, but these are not totally divorced from one another. It appears that, in very diverse historical narratives, there are usually some basic facts that are consistent. For example, the history of World War II can appear very different from various angles, but facts, such as the actual dates of the Nazi invasion of Russia ("Operation Barbarosa"), the landing of the allies in Normandy, and the beginning and end of the Battle of the Bulge should be identical in the different sequential historical accounts. Obviously, what I am referring to here is a legitimate sequence. If fabrications, inventions, and lies are woven in, then, of course, we *will* get an endless series of pasts. Once the line between fiction and reality is crossed, as in any good or bad fiction/fantasy, the possibilities are limitless. Agreement on the validity of a few basic facts, despite the different constructions that arise, is fully compatible with contextual constructionism.

There may be a very big gap between the interpretations of different sequences and the real events that actually took place. Given that the above conceptualization is valid, then what the large number of historical sequences implies is that many (possibly most) of them keep some basic facts intact and delete and add other facts. This process is exactly what creates, eventually, what appear to be different sequences. As we shall see shortly, this peculiar quality of the past is very significant in regard to a major problem in the area of collective memory: the conflict between the continuity and discontinuity perspectives.

Now that we have acquired a common analytical discourse for a meaningful dialogue concerning the past, the next topic we need to discuss is that of myth.

A Few Words about Myths

So far, I have used the word *myth* rather loosely. It is time to try to clarify this term.

The Nature of "Myth." The term *myth* can easily provide an army of scholars with enough ammunition for a long struggle indeed. There are many definitions of myth, in fact too many. Both Cohen (1969) and Doty (1986), as well as others, repeatedly point this out.

Doty should know. His 326-page definitive volume *Mythography* surveys *all* the different theories and provides "a sort of archaeology of mythography" (p. xiv). It is his suggestion (and that of Cohen 1969) that no single approach should be adopted but, rather, that theory should be made to fit the case at hand and "make clear which aspects of myth [one's] own theory is designed to clarify" (p. xiv) because "to say 'myth' . . . is to say so many different things to so many different people that we almost founder in the 'things' at the start" (p. 6). Myth, according to Doty, "is understood as referring to the basic religious or philosophical beliefs of a culture, expressed through ritual behavior or through the graphic or literary arts" (p. 6). He does point out, however, that besides this positive approach, there are other, more negative approaches that emphasize myth as the untrue, the fantastic, and the unreal. "Myth had been understood as deceit, as a falsifying construct, an understanding mirrored in many dictionaries where myth is first described as 'primarily fictitious' " (p. 7). In short, we find the positive and the negative, the serious, the sacred, the fictitious, and the fantastic: the Masada mythical narrative easily fits this conceptualization.

Doty dryly admits, "I now have a list of more than fifty individual definitions, chosen on the basis of eliminating duplications. Fifty!" (p. 9). Obviously, this means that there *is* no single authoritative, definitive, or adequate definition. A nice analytical swamp to get into, if one so wishes.

The inherent ambiguity of the term *myth* does not seem to deter or reduce the interest of social scientists, as well as others, in the concept. For example, an entire issue of *Social Research* was devoted solely to just this topic.[12]

Definitions of Myth. To get a taste of the debate, let us look, briefly, at just how some of the most famous scholars who have studied myth define it. In the 1987 *Encyclopedia of Religion*,[13] edited by Mircea Eliade, the term *myth* is discussed in two separate sections. The first, written by Kees W.

Bolle, deals with religion and myth: "Myth is the word for a story concerning gods and superhuman beings. A myth is an expression of the sacred in words. . . . The language of myth does not induce discussion: it does not argue, but presents" (pp. 261–62). The second section, written by Paul Ricoeur, is focused on history and religion. Ricoeur feels that both history and myth "are . . . narratives, that is to say, arrangements of events into unified stories, which can then be recounted. But myth is a narrative of origin, taking place in primordial time, a time other than that of everyday reality; history is a narrative of recent events, extending progressively to include events that are further in the past but that are, nonetheless, situated in human time" (p. 273). It does not take much to see that neither of these explanations fits the Masada mythical narrative. Victor Turner, however, focused his 1968 discussion on the view of myth as a liminal phenomena. This conception of myth as something that leads people into a period of liminality, necessitating a rethinking and reevaluation of one's cultural ancestry and commitment, fits the Masada mythical narrative very well.

From these general discussions of myth, I tried to find approaches more specific to Judaism and Israel. Interestingly enough, the *Encyclopedia Judaica* also has a definition of myth that is short and to the point: "A myth is a story about the universe that is considered sacred. Such a story deals with the great moments of man's life . . . referring them to events that took place in 'mythical times.' The myth is often recited during a dramatic representation of the event it narrates" (vol. 12:729). The Masada mythical narrative also fits this definition well. Nurith Gertz (1986), in her important paper, also delves into the various definitions of myth. She elects to take a functionalist approach and examines the changes from function to structure in myth among Jews in Palestine and Israel. Gertz also specifically examines what she refers to as Zionist myths. Although she does not discuss the Masada mythical narrative, she does emphasize that a central theme of mythmaking in Palestine and Israel was "the few against the many."[14] This is clearly a theme intimately connected to the Masada mythical narrative. In recent years, two prominent Jewish figures, Elie Wiesel and Shulamit Hareven, have written works, in Hebrew, for a general Israeli audience on the subject of myths.

Wiesel (1988) uses biblical figures as illustrations and calls on Jewish Israelis to abandon their myths. He claims that whereas history is objective, myths have caused the Jews much damage. Shulamit Hareven, in two pieces (1989a: 1989b, based on a public lecture), focuses her discussion on myth and history. She appears to suggest that myths should be learned, discussed, and recognized for what they really are—only myths.

Since I have no desire to become drawn too deeply into this swamp of definitions, counterdefinitions, and debates, I will soon leave this issue behind. First, however, out of deep respect for Doty's awesome effort, I would like to quote his definition, after which I will provide my own definition of myth as it has crystallized from my research on the Masada mythical narrative. In this, I shall be following both Doty's (1986) suggestion and Cohen's (1969). As we shall see, this definition fits very well both with the empirical findings of this research and with its theoretical orientation. Although my own definition contradicts neither Doty's nor Cohen's works (nor Eliade's), I must apologize that there will now be fifty-one available definitions of a "myth."

From Doty (1986:11):

> A mythological corpus consists of (1) a usually complex network of myths that are (2) culturally important (3) imaginative (4) stories, conveying by means of (5) metaphoric and symbolic diction, (6) graphic imagery, and (7) emotional conviction and participation, (8) the primal, foundational accounts (9) of aspects of the real, experienced world and (10) humankind's roles and relative statuses within it.
>
> Mythologies may (11) convey the political and moral values of a culture and (12) provide systems of interpreting (13) individual experience within a universal perspective, which may include (14) the intervention of suprahuman entities as well as (15) aspects of the natural and cultural orders. Myths may be enacted or reflected in (16) rituals, ceremonies, and dramas, and (17) they may provide materials for secondary elaboration, the constituent myth themes having become merely images or reference points for a subsequent story, such as a folktale, historical legend, novella, or prophecy.

This is probably the most inclusive definition available. It is clear that the Masada mythical narrative fits it very well.

Political Myth. Finally, before moving on to my own definition, I will discuss one additional topic—that of the political myth. Here, I shall present two approaches. Tudor (1972) is certainly one of the leading authorities on this subject, and according to him "the question of what constitutes a political myth is surrounded by too much confusion to be capable of a short answer." Noting that "in common usage, the term 'myth' stands for any belief that has no foundation in fact" (p.13), he states: "A myth, I suggest, is an interpretation of what the myth-maker (rightly or wrongly) takes to be hard fact. . . . It remains only to add that there is, from a formal point of view, nothing distinctive about a political myth. . . . What marks a myth as being political is its subject matter" (p. 17). Had Tudor suggested that a myth is whatever the mythmaker *constructs* as a myth, he would have fallen very neatly into the category of strict constructionism, almost in its purest sense. His wording very closely approaches that outlook, but not exactly. Related to political myth is the conceptualization of "politics as a symbolic action" (see Edelman 1971). Although Murray Edelman applies this conceptualization in a different context, the very idea of viewing politics as an activity that has a strong symbolic aspect is quite valid for the Masada mythical narrative. Here it is very clear that a socially constructed myth was used in a political manner and in a highly symbolic fashion, with the aim of preparing a young society for (personal and national) identity formation and action.

Another, crisper approach to political myth was proposed by Friedrich and Brzezinski: "A myth is typically a tale concerned with past events, giving them a special meaning and significance for the present and thereby reinforcing the authority of those who are wielding power in a particular community" (1961:99). This approach seems to fit the Masada mythical narrative like a glove. Furthermore, Friedrich and Brzezinski's emphasis on the idea that myth is used to promote practical purposes supports this conclusion. Political myths may thus be interpreted as myths that are used in and for political processes (e.g., in nation-building processes) and that should be understood within this context.

A Definition of Myth Based on This Research. Nevertheless, it is now my turn to take a shot at the enigmatic and obstinate concept of myth. I will try to develop and present my own approach as it is based on the findings of the present research. From the perspective adopted here, particularly in the previous section, one of the more pressing problems seems to me to be that of creating a distinction between myth and history.

Myth, at the very least, implies something that is "not real": a tale, perhaps a legend; a "story" whose connection to reality is questionable. One of the relevant questions is, of course, *whose* reality? Any empirical study of a myth must answer this question.

So how might we conceptualize a myth within the context of the present study?

A myth is a particular portrayal of a sequence of "events" (real or imaginary) characterized by a number of attributes distinguishing this sequence from a regular historical account:

1. An attitude of sacredness.
2. A high degree of symbolization.

3. A dimension of morality, of an instructive lesson.
4. A frequent demand for action from the listener, either immediately or in the future.
5. A conscious "choice" of specific events and a disregard of others, distinctly different from the historical context.
6. A simple narrative: the moral world is painted simplistically in terms of "good" and "bad."
7. In addition, an impressive site, with an impressive environment, attached to the mythical tale provides a great advantage.

These attributes are what make a mythical tale different from a historical or a historiographical account (at least in the context of this research). Although a mythical "tale" is usually woven out of a historical reality, it is actually very distinct from it.[15] The historical narrative is frequently adjusted and made to fit the moral theme and lesson of the mythical tale so that the myth will appear more credible, consistent, and coherent. Mythical accounts are typically transmitted in an atmosphere that conveys reality and credibility in such a manner (or setting) and by using such props as to induce a willing suspension of disbelief on the part of the receivers. In a sense, mythical tales are aimed at converting and transforming the attitudes and feelings of the receivers (see also Lincoln 1989).

In short, a myth is not meant to report an objective and full truth. A myth is a highly selective sequence of real or imaginary events, constructed in a special and peculiar narrative. It is meant to create attitudes, stir emotions, and help construct particular social realities conducive to the purposes of those transmitting the myth. Hence, there is a tendency to relate mythical tales in specific settings because the atmosphere in which the tale unfolds may have a decisive influence on the listener and on the effective creation of emotions, attitudes, and social constructions of reality. Thus, as Hegy (1991) and others have repeatedly pointed out, myths constitute very central motivating forces in the political, economic, religious, and educational spheres. Myths become particularly important in times of beginnings—for example, in the early stages of a process of the formation of a nation.

Before concluding this section, I must add that our discussion of the Masada mythical narrative indicates that it may also be viewed as a form of what is termed "civil religion" (see, e.g., Liebman and Don-Yehiya 1983). For this, one must accept the validity of the concept of a "civil religion" or, at least, its application in the context of secular rituals, ceremony, and symbolism (see, e.g., Gusfield and Michalowicz 1984). Although an analysis of this approach is not within the scope of the questions raised in this research, future studies might utilize this interesting perspective to conceptualize the Masada mythical narrative.

So far, we have developed a conceptual framework within which we have a set of terms that help us to understand the "past" and "myth," as well as a model within which we can understand *how* this selective sequence of historical events we call the Masada mythical narrative was created.

Myths and Nation Building. The role of myth in processes of nation building is an interesting and important topic. Mythologies were at the symbolic base of nation-building processes of such great empires of the past as Greece and Rome, but not only there.

Smith's important work (1991) incorporates myth into the very definition of the process of nation building (p. 14) and discusses mythology as an essential element of that process. Myths bind people together in a common and integrative belief in a shared past. Thus, myths can play a very important part in shaping personal identities within a process of nation building. Indeed, Ozouf (1988) and Hunt (1988) point out how important for the French Revolution were festivals and rituals, themes very close to myths. Without addressing directly and explicitly the issue of myth, it is not too difficult to interpret much of Anderson's fascinating work (1991) about imagined communities as giving support to the importance of mythologies in the birth of nations.

Both Yael Zerubavel (1980) and Idith Zertal (1994) have noticed that such historical events as Masada, Tel Hai, the Warsaw Ghetto revolt, and the events surrounding the ship *Exodus* (in the summer of 1947) were taken out of their specific historical context and elevated to the level of national myths. As Zertal notes, these myths served as part of a powerful construction of a collective memory in the nation-building process of modern Israel. These myths, notes Zertal, created a new ethos and an identity and image of the "new Jew." In this process, problematic historical events were turned into heroic acts—acts to be looked upon, revered, and imitated.

It is not too difficult to see that there is an interesting convergence at this point between two areas: collective memory and political myth. A social construction of a shared mythical past can certainly serve as a powerfully persuasive ingredient in a process of nation building. Consequently, we should be fully aware of the fact that processes of constructing collective memory are very politicized. Indeed, Portelli's (1991) work provides ample evidence for this observation.

The Masada mythical narrative was an important building block in the symbolic foundation of the modern state of Israel. Generations of young Israeli Jews were socialized into statehood in light of Masada. The Masada mythical narrative helped shape the identity core of hundreds of thousands of young Israelis. In fact, the anger expressed by so many Israelis when they were forced to realize the difference between Josephus Flavius's account and the myth is a powerful testimony to the strength of the need to continue believing in that myth and in the meaning it creates.

The symbolic level in the process of nation building is, simply put, crucial if that process is to be successful. Myths are essential to that symbolization process. As we have seen throughout this book, the Masada mythical narrative serves as a very compelling illustration for this process. Other, similar myths have played analogous roles for other nations and cultures.

Myth Wrecking in Israel

The Masada mythical narrative is not the only myth that has been attacked in recent years. A number of other heroic myths utilized by secular Zionism have also been criticized by some modern scholars.

Zerubavel (1980) has challenged not only the Masada narrative but also the story of Yosef Trumpeldor and Tel Hai (1991a, 1991b). In his own manner, Harkabi (1982) has very critically examined the Bar-Kochva historical (mythical?) narrative, as well as the Great Revolt (1987). Many believe that biblical King Solomon operated copper mines, including mining and smelting (what has become known as "King Solomon's Mines"). Muhly (1987) established that this "historical fact" is nothing but an unsubstantiated myth. Sir Moses Montefiore (1784–1885), a famous British Jewish philanthropist who enjoyed tremendous prestige and helped Jews resettle Eretz Israel, became the focus of two works that questioned his deeds. One of them examined the myth about Montefiore's orange grove in Palestine (Halevi 1976); the other, a more general work, critically examined the man and his deeds, reaching the conclusion that much of what is known about him is factually untrue (Samet 1989). A significant national myth concerning the activity of first-generation Israelis in draining huge malaria-infested swamps was attacked in 1983 by Bar-Gal and Shamai, who stated that although there were swamps, their size was fairly small.[16] Aronoff (1991) has also surveyed quite a number of the myths that were adhered to in the Yishuv and Israel.

What was viewed as "myth-wrecking" activity has caused concern to more than one individual. For example, Tepper (1984) provided a long argument against what he saw as the wrecking of the myths of Tel Hai, Bar-Kochva, the drying of the swamps, and others. His view was that heroic myths are required for a nation.[17]

An interesting and relevant development took place in May of 1992. The May 6 issue of *Haaretz* devoted considerable space (two full pages [pp. 4–5]) to eight discussions concerning the subject of myths, under the title "Myths Do Not Die." Among the topics discussed are the Masada and Tel Hai myths. Of the eight different articles, two are of particular interest. One piece (p. 4) is by journalist Tom Segev, titled "Historian, Do Not Bother." Segev argues that "a myth is not truth. In the worst case, it is a lie that was invented consciously to serve some ideology. In the best case, it is a distortion, perhaps not a conscious one, that reflects an emotional, national, or political need. . . . It portrays the past as bigger than life, frequently in black and white with no gray areas; the good is good and the bad is bad; whoever is not for us is against us." Segev is convinced that all nations cultivate myths, but that as they mature, they can be released from the grip of these myths. Segev implies that those who believe in myths in a fanatic or zealous fashion need a psychiatrist, not a historian.

The other piece, by Avirma Golan (p. 4), is titled "Masada Is Not Our Story." In it, Golan presents the essence of Josephus Flavius's narrative. She points out that, contrary to Zerubavel's (1980) assertion, there never was a consensus about turning Masada into a national symbol, and such major Zionist figures as David Ben-Gurion and Menachem Begin had their reservations. Golan also implies that some Israeli archaeologists (e.g., Yoram Tzafrir and Meir Ben-Dov) have their reservations too. The major thrust of her argument is that Masada does not really fit the Zionist ideology in its essence. Meir Pail, also in *Haaretz* (August 26, 1993, p. 2), stated that the worship of the Masada myth was a big mistake.

Such critical articles about myth wrecking generally and Masada particularly, in what is probably the main forum for the secular Jewish Israeli intelligentsia, are not without significance. They certainly reflect some major reservations (and discontent) of at least a critical part of that intelligentsia with regard to the Masada mythical narrative. This is also the place to note that the message "Masada is not our story" was already echoed in 1983 when Shashar emphatically wrote in *Yediot Ahronot* that it was time to destroy the Masada myth and get rid of the idealization of committing suicide for one's country. In 1985, Shashar repeated his claim but went one step further. He implied there that Josephus cannot be trusted and that the Masada story was a pure invention and an allegory at best.

The myth-wrecking activity in Israel in the last decade is a new, interesting, and important phenomenon indeed (see also *Yediot Ahronot*, November 3, 1994, p. 5). It may be the case that such activity can occur and be published exactly because Israeli society and culture, particularly its intellectual elite, are beginning to look at themselves (and the society in which they live) in a more mature and independent way. In this context, by "mature," I mean that the historical outlook tends to become more complex, giving credit to various nuances and weighing—and being more sensitive to—the various intricacies. This more sensitive, complex view of history is also, by necessity, more critical and much less prone to mythmaking. Thus, what may look like myth-wrecking activity could also be interpreted as an expression of a broader process of social change.

It is interesting to note that there are some people in Israel who seem to want very badly to protect the Masada mythical narrative. A professor of Hebrew literature at the national religious Bar Illan University, Hillel Weiss, defends the Masada mythical narrative at any opportunity he gets—on television and in the printed media (see, e.g., Weiss 1994a and 1994b). He claims that denying the myth by secular Zionist Jews will eventually make it happen, that it will lead to mass suicide in a hopeless war. Weiss suggests what seem to him to be some powerful and alarming contemporary moral and political parallels to the Masada mythical narrative. It is no coincidence that Weiss is very strongly identified with the Israeli political and national religious right. His main 1994b pro-Masada piece was published in *Nekuda*, the journal of the Jewish settlers (In Aza Judea and Samaria or the Occupied West Bank and Aza in a different jargon). There, he accuses that the secular Zionist Jews have basically betrayed what he defines as their cultural heritage. He states that the general process of demythologization, especially about Masada, is a bad and dangerous process from a historical, political, and moral point of view. It is, perhaps, no coincidence that more support in the Masada mythical narrative can be found in that journal (see e.g., Shaskin 1994).

THE MASADA MYTHICAL NARRATIVE AND MORAL ENTREPRENEURSHIP

That the Masada mythical narrative constitutes a bona fide deviance from Josephus Flavius—and a significant one too—is quite obvious. The next question is, how do we conceptualize this particular case of deviance? My suggestion is to view it within the context of moral entrepreneurship, a concept that is well established and developed within the context of the sociological study of deviance.

From the description and analysis provided in previous chapters, it is very clear that the original creation and maintenance of the Masada mythical narrative was initiated by a few moral entrepreneurs in the late 1930s and early 1940s and then carried on by Yadin and others in the early 1960s. There can hardly be any doubt that Shmaria Guttman was the most important of these figures from that early period until the early 1960s, when Yigael Yadin rose to stardom as "Mr. Masada." Certainly, Guttman's active period was much longer than that of Yadin and in many respects more important. However, as Guttman crystallized his moral entrepreneurship, he was not alone and did not act in a vacuum; some additional figures in the background helped him out considerably. In the early 1920s, an excellent translation of Josephus Flavius into Hebrew was published. The translator was an admirer of Josephus Flavius, Dr. Y. N. Simchoni. In 1927, Lamdan published his poem "Masada." In the 1930s, Dr. Yoseph Klosner, a faculty member at Hebrew University, published several documents glorifying Masada. Breslavi's books about Masada also helped. All of these figures were not exactly full moral entrepreneurs in Becker's (1963) sense of the term. However, they all provided a credible background and support to Guttman's moral initiative from both the literary and the scientific fields.

The need of secular Zionist Jews living in the Yishuv (and also after the establishment of the state in 1948) for tales of Jewish heroism explains why this obviously fabricated myth was eagerly embraced by so many. The need for such heroics was so great that Hanoar Haoved Vehalomed went so far as to recommend that a belief in the Masada mythical narrative should be maintained even if the archaeological excavations at Masada were to reveal that Josephus Flavius was wrong.

The Masada mythical narrative has served some very important functions for secular Zionists. This particular group of Jews most certainly felt, during the 1940s and until the mid- to late 1960s, that a symbol of Jewish heroism was badly needed. It is clear that the 1940s were the more important period. By the time that Yadin decided to excavate Masada in the early 1960s, the mythical narrative had pretty much been crystallized and was on the verge of a sharp decline. This conclusion becomes apparent from nearly every interview and relevant document.

What was the situation prevailing during the 1940s in Palestine under the British mandatory rule? The Zionist movement was pushing very hard for Jews to return to their ancient homeland. The ugly and dangerous shadow of Nazi fascism was hanging over Europe. In Palestine, it was clear that the Arabs did not welcome the returning Jews and that an Arab nationalist movement was developing. On top of all this, many Jews, with very little common cultural background (except, that is, Judaism as a religion, and there were differences there too), were arriving in the country. This last factor was magnified tremendously after 1948, when the State of Israel was established and thousands of new immigrants were pouring in. The local Yishuv and its leaders had to deal not only with these differences but also with anti-Semitic stereotypes of Jews (as noncombatants, passive, money exchangers, etc.). Furthermore, the threat and fear of a Nazi invasion during 1940–1942 was ever present.

This threat during the early 1940s and Guttman's moral crusade for the development of the Masada mythical narrative occurred alongside at least two additional conducive factors. The first was the early debate concerning the nature of Zionism. This debate has been charted by Anita Shapira (1992), who contrasts the opposing views on the issue. One such view, expressed by Achad Haam (Asher Tzvi Ginzberg, 1856–1927), was that since the Jews were dispersed from their homeland, they had to depend on their hosts' fair treatment of them and to rely on their own spirituality (that is, on acceptance of Ben-Zakai's choice). An opposing view was expressed by Micha Yoseph Berdyczewski (1865–1921), who pointed out that that attitude bred anti-Semitism. Berdyczewski, in contrast, called for the re-creation of an independent Jewish state. The debate between these two figures went to the very heart of the national character of the Jewish people. During its course, Berdyczewski expressed disagreement with Achad Haam's claim that a major characteristic of the Jewish national morality was its contempt for the use of force and its admiration of spirituality. Berdyczewski renewed old symbols of Jewish heroism. Among his references was a reminder of the Masada narrative as a heroic tale. As Shapira points out (1992:45), it may indeed have been one of the very first references to the Masada narrative by a Jew as a *Jewish heroic tale*. Indeed, Dr. Simchoni, who translated Josephus Flavius into Hebrew, explicitly states, in his introduction to the 1923 first edition (p. 34), that Berdyczewski admired Josephus Flavius and constantly encouraged him to complete the translation. The Berdyczewski–Achad Haam debate echoed the sentiments of many contemporary secular Zionists and preceded both the translation of Josephus Flavius into Hebrew in 1923 and the publication of Lamdan's influential poem "Masada" in 1927.

A second background factor was the presence of another personality who was active during those fateful years in the late 1930s to 1940s: Dr.

Yosef Klosner (1874–1958). Klosner, an historian and literary critic, was one of the prominent figures in the right wing of the Zionist movement. He joined the Hebrew University in 1925 and chaired the Department of Hebrew Literature. His work had a clear focus on the days of the Second Jewish Temple. There can hardly be any question that he *knew* Josephus Flavius's writings very well (chapters 8 [table 8.3] and 9 [table 9.1] include an analysis of his works about Masada). Klosner presented a consistent position throughout his work. He portrayed the Sicarii in a favorable light and helped the mix of Zealots-Sicarii (in the context of Masada) into being. Klosner most certainly viewed the Masada narrative as a heroic one (see his 1937, 1954, and 1963 works).

It is very obvious that during those fateful years there was an urgent need for new, nationalistic Jewish symbols of heroism, and the Masada mythical narrative came into being almost naturally. Because of the tremendous drive of Shmaria Guttman and the exploitation of the site, the Masada mythical narrative was quickly catching on. Guttman first managed to persuade key political and social leaders and then followed this up with two very central youth movements: Hanoar Haoved Vehalomed and Mahanot Haolim. Because the Yishuv was not so big at the time, it was not too difficult, within a relatively short period, to approach whoever it was that needed to be persuaded and to succeed in convincing them. Those exposed to the Masada experience carried the legacy with them into the underground movements, into the Israeli army, and then, later on, into Israeli schools and youth movements. Moreover, the Masada mythical narrative was used—blatantly—to aid the absorption of new immigrants into the newly emerging Israeli culture and to socialize them into the dominant culture (that is, Western) in terms of its symbols. The Masada mythical narrative was constructed, delivered, and believed as an authentic story of supreme heroism in the service of a genuine cause. The narrative emphasized proud Jews fighting for their liberty and land and helped to create and keep a two-thousand-year-old link alive. The physical symbol of this connection was located in a harsh environment that had not changed much since the year 73 A.D. and that provided the narrative with a very powerful element of credibility.

Moreover, during a period in which it was emphasized that the new settlers in Palestine (and later on in Israel) should tour the country as much as possible, Masada became a preferred site. Why Masada? I asked Shmaria Guttman that same question. His response was that Masada indeed provided a heroic story, but he also claimed that there were no other sites available. This is true. There *were* no other appropriate locations at the time. This situation changed as a result of the June 1967 Six-Day War, which facilitated access to many new sites. Moreover, the wars Israel went through in 1948, 1967, and 1973 provided heroic tales of their own. Many of the places associated with these tales were quite easy to reach (e.g., the Western Wall, in Jerusalem) and very gradually the importance of the Masada site and the mythical narrative declined. Furthermore, as Israel became more and more assured of itself as a society, the *need* for the Masada mythical narrative also declined. It *is* a sign of a healthy society that it no longer requires the use of such frightening and horrifying symbols for its self-identity. So at the beginning the need for the Masada mythical narrative clearly existed, and the site of Masada was indeed an excellent instrument for its propagation. But as that need declined, so too did the importance of Masada. In *this* sense and *only* in this sense, Masada may be conceptualized as a case of a positive symbol. It was positive for those individuals who incorporated the Masada mythical narrative into their self-definition of personal and national identity, and it was from the myth that they drew their strength to stand up to some real and utterly horrendous historical challenges.

It is important to remember that until 1948, in addition to Guttman's moral entrepreneurship, there existed solid institutional support from youth movements and, later on, from the Palmach for the perpetuation of the myth. Ideologically, Lehi also supported its promulgation.

Thus, the Masada mythical narrative may be viewed as a positive symbol during the 1940s because it helped a considerable number of Yishuv members to develop a unique personal and national identity. This symbol was accepted, indeed embraced, by some contemporary powerful moral and political leaders as necessary at the time. Though many of the conditions of the early 1940s dissipated with time, the predominant feeling of many Israelis until the mid- and late 1960s was that of a siege mentality. The Masada mythical narrative suited this worldview very well. It was a perspective that emphasized the stand of the few against the many, in a garrison state, armed to the teeth in the midst of a fight for its very survival—against tremendous odds. The memory of the Holocaust, fresh in the 1950s and then revived in the early 1960s by the Jerusalem trial of Adolf Eichmann, strengthened this attitude. However, during the late 1970s (particularly after the peace treaty with Egypt was signed), much of it was already dissipating. The Masada mythical narrative became an ideological burden and could no longer be viewed as a completely positive, problem-free symbol.

Trying to conceptualize "myth" within the framework of "deviance" and "moral entrepreneurship" is an interesting, innovative, and challenging exercise. The only text that I have found that treats myth explicitly as a form of deviance is a fascinating book by Pfuhl (1986). It really should not surprise us to learn that this text treats deviance from the point of view of social constructionism. While discussing the process of mythmaking, Pfuhl is obviously forced into an examination of the issue of moral crusades and crusaders. Why, he asks, should the process of mythmaking initiated by certain moral crusaders be acceptable to the masses? His answer is that

> the crusader's position must appear compatible with others' thoughts, feelings, values, interests, and fears. The morality to be created must be woven into the fabric of the reality already possessed by the crusader's listeners. To achieve this unification, moral entrepreneurs may employ myth. . . .
>   Myths refer to elements within the belief system that people share and in terms of which they explain, interpret, and justify the affairs of everyday life. (1986:79)

Although the examples provided by Pfuhl do not include the Masada mythical narrative, his approach is consistent with the one presented here.

Bronowski (1993) points out that more and more historians are becoming aware of the inherent methodological problems so characteristic of history. Hence, he suggests that the study of memory, rather than history, increases in importance. However, as he points out, memory is much closer to art than to science. Thus, learning about the past through memory (not through history) means giving up on any scientific pretense of socially constructing that past. It also means embracing mythical thinking because one of the major means of memory is indeed myth. If mythical memory is to become a major means of knowing the past—under the justification that it is more faithful, functional, and constructive than dry, factually systematic history—then the use of concepts that have been developed in the area of deviance and moral entrepreneurship will have to be increased (see also Le Goff and Nora 1985; Nora 1993).

THE MASADA MYTH: THE IDENTITY CONTEXT

The moral entrepreneurship mentioned above was directed mostly at young people to help mold a particular type of national identity, a heroic one, to be sure. Although the Masada mythical narrative was not immediately accepted by Jews in Palestine and Israel, eventually it was not only accepted but embraced by both the political and the social elites, as well as the masses. Some words must be devoted to this phenomenon. There is an obvious puzzle here, because the narrative provided by Josephus Flavius is perhaps respectful but is not heroic. To accept the social construction of the Masada mythical narrative, it was necessary either not to have read Josephus Flavius or to have read and simply discounted much of his narrative. Why were people willing to do that?

Providing an answer to this question necessitates the adoption of a functionalist perspective, even in disguise—but I do not wish to disguise it. A basic answer, as Shargel (1979) has suggested, lies in the fact that acceptance of the myth served some very important functions, mostly for the development and crystallization of a new individual and national Jewish, secular Zionist identity. This goal was, no doubt, extremely successful. Direct indications of this are my own anger at discovering that I was lied to and the typical emotional reaction I encountered when I tried to make people aware of the differences between Josephus Flavius's version and what most of them knew as the story of Masada. This emotionally hostile reaction is the best indication of how deeply rooted, to this day, the Masada mythical narrative is in Jewish Israelis' identity maps.[18]

The Masada mythical narrative was created at a time of personal, political, and social turmoil, a period of major social change. Thousands of Jews were returning to what they viewed as their homeland. This return occurred against the background of fiercely growing Arab resistance, pogroms in Europe prior to World War II, the horrific Holocaust, and a general anti-Semitic stereotype of Jews.[19]

Adoption of the second Jewish commonwealth as a period to identify with "makes sense" because it was the last period in which the Jews had their temple and during which a major revolt for political liberty and national sovereignty took place. However, a period of major disaster also marked the destruction of the Second Temple. Furthermore, there still remain some valid questions concerning the political wisdom of that revolt and whether it was at all justified during a period when Rome was at the peak of its military power. The grim and bloody results of the revolt make the adoption of this period as a major symbol for heroism a very problematic issue. The Masada affair is a good reflection of that turbulent period and the problematics involved.

To make this grim and tragic period appear heroic, it was absolutely necessary to introduce major changes into its interpretation. What else is to be expected when the major source of this period is the writings of someone who could easily be viewed as a Jewish traitor and whose own interpretation of the Great Revolt is hardly complimentary?

The answer is exactly that which has been revealed by our research. One begins with a kernel of truth and then builds on it, fabricating the rest to socially construct a myth of heroism.

Using the Masada Mythical Narrative and Problems of Identity

The Masada mythical narrative was used in quite a few areas, especially during the 1930s and 1940s.

Brit Habirionim was a small Jewish group, established by Abba Achimeir, in Palestine of the 1930s. This group was characterized by fascist tendencies and very explicitly adopted the Sicarii as their inspiration. A book of Brit Habirionim is titled *We the Sicarii* and opens with a poem by Uri Zvi Greenberg in which the Sicarii are glorified. The book does not explain who exactly the Sicarii were or what they did.

Lehi, a small prestate underground Jewish organization, drew much of its inspiration from Brit Habirionim, and "Yair," Lehi's legendary leader, chose his pseudonym in honor of the commander of the Sicarii on Masada, Elazar Ben-Yair (see the appendix). The Sicarii thus won popularity during the prestate (1948) days among certain groups. The emphasis was usually placed on their craving for freedom from foreign rule at any cost (including the mass suicide on top of the Masada) and their claims for social justice. Forgotten was their murderous nature, their use of terrorism and political assassination against other Jews, their brutal raid on Ein Gedi, and the fact that the revolt they helped to start ended in a horrendous catastrophe for the Jews.

However, one must also remember that the activities of the Sicarii were much smaller and limited in scope and magnitude when compared to the activities of other similar groups like the Thugs and the Assassins (see, e.g., Rapoport 1984 for a comparison).

Other uses of Masada have been devised in Israel. They include stamps and coins; names of children, ships, streets; bar and bat mitzvahs on top of Masada; pilgrimages and concerts. Masada has thus become an integral part of the modern Jewish Israeli national and individual consciousness.

The basic symbolic idea behind the Masada myth is simple, yet when it is framed within an associative context it becomes complex. It revolves around the idea of proud and self-conscious Jews fighting for their own cultural identity and freedom, in their own land, to the bitter end. It is a narrative of the few against the powerful many, struggling against tremendous odds. It is the story of preference for a liberating and violent death as opposed to a despicable life (most probably in slavery) or, for some, a horrendous death in the Roman arena. The slogan "Masada shall not fall again" (*"Masada lo tipol shenit,"* in Hebrew) can be taken to mean that Jews shall not choose ways that might lead to Masadalike situations and/ or that the idea of fighting at any cost, even in the face of tremendous odds, is preferable. However, the slogan itself reflects the mentality of a besieged nation. Either way, the idea of a glorious death lies behind the Masada myth.

For years the memory of the Sicarii and of Masada was repressed, but the renewal of national Jewish life in Israel sparked an interest in both. Having lived for hundreds of years under foreign rule, far from their homeland, often subjected to virulent anti-Semitic discrimination and persecution, some new Jewish groups most likely derived from memory of the Sicarii a sense of belonging and the conviction that hundreds of years ago, against tremendous odds, Jewish freedom fighters fought and died heroically in Israel. This powerful identification with the Sicarii gave these twentieth-century Jews a vigorous and vital sense of historical continuity and a shared mystical feeling of transcendental integration and resolution. The heroic calamity of Masada only strengthened these feelings. It is thus difficult and improper to downplay the role of the Great Revolt in the collective Jewish consciousness, particularly in the new era beginning around the 1920s–1930s. During this time, in Palestine, the secular Zionist movement was attempting to rebuild a new Jewish culture and society.

Zionism as a pragmatic ideological movement was conceived of and created in the late nineteenth century by *secular* Jews. Its main goal was to advocate an active and militant policy that stipulated that Jews should return to Zion, their natural homeland and the place where they belonged.

The anti-Semitic image of the Jew as it had crystallized in Europe implied that Jews were afraid to fight, exploited their neighbors, and were eternally involved in questionable financial and monetary transactions (in particular by loaning money at high rates of interest). Jews were despised and degraded and described as lazy, mean, and miserable people. Zionism, which emerged against the background of anti-Semitic pogroms and various nationalistic struggles in Europe, was aimed at changing this stereotype in the most radical way. The intention was to create a new type of Jew: one who was willing to fight, was proud, and would work his or her own land. This "experiment" reflected a very sharp historical discontinuity between the cultural milieu of Jews in the Diaspora and the newly emerging Jewish culture in Palestine. The discontinuity denied much of the cultural existence of Jews in the Galut, but it did not deny certain aspects of that existence that seemed to support what was felt to be the new type of Jewish consciousness. For example, acts of heroism were held up as symbols. Moreover, virtually ignoring almost two thousand years of Jewish history, the new resocialization emphasized biblical themes (as if Jewish life in the Diaspora "did not really count") and, in particular, what was considered as the heroic aspect of that biblical past. This in itself provided a sharp discontinuity with Jewish existence in the Diaspora. Jewish scholarship for almost two thousand years was focused on the Talmud. The new secular Zionism focused on the Bible. The Talmud was too reminiscent of a cultural existence with which the new cultural entrepreneurs felt uneasy. It is thus no mere coincidence that David Ben-Gurion's interest and support for biblical studies led to a biblical cult in Israel. Likewise, it is no coincidence that another famous military and political leader, Moshe Dayan, titled his 1978 book *To Live with the Bible*. When the original source was not heroic enough, a new narrative was concocted. The Masada myth fits this pattern well.

Thus, the modern attempt to remold a new type of nationalistic, secular Jew involved some profound social and political changes for Jewish collective life, as well as profound changes in the personal identity and consciousness of Jewish individuals. A major part of this process was to negate and deny the very legitimacy of the "Yehudi galuti," meaning the Jew who lived in the Diaspora. One must hastily add that much of the attempt to create this new Jew was aimed at negating the traditional European anti-Semitic stereotype of the Jew as well.

It is interesting to quote, at this particular point, the words of Zalman Shazar, Israel's president in 1963. Shazar arrived to Masada by helicopter to attend the ceremony inaugurating the second season of the excavations. He said, among other things, that "at this time when we are trying to renew the heroic period of our nation's history, the story of Masada should penetrate into every home in the country" (quoted in Silberman 1993:285).

Masada, the Sicarii, and the Great Revolt all joined together to play a crucial role in this attempt, because Masada was used as both a powerful symbol and an overwhelming physical site in the socialization process of Jewish youth in Palestine and then later on in Israel. Masada was a place that almost every youngster in Israel knew about, and most of them climbed to the top of the ancient fortress. It became a symbol of Jewish heroism and martyrdom. And yet, many of the most unpleasant aspects of the Sicarii deeds and policies were totally repressed in the modern era. In a strange parallel to the acts of the Sicarii, most of the political assassinations committed by the three prestate Jewish underground groups were of other Jews. Most political assassinations were carried out by groups for whom Masada and the Sicarii were very central socialization symbols (see Ben-Yehuda 1993). Moreover, during the late 1980s and early 1990s a mysterious group calling itself Sicarikin appeared in modern Israel. Its anonymous member or members made quite a few threats and even perpetrated more serious acts of violence (e.g., burning the doors of apartments) against Israeli figures who they felt were favoring or sympathetic to the Arab-Palestinian political position regarding the Israeli occupied territories.

It is also interesting to note that the Israeli Mossad assassination unit was named *Metzada*, or Masada (see Hoy and Ostrovsky 1990:34, 117–119).

It is time now to return to the issue brought up at the beginning of this chapter, the dispute within the field of collective memory, and to examine this controversy in light of the conceptualization we have discussed so far.

CONCLUDING DISCUSSION

Combining our discussions of the model developed originally by Allport and Postman with those concerning the nature of the past and myth, we can now look at the Masada mythical narrative in detail and examine this particular socially constructed sequence of "historical" events in light of the analytical debate within collective memory.

To recapitulate, we first must remind ourselves what exactly the nature of the Masada mythical narrative is. First of all, it is a *very* shortened version of the original narrative provided by Josephus Flavius. This mythical narrative typically condenses a very complex account into a few simplified sentences. These sentences project the imagery and create the effect of a heroic tale. This is achieved by the use of words and expressions that explicitly project heroism and by a consistently positive description of the events on Masada.

Collective Memory: The Continuity Perspective

A very salient empirical observation we need to make at the outset is that this research gives clear and strong support to the *continuity* perspective in collective memory. That is to say that despite the fact that the Masada mythical narrative is based on a rather clever social construction, the *basic* historical facts appear in the mythical narrative most of the time.

What then are ingredients of the Masada mythical narrative that are, more or less, faithful to the original narrative? First, that Jewish rebels who took part in the Great Revolt against the Roman Empire found themselves at the end of the rebellion on Masada; second, that the Roman imperial army launched a siege on the mountain to conquer the place and capture the rebels; third, that when the rebels realized that there was no more hope of either winning or holding out against the Roman army, they chose to kill themselves rather than surrender and become wretched slaves. These details can be found in nearly all forms of the mythical narrative, both written and oral. Thus, it is indeed easy to be impressed with the heroism of the rebels on top of Masada. This is, of course, a general account. The various forms of the Masada mythical narrative may contain additional historical facts, such as the number of rebels on top of the doomed fortress or further details concerning the suicide.

An important point needs to be made here: a geographically specific location and archaeological artifacts obviously tend to magnify and support the *continuity* perspective. If a mythical tale can be combined and directly connected to a geographically specific location, the credibility of that tale may be magnified tremendously. Even Halbwachs was fully aware of this possibility as he traveled to the place where this book was written—Jerusalem—to see for himself the social construction of collective memory on site (see Coser 1992:52–53; 193–235). A geographical location gives a tangible and strong sense of continuity between the past and the present. Being able to pinpoint the mythical tale to a specific location is probably one of the most powerful combinations achievable in the social construction of a myth. Moreover, when some archaeological artifacts are to be found in the geographical location, that powerful combination is magnified. Archaeological artifacts can give some mighty support to verbal narratives. Of course, a geographical location coupled with archaeological artifacts limit the more wild imaginary possibilities of mythmaking. Masada is a very good illustration of the creation of a mythical narrative linked very intimately to a specific site. Fortunately for the mythmakers, the location of Masada is in a fantastic landscape that actually helped the creation of the myth. However, it is also quite possible that the fact that Masada *as a site* was accessible, excavated (and later reconstructed), and visited by millions of tourists meant that *some* important aspects of Josephus Flavius's original account had to be preserved. That is, the chance to go wild with some totally fantastic mythical tale about Masada was limited by the very existence of the site.[20] In fact, an interesting hypothesis may be generated by a comparison of historical myths that are attached to geographical and archaeological sites and those that are not, by measuring the "accuracy" of the myths. If the hypothesis holds true, then we should find more elements of *continuity* in myths attached to archaeological sites and less deviation from their related historical narratives.

I would like to make here one observation regarding the commonly used expression "the Masada myth." It is my impression that when people use this expression, the overwhelming majority have one troubling item on their minds—the suicide. People seem to find it difficult to allow themselves to be socialized into an acceptance of suicide. So the expression "myth," in its popular usage in relation to Masada, seems to me to express discontent and deliberation concerning this particular issue.

Thus, in the main, Schwartz's suggestion that the element of continuity must be taken into consideration as an important component of collective memory receives nice solid support and corroboration in this study. Moreover, the historical elements that have remained in the mythical narrative are not marginal; they are very central to the original narrative too. So the preservation of central historical themes may easily be observed in this study. That the past, in this case, has provided solid support for the present is obvious.

Collective Memory: The Discontinuity Perspective

However, the past did not simply provide support on its own. The support was also constructed into the myth. This brings me to the second perspective in collective memory, the *discontinuity* perspective. Might we also say that the Masada mythical narrative was socially constructed in discontinuity with the past? Was the "past" molded in such a way as to answer the needs of the present? Again, Barry Schwartz's observation that this process also occurs and must be taken into consideration has received full empirical support.

An examination of the social construction of the Masada mythical narrative requires us to take a look at the deviations from the original narrative, omissions as well as additions. On the one hand, many "facts" have been left out of the mythical version—elements that, if included, could very easily destroy the foundations of the heroic mythical narrative. On the other hand, additions have been made, either as part of a liberal interpretation or as simple fabrication. After discussing these changes, we will comment on their significance.

The first significant piece of information that is omitted is the fact that the events at Masada were the final act in a failed and disastrous revolt against the Roman empire. The wisdom of that revolt and the questionable way in which it was organized and fought are typically not examined. Generally added to this omission is the fabrication that the rebels on Masada arrived there *after* the destruction of Jerusalem. This is significant since it implies that these "poor heroes," who fought so hard in Jerusalem, were barely able to escape the Roman army but, having succeeded in doing so, then chose to continue the fight elsewhere. Almost completely ignored is the fact that the Sicarii on Masada were forced to leave the city by the other Jews in Jerusalem who had had enough of them and their leader, Menachem. The Sicarii were, in fact, forced to flee Jerusalem *before* the Roman army put a siege on the city. It was at this time that they found refuge on top of Masada.

Second, the true identity and nature of the "rebels" on Masada is not usually revealed. As we have seen, they were Sicarii, and what Josephus Flavius has to say about them is not exactly flattering. They were a group of thieves and assassins who killed and robbed other Jews. Very few accounts of the events mention them or their nature. The terms generally used to describe them, such as "defenders of Masada," "fighters of Masada," and, most frequently, "Zealots," are deliberately deceptive.[21] The last term—following Josephus Flavius—is simply inaccurate.

Third, the raids carried out by the Sicarii at Masada on nearby Jewish (?) villages and the massacre of the settlers at Ein Gedi (which testifies to the nature of the Sicarii as brutal assassins and robbers or terrorists [see Horsley 1979b; Rapoport 1984]) is almost universally ignored.

Fourth, the length of the Roman siege of Masada, most probably between four and eight months, at least in accordance with Josephus Flavius, tends to be ignored. The siege is usually described vaguely as "long," as having "taken years," or as having lasted between one to three (more typical) years.

Fifth, the fact that no battles around Masada are described by Josephus Flavius, as well as the implied possibility that the Sicarii may have been less than enthusiastic about fighting the Roman army, is ignored. On the contrary, many versions of the mythical narrative either imply or state explicitly that those on Masada during the siege fought the Roman tenth legion, carrying out raids on its troops and its war machines. Thus, a real battle is hinted at. However, this is pure fabrication that archaeological excavations have failed to confirm (and have even negated). It is probable that there may have been a fight in the last stage of the siege, when the Romans were actually in the process of breaching the wall, but there was no opposition from the besieged prior to this. Some creative writers have even suggested that Masada was the center of operations against the Romans. This is pure invention.

Sixth, attempts are made to "undo" the suicide either by using expressions that ignore the exact nature of the act, such as "died heroically," or "chose death over slavery," or by emphasizing that they killed each other and not themselves, that is, of course, except for the last person.

Seventh, the hesitation of the rebels to commit suicide and the fact that it took Elazar Ben-Yair *two* speeches to persuade them to do so is typically disregarded. Only one speech, if any, is usually mentioned. This, of course, is much more consistent with a tale of heroism; after all, heroes do not hesitate.

Eighth, Josephus Flavius's report of seven survivors is rarely mentioned, and it is often emphasized that all of those present on Masada committed suicide. Usually the whole matter is ignored; at times, mention is made of "one survivor" (an "old woman") or of "no survivors." Once again, this approach suits the heroic theme much better: heroes do not hide underground cowering in fear for their own survival.

Finally, the choices left open to the rebels on Masada are usually presented as having been limited to two: surrender or death (meaning suicide). Other possible (and glorious) alternatives, such as fighting to the end or concentrating forces in one spot in an attempt to create a diversion that could allow for the escape of many, including the women and children (as suggested by Weiss-Rosmarin), are completely ignored, as is the possibility (albeit less desirable one) of trying to negotiate with the Romans (in fact, such a negotiation did take place at Macherus).

Omission and addition are not the only methods used in the social construction of the mythical narrative. Emphasis has also played an important role. For example, most sources that disseminate the Masada myth present a picture of a small group of rebels against a huge Roman army. Sometimes, even figures are provided: 967 rebels against thousands (10,000–15,000) of Roman soldiers. Although these figures are most probably accurate, their very emphasis tends to reinforce an element that is one of the hallmarks of modern Israeli Jewish identity—the struggle of "the few against the many" (see, e.g., Gertz 1984).

Collective Memory: An Integration

Returning, therefore, to the two perspectives discussed earlier, it is interesting and significant to note that the Masada mythical narrative provides a sense of both *continuity* and *discontinuity* from another angle also. The continuity lies in the obvious attempt to create an identification between the rebels trapped on Masada and the Palestinian/Israeli Jews of this century. The discontinuity, strange as it may seem, is reflected in

Lamdan's line "Masada shall not fall again!" It is embodied in this very strong statement, which expresses the conviction that what happened to the original Masada will *not* happen again.

Moreover, the continuity/discontinuity dichotomy is clearly not anchored in the theoretical problems characteristic of collective memories. The difficulty here emanates *directly* from the very nature of the "past." As we pointed out earlier in this chapter, the main characteristic of history is that it is composed of selected sequences of events. The large number of sequences dictates, obviously, that there will be a discontinuity effect in remembering the past. However, many of these sequences (possibly a majority of them) share certain common elements. Without this commonality, we would have not just different sequences but, rather, altogether different histories. Hence, the continuity/discontinuity problem is characteristic of the way we remember and construct the "past" itself.

Furthermore, this particular conceptualization places the problem of collective memory versus collective forgetting within a different perspective. Collective memory and collective forgetting can be thought of as two ends of the same process—that of selecting historical facts and events. Collective forgetting is thus never complete, because as long as there are groups that remember, a memory can be adopted and revived by other groups as well. Remembering is possible only when a memory is not totally forgotten. If the recollection of a particular event is "erased" from the collective memory altogether, then its retrieval will be virtually impossible. Thus, remembering and forgetting are matters related to two other important variables: the nature of the specific historical sequence selected to be remembered and the competition between different groups over who remembers what. In this study, we can very easily see that Orthodox Judaism chose, by and large, to suppress the memory of Masada. Fortunately or unfortunately, depending on one's point of view, there were other groups that chose to remember Masada. Hence, as secular Zionism was developing, it was able to *revive* the memory of Masada. However, the main figures responsible for this revival also *changed* the original sequence as provided by Josephus Flavius and thus created the Masada mythical narrative.

With this conceptualization in mind, this study has given us the opportunity to examine just how continuity and discontinuity are created in reality, by using the Allport and Postman model.[22] If I want to synthesize and reconstruct the Masada mythical narrative, with its preservation of true facts, its omissions, and its additions, into an ideal type, it might look something like this: "After the destruction of Jerusalem by the Romans, the remaining Zealots escaped to Masada. The Romans put a siege on Masada. The Zealots valiantly fought and raided the Roman positions over a period of three years. However, when they realized that there was no longer any hope of winning and that the choice was either death or wretched slavery, they all chose to kill themselves."

Thus, by preserving *some* elements, by ignoring—in a systematic fashion—the more problematic aspects and by adding liberal interpretations and fabrications, the heroic Masada mythical narrative was formed. However, although this was the primary method of its creation, it was not the only one. The repeated and consistent use of words such as *courage, daring, heroism, bravery, boldness, glory,* and *honor* has undoubtedly colored the narrative. Furthermore, the emphasis on the "last stand" (a la Yigael Yadin) and on a "no choice" situation have created sympathy and helped to transform a painful and colossal defeat into some sort of moral victory.

As Zerubavel points out (1980:67–70; see also her 1994 paper), the Holocaust in Europe provided much impetus and strength to the promulgation of the Masada mythical narrative. As the myth goes, the defenders of Masada had no choice and were locked into a final stand, at which point they chose death. In Europe, the Jews were in fact caught in a diabolically real situation of no choice. Moreover, most were deceived into believing that they were not going to be exterminated. A last-stand fight to the end was, unfortunately, a path chosen by very few European Jews. The comparison, however, was quite valid in many Israeli minds, and in it, the rebels of Masada typically came out in a favorable light. As I have pointed out earlier, I find this comparison totally misleading. First, it is typically made with the Masada mythical narrative and not with Josephus's account. So it is a comparison between a socially constructed image and reality. Second, European Jews were *not* Sicarii, and they did *not* rebel for national independence; they were massacred because they were Jews and for no other reason. Third, those Jews who did stage a final fight (e.g., the Warsaw ghetto revolt) were, in my view, real heroes. No comparison whatsoever to the Sicarii on Masada is called for here.

The fact that the past is not just "given" but is *socially constructed* seems also to constitute an empirically proven fact. There is really no *one,* indisputable "past." The past is indeed an endless collection of selected sequential events that can be molded in various ways. This, of course, does not mean that there are no indisputable facts concerning such a past. However, the context within which these facts are presented and the way in which they are portrayed are crucial determinants (remember how that tour guide in Masada "undid" the suicide?).

So far, we have established, empirically, that Barry Schwartz's proposal that sociological interpretations in collective memory should utilize both the *continuity* and *discontinuity* perspectives together, in an integrative way, is wise, useful, and analytically sound. On the one hand, the Masada mythical narrative provides deceit, manipulation, and fabrication on an impressive scale. On the other hand, some of the main elements of Josephus Flavius's original narrative are still present.

The Masada Myth as a Form of Deviance and Moral Entrepreneurship

That the Masada mythical narrative, as compared to the original account provided by Joseph Flavius, is quite deviant is obvious. What created the myth were modern omissions and additions, inventions and fabrications, on a large scale of the original narrative. This deviant belief system began to emerge and flourish in the late 1920s and lasted well into the 1960s. From the point of view of early Zionism, the moral entrepreneurship leading to this myth was harnessed to help create a new strong individual and national identity and as a political statement affirming the Jewish connection to the land of Israel.

A Few Words about Fabrications

One final matter needs to be pursued here: the issue of fabrication. The findings of this study necessitate asking an important question: When is a distortion on such a large scale that we can comfortably say that only one theoretical approach—that which focuses on fabrication—fits the phenomenon? Or when is a distortion on such a small scale that we can use a different theoretical discourse to interpret the phenomenon (one that would probably use lots of "ifs," "buts," and "howevers")? This problem is not limited to the field of collective memory. A somewhat similar difficulty exists in the sociology and philosophy of science. There, the problem of deciding whether a particular theoretical and/or empirical discovery constitutes a bona fide "revolution" or, instead, a natural "evolution" is not an easy one to solve. Basically, this is an argument between the Kuhnian perception of science and the so-called conservative perception of science.[23] I encountered a similar problem in one of my previous works, concerning the fourteenth-to-seventeenth-century European witch craze (Ben-Yehuda 1980, 1985). There, the question was whether the witch hunt continued older themes or involved a fabrication on such a scale that a totally new concept of "witch" was actually created. In that study, I was persuaded that the "theory" behind the witch craze (the so-called demonology) was a rather complete fabrication. Can we make a similar argument about the Masada mythical narrative?

The real question, I feel, is whether enough *important* elements of the original Masada narrative were manipulated in such a way as to justify the label "fabrication" or, alternatively, whether not enough elements were fabricated, so that such a claim cannot be justified.

On the face of it, it seems that the charge of fabrication is justified. When we examine the main ingredients of Josephus Flavius's narrative about both the Great Revolt and Masada, the issue of heroism does not arise so simply. On the contrary, the narrative conveys a story of doomed revolt, of majestic failure, of massive massacres of Jews, of opposing factions of Jews fighting and killing one another, and, finally, of collective suicide (an act not looked upon favorably in the Jewish faith) by a group of terrorists and assassins. Even the use of the word *fighters* to describe these Sicarii is problematic. No battles or fights are mentioned by Josephus in connection to Masada. Moreover, when Shimon left Masada to join the Jewish rebel forces against the Romans, the Sicarii refused to join him. Reading this story raises the immediate question of how such a horrible story could become a positive symbol. After all, the heroism in the context of the Masada narrative is not at all self-evident. Furthermore, some very major elements in the original narrative were simply discarded because they did not fit a heroic tale, and the heroic tale itself was constructed and presented in such a way that some very important details in Josephus's original narrative were simply twisted beyond recognition, as we have seen earlier. Do these "changes" necessarily lead to the conclusion or decision that the Masada mythical narrative provides more discontinuity (and fabrication) than continuity? It seems that the answer to this question is positive.

Overall, Barry Schwartz's proposal for an analytical integration was confirmed very well in this study. It is just that it seems to me, perhaps to a large extent because of my personal bias on this issue, that if we put the continuity and the discontinuity perspectives on a scale—in the context of this study—we find a tilt towards the discontinuity, or social construction, side of the scale.

Contextual Constructionism

This discussion brings me to the theoretical framework used in this research, that of contextual constructionism. Clearly, Barry Schwartz's suggestion to integrate the continuity and the discontinuity perspectives into the same analysis can be interpreted as a call for the use of contextual constructionism. Such an application means that we can reach an agreement concerning the basic facts of the Masada historical narrative (the *continuity* perspective) and, on this basis, examine the different social constructions of the Masada mythical narrative (the *discontinuity* perspective). In the present research, we have indeed tried to do exactly this.

Chapter Fourteen

Summary and a Personal Note

THIS STUDY WAS occasioned by two puzzles, one personal, the other professional. On the personal level, the curiosity and anger that motivated much of this research effort have been answered. More specifically, the personal question posed in the first chapter of this book shall also be answered at the end of the chapter.

On the professional level, we now know that the Masada myth is a particular selective historically invented sequence (narrative) based, partially, on Josephus Flavius's account, minus some very important details and supplemented by items ranging from a rather liberal interpretation of his writings to sheer fabrication. The way in which this particular sequence was socially constructed can be understood in terms of leveling, sharpening, and assimilation. The Allport and Postman model that was used in this context was very helpful in conceptualizing the process.

In this book, we analyzed the way in which the Masada mythical narrative was socially constructed by Jews in British-occupied Palestine and in the State of Israel. Hence, most of the emphasis was placed on social activities in this region and on texts in the Hebrew language. However, the non-Hebrew-speaking person, in Israel and abroad, has also been exposed to much of the same myth. Two of the more popular books in English—Yadin (1966) and Pearlman (1967)—present a magnificent example of the Masada mythical narrative. The debate in the more academic journals did not reach most interested parties, and the discussion in the popular Jewish press (e.g., in the *Jewish Spectator*) may have only helped to confuse the issue.

The Masada mythical narrative was consciously invented, fabricated, and supported by key moral entrepreneurs and organizations in the Yishuv. At the time, central Jewish leaders (see, e.g., Guttman's interview) were very reluctant to use this rather questionable tale. Much of the success in its acceptance can be attributed to these key moral entrepreneurs and to strong grass-roots support, which was manipulated by these entrepreneurs. After 1948, the existence of this very same Masada mythical narrative was supported by the central Israeli regime, as well as by key political, social, military, and academic figures. This "tale" spoke to contemporaries; it made sense; it explained things; it allowed for meaningful allegories and gave a strong sense of personal and national identity, as well as a feeling of continuity with the past. Moreover, some of these entrepreneurs enjoyed tremendous popularity and prestige as historians and archaeologists (e.g., Guttman, Klosner, Yadin), which made accepting their view rather easy. In addition, the State of Israel lent an institutional support to the maintenance of the myth.

The adoption of the Masada mythical narrative first by a few very central youth movements and later in the regular school curriculum was a cornerstone in the process of making Masada such an important national symbol for secular Zionism. It became a crucial element of socializing young Jewish Zionists into a new national and historical Jewish identity.

> In reality, the Zionist education [in Palestine and Israel] attempted to replace the consciousness of destruction and messianism. [This consciousness] was swinging between longings to the past, future utopian hopes, [and] coping with the present. Zionism tried to transform the major symbol of the destruction, the Wailing Wall, to a new national symbol: Masada. [This new symbol was supposed to be] an expression for a nation that fights for its liberty to the bitter end, because it refuses to accept the option of living in the Diaspora. The assumption was, better death with independence than enslavement. This is the semiotic meaning that turned Masada into a symbol for the youth movements, as well as their place of pilgrimage. [They] and the Hagana's units made [on Masada] their famous swearing-in ceremonies. (Shaked 1993:30)

As Shaked points out, there is a contradiction between a destruction (or holocaust) that can be followed by a Diaspora and a creation of a national mentality of mourning and messianic hope, on the one hand, and an option of a struggle that negates the option of the Diaspora on the other hand. Shaked argues that this contradiction was the central theme that the Zionist movement capitalized on. In this contradiction, Masada plays a central symbolic role. As Shaked indicates, the Diaspora option was viewed with deep contempt by many of the important Zionists who were the main political and ideological figures in the struggle for the creation of the State of Israel, as well as among a whole generation, that of fighters in the 1948 war for independence.

The process of socially constructing the Masada mythical narrative has been conceptualized within the sociological study of collective memory. We used Allport and Postman's social psychological model of leveling, sharpening, and assimilation to explain the very process of how the myth was created.

The Masada mythical narrative was constructed as a central and national symbol of heroism for the new secular Zionist culture that was crystallizing during the nation-building process taking place in Palestine since the 1920s and in the State of Israel after 1948. In Becker's (1986) terminology, the Masada mythical narrative was a central element in what he refers to as the cultural "doing together" of this newly emerging secular Zionist culture. The Masada mythical narrative most certainly played an important role in shaping the national and personal identity of many young Jewish Israelis. For that population, the Masada mythical narrative was definitely considered a positive and heroic symbol. That lesson was most frequently driven into people's minds by using the dramatics of a trek in the Judean desert, a climb to the ancient fortress early in the morning, and participation in an awe-inspiring sight-and-sound show about the Great Revolt and Masada.

The way we conducted this study was to document the original narrative provided by Josephus Flavius, which is the *only* detailed source available concerning Masada. Then we examined in detail how this original narrative was leveled, sharpened, and assimilated into the Masada mythical narrative. We have achieved this by dissecting Josephus Flavius's version into its main ingredients and examining how many of these elements were represented in the mythical narrative and to what degree of accuracy. Furthermore, we also examined the way the Masada topic was utilized in most of the important areas of Israeli culture: excavations, youth movements, the prestate Jewish underground movements, the Israeli army, educational and history textbooks, the media, tourism, and the arts. We could see how, in each of these areas of cultural life, the Masada mythical narrative was created, re-created, and maintained; how a very complex, not always clear narrative was reduced to a short, simplified, and very clear account; and how a narrative about a horrendous failure that culminated in mass destruction and suicide was reconstructed and fabricated into a heroic story.

It is difficult indeed to think that this process was unique to the newly emerging Jewish Zionist culture in Palestine and Israel. Indeed, the *discontinuity* perspective in the sociological area of collective memory has enough documentation to show the universality of this process. Nevertheless, the *continuity* perspective also received an impressive confirmation in this study. Therefore, the universal generalization that seems to emerge from this study, in accordance with Barry Schwartz's novel suggestion, is that the social process of collective memory is composed of two complementary processes: that of preservation and that of invention and fabrication. Judging from the results of this study and a few others (e.g., Ben-Yehuda 1980; Lofaro and Cummings 1989), it may be that the balance tips toward the *discontinuity* perspective, that is, toward the invention/fabrication side. In this way, we not only placed our study squarely within the field of collective memory; we also used this occasion to help ourselves examine a major controversy in that area and to see that Barry Schwartz's suggestion for solving this controversy is indeed a fruitful and valid one.

Moreover, since 1985, I have been involved in an ongoing attempt to demonstrate that the sociological conceptualization of deviance should be expanded and reframed within mainstream sociology. I have argued that the sociological conceptualization of deviance must consider total social structures and/or processes by examining behavioral patterns referred to as deviance as a relative phenomenon and as part of larger social processes of change and stability in the realm of boundaries of symbolic-moral universes (Ben-Yehuda 1990:5). In a major way, this study most certainly continues that attempt and should be viewed as another link in a chain. It provides us with a golden opportunity of doing a cultural study that examines a very central societal belief system, in the form of a vital myth, within the context of conceptualizing this particular myth also as a unique form of deviance.

As promised in the first chapters of this book, it has been structured according to a "natural history" approach, paying full attention to contextual constructionism. We gave the basic empirical information, and we examined the deviations from that information as they were made by the social constructionists of the Masada mythical narrative.

A PERSONAL NOTE

I began this book with an explanation of how and why I had become involved in this project in the first place. That explanation had to do with the feeling of having been deceived about a very major issue. Eight years later, with the entire study behind me, what now is my personal feeling about the Masada mythical narrative?

The first, most important feeling is that I have solved the puzzle of the myth. I now know how, why, and by whom it was created, and I also know how it has lost its prominent position. In terms of my professional identity as a sociologist, I am satisfied.

As a Jewish Israeli, I find the experience more difficult to summarize. Much of the original anger and resentment are still there. This resentment is reflected, rather frequently, by other Israelis with whom I discuss the subject. Whenever I talk with a friend or acquaintance and am asked what my research is about and I reply "Masada," I am asked to explain. I usually respond with a question and inquire of the person asking what he or she knows about Masada. In the overwhelming number of cases (and I have gone through this ritual countless times), the person will repeat the myth. After all, this is what they have been taught and all they know. This, of course, is an intellectual trap I have set. In response to the version of the mythical narrative they have related, I provide them with Josephus's account, and then it is easier for me to explain my research. Time after time, these people are drawn into the conversation, which usually elicits expressions ranging from mild disbelief to (much more frequently) anger and open hostility. My worst encounters have typically been with history teachers. In one case, a particular teacher avoided me for a number of months following a Masada conversation. This angry reaction, very similar to my own 1987 response, saddens me. As much as I was disturbed in 1987, now I experience feelings of remorse. Obviously, the realization that a major element of one's personal and national identity was based on a biased and falsified myth is not an easy thing to deal with. The strong emotions evinced (from some of our interviewees as well) have demonstrated to me that my original reaction to the discovery of the myth was not unique. It is sad, even more so because, while one can easily see how and why there was a need for the myth between the 1940s and the 1960s, it is quite evident that it is really no longer required in the Israel of today.

This emotional reaction raised another question. At this point I began to ask myself, Why is "truth" so "dangerous" for a myth? Why is there a "need" for unrealistic, fabricated myths?

In the case of the Masada mythical narrative, the "truth" is very obvious and easy to find. It is right there in Josephus Flavius's writings, for whoever wants to bother to read it. It is unpleasant, of course, but it is there. Still, why do people prefer the fabricated myth? It is "better" in the sense that it has a conclusion that Josephus Flavius's version does not provide—the mythical narrative is dressed in an immense and awesome cloak of heroism and is tailored to the cultural needs of the Yishuv and, later on, of the state. In this sense, the Masada mythical narrative is seductive. It contains a positive message that is easy to understand. But why are people so eager to embrace this fabrication? Because we like fairy tales? The more I thought about it, the more enigmatic it became. Of course, people, nations, tribes, and groups all nourish myths. This much we know as an empirical fact. Such selective and biased historical sequences are loved, a fact that must have something to do with human consciousness and social settings.

As I have shown elsewhere, "institutional conceptualizations" of morality are easily embraced by masses, given conditions of uncertainty and the need to search for answers (e.g., see 1980, 1985, 1986). The ascendance of myths of heroism must also characterize periods when the collective celebrates its dominance—in other words, when enough moral entrepreneurs have the power to impose their perception of morality on an entire culture. The creation of myths under these conditions requires altruistic behavior and sacrifice on the part of the collective (as defined by those in power). This hypothesis implies that such heroic "myths" will rise to ascendance whenever there is a lack of attention to individual human rights and to humanity itself. If true, this formulation leads to an interesting paradox. People are told that they want "freedom" (a very subjective term), and so an organized "institutional" perception about the nature of that freedom may arise. This perception, however, will typically deprive those believing in it and acting on its behalf of their freedom in the most basic way. The Masada mythical narrative implies, for example, that national, personal, and religious freedom may require suicide. If so, what exactly *is* the meaning of freedom? Thus, in answer to the previous query, it may be that "truth" and "myth" are actually antagonistic, because a myth is always collective and truth is always individualistic. Thus, truth means freedom, whereas myth means deception, and the liberating power of a heroic myth is really a fallacy, whereas the true liberation may lie in the opposite direction.

Moreover, my own anger, as well as that of others, was used in this work as a social indicator—that is, as one of the best measures for demonstrating the nature and type of emotional reaction evinced by a realization that a major element of one's national and social identity is based on a very biased and falsified mythical narrative.

With the understanding of and solution to the Masada puzzle came the reconciliation and comfort involved in knowing why something, difficult as it is to accept, is the way it is. I am much more calm today about Masada than I was in 1987. I know, understand, and even sympathize with the moral entrepreneurs who made Masada into the myth it has become.

I still very strongly feel that Masada is one of the most impressive sites one may visit. I would encourage any reader of this book, given the opportunity, to visit the place. Every moment there is well spent. I also know the Masada mythical narrative for what it really is: a heroic myth that actually contains very little heroics; a doomed and failed revolt; the destruction of the Jewish Second Temple and Jerusalem; the massacre of a large number of Jews; a group of Sicarii who killed other Jews and escaped to Masada; the massacre in Ein Gedi; the lack of battles around Masada; and finally a collective suicide (instead of a brave fight to the end). These are not events for Jews to be very proud of.

Ideologically, the original Masada narrative should be told. There is a bitter lesson in that narrative. The slogan "Masada shall not fall again" has for me a meaning very similar to that given to it by many people today. It means "take another look at the whole story. Be careful not to become cornered like that again." The lesson is *not* that Masada shall not fall again, because once a Masada situation is created, the Masada end may not be far behind. The real historical wisdom is not to even reach a Masada situation.

Appendix

Notes

Bibliography

Index

Appendix

Main Jewish Underground
Groups in Palestine, 1920–1948

Zionism as a pragmatic ideological movement was conceived of and created in the late nineteenth century by secular Jews as a reaction to traditional and virulent European anti-Semitism. Zionism's main goal was to advocate an active and militant policy that Jews should return to Zion, their homeland and natural place.

Since the sixteenth century, Palestine had been part of the Ottoman Empire. The first Zionist immigration wave to Palestine occurred between 1882 and 1903. It was based on settling Jews in small agricultural communities. More immigration followed, as did the crystallization of the Zionist movement in Europe and the establishment of a Zionist political lobby, which eventually directed itself toward helping to establish a new Jewish state.

When World War I began, the Jewish population in Palestine consisted of approximately eighty-five thousand people, of whom only twelve thousand lived in rural villages. The British army, commanded by General Allenby, defeated the Turkish army and conquered Palestine. Jerusalem itself surrendered in December of 1917, and the British ruled Palestine until 1948.

The Zionist effort began to crystallize under the Turkish occupation; the fight for Jewish independence, culminating in the establishment of the State of Israel in 1948, took place under the British occupation. Hashomer was one of the first Jewish defense organizations that was established during the Turkish occupation, and it operated mostly in the northern part of the country. It was dissolved in the early 1920s with the establishment of the Hagana.

The main conflicts during the British occupation involved several issues. A major conflict developed with the British. Another struggle developed with the Palestinian Arab national movement, which was also undergoing its own process of crystallization. In addition, major struggles occurred between different factions within the Jewish community in Palestine. There was conflict between the older and more established Jews and the new immigrants; between left and right (socialists vs. capitalists); between more and less militant groups. During this period, three rival major Jewish underground groups emerged: the Hagana (in 1921), Etzel (also known as the Irgun, in 1931) and Lehi (also known as the Stern Gang, in

1940). The goal of all three groups was the establishment of a new Jewish State. However, they were divided as to the appropriate strategy for achieving this goal. The intensity of the struggle between these groups sometimes reached dangerous proportions, but at other times they cooperated. All three groups used military and guerrilla tactics against the Arabs, the British, and one another.

In 1948, the British left Palestine, and the bloodiest war in the history of the newly established Jewish state began between the Jews and the Arabs. That war ended with the formal establishment of Israel as a sovereign and independent state.

THE HAGANA

The largest and most influential prestate Jewish underground group was the Hagana (meaning "defense"). Unlike the other prestate underground groups, the Hagana was the operational arm of a political organization, the Jewish Agency,[1] and was used and controlled by that organization. The Hagana was a big and complex organization with many diversified units. Many books have been written on the history of the Hagana. The reader is referred to S.T.H.; M. Cohen 1981; Pail 1979. For a short review, see Rabinov 1969. I shall provide here a *very* brief sketch of the Hagana, based on Rabinov 1969; the more curious reader is urged to read the eight volumes of S.T.H., the history of the Hagana.

Generally speaking, the history of the Hagana parallels the history of the renewed Jewish settlement in Palestine. In the early days of the settlement (as well as from lessons learned in Europe), the need for a Jewish defense organization became evident. Bar Giora, Hashomer, and the "Hakibbutz" were such primary organizations. The beginning of the Hagana can be traced to 1919–1921. After the Arab attacks on Jews in Palestine in May of 1921, the social kernel for the Hagana crystallized. The Hagana drew its membership from large groups of politically left-oriented Jews in Palestine and was intimately associated with the labor union, the Histadrut. The first commanding committee of the Hagana was created in 1921.

The Arab attacks on Jews in 1929 caught the Hagana (as well as the British Army) by surprise. Ex-members of Hashomer (a Jewish defense organization that no longer existed in 1929) helped the Hagana in attempts to cope with the Arab attacks. The defense concept that evolved emphasized a *national* (not local) basis of organization. The Jewish Agency decided to take responsibility for the Hagana.

In the 1930s, the Hagana experienced a severe crisis: some of its old and most experienced commanders refused to accept the moral and military authority of the Jewish Agency. Consequently, a few of these commanders were asked to leave their command posts. The situation was more severe in Jerusalem, where a group headed by Avraham Tehomey (and others) split from the Hagana and created another organization (Hagana, or Irgun Beit), which later became the Etzel.

In the early 1930s, the Hagana created the National Command (*Mifkada*

Artzit). In those years, the Hagana emerged and crystallized as a national organization. It began to provide military courses for its recruits, purchase weapons, and establish a modest basis for a military industry, as well as building the foundations of departments of medicine, law, and intelligence and participating in attempts to help bring Jewish immigrants to Palestine (Aliya).

When Arab attacks on the Yishuv (Jewish community in Palestine) were renewed again in 1936, the Hagana was more prepared. It gradually moved from a local, static defense to a dynamic, more aggressive defense based on strike forces. In 1937, strike forces were created (Posh—*Pelugot Sadeh*), and in 1939, they were replaced by other units. In 1938, a British officer, Charles Orde Wingate, helped to create, train, and lead carefully selected strike force units that specialized in night assaults. During those years, the Hagana participated in a massive effort to create new Jewish settlements.

The events of the late 1930s helped the Hagana to reorganize and create a vital organization, as well as to establish new patterns of defense and assault.

The year 1939 witnessed the nomination of the first head of the Hagana's National Command, Yohanan Rattner, and the establishment of the Matcal, the general military command of the Hagana (this name is still used today to refer to the Israeli's army headquarters). Yaacov Dori was nominated as the first chief of staff.

The Hagana began to use its newly established and organized military power from 1938 to 1939. It created a special strike force, the Pum (*Peulot Meyuchadot,* meaning "special action"), in 1939, to act against Arab terrorism and against the British occupation forces.

The basic policy of the Jewish leadership during World War II was not to interfere with the British war effort, which was aimed at crushing the Nazis. The Jewish Agency pressed the British authorities to create a Jewish Brigade. The idea was to help create a partnership with the British so that after the war, the British government would help to establish a Jewish state. The British, however, tried to dismantle the Hagana. They were not very successful. Clearly, the British authorities suspected that the military experience gained by Jews in combat in a special brigade might later be channeled into the Jewish struggle for statehood. These suspicions were not baseless.

Changes in British personnel, as well as the bad situation of the British Army in North Africa in 1941, helped to create better relations between the Hagana and the British authorities. On May 19, 1941, the Hagana created the Palmach (*Pelugot Machatz,* meaning "shock or storm troops"). It consisted of a brigade of strike and assault units. Contrary to other units of the Hagana that were mobilized on demand, the Palmach was the Hagana's only military structure that was mobilized all the time. The British military felt that the Palmach was a very reliable force and used it in some combat during 1941–1942. The British victory at El Alamein, in November of 1942, ended this period of cooperation, and the Palmach went underground. The British Army eventually established a Jewish Brigade within the British Army in 1944.

As World War II was coming to an end, there were increasing signs of an anti-Zionist British policy (e.g., fierce objection to the mass immigration of Jews to Palestine). Consequently, the Hagana and the Palmach turned more and more to actions against the British. Thus, the British Army tried, on June 29, 1948 ("Black Saturday"), to disarm the Hagana and the Palmach by force. That attempt was not successful, although thousands of members were arrested.

The Palmach, by now a legend itself, grew into a very strong military organization. When the State of Israel was established in 1948, the Palmach's brigades carried most of the weight of the bloody defense against the attack by Israel's Arab neighbors in what became known as the Israeli War of Independence. The Hagana contributed between forty thousand and sixty thousand soldiers to the newly established Israeli army.

ETZEL: IRGUN TZVAI LEUMI (National Military Organization)

The basic aim of the Zionist movement was the re-creation of a Jewish state. Theodore Herzl, the founding father of Zionism, expressed this goal very forcefully in Basel, Switzerland, in 1897, when the first Zionist Congress convened.

Beginning in 1925, Zeev Jabotinski headed the opposition to the established, left-wing Zionist movement. This opposition demanded a revision in the Zionist movement's means and goals, while it shared the idea that Jews should re-create their own state. The main demands for a "revision" focused on a much more aggressive, determined, and dynamic policy, as well as on emphasizing an aggressive orientation. The contradiction and friction between this opposition and the main body of the Zionist movement grew till a real faction began to gain momentum in 1931, culminating in the 1935 elections. At that time, a new right-wing Zionist organization was created (Niv, vol. 1; S.T.H., vol. 2, part 1, pp. 488–99).

In 1931, a group with fascist inclinations calling itself "Brit Habirionim," led by Abba Achimeir, was created. The group was eventually dissolved in 1933 after some of its key members were arrested by the British and the remainder stigmatized by the Hagana. It was charged that this group was involved in the assassination of a major Jewish political leader, Haim Arlosoroff, in 1933.

In the spring of 1931, Avraham Tehomey and a few others, who felt totally dissatisfied with and alienated from the Hagana, broke away and created an independent defense organization in Jerusalem (Irgun Beit). This was the actual beginning of Etzel, which, in contrast to the left-wing Hagana, was a right-wing, active defense group affiliated with the revisionist faction. The initial group consisted of around three hundred members and had branches in Jerusalem and other locations. Such figures as David Raziel, Abraham Stern, and Avraham Tehomey were very active in this group.[2]

Following the Arab riots of 1936, the Etzel was once again divided. Against the background of a deep ideological controversy, about half its members (around 1500), together with Tehomey, reunited with the Hagana in April 1937, while the other half, led mostly by Abraham Stern, David Raziel, and Moshe Rosenberg, emerged as the new Etzel. Robert Bitker became the first commander of this group but was asked to leave his command in October of 1937 and was replaced by Moshe Rosenberg. Etzel in 1937 was no larger than two thousand members.[3] Rosenberg quit his position on May 28, 1938,[4] and David Raziel became the commander of the Etzel.

In May of 1939, David Raziel was arrested by the British (Niv, 2:235), and Hanoch Kalai became the temporary commander of Etzel (ibid., p. 736). On September 1, 1939, the five high commanders of Etzel were arrested by the British. As the Second World War began, Raziel and Jabotinski decided that Etzel would not oppose the British regime anymore but would instead join their efforts to fight Nazi Germany. This policy was rejected by Abraham Stern and others. On June 19, 1940, after most of Etzel's commanders, including Stern, were released from British jail (on June 18, 1940), there was a meeting in Tel Aviv (Yevin 1986:187) in which severe and harsh accusations were directed at Raziel. Subsequently, he resigned.

Jabotinski did not accept Raziel's resignation but renominated him as commander (July 17, 1940). Abraham Stern did not accept this decision and continued to crystallize a group of members around him. Stern was elected commander (Niv, 3:43) of Etzel on June 19, 1949. As can be seen, Jabotinsky's instructions did not make much difference, for Etzel was in a real crisis. The crisis was ideological and was not only a clash between different personalities and temperaments.

Stern's group basically rejected Jabotinski's and Raziel's position that cooperation with the British was required and that a lowering of the level of guerrilla warfare was necessary as long as British were fighting the Nazis. Stern's group was composed of members who wanted to continue the fight against the British on an active basis. It appears that this particular group may have been somewhat inclined toward possible limited cooperation with the Italians (Yevin 201–13).

On June 26, 1940, Stern initiated the publication of a document (no. 112) that stated that Etzel would not cooperate with the British and that encouraged Jews to evade the draft to the British army.[5] This document endorsed an active and aggressive approach, in contrast to what it portrayed as the passivity of the Hagana. Stern's group wanted to end the connections with British intelligence, disconnect from the leaders of the revisionist movement, and renew the struggle against the British (Lankin 1980:52–54; Yellin-Mor 1974:57–70; Yevin 1986).

Jabotinski died on August 3, 1940, but his death did not end the controversy. In the same month (August 14, Bauer 1966:112), Stern and his group left Etzel (a process that actually had begun already in March of 1940) to establish Lehi.

This crisis was painful for both Etzel and Lehi and continued to serve as a seedbed for animosity. Yevin (1986:106) states that Etzel had around two thousand members after the split in the summer of 1940.

Etzel reorganized and regrouped under the renewed leadership of Raziel. In 1941, a pro-Nazi revolution began in Iraq. Haj Amin Al-Husseini, the Arab mufti was actively involved in it. The British asked Etzel to help them deal with this problem, and Raziel and a few others volunteered to go east. There Raziel died during an air raid on May 20, 1941.[6] After his death, Etzel was under the command of a group of Etzel's commanders, led by Yaacov Meridor.

During 1941–1943, Etzel was in a very problematic state, socially, politically, and operationally attempting to redefine itself. As part of this reorganization, on December 1, 1943, Meridor quit his position, admitting that "nothing of significance was achieved in the last two years"; on January 1, 1944, Menachem Begin was appointed as the last commander-in-chief of Etzel (S.T.H. vol. 3, part 1, p. 493).

Under Begin's leadership, Etzel entered a period of renewed activity. Operations were carried out against British and Arab targets (ibid., 520–43; Livni 1987; Niv, vols. 3–6). During 1945–1946, Etzel enjoyed a membership of about two thousand members. During 1945–1947 more activities followed (see also, e.g., Begin 1950; Meridor 1950). When the Israeli Army (IDF) was created in 1948 and the Lehi, Hagana, and Etzel basically ended their separate and independent existences, Etzel had between three thousand and five thousand members to contribute to the new force. Amongst these troops, about three thousand were actual fully trained soldiers.[7] After 1948 Menachem Begin formed a political party, Herut, and developed a long political career. This career came to a peak when Begin served as Israel's prime minister in 1977–1983.

LEHI: LOHAMEI HERUT ISRAEL ("Fighters for the Freedom of Israel")

In August of 1940, the split of Stern's group from Etzel was final. Stern's group saw itself as a continuation of Etzel and even called itself "Etzel in Israel." Its explicit goal was to be the main faction that would politically control Palestine by force of weapons, in the name of the "fighting Jews." In September of 1940, Abraham Stern changed the name of the group to Lehi (Yevin 1986:210).

In September of 1940, Stern published Lehi's first announcement (Yevin 1986:315), and in November of 1940, the movement's "principles" (Yevin 1986: 316). Both documents clearly delineate the symbolic-moral universe and boundaries of Stern's Lehi. The documents are saturated with mystical statements regarding the divine nature of the people of Israel and their divine right to their land, based totally on biblical sources, even to the point of advocating the building of a third Jewish Temple. Stern changed his name to AVI—Abraham Ben Yair. He explained his choice of this particular name as a symbol that continued the tradition of the Sicarii. Stern's new name was a tribute to the last commander of the Sicarii on top of the doomed fortress of Masada, Elazar Ben-Yair. Stern very quickly became identified as "Yair."

In the summer of 1940, following the split from Etzel, Yair found himself commanding a very devoted, talented, and dedicated group of zealots, including some of the best, most qualified and experienced commanders of Etzel. On September

16, 1940, Lehi committed a most successful bank robbery in Bank APAK (Anglo-Palestine Bank) on Ben-Yehuda Street in Tel Aviv. As a result of this robbery, Lehi acquired a very large amount of money, which gave the young organization a decent start as an underground revolutionary movement.[8]

In comparison to the Hagana and Etzel, Lehi always remained a much smaller organization. It was estimated that in 1946, the Hagana comprised about eighty thousand members; Etzel, about one thousand active members (plus around four thousand in the reserves); and Lehi, around two hundred members (Avidar 1970:232).

In the early 1940s, the attrition rate from Lehi was apparently very high. Many felt that the split of Etzel into two organizations was useless, and many of its members were unemployed and had to find jobs; hence, they could not devote their time to Lehi. Moreover, the atmosphere of mutual suspicion became unbearable (Yevin 1986:215). Yair was apparently not very effective in closing his ranks and keeping his initial advantage. Lehi began to transform itself into a small, unique type of organization, almost a sect.

One of Yair's main efforts was ideological. He tried to make the symbolic-moral boundaries of Lehi distinct. He met (probably in 1941) with Abba Achimeir, who, in 1933, had led the semifascist and defunct "Brit Habirionim" (Yevin 1986:253). He also met with Israel Eldad-Sheib, who later became Lehi's ideologist, and with Uriel Shelach, who was then a bubbling and stormy Israeli poet. He had first met Shelach at Hebrew University, where they studied together. Shelach was on his way to developing a unique moral perception and a symbolic-moral universe that was supposed to help a new type of Jew into being. Shelach's followers later became known as the "Canaanites." Shelach helped to draft some of Etzel's and Yair's publications (Yevin 1986:98–99, 106). He was also involved in some of the ideological debates between contemporary leaders of Etzel (ibid., 209–10). After Yair was killed, Shelach wrote a powerful poem in his memory (see, e.g., Yevin 1986:7–8).

Between 1940 and 1942, Lehi, under the leadership of Stern, committed quite a number of anti-British and other (urban) guerrilla activities ("terrorism" in a less sympathetic language), including robberies and acts of personal terrorism. Lehi did not accept the idea that the raging Second World War called for temporary cooperation with the British occupation army. Its core ideology was focused on a relentless struggle with the British, with the spice of mysticism and elements of messianism. Lehi explicitly wanted to chase the British out of Palestine and reestablish a Jewish state, the sooner the better.

Lehi at this time was a small group, not popular with the British, the Hagana, or Etzel. Consequently, its members were persecuted. When British intelligence discovered Stern's hiding place, on February 12, 1942, a British officer named Morton shot him to death. At the time of Stern's death, most of Lehi's members were already in prison, and the movement was in an advanced state of disintegration.

In September of 1942, Yitzhak Yazernitzki-Shamir and Eliahu Giladi escaped from the British detention camp in Mazra and, together with Yehoshua Cohen, Anshell Shpillman, and others, re-formed Lehi. After the assassination of Giladi, in the summer of 1943 (see Ben-Yehuda 1993:178–85), a collective leadership for Lehi began to emerge. The group was headed by Shamir, Eldad-Sheib, and Nathan Yellin-Mor (after his escape from the British detention camp in Latrun on November 1, 1943). Sheib was arrested by the British in April 1944, and in July 1946, Shamir too was arrested. Hence, the period of time when the three actually led Lehi together was short, and command responsibility fell mostly on the shoulders of Shamir and Yellin-Mor.

Shamir and Yellin-Mor understood quite well that it would be impossible for Lehi to behave as it had while under Stern's leadership. They realized the need for popular and widespread support, and they acted in that direction. Hence, from the autumn of 1942 until 1944, Lehi carried out many acts, focusing again on personal terrorism. A turning point was the November 6, 1944, assassination of Baron Walter Moyne (see Ben-Yehuda 1993:206–11). As a result, the crackdown on Lehi once again began, and the organization was forced to tone down some of its activities.

Between the autumn of 1945 and September 1946, all three underground Jewish groups in Palestine cooperated in the struggle against the British. This cooperation collapsed in September 1946, and Lehi continued its own independent activities.

When the State of Israel was established in 1948, Lehi accepted the authority of the new state, and it formally disbanded on May 29, 1948, contributing eight hundred members to the Israeli Army.

After Lehi formally ceased to exist, some of its members continued their subversive activities. The assassination of Count Folke Bernadotte in Jerusalem on September 17, 1948 (see Ben-Yehuda 1993:267–74), is one example. This assassination roused such a severe reaction from the new Israeli government that actions were taken that put an end to the existence of even the more militant remnants of Lehi.[9]

In the 1950s, some militant groups continued to exist, and political assassinations were carried out by former members of Lehi, including the assassination attempts against David Zvi Pinkas (in Tel Aviv on the night between June 21 and June 22, 1952; see Ben-Yehuda 1993:276–78) and Dr. Rudolf Kasztner (in Tel Aviv on March 2, 1957; see Ben-Yehuda 1993:278–84). The last case of assassination certainly gained much support and legitimization from Sheib, who continued to harbor and maintain his right-wing ideology.

Lehi tried to establish a political party after 1948, but the attempt failed. Shamir began a late and very successful political career; in 1970, he joined the Herut party and became a parliament member for Gahal (Begin's party) in 1973. In 1977, he was elected as the chairman of the Knesset. In 1980, Shamir was appointed minister of foreign affairs. He became Israel's prime minister from October 1983 until September 1984 and then again from October 1986 until June 1992.

Notes

CHAPTER ONE. INTRODUCTION: THE RESEARCH PUZZLE

1. Following that paper, both Dan Ben-Amos (pp. 76–78) and Don Handelman (pp. 78–79) provide short and critical responses. For another analysis using the concept of Dialogic Narrative (as used by Bruner and Gorfain), this time concerning Israeli settlements, see Katriel and Shenhar 1990.

2. I am only using his works that were translated into Hebrew. Apparently, he wrote much in French about exactly this problem. However, because of problems in accessibility, I could not use these French writings.

3. For more about this see Ben-Yehuda 1983; Best 1989, 1990; Goode 1989; Rafter 1990; Jenkins 1992:1–3; Goode and Ben-Yehuda 1994.

4. Unless there is an empirically substantiated claim that Josephus Flavius's work is fatally flawed or totally fabricated, a claim not made so far. However, even if such a credible claim is being made, it is irrelevant for this study. The reason is that when the Masada mythical narrative was created and used, at least until 1992, no such claim was made, and the creation, maintenance, and decline of the Masada mythical narrative had absolutely nothing to do with such an unmade claim.

CHAPTER TWO. THE HISTORICAL EVENTS OF MASADA

1. E.g., see Kasher 1983; Avi-Yonah and Beres 1983; Stern 1984; Horsley and Hanson 1985:118–127, 190–243.

2. For short biographical sketches of Josephus Flavius, the man, his deeds, and his writings, see *Encyclopedia Judaica*, 1971, vol. 10, pp. 251–264, and the *Jewish Encyclopedia*, vol. 8. For more on Josephus's writings, see Aberbach 1985; Feldman 1984; Flusser 1985; Horsley 1979a; Rajak 1983; Rapoport 1982; Stern 1987; Stone 1984; Thackeray 1968. There have been literally thousands of works about Josephus Flavius, and it is impossible for this study to delve into all of them. As we shall see later, the issue is not the accuracy of Josephus Flavius but rather how his work was remolded. Nevertheless, the curious reader is referred to Feldman's summarizing works from 1984 (about 1000 pages) and 1986 (about 700 pages).

3. However, and for the sake of fairness, let us note some of the possible inaccuracies in Josephus's account. There are seven more tangible and fact-related issues with which, on the face of it, Josephus may have a credibility problem regarding Masada (see also Feldman 1984:772–789). It is important to note that none of these issues, to the best of my knowledge, affected, in any meaningful way, the development of the Masada mythical narrative.

The first issue concerns Elazar Ben-Yair's speeches. This is a commonly attacked item. Josephus Flavius was probably not even near Masada when the fortress fell, and the tape recorder was not invented until about 1800 years later. How does he *know* what Elazar Ben-Yair said? There are two answers to this puzzle. First, two women survivors were the direct source for the speeches. Second, Josephus Flavius must have been an intimate acquaintance of the Jewish parties in the Great Revolt. He had been the commander of the Galilee, and he must have known many (or all) of the leaders personally. He could easily have guessed what they *might* have said under such difficult circumstances. However, the issue of the speeches returns every time anew to haunt his credibility.

The second issue is the color of Masada's casemate wall. Josephus states that the wall "was composed of white stone" (book 6, chapter 8, p. 599). In fact, Yadin's excavations disclosed that it was composed of "hard dolomite stone which was quarried on Masada" (Yadin 1966:141). It is possible that for an outside observer the wall appeared white because it was covered with a white plaster (ibid.).

The third issue is the height of Masada's casemate wall. According to Josephus it was six meters high (book 6, chapter 8, p. 599; see also Yadin 1966:141 and Livne 1986:119). In fact, the height of the wall was not uniform, and its height was only five meters. Again, the exaggeration here may be due to a mistake by an outside observer, perhaps looking at Masada from its bottom up.

The fourth issue is that Josephus states that the wall had thirty-eight towers (book 6, chapter 8, p. 599), whereas according to Livne (1986:119), not more than thirty towers were identified in the excavations. Either Josephus made a mistake here or the archaeologists did.

The fifth issue is that while Josephus states that the Sicarii started one big fire on the last night, the excavations revealed many fires (see also S. Cohen 1988).

The first four problems (and possibly also the fifth) are not generally viewed as too severe. A more difficult issue is the sixth: The largest building (and perhaps one of the oldest buildings) on Masada is the western palace, built by Herod too (Livne 1986:31, 36–37, and Netzer 1983 imply that the early construction may have begun already by the Hasmoneans. In an interview [November 4, 1993] Netzer stated that there is no evidence for this hypothesis. The problem is thus of dating the construction). Puzzling is the fact that Josephus does not mention this palace (Yadin 1966:42, 117; Livne 1986:158). This is even more puzzling because the Roman breach to Masada occurred not too far away from that palace. The majestic palaces Josephus describes are those on the northern stairlike slope of Masada. A strange omission indeed (Yadin [1966:119] feels that Josephus's description simply concentrated on the "wonderous palace-villa at the northern point").

The seventh issue is that, as Gill (1993) argues, contrary to Josephus Flavius's narrative, the Romans did not build all of the huge structure that looks like the siege ramp (on the west side of Masada). Building that structure must have involved a tremendous amount of work. On the basis of his geological survey, Gill claims that the artificial siege ramp was built on a big natural spur. This claim is supported by Josephus, who states that on the western approach to Masada "there was a certain eminency of the rock, very broad and very eminent" (p. 600), and by Livne (1986:82), who confirms this. If true, this means that the effort of building the siege ramp was not as hard and could be accomplished in a relatively short period of time. In a counterargument, Ben-Dov (1993), quoting anonymous archaeologists, claims that all of the siege ramp is indeed an artificial structure (see also Netzer 1994). The paper by Gill is, to some extent, puzzling. Josephus Flavius *can* be read as stating that there *was* a spur ("eminency"?) on the western side of Masada, on which the Roman tenth legion built the siege ramp. Why does Gill seem to assume that it is not mentioned there? My guess is that Gill was, perhaps more than anything else, influenced by Yadin's book. Although he does not state it very explicitly, Yadin gives the impression in his 1966 book (pp. 220–23) that the Romans built the whole structure on the western side of Masada. In no place does Yadin state explicitly that there was a natural, very large spur on the western side of Masada, leading to the top of the mountain. Of course, building that siege ramp was quite an impressive effort, but it was surely not as impressive as building the whole thing by themselves would have been.

4. Throughout the text, when a reference to Josephus Flavius is made, the text used is, unless stated otherwise, *The Complete Works of Josephus,* by Josephus Flavius, translated into English by Wm. Whiston. I used the 1981 edition, published by Kregel (Grand Rapids, Mich.).

5. See also, e.g., Aberbach 1985; Flusser 1985; Hangel 1983; Horsley 1979a; Rapoport 1982, 1984, 1988; Safrai 1970; Smith 1971, 1983; Stern 1973, 1983, 1984, 1987, 1989. For a more general perspective see Smallwood 1976 and Grant 1973.

6. *Wars of the Jews,* book 7, chapter 8, section 3, p. 509.

7. Probably, but not for sure, Alexander Jannaeus. See p. 4 in Cotton and Geiger 1989.

8. *Wars of the Jews,* book 4, chapter 7, section 2, p. 537.

9. *Wars of the Jews,* book 7, chapter 8, section 4, pp. 599–600.

10. For a short review, see Livne 1986:123–28 and Yadin 1966:231–46.

11. Minus, of course, the modern roads and structures, the cable car, and the receding Dead Sea.

12. The version I give here of the capture of Masada by the Sicarii is the standard and accepted version. Josephus Flavius himself does not provide a very clear

or consistent account about the events leading to the capture of Masada. For example, it is not clear from his description whether Menachem's forces were the forces that captured Masada the first time or whether these were other forces (the implication is that around 66 A.D. Masada was captured twice). Also, it is not clear whether when Menachem's men took the weapons from Masada they left a garrison there or not, and it is not clear whether upon their return to Masada Elazar Ben-Yair and his men had to recapture it or not. Thus, Josephus Flavius states that "he [Elazar Ben-Yair] and his *Sicarii* got possession of the fortress [Masada] by treachery" (*Wars of the Jews*, book 5, chapter 7, section 4, p. 599). For more details about this rather messy historical sequence of events, see Horsley and Hanson 1985:212; Cotton and Geiger 1989:1–24; and Cotton and Preiss 1990.

13. *Wars of the Jews*, book 2, section 9, p. 492. I used the names as they appear in the Hebrew translation of Simchoni.

14. *The History of the Wars between the Jews and the Romans*, book 4, chapter 7, section 2, p. 537. The looting and robberies were also carried out by Simeon the son of Giora. See *Wars of the Jews*, book 4, chapter 9, section 3. Hoenig 1970; Spero 1970; Zeitlin 1965 and 1967.

15. *Wars of the Jews*, book 7, chapter 6.

16. *Wars of the Jews*, book 6, chapter 8.

17. See also Dvir 1966 (although he somewhat tries to blur this point); Livne 1986:14.

18. *Wars of the Jews*, book 4, chapter 7, section 2, p. 537.

19. For more about the end of Masada, from an archaeological and architectonic point of view, see Netzer's fascinating work 1991.

20. *Wars of the Jews*, book 5, chapter 9, p. 603.

21. Josephus Flavius (book 5, chapter 9, section 1, p. 603) states that the collective suicide on top of Masada took place on the "fifteenth day of the month [Xanthicus] Nisan." Alas, he does not state in which year. Most researchers assume that this was 73 A.D. However, in 1969, Werner Eck suggested that the year 74 A.D. was probably more accurate. A debate ensued around this issue. One problem with accepting Eck's new date of 74 A.D., among other things, is that it may create problems in dating other events. The debate ended with 73 A.D. still being considered the correct year (for a review of the debate see Jones 1974; Stern 1989:370 n. 17; and Cotton and Geiger 1989:21–24). The currently accepted version is that the siege of Masada began in the winter of 72–73 A.D. and ended in the spring of 73 A.D., a matter of just a few months (see also Feldman's review 1984:789–790).

22. See also Avi-Yonah and Beres 1983; Kasher 1983; Rapoport 1984; and Stern 1983, 1984.

23. *Wars of the Jews*, book 2, chapter 17, parts 2 and 8. See footnote 12.

24. *Wars of the Jews*, book 4, chapter 7, part 2, p. 537.

25. *Wars of the Jews*, book 7, chapter 6.

26. See *Wars of the Jews*, book 4, chapter 9, part 3, p. 541.

27. See also Horsley and Hanson 1985:214.

28. I refer here, of course, to the (mythical?) perception that Davy Crockett chose not to surrender to the Mexican General Santa Anna at the Alamo and that he and his men were killed in the final battle. I used the word "myth" before because some of the authors in Lofaro and Cummings's 1989 volume imply that Davy Crockett did in fact surrender when the situation became hopeless but that the force in the Alamo was killed regardless. For some interesting notes in regard to a comparison of Masada to the Alamo, see Bruner and Gorfain 1984: 70–71.

29. The German offensive in the Ardennes (Battle of the Bulge) began on December 16, 1944. Bastogne, a French town, was surrounded by German forces. On December 21, 1944, the commander of the Forty-Seventh Panzer Division passed on an ultimatum to the American commander in Bastogne to surrender or die. The acting American commander of the 101st Airborne Division, Brigadier General Anthony C. McAuliffe, replied: "Nuts!" The American forces in Bastogne staged a stubborn—and effective—defense that held the German forces for eight days. The forces of General George S. Patton, commander of the Third Army, ended the German siege on Bastogne on December 26, 1944.

30. In the Central Pacific. The American base there was defended by a marine force of about four hundred soldiers, commanded by Major James Devereux. The first Japanese attack on the island took place on December 7, 1941 (an air raid). The island fell to landing Japanese troops on December 23, 1941. Although there were survivors from that battle (who were sent to Japanese prisoner-of-war camps), there is no question that the U.S. Marines staged a heroic fight for as long as they possibly could.

31. *Wars of the Jews,* book 5, chapter 9, p. 603.

32. Hawkes (1929:204) estimates that 3,500 soldiers of the tenth Roman legion and 3000 auxiliari soldiers participated in the siege. Looking at the remnants of the Roman army camps around Masada, Yadin (1966:218) estimates that

> the built camps alone could house almost 9,000 troops, including the legion.
> But there is no doubt that the entire besieging force was very much larger,
> probably reaching 15,000 men if we add to the fighting units the thousands of
> Jewish prisoners who, according to Josephus, were used to bring water and
> food and apparently also to work on construction.

The size and structure of a Roman legion fluctuated between 5 B.C. and 5 A.D. However, it seems safe to assume that the average size of a legion throughout this period was around 6000 soldiers. If indeed the size of the tenth Roman legion was about 6000 warriors, it seems safe to assume that the legion with the auxiliary logistic forces (and the prisoners and slaves) may have numbered around 10,000 (see also Magness 1992:64; Richmond 1962; and for a more general perspective see Luttwak 1976). Shatzman (1993) estimates the size of the Roman army at around 7,000–8,000 soldiers. I am very grateful to Professor Ernest David Coleman from the Department of Classical Studies, Tel Aviv University, who helped to guide me through this complex question.

33.   Two almost identical ancient Roman inscriptions from 81 A.D. were found in Urbs Salvia (in northern Italy, south of Ancona) in the late 1950s. These inscriptions describe the career of L. Flavius Silva Nonius Bassus. The inscriptions do not mention conquering Masada at all. It is stated that Flavius Silva was in charge of the "provinciae Iudaeae" and that during his career he commanded two Roman legions: the twenty-first legion (Rapacis) and the fourth (Scythicae). Interestingly, it is not stated that he commanded the tenth legion (Fretensis). If so, it is possible that Flavius Silva gave the orders to the tenth legion and intervened in strategic and tactical decisions but that the Roman tenth legion was actually commanded by another person during the siege on, and conquering of, Masada. (See *Annee Epigraphique* 1969/70, section 183; Pauly-Wissowa, *Paulys Realincyclopädie Der Classischen Altertums-Wissenschaft,* Supplementband 14, München, 1974, pp. 121–22, entry 181). I am very grateful to Shmuel Sermoneta-Gertel from the Department of Classical Studies at Hebrew University, who helped me with this issue.

34.   Just as an example, the old trick of putting Josephus Flavius on trial, so popular in the past among members of youth movements, was recently repeated. On Thursday, October 8, 1992, the Israeli Television, during prime time, devoted a whole program to a mock trial of Josephus Flavius.

35.   See Feldman's 1975 paper for a summary of some of the major issues.

36.   See, for a short explanation and some historical illustrations, the *Encyclopedia Judaica,* vol. 10, pp. 977–86; Ben-Sasson 1974; and Yuval 1993. See also Goren's (1985) and Zerubavel's work (1980:95–107), for a discussion of the concept within the context of the Masada narrative, and Paine (1991:12–14). The fact is that Jews did sometimes commit suicide. See, for example, the collective suicide in York, March 16, 1190, or the suicides at Yodfat and Gamla, also described by Josephus Flavius (about Gamla, see also Syon 1992).

Among those objecting to the view of Masada as a case of Kiddush Hashem we find Frimer (1971:33), Hoenig (1970, 1972), Weiss-Rosmarin (1966), and Heller (1968). From different points of view, they all deny this interpretation. Among those advocating the interpretation we find Kolitz (1971), Frimer (1971:28–30), and Goren (1985 and quoted by Frimer [1971:31]). As Zerubavel indicates, Goren's position was also attacked. See Zerubavel 1980:104–5); Rabinowitz 1970; Spero 1970, 1971.

Frimer (1971:33) points out that the number of those denying that the rebels of Masada should be viewed as giving their life for Kiddush Hashem outnumber the advocates. In any event, very little of this debate, taking place in scholarly journals, has reached the attention of the Israeli public. Moreover, the debate did not end in a swift and decisive verdict.

37.   Stern's discussion of this suicide, in a comparative context, is probably the most comprehensive available.

38.   There are a few versions concerning his escape. See also Lewis 1975:20–21; Zerubavel 1980:107–16; Kedar 1982:59–60. For some more readings on Ben-Zakai and Yavneh, see Neusner 1970 and G. Alon 1967:219–52.

39. For a most interesting discussion of this Masada-Yavneh contrast and its possible implications for Judaism generally and contemporary Judaism particularly, see Weiss-Rosmarin 1966, 1967; *The Spirit of Masada*, 1967. Obviously, the contrast between Yavneh (read "survival") and Masada (read "death") is unavoidable. See also note 38 above.

CHAPTER THREE. EXCAVATIONS OF MASADA

1. See Yadin 1966:245; Livne 1986:128. The discoveries and excavations of Shmaria Guttman and Azaria Alon appeared between 1952 and 1954 in a series of papers called "*Mefarkei Metzada*" (meaning "the dismantlers of Masada") that were published in *Mebifnim*, the quarterly journal of the Kibbutz Hameuchad (vols. 16 and 17).

2. The fact that the first efforts in excavating Masada and the first major discoveries in the modern period were made by amateurs and interested individuals is not confined only to archaeology. Lankford (1981) documented the major (albeit usually neglected) advances that amateurs have made in astronomy and astrophysics. It was the amateurs who were willing to take risks in the early days of the discipline and to invest their time and resources in something in which they believed. I have shown (1990:181–219) that a similar process took place in the early days of radio astronomy.

3. See Livne 1986:129; Yadin 1970:129; Netzer 1990:185–86. The report about these excavations was published (in Hebrew) in a 1956 special issue of the quarterly journal *Hadshot Hahevra Lehakirat Eretz Israel Veatikoteha* ("News of the [Israeli] Society for Researching Eretz Israel and its Antiquities").

4. For more on the paths to and around Masada, see Livne 1990.

5. See *Encyclopedia Judaica*, vol. 16, pp. 694–96.

6. See, e.g., Netzer 1990:187–89; Livne 1986:130–32.

7. For one experiential report written in English, see Kossoff 1973.

8. See, e.g., the reactions of Weiss-Rosmarin in 1966 and 1967 for an illustration.

9. *Wars of the Jews*, book 6, chapter 9, p. 603. However, this issue is not a simple one. For more on the inscriptions, see volume 1 of the final report on Masada's excavations (Aviram, Foerster, and Netzer 1989) and specifically pp. 28–31 about the ostracon carrying the inscription "Ben-Yair" (ostracon no. 431). As the report points out, it is not clear whether the inscription is "Ben-Yair" or "*Bnei Or*" (meaning "the sons of light"). Moreover, more ostraca were found in the excavations than were described by Josephus Flavius, and the "explanation" that the ostraca found were the lots described by him hinges on Yadin's credibility.

10. Louis M. Feldman (1975), "Masada: A Critique of Recent Scholarship," in *Christianity, Judaism, and Graeco-Roman Cults: Studies for Morton Smith at Sixty*, vol. 3, ed. Jacob Neusner, p. 218. Leiden. Quoted by Aviram, Foerster, and Netzer, 1989, p. 1.

11. E.g., Yadin 1965, 1966, 1970. See also a progress report by Rabinowitz 1990.

12. See Feldman's review 1984:765–69. Aviram, Foerster, and Netzer edited the three volumes, two of which were published in 1989 and the third in 1991. The first volume contains chapters written by Yigael Yadin and Joseph Naveh on the ostraca and inscriptions and by Yaacov Meshorer on the coins found in the excavations. The second volume, written by Hannah M. Cotton and Joseph Geiger, consists of an examination of the Latin and Greek documents found at Masada. The third volume, the largest of the three, written by Ehud Netzer, describes the buildings, stratigraphy, and architecture of Masada. In the summer of 1994, volume 4 (about four hundred pages in length) was published. This volume focused on the oil lanterns, fabrics, wood products, catapult stones, and skeletons found at Masada. Volume 5 (possibly the last), prepared in 1994, will focus on the architecture and art found at Masada. As is becoming clearer and clearer, the scientific importance of Masada lies not so much with the Sicarii as with important discoveries in other areas, such as coins, scriptures, collections of fabric materials, Herodian architecture, and Roman army siege tactics.

13. For a presentation of the accusations and a counterargument, see Shanks 1986. One can very easily interpret the delayed publications about the Masada excavations as supporting Shanks's counterarguments. In this context, it is interesting that the editors of the first volume of the final report of Yadin's excavations note that it is quite obvious that Yadin did not leave a manuscript as the final report of the excavations (see Aviram, Foerster, and Netzer 1989a:1–2).

14. In fact, he emphasizes the point made by many other researchers, which seems to be agreeable to him, that archaeology helped into being a "new system of beliefs" (p. 27, first footnote).

15. One of the interesting questions, of course, is how deep one wishes to dig. Different strata can substantiate different national claims.

16. *Bamachane* is the official weekly magazine of the Israeli Defense Forces.

CHAPTER FOUR. SHMARIA GUTTMAN

1. The name appears sometimes as Shmariahu or Shmaryahu and at other times as Shmaria. Since 'Shmaria' seems to be most frequently used, I too shall use it.

2. The following is based on Shashar 1987 and on an interview with Shmaria Guttman on January 29, 1987, in his home at Kibbutz Naan.

3. Guttman refers here to the "Plan for the North," which will be discussed in chapter 6 in the section describing Masada in the Palmach. Basically, the idea was to prepare contingency defense plans in case the Nazi Wehrmacht's Afrika Korps reached Palestine.

4. What Josephus Flavius really says is, "A few there were of them who

privately escaped to Masada, among whom was Elazar, the son of Jarius, who was kin to Manahem, and acted the part of a tyrant at Masada afterward" (*Wars of the Jews,* book 2, chapter 17, p. 492.

5. *Wars of the Jews,* book 4, chapter 7, p. 537.

CHAPTER FIVE. MASADA AND YOUTH MOVEMENTS

1. For more on youth movements, see Adler 1962; Adler and Kahane 1974; Ichilov 1976, 1984; Naor 1989; Peres 1969; Shapira, Adler, Lerner, and Peleg 1979.

2. For the first trip to Masada by the Noar Oved in 1933, see pp. 251–53; for photos of treks to Masada, see pp. 151, 252.

3. This part is based on an unpublished paper by David Cohen and Debbi Mazo, "The Masada Myth in the Youth Movement Hanoar Haoved Vehalomed," submitted in August 1989 in my seminar on the Masada Myth. I am very grateful to Mr. Cohen and Ms. Mazo for their permission to use parts of the paper.

4. Interview with Shmaria Guttman, Kibbutz Naan, January 29, 1987.

5. A group of young members who prepare themselves either to build a new settlement or to join an existing one.

6. *The Desert of Judea: A Hanukkah Trip,* p. 33 (in Hebrew).

7. *Trips in the Judea Desert* (in Hebrew), Hanukkah 1985, Hanoar Haoved Vehalomed, p. 20.

8. This interview and others were conducted in May 1989 by David Cohen and Debbi Mazo.

9. This part is based on two unpublished seminar papers. One is by Uri Bitan, "Masada in the Movement 'Mahanot Haolim' during the Period of the Mandate: Perception, Class, and Symbolization," submitted in January 1990 in my course on the Masada Myth. The other is by Ofra Elad, "The Masada Myth in the Youth Movements [in Israel] during the Thirties and Forties," submitted in October 1989 to Prof. Anita Shapira, Tel Aviv University, in an M.A.-level seminar, "The Eretz Israel Youth, 1936–1948." I am very grateful to Mr. Bitan and to Ms. Elad for their permission to use parts of their papers.

10. See Shlomo Bachar's review in Naor 1989:49–61 and Bitan 1990 (see footnote 9).

11. P. 9. See note 9 above.

12. Lamdan's attitude to Masada is quite problematic and ambivalent. I will say more about this issue in the chapter about Masada and the arts.

13. For more on this, see Segev 1991. See also Roskies 1984.

14. See Bitan, pp. 17–18.

15. A Jewish kibbutz that was settled in the northern region of the Dead Sea in 1939, near the outlet of the Jordan River into the sea.

16. Pp. 28–29. See note 9 above.

17. I am very grateful to Iris Wolf for collecting the post-1948 information.

18. The Hebrew term used in the report is *tzorer*. I translated it as "enemy" (it could also be translated as "oppressor"). However, in the 1950 Israeli context, the word *tzorer* means "Nazi."

19. I must remind the reader here that, in fact, Masada *was* conquered by the Romans. The use of this terminology must have been metaphorical. If the word *Masada* is replaced with the word *Israel*, the intention of H. Dan, who wrote that report, may be more obvious.

20. Referring, of course, to the famous Italian leaning tower.

21. August 3, 1992, interview by Iris Wolf.

22. For more on the development of Hatzofim, see Hemda Alon, 1989.

23. There were a few reasons for that: one, they did not see much point in joining the Arabs, who objected to the national aspirations of the Jews; two, joining the British-oriented Baden-Pauli movement meant conceding some of their unique features. For example, the integrated coed groups would have to be split up into separate groups of boys and girls, and the multiage integration would have to be broken up into homogeneous-age groups. Swearing an oath to God was totally unacceptable for the secular Scouts but allowed for the religious Scouts. Finally, entering the international organization meant giving up the dream of unifying the Jewish youth of the world into one movement, of which the Israeli Hatzofim would be the center (Hemda Alon 1989:21).

24. I am very grateful to Yossi Bar-Nachum, who collected the information for this part.

25. A special series published by Hatzofim about tours.

26. On the night between May 31, 1993, and June 1, 1993, I went through a strange and ironic experience. My son, Tzach, was studying then in the Gymnasia Ivrit (seventh grade) in Jerusalem. The school organized the eight classes in his cohort to visit Masada as a bar mitzvah trip. I was asked by his teacher to make a speech there congratulating the kids on behalf of the parents. We left Jerusalem at half past midnight and drove, via Arad, to the western side of Masada, a hefty two-and-a-half-hour drive in seven very comfortable air-conditioned buses. Upon arriving, we saw the sight-and-sound show (explained in the voice of the late Professor Yadin). After my speech (I deliberately ignored Masada and talked about a hopeful future), the kids prepared a dance show, and then we climbed up the Roman siege ramp to Masada to witness the majestic sunrise in the east. After an hour, we climbed down via the snake path to the buses and drove back to Jerusalem. The experience of being awake during the whole night there, the physical effort of climbing up and down, and the ceremonies provided, at least for me, a very eerie and ironic feeling.

27. *Heye Nachon*, November 1957, 42:12.

28. *Heye Nachon*, 1966, 13(19): 8.

29. I am very grateful to Ms. Iris Wolf, who collected the information for this section and the one on Beitar.

30. See Ben-Nachum 1988 for a short review of the history and structure of Hashomer Hatzair.

31. Meaning, in Hebrew, "on the wall."

32. *Al Hachoma,* October 1, 1958, 13(115): 15.

33. *Al Hachoma,* October-November 1943, pp. 6–7.

34. Basically, the cohort referred to as the "Sons of Masada" in Hashomer Hatzair was kept as such until the 1960s. It had a special sign, different from the sign of the other cohorts in Hashomer Hatzair (a July 1992 interview by Ms. Iris Wolf with Mr. Roni Giter, chief of education in Hashomer Hatzair).

35. A January 30, 1991, interview by Mr. Yossi Bar-Nachum with Mr. Avi Navon, then chief of the department of Yediat Haaretz in the Brit Hatnua Hakibbutzit (the alliance of the Kibbutz movement).

36. See *Al Hachoma,* May 5, 1956, 2(104): 10–12 (Hebrew).

37. See *Al Hachoma,* March 10, 1957, 7(109): 2, and *Al Hachoma,* June 13, 1957, 8(110): 6–7 (Hebrew).

38. *Al Hachoma,* February 17, 1958, 11(113): 6–7. (Hebrew).

39. *Al Hachoma,* October 1, 1958, 13(115): 15. (Hebrew).

40. *Al Hachoma,* January 23, 1960, 20(122): 4–5. (Hebrew).

41. *Al Hachoma,* May 20, 1967, 1(190): 7, 14; *Al Hachoma,* December 20, 1967, 5(194): 4–5. (Hebrew).

42. A major daily Hebrew newspaper in Israel.

43. Or the Israeli-occupied (since 1967) West Bank. Even the different names one uses to describe this area have become politically loaded within the context of the Arab-Israeli conflict.

44. This part (about Bnei Akiva and Ezra) is based on an unpublished paper by Rachel Cohen, "Why Doesn't the Masada Myth Exist in the Religious Youth Movements Bnei Akiva and Ezra?" submitted in July 1990 in my course "Culture, Myth, and Deviance." Interviews with Yochanan Ben-Yaacov and Shmuel Shneler were conducted in winter 1989 by Ms. Cohen. I am very grateful for her permission to use parts of this paper.

45. Most of the information is based on interviews given to Rachel Cohen (see previous note). The interviewees were Yonah Goodman, in charge of educational materials in the movement; Simcha Luz, who planned the trek to Masada in 1961; and Yochanan Ben-Yaacov, who is considered one of the ideologists of the movement. They were interviewed by Rachel Cohen in the winter of 1989.

46. In that case, obviously, the finger is pointed at Yochanan Ben-Zakai.

47. See previous note and notes 38 and 39 in chapter 2.

48. In Hebrew, *Hag umoed bebeitar.*

49. 1 (1–6): 415–36. The same play was republished in 1955. See the relevant discussion in chapter 10 (and table 10.2).

50. *Shichva.*

51. Edited by Aryeh Bachar.

52. The article was titled "Masada Reveals Its Secrets"; see pp. 3, 15.

CHAPTER SIX: MASADA AND THE PRE-STATE JEWISH
UNDERGROUND GROUPS

1. This part is based on Menachem Sofer's 1990 paper titled "Masada in the Underground Groups: Hagana, Palmach, Etzel, Brit Habirionim, and Lehi," submitted in my 1990 seminar "Culture, Myth, and Deviance." I am very grateful to Mr. Sofer for his permission to use parts of his paper.

2. See Y. Tabenkin, "Tisha Beav," *Devarim*, 1972, 2:39 (Hebrew).

3. See Yehoshua Cohen, "Masada as a Revitalizing Power," in *Masada as an Educational Value* (Yad Tabenkin, 1986) (Hebrew). See p. 16 there.

4. Y. Tabenkin in *Devarim*, 2:318 (Hebrew).

5. *To the Young Member* (*Palmach*), November–December 1944, no. 25, from a letter of a *havera* (a female member).

6. "To Masada," in *Bamivchan*, December 1944, no. 51. That last sentence clearly expresses an ambivalence about the issue of suicide.

7. The "Nebi Daniel" convoy.

8. *Palmach Harel*, March 29, 1949, 3:11.

9. Once, on May 27, 1940, and a second time in a convention that took place between August 7 and 8, 1940. The quote below is crystallized from the two speeches (see Brener 1984:23).

10. For more concerning the "Masada on the Carmel" plan, see Brener 1984; Gelber 1990; Eshed 1988:75; Segev 1991:62. For an unclear reason, Segev prefers to treat this plan as a "fantasy" and as yet another example of the haughtiness on the part of Jews in Palestine toward Jews in Europe, especially the expression used by Greenboim. The "Plan of the North" was given a rather dramatic presentation when, on June 3, 1971, at 12:05, the main station of the Israeli state-controlled radio transmitted a program (edited by Yehuda Kaveh) on the plan. It is interesting to note that the radio program did not mention Masada. The analogy used in the program was to Moussa-Dag. See also *The Jerusalem Post Magazine*, October 19, 1984, p. 10.

11. Niv 3:101 confirms the existence of the plan but also mentions that it had no enthusiastic supporters. Gilad (1955, 1:18–20) also discusses the "New 'Masada' Plan," stating very clearly that "the sharp association to the ancient 'Masada' affair came up by itself." Gilad explicitly states that, contrary to Masada, the only choice for the Palmach was to fight (see also Alon 1985:23).

12. For more on this particular issue, see Gurevitz and Aran's 1991 paper.

13. It is interesting to note again Segev's response. Whereas he referred to the "Plan of the North" as a fantasy, no such (or similar) expressions are used by him in referring to the Etzel's plan for a second Masada. Although he makes it clear that the Palmach and Etzel intended to fight to the end, he refers to both plans as "suicidal." He does not seem to be aware of the difference between "suicide" and "fighting to the end" (Segev 1991:62).

14. *Hametzuda,* 1932–1942; *Herut,* 1942–1948, no. 62, September 1946.

15. "Judea, Rome, and Brittany," *Herut* 61 (September 1946), in *Hametzuda* (Tel Aviv: Hadar and the Jabotinski Institute, 1978) (Hebrew).

16. Meaning, in Hebrew, "Alliance of the Hoodlums" (or "Hooligans"). For a bibliographical survey of that group, see Amrami 1975:19–25.

17. The Jewish foreign minister in Weimar Germany. He was assassinated on June 24, 1922.

18. Members of the Communist Party, Weimar Germany, assassinated in January 1919.

19. See *Lehi-Ketavim,* Committee for the Publication of Lehi's Written Works, 1:515–17 (1960).

20. "This is the Way that the Fighters for Life Die," *Hamaas* 42, Iyar 1947. See also *Lehi-Ketavim* 2:465–66 (1982). Tel Aviv: Yair Publications (all in Hebrew).

21. See *Hamaas* 32 or *Lehi-Ketavim* 2:362–63. One cannot fail to notice the similarity between this position and Abba Achimair's.

CHAPTER SEVEN. MASADA AND THE ISRAELI ARMY (IDF)

1. I am very grateful to the IDF spokesman, Public Relations Office, for allowing us access to interview army officers and for providing archive materials. I am particularly grateful to Uri Algom and Noah Hershko, who helped us in every possible way they could. This is also the occasion to express my gratitude to the officers who granted us interviews: Avraham Adan ("Bren"); Yitzhak Arad ("Tolka"); Moshe Bar-Kochva ("Bril"); Yitzhak Ben-Ari; Shaul Bevar; Rafael Eitan ("Raful"); Rabbi Shlomo Goren; Menashe Harel; Yaacov Heichal; Shmuel Lalkin; Yehoshua Levinson; Moshe Nativ; Elchanan Oren; Amnon Reshef; Herzel Shaffir; Elchanan Yishai; and Rechavam Zeevi ("Gandhi"). I am particularly grateful to Anat Kaminer, who was most effective with the interviews and summary of the information.

2. Ben-Ari was then commander of Company C and later commander of Battalion 46. Interview from January 1, 1990.

3. Shmuel Lalkin was then commander of reconnaissance (Scouts), Company 135 of Armored Brigade no. 7. Interview from December 3, 1991.

4. Interview from November 18, 1991.

5. Around 1953, Bar-Kochva was a company commander in Battalion no. 79 and later its commander. In 1957, he served as deputy commander of Battalion 82. Interview from December 2, 1991.

6. According to Yaacov Heichal, then head of chambers of commander of Armored Brigade no. 7. The first documents we were able to locate in the IDF archives regarding a ceremony on Masada date back to 1961. A document dated September 21 from A. Zeev, then chief education officer, to the commander of the

armored units, suggests that the slogan for the swearing-in ceremony on Masada would include a direct address to the "heroes of Masada: 'You were not the last warriors; (as Elazar Ben-Yair stated) we exist and fight.' "

7.   Bevar was chief education officer for the IDF's armored units after 1956. Chief of armored units at that time was David Elazar ("Dado"). Interview on March 14, 1990.

8.   In 1956, Adan was commander of Battalion no. 82 and later commander of Armored Brigade no. 7. Interview on November 17, 1991.

9.   Shaffir was commander of Armored Brigade no. 7 after Avraham Adan ("Bren").

10.   This is confirmed from the interviews of Yaacov Heichal (who was head of chambers [Ralash] of commander of Armored Brigade no. 7 [then "Dado"]. Interview on March 6, 1990); Rabbi Shlomo Goren (chief rabbi of the Israeli Army between 1948 and 1972. Interview from November 17, 1992); Moshe Nativ (platoon commander in Armored Brigade no. 7 between 1953 and 1954. Interview on February 8, 1992); and Rechavam Zeevi ("Gandhi") (one of Palmach's most famous scouts. Interview from January 21, 1990). Hanoch Bartov, "Dado" 's biographer, indeed stated (1979, 1:101–2) that it was "Dado" who emphasized the treks to the Judean desert and the climbs to Masada, including the swearing-in ceremonies.

11.   Reshef was the commander of the IDF's armored units after Mussa Peled. Interview from February 1992.

12.   In other words, a Pakal Tekes was created.

13.   "Oy" in the original.

14.   In his interview, "Raful" did not confirm this.

15.   Interview on January 1, 1990.

16.   Ben-Ari refers here to the 1982 book by Y. Harkabi. In it, Harkabi examines, very critically, the Bar-Kochva revolt and basically suggests that the revolt was not useful and should have been avoided.

17.   Ben-Ari refers here to the biblical narrative concerning Samson: "Tamut nafshi im pelishtim!"—that is, to kill oneself together with the enemy.

18.   The "we" and "us" Rabbi Goren uses refer to observant Jews, as opposed to the secular Jews he was talking to.

19.   Jewish martyrdom.

20.   A place where some famous battles took place during Israel's 1948 War of Independence. The site is located near the highway between Jerusalem and Tel Aviv, about twenty-six kilometers west of Jerusalem. It has a British-constructed "Tigert" police fortress (on the Latrun battle see Shapira 1994).

21.   Interview from April 27, 1992.

22.   Amutat Hashirion.

23.   A military section of the IDF that trained prerecruitment adolescents in a variety of military-related activities in preparation for military service. Some Gadna forces took an active combat role during the 1948 war. The Gadna em-

phasized in its training values of trekking and touring the land, of getting to know the country via field trips (for a short description, see Haber and Schiff 1976:109–10).

24. *Niv-Alumim,* 1948, no. 14, p. 2.

25. The trek to Masada began on March 20, 1950, in two columns, each consisting of about 500 adolescents. They all arrived at Masada on March 23. They climbed Masada early in the morning and from the top of the mountain used the wireless transmitters they carried to send greetings from the Gadna to the Israeli president, prime minister, and chief of staff of the IDF. This was not the only trek. On March 30, 1955, another 1300 Gadna members repeated the operation.

26. The IDF archive has a soundless short movie called *The Trek of the 1000 Gadnaim,* dated 1950 and produced by the IDF's filming unit.

27. Oren was the chief instruction officer in the Gadna. Interview from November 17, 1991.

28. Interview from November 17, 1992.

CHAPTER EIGHT. MASADA IN TEXTBOOKS

1. This part is based on an unpublished paper by Ehud Pekler, "The Masada Myth in Textbooks," submitted in September 1989 in my seminar on the Masada myth. I am very grateful to Mr. Pekler for his permission to use parts of his paper.

2. This approach found its expression in his different writings about Masada in 1965, 1966, 1970, 1971, 1972, and 1980.

3. Yonatan Ratosh (also known as Uriel Shelach) was an interesting and stormy poet with some innovative ideas about the direction in which the new Jewish identity in Palestine and later in Israel should be developing. He was effective in establishing a group that became known as the "Canaanites." The "Canaanites" were a small group of young idealists whose main goal was to create a new type of Jewish identity—both individual and collective—in Palestine and Israel. They called themselves the "Young Hebrews," tried to reject the use of symbols associated with the Jewish existence in the Diaspora, and wanted to create a new, proud, nationalistic-secular and free Jew. This group explicitly demanded, among other things, a full and total separation of religion and state. For some background materials on the group, see Gertz and Weisbroad 1986; Ratosh 1976; and Shavit 1984.

CHAPTER NINE. MASADA, THE MEDIA, AND TOURISM

1. Before his academic career, Yadin was chief of staff of the Israeli Army.

2. This part is based on Tal Ben-Shatz and Yossi Bar-Nachum's unpublished paper titled "The Masada Myth in the Written Media," submitted in my 1990 seminar "Culture, Myth, and Deviance." I am very grateful to Ms. Ben-Shatz and to Mr. Bar-Nachum for their permission to use parts of the paper.

3. See *Maariv*, November 29, 1963. The weekend editions of *The Observer* during the period of the excavations (1963–1964) carried large pieces about the operation.

4. See *Wars of the Jews*, book 7, chapter 8, p. 599.

5. See *Wars of the Jews*, book 7, chapter 9, p. 603.

6. One of the main divisions among Israeli Jews.

7. "Dado," then commander of the Israeli Army armored units and later the Israeli chief of staff.

8. This part is based on an unpublished paper by Moulli Brog, "*Masada— A Site and a Symbol: A Study of the Literature of Yediat Haaretz*," submitted in November 1989 in my seminar on the Masada myth. I am very grateful to Mr. Brog for his permission to use parts of his paper. The basic table was prepared, diligently and enthusiastically, by Iris Wolf. I am very grateful to Ms. Wolf for her most fruitful efforts.

9. In Shaul Tchernichovski, *Poems* (Jerusalem: Shocken, 1950) (Hebrew), p. 466. Although the poem refers to a different landscape than that of the Holy Land, the idea is valid for both.

10. On Masada within the concept of *Yediat Haaretz*, see Benvenisti 1988:151–52.

11. Retrospectively, one cannot avoid making the comment that their original reaction may have been indeed correct. They were all skeptical about using the failed revolt, the Sicarii, and the suicide as positive national symbols. However, the social construction of the Masada mythical narrative was *so* successful that much of their objections simply evaporated in light of the new overhauled narrative.

12. *Wars of the Jews*, book 7, chapter 9, p. 603.

13. See, for example, *Hadassah Magazine*, April 1967, 48:10.

14. See, for example, an advertisement in the March 3, 1991, issue of *The New York Times Magazine* ("Sophisticated Vacation Guide" section). There, a travel agency (called Tova Gilead, Inc.) advertised that it specialized in organizing "Bar-Bat Mitzvah" ceremonies on Masada. A major attraction is that the remains of the synagogue on top of Masada are presented as the oldest known synagogue in the world. Thus, the celebration of "Bar (or Bat) Mitzvahs" on top of Masada is a very persistent tourist-supported custom. For example, according to El Al (Israel national airline), in only the first half of 1993 the company flew eight hundred young adolescents and their families to Israel to have their "Bar (or Bat) Mitzvah" on Masada (*Haaretz*, August 4, 1993, p. 8).

15. See, for examples, *Haaretz*, October 14, 1988, p. 2; *Hadashot*, October 16, 1988, p. 17. Clearly, the most intensive coverage was by *Yediot Ahronot*, weekly magazine, October 21, 1988, pp. 28–29 and 30–31. Yigael Tomarkin had some sarcastic and acid remarks about that event; see his 1988 article.

16. A much less dramatic event, much more commercial but interesting nevertheless, occurred in September 1993. At that time, the American singer Michael

Jackson visited Israel. He was flown by helicopter to Masada, where pictures of him drinking cans of Coca-Cola were taken. His sister La Toya visited Israel in December and, naturally, visited Masada.

CHAPTER TEN. MASADA IN CHILDREN'S LITERATURE AND IN ART

1. This part is based on an unpublished paper by Tali Geiger, "The Myth of Masada in Children's Literature," submitted in September 1989 in my seminar on the Masada myth. I am very grateful to Ms. Geiger for her permission to use parts of this paper.

2. These Hebrew books are by Breslavski 1941; Gafni 1970; Habron 1962; Hailan 1973; Hertzberg 1964; Ron-Feder 1982; Tzoref 1960. All the books are identified in the table by the author's name and year of publication.

3. These stories (all in Hebrew) appeared in a children's weekly magazine called *Davar Leyladim* (*"Davar* for Children"). Of these five stories, four appeared in the section of the magazine that focused on the geography and knowledge of Israel. The stories are identified in the table by the name of the story, the author, the year, and an asterisk. The stories are

Dan Shirei, "To Masada," 1947, 18(7): 96–97.

B. Meizel, "To Masada," Feb. 12, 1942, 12(21): 162.

Shimeon Tzabar, "How I Walked with the *Gadnaim* to Masada," April 12, 1950, 20(30): 557–61.

Beno, "A Trek to the Fortress of Masada," 1949–1950.

Avi Shmuel, "The Gospel of Masada (An Ancient Legend)," May 7, 1942, 12(33): 259.

4. The term *sabra* refers to an Israeli-born Jew raised in Israel. The word *sabres* means the thorn-covered sweet fruit of a type of cactus plant typically used in older Arab villages for fencing.

5. Interview given to Tali Geiger in the spring of 1989.

6. See Geiger's paper, "The Myth of Masada in Children's Literature," submitted in September 1989 in my seminar on the Masada myth.

7. This part is based on Sigal Shenkar and Yael Dover's 1989 paper titled "The Masada Myth in the Arts," submitted in my seminar on the Masada myth. I am very grateful to Ms. Shenkar and Ms. Dover for their permission to use parts of this paper.

8. It was probably written in 953 A.D. See Flusser's introduction to the second volume; see also *Encyclopedia Judaica,* 10:296–98.

9. The major part of this revolt began on April 19, 1943, and ended on May 16, 1943. The Jewish fighters' headquarters fell to the Germans on May 8.

10. I am very grateful to Suanne Kelman from Toronto, who told me about the play and sent me the theater book.

11. *Masada* opened at the Great Canadian Theatre Company in Ottawa, Canada, on January 31, 1990.

12. High words indeed. Reading this reminded me of an old saying that some North American Jews are willing to fight to the last Israeli.

In more realistic terms, the words that Milner puts in the mouth of the actor simply ignore military, economical, and social realities. It is frightening to think that a similar argumentation may have been made before the beginning of the Great Revolt, to justify that doomed revolt.

Finally, one must simply be reminded that, despite the last lines, the "Zealots" indeed "died a thousand deaths"—but they also lost the war.

13. See *Encyclopedia Judaica,* 1971, 10:1363–65.

14. From an interview conducted by Shenkar and Dover (see note 7 above).

15. See *Haaretz,* May 31, 1973. There are reports about two other Masada movies that might have been made earlier: Danny Kaye was involved in a TV movie about Masada (*Haaretz,* June 24, 1966), and Yigael Ephrati, an Israeli artist, made a short film about Masada (*Haaretz,* October 10, 1970). We could not find these movies.

16. See *Haaretz,* October 27, 1976.

17. See *Haaretz,* December 26, 1978, and February 1, 1979.

18. See *Haaretz,* March 30, 1981, and April 6, 1981.

19. See *Haaretz* June 5, 1979; September 30, 1979; November 15, 1979.

20. Gideon Samet, "Masada is Not a Japanese Car," *Haaretz,* April 10, 1981.

CHAPTER ELEVEN. THE MASADA MYTHICAL NARRATIVE

1. See Rabinowitz 1970; Nerya 1961; Hoenig 1972; Frimer 1971; Heller 1968; and the review presented by Feldman 1984:769–72. The 1948 *Sefer Haagada* ("The Book of Legend"), edited by H. N. Bialik and Y. H. Ravnitzky (Tel Aviv: Dvir, 1948) (Hebrew), mentions a few items perhaps associated with Josephus Flavius's account. On page 143 the "hoodlums" are mentioned as opposing any peace settlement with the Romans. On pages 143–44 the "hoodlums" are again mentioned, this time as led by one Abba Sicra ("head of the hoodlums of Jerusalem"). It is written that they opposed any settlement with the Romans. Another item (in Yuma 9) states that the second temple was destroyed because of hatred between the Jews. Are the "Sicarii" the same as the "hoodlums"? It is not at all clear.

2. See the chapter on the media and tourism. That booklet is analyzed in the table there.

3. See note 2 in chapter 9.

4. *Haaretz,* same date.

5. *Haaretz,* same date.

6. See *Haaretz,* February 12, 1971; *Haaretz,* February 18, 1971 (p. 2). For a retrospective summary of the religious position, see *Hamodea,* February 19, 1971, p. 2.

7. *Haaretz,* February 18, 1971 (p. 2).

8. *Haaretz,* February 12, 1971 (he was responding to earlier claims). On this issue, see Prager's (1971) interesting (and excessively lengthy) open letter to Yadin.

9. Shlomo Lorentz (from the ultra Orthodox Jewish party Agoy), an old-time veteran of the idea that Israel should be a Jewish theocracy. The vote was twenty-three against eleven. See *Haaretz,* March 25, 1971; *Hamodea,* March 24, front page, and March 25, front page, 1971; and *Hatzophe,* February 19, supplement, p. 3, and March 25, p. 2, 1971. Both *Hamodea* (an ultra-Orthodox newspaper) and *Hatzophe* (a national religious newspaper) emphasized that the rebels on Masada were observant Jews and that, hence, letting the cable car run there on Saturdays was even more offensive.

10. *Haaretz,* October 20, 1963.

11. See, for example, *Haaretz,* October 24, 1963, "Letters to the Editor."

12. Yadin's book (1966:193–94) reports on finding twenty-five skeletons. By process of elimination, he states that the skeletons "can only be of the defenders of Masada" (p. 194).

13. *Haaretz,* March 23, 1967.

14. *Haaretz,* February 20, 1968, and March 28, 1968, respectively. See also *Hamodea,* February 20, 1968, p. 4, and March 28, 1968, p. 1.

15. *Haaretz,* March 4, 1969. See also *Hamodea,* same date, p. 4.

16. *Haaretz,* March 10, 1969.

17. Clearly, that spokesman must never have read Josephus Flavius.

18. *Haaretz,* March 17, 1969.

19. *Haaretz,* July 1, 1969.

20. *Haaretz,* July 7, 8, and 10, 1969. See also *Hamodea,* July 7, 1969, p. 4.

21. See Zeitlin 1965:270, 313; 1967:251–70; Shargel 1979:368; Rotstein 1973:16; Smallwood 1976:338; Weiss-Rosmarin 1966:5–6.

22. Zerubavel (1980:122) feels that in at least one of the criticisms of Lamdan's 1927 Masada poem, by Shlomo Zemach, a reference to a possible "Masada complex" can be found. I tend to disagree. Zemach's work is basically a criticism of an ambivalent, complex poem. The "Masada complex" is more of a political criticism and needs, I think, to be kept in that framework.

23. 7 (52): 2 (December 27, 1963).

24. And to think that this was written twenty-seven months before the October 1973 Yom Kippur War is simply hair-raising. One is left wondering what could have happened had Golda Meir agreed to the reopening of the canal. For some background information of the period up to 1970, see Schueftan 1989.

25. "The Masada Complex," *Haaretz,* April 22, 1973, p. 16. See also his 1982 paper (in English).

26. He actually stated that the Israeli army could capture Cairo, Damascus, and Beirut "in brief order if it ever chose to do so" (p. 24). I simply cannot avoid stating that from a 1995 perspective, this statement looks incredibly arrogant and flamboyant.

27. "Between Masada and Jabel Ataka," *Haaretz*, November 5, 1973, p. 5.

28. See Natan Riban's article, "Masada Is Not a Complex—It Is a Reminder," *Haaretz*, March 23, 1975, p. 3.

29. Including Shmaria Guttman, Uri Yaffe, Menashe Harel, Ephraim Bloch, Azaria Alon, and Yossi Feldman.

30. Fishbane continued to report on this matter and related issues in *Davar*, August 14, 1992 (p. 20), quoting other teachers who agree with Erelli. In a letter to the editor, Gabriel Knoler (who identifies himself as a "teacher of history for more than thirty years") agrees with the criticism but maintains that a nation needs myths (see *Davar*, August 31, 1992, the "Responses" section [Hebrew]).

31. Most of Ben-Yosef's views appeared on February 7, 1992. Most of the reactions appeared a week later.

32. Although there is no shred of evidence to support this strange assertion, if it *is* true, it raises yet other bothersome questions. First, if lots were drawn, how come Elazar Ben-Yair, the Sicarii commander, was the last to survive? Did he not trust his people to do as he urged them to (that is, to kill one another)? Did he remain alive to the last just to be sure that no one escaped?

33. I must say that I find Meshel's personal attack on Safi Ben-Yosef deplorable, as much as I feel very uncomfortable with Shavit's attempt to define the boundaries of the research about Masada. That kind of forceful censorship is simply inappropriate. Ben-Yosef most certainly has the right—indeed the obligation—to voice his views. Regarding the content of his argument, I find myself in total agreement with all the criticisms against it. I find Ben-Yosef's argument fantastic and simply not supported by the evidence we have. To accept this argument means to discard too many credible archaeological findings and declare Josephus a "liar." If the Masada mythical narrative twisted Josephus Flavius's account, Ben-Yosef does a similar thing, but in the opposite direction: he discounts *all* of Josephus's narrative. In my view, this is just as bad as the myth-making. We should take, I believe, two things as given. One is the *only* narrative available about Masada—Josephus Flavius's. The other is the archaeological evidence. If we declare Josephus to be a "liar," Masada simply disappears. In that case, any fantasy about the rock can be created to make sense. And Weiss-Rosmarin already tried that prescription years ago.

34. E.g., contrary to Dimitrovsky's 1968 uncritical paper, Yadin Roman's 1987 work provides a fairly nonmythical, critical, accurate, and simple-language account of the Masada affair, with most of the problems mentioned too.

35. For supporting evidence on this particular issue, in the context of a collective memory study, see Schuman and Scott 1989 and Elder, Gimbel, and Sweat 1988. Some of the interviews conducted by Yael Zerubavel concerning visits to Masada seem to support this hypothesis. For example, she states explicitly that the "Masada experience" was *much* stronger for the parents than for their children (Zerubavel 1980:48–49).

CHAPTER TWELVE. METHODOLOGICAL FRAMING

1. One is almost tempted to try to apply (and compare) the formulations about "legends" (see, e.g., Goode 1992:303–48 for a summary) and legends and rumor (see, e.g., Mullen 1972). However, having examined both, I have reached the conclusion that the Masada mythical narrative cannot possibly be treated (or seen as) a "(modern) legend" (and, hence, compared to other legends, modern or not).

CHAPTER THIRTEEN. THEORETICAL INTERPRETATION

1. Barry Schwartz has summarized in his various papers, particularly in his 1991 work, the different theoretical stands. I shall refer below only to the essence of his argument and repeat the bibliographical references in the following two notes. I did not see much point in discussing in detail the particulars of the argument because of Schwartz's excellent summaries. See Schwartz 1982, 1990, and 1991 and Schwartz, Zerubavel, and Barnett 1986. See also Gillis 1994 and Irwin-Zarecka 1994.

2. These scholars' works are typically more directly focused on remembering and collective memory and include Bromley 1988; Hobsbawm and Ranger 1983; Le Goff and Nora 1985; Lewis 1975 (see also Shavit 1990); Lowenthal 1987, 1989; Mead 1929 (see also Maines, Sugrue, and Katovich 1983); Schuman and Scott 1989; Schwartz 1982; and Mosse's 1990 fascinating work about how the grim realities of wars have been transformed into a positive myth. On the survival of reputation, consult also Lang and Lang 1988; Thelen 1989; Tuchman and Fortin 1984. A supporting argument for this stand can also be found in Costonis 1989. Some more support for the social constructionist approach in a different context (and more so in "oral histories") can be found in Hareven 1978. Mary Douglas's work (1986:81–90) also supports this hypothesis and approach by suggesting the framing of the integration of the concept of "memory" within a social context.

3. Some of the scholars whose work seems to support this stand did not write papers directly focused on the issue of collective memory. However, their work has a very clear and direct relation to the field—for example, Shils's work on tradition. Thus, among the scholars whose work can be taken as supporting this position, one can find Burke's work on the French Revolution, 1940:29; Durkheim's work on religion, 1965:415, 420; Joseph de Maistre, see Lively 1965; Nisbet 1978; Schudson's much more focused work on the past versus the present, 1989; and Shils's work on tradition, 1981. A more indirect support for this position can be found in Bellah, Madsen, Sullivan, Swidler, and Tipton 1985:152–55.

4. This suggestion echoes a much broader, Durkheimian approach that stipulates that stability and change are two necessary and complementary aspects of any culture where members "do things together" (Becker 1986). For more on this particular issue, see Ben-Yehuda 1985:3–10.

5. This section is based on Ben-Yehuda 1983. See also Hall 1992.

6. E.g., Nagel 1961, pp. 549, 572–73, 581; Carr 1961, pp. 113–43.

7. In Nagel 1961:581 n. 26.

8. Kurt Gödel's theorem (Nagel and Newman 1958:6) implies that within a particular system, it is logically impossible to determine all of the rules needed to describe and explain that system; to do so, it is necessary to leave the system and to select only a few of the rules.

Gouldner (1968) has suggested that a similar problem exists in sociological research also.

9. The issue of alternative histories is an intriguing one. In fact, one of sociology's "totemic fathers," Max Weber, evidently advocated the use of this type of intellectual game, in which such questions are asked as "What if . . . ?" Very few sociologists ask themselves this question nowadays (especially in the professional journals); however, simulation games have indeed become an integral part of some disciplines (the military and social psychology, political science, and the like). Both classic and modern science fiction have made heavy use of such games, especially "what if" questions, as evidenced in stories of parallel universes, time travel, and so forth. One such interesting tale can be found in Eisenstein's (1979) book *Shadow of Earth,* based on the defeat of the Spanish Armada by the English fleet in 1588, in the battle that led the way to England's rise and Spain's decline. Eisenstein's book postulates what would have happened if, instead, the Armada had won the battle, conquered England, and assured Spain's domination of the world. Another similar "what if" story is the now famous British TV series "An Englishman's Castle." For a thorough survey of possible, though fictional, so-called "alternative histories," see Hacker and Chamberlain 1981.

10. Although the topic of "alternative histories" has been mentioned above (see the previous note), the subject of historical alternatives must also be given proper attention. Some of the most important work in the area of historical alternatives was suggested by Fogel (1964) and Fogel and Engerman (1971, 1974). Fogel (1964) suggested a historical analysis based on the analytical and quantitative techniques of modern economics. Using such an analysis, he provided a critical evaluation of the proposition that railroads were indispensable for American economic growth during the nineteenth century. Fogel and Engerman (1971) also suggested alternative interpretations of historical economic processes, and they examined the economics of slavery (1974). In a sense, what Fogel tried to do was to build historical alternatives, very rigorously and mathematically. Although numerous criticisms have been leveled against his work, debating its accuracy, validity, and usefulness, one cannot but admire the rigorous method used by Fogel and its excellence (for more on this, see Ben-Yehuda 1983). His elaborate formulations are only restricted to economic history and to cases in which actual numerical data could be found.

11. It is interesting to note that Stinchombe, a sociologist, stated (1978:7) that "the central operation for building theories of history is seeking causally sig-

nificant analogies between instances." Stinchombe, however, was acutely aware of the selection problem in historical research and also stated that "the problem is . . . that if a scholar is going to select only one aspect of an instance . . . to make him comparable . . . that scholar better have hold of the causally relevant aspects" (p. 6).

12. Summer 1985, vol. 52, no. 2.

13. New York: Macmillan vol. 10.

14. Why Gertz feels that this is a *myth* is not entirely clear.

15. A myth is really based on the ability of human beings to symbolize. Most people think of a myth as something in the "past." However, a future myth, (e.g., utopia) *can* be conceptualized. Such a future mythical "image" of a society *can* drive people to act—for example, Zionism.

16. That myth wrecking was, apparently, a bit too difficult to digest. Indeed, issue 30 of *Cathedra* (December 1983) devotes a whole section to a debate about this swamp issue. This section takes pages 161–95 of the issue, thirty-four pages in all. The original is twelve pages.

17. Commenting on this "myth-wrecking" issue and the presence of myth in the research about Eretz Israel, Israel Bartal noted that Jews may have the "Phoenix Syndrome"; that is, they are used to failures because in only very rare and short periods did they enjoy national and political independence. Thus, falling and rising again may be a typical Jewish cultural experience. He pointed out that, indeed, specific historical sequences were warped for national purposes (by historians too) but also that the ability to examine these myths critically is a sign of maturity. Myths, according to Bartal, seem to be manufactured when the connection between the people and the land is shaky (1990). Also, it is quite possible that with the rise of the new Israeli Historical Revisionism, researchers became more critical and suspicious of myths (for a short review about Israeli Historical Revisionism, see Slater 1991).

18. For some interesting statements about myth and identity, see Bruner 1960.

19. For some more on the Jewish and national identity, see Avineri 1981; Ben Ezer 1974; Berkovitz 1979; Dominguez 1989; Elon 1981; Gorni 1966; Gurevitz and Aran 1991; Hareven 1988a, 1988b; Horowitz and Lissak 1989; Liebman 1978; Liebman and Don-Yehiya 1983; Segre 1980.

20. More support for this idea can be found in Layton 1989.

21. Both Zeitlin (1968) and Hoenig (1970, 1972) also emphasize this point.

22. Zerubavel (1980:286–87) uses the much more general terms "editing" and "coloring" to describe this process. I find that the details, as conceptualized within the Allport and Postman model, provide a more powerful and accurate analytical analogy.

23. The orthodox view portrays the sciences as developing in a linear and progressive manner, built up by accumulation of data in a continuous effort to discover the truth. Kuhn suggested that while science develops from something,

it does not evolve toward anything specific. According to Kuhn (1962), what he calls "normal science" enjoys widespread acceptance by the particular scientific community that shares a specific theoretical and empirical paradigm. This paradigm provides guidelines for research methodologies and for prioritizing research goals, and it establishes criteria for accepting or rejecting data and hypotheses. According to Kuhn, the history of science can be characterized by the dominance of specific paradigms. A scientific paradigm constitutes, for a longer or shorter period of time, the worldview, or the definition of reality, of specific scientific disciplines. While a specific paradigm reigns, it will provide criteria for what is "sensible" and what is "nonsense." Phlogiston theory in chemistry, relativity in physics, Parsonian or ethnomethodological theory in sociology, psychoanalysis in psychology, and the idea that the earth is the center of the universe can all be used as examples of specific paradigms. Ultimately, the existence and persistence of many anomalies will force an entire field into a state of crisis. This crisis situation generates questions relating to the very basic assumptions, validity, and reliability of a specific paradigm. Kuhn stated that a crisis situation is solved by what he calls a scientific revolution, which creates a new paradigm that will dominate the field until the next revolution occurs.

The Kuhnian conception provides a very different view from the one fostered by orthodox science. As empirical historical analyses indicate, however, the Kuhnian view is not always valid. Furthermore, Kuhn's account takes very little note (if any) of the social processes involved in a scientific revolution.

APPENDIX: MAIN JEWISH UNDERGROUND GROUPS IN PALESTINE, 1920–1948

This appendix is based on Nachman Ben-Yehuda, *Political Assassinations by Jews: A Rhetorical Device for Justice* (Albany: State University of New York Press, 1993), pp. 88–97, 425–426.

1. The Zionist Federation is the administrative framework of the World Zionist movement. It was established at Dr. Theodore Herzel's (1860–1904) initiative at the first Zionist Congress in Basel (Switzerland) in 1897. The Zionist Federation was recognized by the British mandate authorities as the Jewish Agency. According to article 4 of the 1922 Mandate over Palestine, the main function of the Jewish Agency was to advise and help in creating and building a national homeland for the Jews and in matters concerning Jewish settlement in Palestine.

2. Niv, 1:156–94; S.T.H., vol. 2, part 1, pp. 574–85 and vol. 2, part 1, pp. 420–34.

3. See Yevin 1986:105–6; Niv, 2:17–20; S.T.H., vol. 2, part 2, pp. 722–34.

4. Niv., 2:75; Yevin 1986:125–30.

5. Niv, 3:45–46; Yevin 1986:190, 310–11; Livni 1987:25–26.

6. Apparently, it was a German air raid. See Niv, 3:72–77; Yevin 1986: 223–38; S.T.H., vol. 3, part 1, pp. 481–82; Naor 1990:265–79.

7. S.T.H. vol. 3, part two, p. 1541; M. Cohen [ed.] 1981:534–35. For a

bibliographical review and a history of Etzel, see Amrami 1975:29–70; Niv 1965–1980; Begin 1950; Livni 1987.

8. S.T.H., vol. 3, part 1, p. 494; Eliav 1983:171–78.

9. For the history of Lehi, consult Amrami 1975:73–90; Banai 1958; Eliav 1983; Gilboa 1986; Harel 1979; Harel 1985; 1987:193–205; Heller 1989; Katz 1987; Niv, information dispersed in all six volumes; Shavit 1987:153–79; S.T.H., vol. 3, part 1, pp. 474–543; Shomron 1985; Weinshall 1978; Yevin 1986; Yellin-Mor 1974.

Bibliography

Note: The names of the Hebrew books either are translated into English by the author or are as given in English in the book. Hebrew books are identified as such at the end of the reference.

Aberbach, Moses. 1967. "Josephus: Patriot or Traitor?" *Jewish Heritage* pp. 10(2):13–19.

Aberbach, Moses. 1985. "Josephus and His Critics—A Reassessment." *Midstream* 31(5): 25–29.

Achimeir, Abba. 1972. *Brit Habirionim.* Tel Aviv: Committee for the Publication of the Writings of Ahimair (Hebrew).

Achimeir, Joseph, and Shmuel Shatzki. 1978. *We Are Sicarii.* Tel Aviv: Nitzanim (Hebrew).

Adar, Shaul. 1993. "Masada Syndrome." *Kol Hair,* April 16, p. 9 (Hebrew).

Adler, Haim. 1962. *The Youth Movement in Israeli Society.* Jerusalem: Ministry of Culture and Education and the Sald Institute (Hebrew).

Adler, Haim, and Reuven Kahane. 1974. "The Social Profile of the Youth." In *The Israeli Society in Israel, 1967–1973,* ed. Reuven Kahane and Simcha Kopfshtein, pp. 288–95. Jerusalem: Academon (Hebrew).

Admoni, Yael. 1989. "I Wanted Menachem, the Extreme Sicarii, to Know in the End That He Was Wrong." *Yerushalayim,* May 19, pp. 8–9 (Hebrew).

Agurski, Michael. 1984. "Conditions of Imitation." *Haaretz,* May 11, weekend supplement, pp. 17, 36 (Hebrew).

Aharoni, Yochanan. 1958. *Masada.* Israeli Army, Chief Education Officer, Maarachot (Hebrew).

Ahia, B., and M. Harpaz. 1959. *The History of the People of Israel.* 3d ed. Tel Aviv: Joseph Serebreck (Hebrew).

Ahia, B., and M. Harpaz. 1968. *Korot Israel.* Tel Aviv: Niv (Hebrew).

Ailon, Giora. 1992. "We Stood on Masada, and Ben-Gurion Told Me: 'You Were Right.' " *Jerusalem,* February 14, pp. 27–29 (Hebrew).

Allport, Gordon W., and Leo F. Postman. 1945. "The Basic Psychology of Rumor." *Transactions of the New York Academy of Sciences,* 2d ser., 8:61–81.

350

Allport, Gordon W., and Leo F. Postman. 1947. *The Psychology of Rumor.* New York: Henry Holt.

Alon, Azaria. 1969. *Paths in the Desert.* Tel Aviv: Hakibbutz Hameuchad (Hebrew).

Alon, Azaria. 1990. "What Was the Judean Desert for Us?" In *The Dead Sea and the Judean Desert, 1990–1967,* Idan Series, ed. Mordechai Naor, pp. 270–275. Jerusalem: Yad Yitzhak Ben-Tzvi (Hebrew).

Alon, Gedaliah. 1967. *Studies in the History of Israel.* Tel Aviv: Hakibbutz Hameuchad (Hebrew).

Alon, Hemda. 1989. "The Scout Movement from its Beginning till the 1960s." In *Youth Movements, 1920–1960,* Idan Series vol. 13, ed. Mordechai Naor, pp. 19–36. Jerusalem: Yad Yitzhak Ben-Tzvi (Hebrew).

Aloni, Yaacov. 1984. "Historical Myth—Added Value to Historical Truth." *Moreshet Derech* (journal of the Association of Tour Guides in Israel) 8 (November-December): 30 (Hebrew).

Alter, Robert. 1973. "The Masada Complex." *Commentary* 56:19–24.

Amrami, Yaakov (Yoel). 1975. *Practical Bibliography.* Tel Aviv: Hadar (Hebrew).

Anderson, Benedict. 1991. *Imagined Communities: Reflections on the Origin and Spread of Nationalism.* London: Verso.

Argov, Gershon, and Yitzhak Spivak. 1963. *The Generations of the People of Israel.* Tel Aviv: Yesod (Hebrew).

Aronoff, Myron J. 1991. "Myths, Symbols, and Rituals of the Emerging State." In *New Perspectives on Israeli History,* ed. Laurence J. Silberstein, pp. 175–192. New York: New York University Press.

Asaf, M. 1939. "Do Not Murder. Without Interpretations." In *Against Terrorism,* pp. 19–20. Jerusalem: N. p., August (Hebrew).

Avidar, Joseph. 1970. *On the Road to Zahal—Memories.* Tel Aviv: Maarachot (Hebrew).

Avidor, M., and Y. Spivak. 1950. *The History of the People of Israel in Its Country and in Foreign Lands,* part 2. Tel Aviv: Masada (Hebrew).

Avineri, Shlomo. 1981. *The Making of Modern Zionism: The Intellectual Origins of the Jewish State.* New York: Basic Books.

Aviram, Joseph, Gideon Foerster, and Ehud Netzer, eds. 1989a. *Masada I: The Yigael Yadin Excavations, 1963–1965. Final Report.* Jerusalem: Israel Exploration Society and the Hebrew University of Jerusalem.

Aviram, Joseph, Gideon Foerster, and Ehud Netzer, eds. 1989b. *Masada II: The Yigael Yadin Excavations, 1963–1965. Final Report.* Jerusalem: Israel Exploration Society and the Hebrew University of Jerusalem.

Aviram, Joseph, Gideon Foerster, and Ehud Netzer, eds. 1991. *Masada III: The Yigael Yadin Excavations, 1963–1965. Final Report.* Jerusalem: Israel Exploration Society and the Hebrew University of Jerusalem.

Avi-Tamar, Yoram (Yoram Tzafrir). 1989. *The Sign of the Sword.* Jerusalem: Carta (Hebrew).

Avivi, B., and N. Perski. 1951. *The History of Our People.* Tel Aviv: Yavneh (Hebrew).

Avivi, B., and N. Perski. 1955. *The History of Israel.* Tel Aviv: Yavneh (Hebrew).

Avi-Yonah, Michael, ed. 1974. *Carta Atlas for the Period of the Second Temple, Mishna, and Talmud.* In *Carta Atlas for the History of Eretz Israel.* Jerusalem: Carta (Hebrew).

Avi-Yonah, Michael, and Zvi Beres, eds. 1983. *Society and Religion During the Period of the Second Temple.* Tel Aviv and Jerusalem: Alexander Peli and Am Oved (Hebrew).

Azarya, Victor. 1983. "The Israeli Armed Forces." In *The Political Education of Soldiers,* ed. M. Janowitz and S. D. Wesbrook, pp. 99–127. Beverly Hills, Calif.: Sage Publications.

Bachar, Shlomo ("Gom"). 1989. "Hamachanot Haolim—Tenuat Hanoar Halomed" (The immigration camps—the Learning Youth Movement). In *Youth Movements, 1920–1960,* Idan Series, vol. 13, ed. Mordechai Naor, pp. 49–61. Jerusalem: Yad Yitzhak Ben-Tzvi (Hebrew).

Banai, Yaacov. 1958. *Anonymous Soldiers.* Tel Aviv: Hug Yedidim (Hebrew).

Bar-Droma, H. 1937. *Masada.* Lanoar, Library of Eretz Israel, booklet 62, pp. 34–82. Tel Aviv: Omanut (Hebrew).

Bar-Gal, Yoram, and Shmuel Shamai. 1983. "The Israel Valley Swamps—Legend and Reality." *Cathedra* 27:163–174 (Hebrew).

Bar-Lev, Mordechai. 1989. "Bnei Akiva—The Religious Pioneeer Youth Movement." In *Youth Movements, 1920–1960,* Idan series, vol. 13, ed. Mordechai Naor, pp. 75–91. Jerusalem: Yad Yitzhak Ben-Tzvi (Hebrew).

Bar-Tal, Daniel. 1986. "The Masada Syndrome: A Case of Central Belief." In *Stress and Coping in Time of War,* ed. Norman A. Milgram, pp. 32–51. New York: Brunner/Mazel.

Bartal, Israel. 1990. *The Presence of the Myth in the Study of Eretz Israel: The Case of 'Cathedra.'* Paper presented at the Van Leer Institute, Jerusalem, March 22 (Hebrew).

Bartal, Israel. 1992. "Sixty Seconds about Judaism." *Haaretz,* June 5, p. 1 (Hebrew).

Bartov, Hanoch. 1979. *Dado—Forty-Eight Years and Twenty More Days.* Tel Aviv: Maariv (Hebrew).

Baseman, Bob. n. d. *Masada: Pictorial Guide and Souvenir.* N. p.

Batz, Sarah, and Tzippora Lapid. 1976. *Masada and a Short Survey about the Period of the Second Temple in Light Hebrew.* N.p.: Sarah Batz (Hebrew).

Bauer, Yehuda. 1966. *Diplomacy and Underground in Zionist Policy, 1939–1945.* Merchavia: Sifriat Poalim (Hebrew).

Becker, Howard S. 1986. *Doing Things Together: Selected Papers.* Evanston, Ill.: Northwestern University Press.

Begin, Menachem. 1950. *The Revolt.* Jerusalem: Achiasaf (Hebrew).

Bellah, Robert N., Richard Madsen, William M. Sullivan, Ann Swidler, and Steven M. Tipton. 1985. *Habits of the Heart.* New York: Harper and Row.

Ben-Amitai, Levi. 1979. *Poems.* Tel Aviv: Am Oved (Hebrew).

Ben-Dov, Meir. 1993. "In Contradiction to the Claim Made by Geologist Dan Gill, Archaeologists Claim the Masada Siege Ramp is Manmade." *Haaretz,* August 13, p. 6 (Hebrew).

Ben Ezer, Ehud, ed. 1974. *Unease in Zion.* Jerusalem: Jerusalem Academic Press.

Ben-Gurion, David. 1993. "Not Masada and Not Vichy." In *Toward the End of the Mandate: Memories from the Literary Remains, June 29, 1946–March 1947,* ed. Meir Avizohar, pp. 153–88. Tel Aviv: Am Oved (Hebrew).

Ben-Nachum, Yizhar. 1989. "Hashomer Hatzair—Scouting, Actualization, and Political Involvement." In *Youth Movements, 1920–1960,* Idan Series, vol. 13, ed. Mordechai Naor, pp. 62–74 (Hebrew).

Ben-Sasson, H. H., ed. 1972. *The History of the People of Israel.* Tel Aviv: Dvir (Hebrew).

Ben-Sasson, H. H. 1974. "Kiddush Hashem: To Die For the Glory of God and His People." In *Trial and Achievement: Currents in Jewish History (from 313)* pp. 209–18. Jerusalem: Keter (Hebrew).

Benvenisti, David and Meron (1957–1958). In *A Guiding Booklet for Tours for the Teacher and Guide,* vol. 5, "The Negev and the Dead Sea." pp. 51–58. Jerusalem: Government Printing Office (Hebrew).

Benvenisti, David and Meron. 1959. *Instruction Booklets for Tours, for the Teacher and Youth Guides.* Booklet 5, *The Negev and the Dead Sea.* Jerusalem: Ministry of Culture and Education, Government Printing House (Hebrew).

Benvenisti, Meron. 1988. *The Sling and the Club,* Jerusalem: Keter (Hebrew).

Ben-Yehuda, B., and Y. Shochat, eds. 1974. *The Days of Herod and the Great Revolt.* Ramat Gan: Masada (Hebrew).

Ben-Yehuda, Nachman. 1980. "The European Witch Craze of the Fourteenth to Seventeenth Centuries: A Sociologist's Perspective." *American Journal of Sociology* 86 (1): 1–31.

Ben-Yehuda, Nachman. 1983. "History, Selection, and Randomness—Towards an Analysis of Social Historical Explanations." *Quality and Quantity* 17, pp. 347–67.

Ben-Yehuda, Nachman. 1985. *Deviance and Moral Boundaries: Witchcraft, the Occult, Science Fiction, Deviant Sciences and Scientists.* Chicago: University of Chicago Press.

Ben-Yehuda, Nachman. 1986. "The Sociology of Moral Panics: Toward A New Synthesis." *The Sociological Quarterly* 27(4): 495–513.

Ben-Yehuda, Nachman. 1990. *The Politics and Morality of Deviance.* Albany: State University of New York Press.

Ben-Yehuda, Nachman. 1993. *Political Assassinations by Jews: A Rhetorical Device for Justice.* Albany: State University of New York Press.

Ben-Yoseph, Reuven. 1978. *Noon in Jerusalem: Poems.* Tel Aviv: Shelach (Hebrew).

Ben-Zakai, Y. 1946. *Against the Terrorist Groups: Etzel and Lehi—Their Way and Worldview.* Tel Aviv: Center of the Workers' Party, Hashomer Hatzair in Eretz Israel (Hebrew).

Benziman, Yotam. 1994. "Like the Broken Ceramic." *Kol Hair,* June 17, pp. 54–59 (Hebrew).

Berkovitz, Eliezer. 1979. "Identity Problems in the State of Israel." *Judaism* 28(3): 334–344.

Berkowitz, L. 1971. "Reporting an Experiment: A Case Study in Levelling, Sharpening, and Assimilation." *Journal of Experimental Social Psychology* 7:237–243.

Best, Joel, ed. 1989. *Images of Issues: Typifying Contemporary Social Problems.* New York: Aldine de Gruyter.

Best, Joel. 1990. *Threatened Children.* Chicago: University of Chicago Press.

Best, Joel. 1993. "But Seriously, Folks: The Limitations of the Strict Constructionist Interpretation of Social Problems." In *Constructionist Controversies: Issues in Social Problems Theory,* ed. Gale Miller and James A. Holstein, pp. 109–127. New York: Aldine de Gruyter.

Biltzky, Israel Haim. 1976. "H. Leivick: A False Name—The Visual Dramaturgy of H. Leivick." Ph.D. diss., Tel Aviv University (Hebrew).

Biltzky, Israel Haim. 1979. *H. Leivick: Visionary Dramaturgy.* Tel Aviv: Hakibbutz Hameuchad (Hebrew).

Bir, Aharon. 1969. *With a Wandering Cane: A Guide for Trips in the Land.* Jerusalem: World Zionist Organization, Department for Religious Education in the Diaspora pp. 97–102. (Hebrew).

Bir, Aharon. 1976. *Eretz Israel. Traveling in the Spring Country.* Jerusalem: World Zionist Organization, Department for Religious Education in the Diaspora (Hebrew).

Bitan, Dan. 1990. "Masada—The Symbol and the Myth." In *The Dead Sea and the Judean Desert, 1900–1967,* Idan Series, vol. 13, ed. Mordechai Naor, pp. 221–35. Jerusalem: Yad Yitzhak Ben-Tzvi (Hebrew).

Blank, A., and Y. Kutcher. 1933. *Our People: An Israeli History.* Kishinov: Ascola (Hebrew).

Blaushild, Tamara. 1985. "The Rise and Fall of Yitzhak Lamdan's Poem 'Masada.' " Master's thesis, Tel Aviv University (Hebrew).

Brener, Uri, ed. 1984. *In the Face of the Threat of a German Invasion to Eretz Israel in the Years 1940–1942; Sources and Testimonies.* 2d ed., ed. Orna Makover-Katlav. Efal: Yad Tabenkin (Hebrew).

Breslavski, Moshe. 1941. *When Masada Fell.* Tel Aviv: Am Oved (Hebrew).

Breslavski, Yoseph. 1944. *Masada.* Tel Aviv: Hakibbutz Hameuchad (Hebrew).

Breslavi, Yoseph. 1955. "Did You Know the Land?" In *The Dead Sea, Around and Around,* pp. 297–448. Tel Aviv: Hakibbutz Hameuchad (Hebrew).

Bromley, Roger. 1988. *Lost Narratives: Popular Fictions, Politics, and Recent History.* London: Routledge.

Bronowski, Yoram. 1993. "Legends of Memory, History of Forgetting." *Haaretz,* October 1, p. 5 (Hebrew).

Bruner, Edward M., and Phyllis Gorfain. 1984. "Dialogic Narration and the Paradoxes of Masada." In *Text, Play, and Story: The Construction and Reconstruction of Self and Society,* ed. Stuart Plattner and Edward M. Bruner, pp. 56–75. Washington: American Ethnological Society.

Bruner, Jerome. 1960. "Myth and Identity." In *Myth and Mythmaking,* ed. Henry A. Murray, pp. 276–87. New York: Braziller.

Burke, Edmund [1790] 1940. *Reflections on the French Revolution.* Reprint. London: J. M. Dent.

Butrimovich, Yigael. 1972. *PAZ Guide to the Roads.* Tel Aviv: Levanda Press (Hebrew).

Carr, E. H. 1961. *What Is History?* New York: Vintage Books.

Cohen, Mordechai (Marko), ed. 1981. *Chapters in the History of Eretz Israel,* vol. 2. Tel Aviv: Ministry of Defense (Hebrew).

Cohen, Percy S. 1969. "Theories of Myth." *Man,* n. s. 4:337–53.

Cohen, Pinhas, and David Benvenisti. 1938. *A Road Guide in Eretz Israel for the Traveller, Teacher, and Tourist.* Jerusalem: Pinhas Cohen and David Benvenisti, pp. 366–67 (Hebrew).

Cohen, Shaye D. 1982. "Masada: Literary Tradition, Archaeological Remains, and the Credibility of Josephus." *Journal of Jewish Studies* 33(1–2): 385–405.

Cohen, Shaye D. 1988. "What Really Happened at Masada?" *Moment,* July/August, pp. 28–35.

Connerton, Paul. 1989. *How Societies Remember.* Cambridge: Cambridge University Press.

Coser, Lewis A. ed. 1992. *Maurice Halbwachs, On Collective Memory.* Chicago: University of Chicago Press.

Costonis, John J. 1989. *Icons and Aliens: Law, Aesthetics, and Environmental Change.* Urbana: University of Illinois Press.

Cotton, Hanna M., and Joseph Geiger. 1989. "The Latin and Greek Documents." In *MASADA II: The Yigael Yadin Excavations, 1963–1965. Final Report.* ed. Joseph Aviram, Gideon Foerster, and Ehud Netzer. Jerusalem: Israel Exploration Society and the Hebrew University of Jerusalem.

Cotton, Hanna, and Yehonatan Preiss. 1990. "Who conquered Masada in 66 A.D. and who occupied it until it fell?" *Zion* 55:449–54 (Hebrew).

Dayan, Moshe. 1978. *To Live with the Bible.* Jerusalem: Edanim Publishers (Hebrew).

Dayan, Moshe (ed). 1983. *Masada.* Paris: Armand and Georges Israel.

Dimitrovsky, Zalman. 1968. "Masada." *Conservative Judaism* 22(3): 36–47.

Dominguez, Virginia R. 1989. *Selfhood and Peoplehood in Contemporary Israel.* Madison: University of Wisconsin Press.

Donevitz, Nathan. 1976. "History in a Pleasant Way." *Haaretz,* April 16, Supplement, p. 15 (Hebrew).

Donevitz, Nathan. 1984. "The First Flute." *Haaretz,* February 24, Supplement, p. 29 (Hebrew).

Doty, William G. 1986. *Mythography: The Study of Myths and Rituals.* Tuscaloosa: University of Alabama Press.

Douglas, Mary. 1986. *How Institutions Think.* London: Routledge and Kegan Paul.

Dukin, Amit. 1992. "Masada Falls Again." *Kol Hair,* February 7, pp. 35–37 (Hebrew). Same piece appeared in *Hair,* February 7, pp. 34–37 (Hebrew).

Dubnov, Shimon. 1958. *The History of Am Olam,* vol. 2. Tel Aviv: Dvir (Hebrew).

Dubnov, Shimon. 1967. *History of the Jews,* vol. 1, South Brunswick, N.Y.: Thomas Yoseloff.

Durkheim, Emile [1912] 1965. *The Elemantary Forms of the Religious Life.* Reprint. New York: Free Press.

Dvir, Uri. 1977. *Where Shall We Tour This Week?* Tel Aviv: A. Lewin-Epstein (Hebrew).

Dvir, Yehuda. 1966. "The Ideological Face of the Heroes of Masada." *Hauma* 4(15): 327–46 (Hebrew).

Echad, K. 1947. "The Masada Ritual as a Device for Defeatism." *Moledet,* Heshvan, p. 1 (Hebrew).

Edelman, Murray. 1971. *Politics as Symbolic Action.* Chicago: Markham.

Einstein, Albert. 1968. *Relativity.* New York: Crown.

Eisenstein, Phyllis. 1979. *Shadow of Earth.* New York: Dell.

Elad, Ofra. 1989. "The Masada Myth among the Youth Movements in the Land during the 1930s and 1940s." Paper submitted to Professor Anita Shapira in her seminar "Eretz Israeli Youth, 1936–1948," Tel Aviv University (Hebrew).

Eldad-Sheib, Israel. 1988. *Hegionot Hag.* Tel Aviv: Yair Publications and the Midrasha Leumit (Hebrew).

Elder, Glen H., Cynthia Gimbel, and Rachel Sweat. 1988. *Collective Memories of Wartime Experience.* Paper presented at the 1988 American Sociological Association annual meeting, Atlanta, August.

Elgazi, Yoseph, 1995. "Without Parameters for Human Suffering." *Haaretz,* January 19, p. 2 (Hebrew).

Eliav, Yaacov. 1983. *Wanted.* Jerusalem: Bamachteret (Hebrew).

Eliraz, Israel. 1977. " 'Masada' in the Ballet Festival in Vienna." *Bamah* 73–74 (126–27): 95–98 (Hebrew).

Elon, Amos. 1981. *The Israelis: Founders and Sons.* Jerusalem: Adam (Hebrew).

Encyclopedia Hebraica. 1965–1988. 35 vols. Jerusalem: Peli (Hebrew).

Encyclopedia Judaica. 1971 16 vols. Jerusalem: Keter.

Encyclopedia of Zionism and Israel. 1971. New York: Herzl.

Erelli, Neri. 1983. "Legacy and Myth in Israeli Heroism." *Mebifnim, 1-1-2:*183–87 (Hebrew).

Erelli, Neri. 1986. "In Favor of an Objective Instruction, and against the Zealots," and dialogue. In *Masada as an Educational Value: The Transcription of a Day of Deliberations on the Topic Dated October 31, 1985,* ed. Penina Hillman and Amnon Magen, pp. 12–15, 19–26. Efal, Yad Tabenkin: United Kibbutz Movement (Hebrew).

Eshed, Hagai. 1988. *A One-Man Mossad: Reuven Shiloach, The Father of Israeli Intelligence.* Tel Aviv: Edanim (Hebrew).

Evron, Boas. 1971. "We Are Not Being Annihilated." *Yediot Ahronot,* December 3, p. 16 (Hebrew).

Facts about Israel. 1985. Jerusalem: Ministry of Foreign Affairs, Information Division.

Feldman, Louis H. 1973. "Masada: A Critique of Recent Scholarship." *Commentary* 53: 218–48.

Feldman, Louis H. 1984. *Josephus and Modern Scholarship (1937–1980).* New York: Walter de Gruyter.

Feldman, Louis H. 1986. *A Supplementary Bibliography.* New York: Garland.

Ferris, Timothy. 1977. *The Red Limit.* New York: William Morrow.

Finley, M. I. 1966. "Josephus and the Bandits." *New Statesman,* December 2, pp. 832–33.

Fishbane, Yael. 1992. "The Period of the Second Jewish Temple as a National Allegory." *Davar,* August 30, pp. 9–10 (Hebrew).

Fisher, Shlomo, ed. 1985. *Jewish Society in the Days of the Second Temple.* Jerusalem: Institute for Jewish Education (Hebrew).

Flusser, David. 1985. *Josephus Flavius.* Tel Aviv: Ministry of Defense, Radio transmitted University (Hebrew).

Flusser, David. 1993. "The Dead People of Masada in Their Own Eyes and the Eyes of the People of Their Own Generation." In *Jews and Judaism in the Days of the Second Temple, the Mishna, and the Talmud: Studies in Honor of Shmuel Safrai,* ed. Aharon Oppenheimer, Yeshayahu Gafni, and Menachem Stern, pp. 116–46. Jerusalem: Yad Yitzhak Ben-Tzvi (Hebrew).

Fogel, R. W. 1964. *Railroads and American Economic Growth: Essays in Econometric History.* Baltimore: Johns Hopkins Press.

Fogel, R. W., and S. L. Engerman, eds. 1971. *The Reinterpretation of American Economic History.* New York: Harper and Row.

Frankel, Jonathan, ed. 1994. *Reshaping the Past: Jewish History and the Historians.* Studies in Contemporary Jewry, vol. 10. New York: Oxford University Press.

Freilich, Y. 1962. *Masada and Rome.* Ed. and trans. M. Aram. Tel Aviv: Y. L. Peretz (Hebrew).

Friedrich, C. J., and Z. L. Brzezinski. 1961. *Totalitarian Dictatorship and Autocracy.* New York: Frederick A. Praeger.

Frimer, Dov I. 1971. "Masada—In Light of Halakha." *Tradition* 12(1): 27–43.

Gafni, Shraga. 1970. *The Glory of Masada.* Tel Aviv: Amichai (Hebrew).

Geertz, Clifford. 1964. "Ideology as a Cultural System." In *Ideology and Discontent,* ed. David Apter, pp. 47–76. New York: Free Press.

Gelber, Yoav. 1990. *Masada: The Defense of Palestine during World War II.* Ramat Gan: Bar Illan University Press (Hebrew).

Gertz, Nurith. 1984. "The Few against The Many." *Jerusalem Quarterly* 30:94–104.

Gertz, Nurith. 1986. "Social Myths in Literary and Political Texts." *Poetics Today* 7(4): 621–39.

Gertz, Nurith, and Rachel Weisbroad, eds. 1986. *The Canaanite Group: Literature and Ideology.* Tel Aviv: Everyman's University (Hebrew).

Geva, Shulamit. 1992. "Israeli Biblical Archaeology at its Beginning." *Zemanim* 42:93–102 (Hebrew).

Geva, Shulamit. 1994. "Biblical Archaeology." *Haaretz,* November 11, weekend supplement, pp. 50–52 (Hebrew).

Gilad, Zerubavel. 1955. *The Palmach Book,* 3d ed. Tel Aviv: Hakibbutz Hameuchad (Hebrew).

Gilboa (Polany), Yaacov. 1986. *As You Walk the Fields of Terror.* Tel Aviv: Yair (Hebrew).

Gill, Dan. 1993. "A Natural Spur at Masada." *Nature* 364(6438): 569–70.

Gillis, John. ed. 1994. *Commemorations: The Politics of National Identity.* Princeton: Princeton University Press.

Glis, Y. 1964. "Masada is not a symbol." *Hamodea,* December 4, p. 2 (Hebrew).

Gonen, Jay Y. 1975. *A Psychohistory of Zionism.* New York: Mason/Charter.

Goode, Erich. 1989. "The American Drug Panic of the 1980s: Social Construction or Objective Threat?" *Violence, Aggression, and Terrorism* 3(4): 327–48 (reprinted in *International Journal of the Addictions,* 1990, 25(9): 1083–98).

Goode, Erich. 1992. *Collective Behavior.* Fort Worth: Harcourt Brace Jovanovich.

Goode, Erich, and Nachman Ben-Yehuda. 1994. *Moral Panics.* Oxford: Blackwell.

Gordis, Reuven. 1968. "About the Heroism of the Defenders of Masada." *Hadoar,* October 25, 48(40): 756–57 (Hebrew).

Goren, Shlomo. 1985. "The Heroism of Masada in Light of the Halacha." In *Masada in a Historic View,* a collection of articles for a conference, "With Shmaria Guttman on Masada," inner document, kibbutz movement, Mador Leyediat Haaretz, pp. 41–46 (Hebrew).

Gorni, Yoseph. 1966. "The Romantic Element in the Ideology of the Second Aliya." *Asufot* (January) 10: 55–74 (Hebrew).

Gouldner, A. W. 1968. "The Sociologist as a Partisan: Sociology and the Welfare State. *American Sociologist* 3: 103–116.

Grant, Michael. 1973. *The Jews in the Roman World.* London: Weidenfeld and Nicholson.

Graetz, Heinrich. *History of the Jews,* vol. 2. Philadelphia: Jewish Publication Society of America.

Gretz, Tzvi. 1972. *The Book of the History of Israel,* part 2. Jerusalem: Makor (Hebrew).

Grazovsky, Yehuda. 1900. *A Shortened Version of the History of the People of Israel*. Warsaw: Tushia (Hebrew).

Gregory, Stanford W., and Jerry M. Lewis. 1988. "Symbols of Collective Memory: The Social Process of Memorializing May 4, 1970, at Kent State University." *Symbolic Interaction* 11(2): 213–33.

Gurevitz, Zali, and Gideon Aran. 1991. "On the Place (Israeli Anthropology)." *Alpaim* 4:9–44 (Hebrew).

Gusfield, Joseph R., and Jerzy Michalowicz. 1984. "Secular Symbolism: Studies of Ritual, Ceremony, and the Symbolic Order in Modern Life." *Annual Review of Sociology*, ed. Ralph H. Turner and James F. Short, Jr., pp. 417–35. Palo Alto, Calif.: Annual Reviews.

Guttman, Israel. 1963. *The Revolt of the Besieged: Mordechai Anilewitz and the Warsaw Ghetto Revolt*. Merhavia: Sifriat Poalim (Hebrew).

Guttman, Shmaria. 1954. "The Dismantlers of Masada." *Mebifnim* 17(4): 521–34 (Hebrew).

Guttman, Shmaria. 1964. *With Masada*. Tel Aviv: Hakibbutz Hameuchad (Hebrew).

Guttman, Shmaria. 1986. "Historical Survey." In *Masada as an Educational Value: The Transcription of a Day of Deliberations on the Topic Dated October 31, 1985*, ed. Penina Hillman and Amnon Magen, pp. 5–11. Efal, Yad Tabenkin: United Kibbutz Movement (Hebrew).

Haber, Eitan, and Zeev Schiff, eds. 1976. *Israel, Army, and Defense: A Dictionary*. Tel Aviv: Zmora, Bitan, Modan (Hebrew).

Haberman, Clyde. 1995. "Meet a New (and Younger) Breed of Israelis." *New York Times*, January 12, pp. A1, A10.

Habron, Rina. 1962. *A Trek to the Judean Desert*. Tel Aviv: Hakibbutz Hameuchad (Hebrew).

Hacker, B. C., and G. B. Chamberlain. 1981. "Pasts That Might Have Been: An Annotated Bibliography of Alternative History." *Extrapolation* 22: 334–79.

Hadas-Lebel, Mireille. 1993. *Flavius Josephus: Eyewitness to Rome's First-Century Conquest of Judaea*. Trans. Richard Miller. London: Macmillan.

Haelion, Yaacov. 1981. "Masada That Never Was." *Maariv*, July 10, pp. 21–24 (Hebrew).

Hailan, Tzvi. 1973. *Following the Zealots to Masada*. Tel Aniv: Yoseph Serebrek (Hebrew).

Haimi, Avinoam. 1967. *Yoseph Ben-Matityahu's Masada*. Ramat Gan: Masada (Hebrew).

Halbwachs, Maurice [1950] 1980. *The Collective Memory*. Reprint. New York: Harper and Row.

Halevi, Shoshana. 1976. "The Montefiori Orange Grove." *Cathedra* 2:153–67 (Hebrew).

Hall, John R. 1992. "Where History and Sociology Meet: Forms of Discourse and Sociohistorical Inquiry." *Sociological Theory* 10(2): 164–93.

Hameiri, Avigdor [1933] 1955. "Masada—The Last Pesach Sacrifice in Judea." Reprint. *Moznaim* 5:268–83 (Hebrew).

Hangel, Martin. 1983. "Zealots and Sicarii" In *The Great Revolt: Reasons and Circumstances for Its Occurrence,* ed. Arieh Kasher, pp. 339–64. Jerusalem: Mercaz Zalman Shazar (Hebrew).

Harel, Israel. 1979. "Dr. Israel Eldad (Sheib): 'Begin in a Sad Episode.' " *Monitin* 13 (September): 56–63, 87, 144 (Hebrew).

Harel, Isser. 1985. *The Truth about the Kasztner Murder.* Jerusalem: Edanim (Hebrew).

Harel, Isser. 1987. *Soviet Espionage: Communism in Israel.* Jerusalem: Edanim (Hebrew).

Harel, Menache. 1960. *These Are My Trips in the Land: A Guide for Trips in Israel,* vol. 2, pp. 445–49. Tel Aviv: Am Oved (Hebrew).

Harel, Menache. 1971. *Voyages in the Judean Desert and the Dead Sea.* Tel Aviv: Am Oved (Hebrew).

Harel, Menashe. 1963. *The Judean Desert and South Dead Sea.* Jerusalem: Ministry of Culture and Education, the Szald Institute, Department for Youth (Hebrew).

Hareven, Shulamit. 1988a. "The First 40 Years: Real and Less Real Tensions," *Yediot Ahronot,* February 12, pp. 6–7, 14 (Hebrew).

Hareven, Shulamit. 1988b. "The First 40 Years: The Individual against the Collective." *Yediot Ahronot,* February 19, pp. 4–5 (Hebrew).

Hareven, Shulamit. 1989a. "What Shall We Do with a Myth?" *Yediot Ahronot,* April 19, weekend magazine, pp. 28–29 (Hebrew).

Hareven, Shulamit. 1989b. "What Shall We Do with a Myth?" *Yediot Ahronot,* April 21, weekend supplement, p. 22 (Hebrew).

Hareven, Tamara K. 1978. "The Search for Generational Memory: Tribal Rites in Industrial Society." *Daedalus* 107(4): 137–49.

Harkabi, Yehoshafat. 1982. *Vision, No Fantasy: Realism in International Relations.* Jerusalem: Domino (Hebrew).

Harkabi, Yehoshafat. 1987. *The Validity of Reality: National and Educational Lessons from Yirmiyahu, the Great Revolt, and the Bar Kochba revolt.* Jerusalem: Van Leer Institute (Hebrew).

Harker, Ronald. 1967. "Masada Shall Not Fall Again." *Jewish Heritage,* Fall, pp. 5–12.

Harnik, Noa. 1993. "This Was Escaping to Save Our Souls." *Jerusalem,* September 15, pp. 20–23 (Hebrew).

Hawkes, C. 1929. "The Roman Siege of Masada." *Antiquity* 3:195–213.

Hazan, L. 1939. *The History Of Israel.* Tel Aviv: Dvir (Hebrew).

Hazaz, Haim. 1963. *In One Collar.* Tel Aviv: Am Oved (Hebrew).

Hecht, Immanuel. 1904. *The Book of the History of the Jews.* Berditchev: N. p. (Hebrew).

Hegy, Pierre. 1991. *Myth as Foundation for Society and Values: A Sociological Analysis.* Lewiston, N.Y.: Edwin Mellen Press.

Heller, Bernard. 1968. "Masada and the Talmud." *Tradition* 10(2): 31–34.

Heller, Joseph. 1989. *Lehi: Ideology and Politics, 1940–1949.* Jerusalem: Mercaz Zalman Shazar and Keter (Hebrew).

Hendel, Michael. 1961. *Social and Cultural History: Israel and Its Peoples,* part 1. Tel Aviv: Yehoshua Chechik (Hebrew).

Hendel, Michael. 1961. *Social and Cultural History: Israel and the Nations,* part 1, vol. 1. Tel Aviv: Yehoshua Tchechik (Hebrew).

Hendel, Michael, and A. Shochat. 1954. *Sources for the Study of General and Israeli History,* 2d ed. Tel Aviv: Yehoshua Tchechik (Hebrew).

Hertzberg, Yitzhak. 1964. *Masada: A Heroic Tale of Israel, a Historic Tale,* Tel Aviv: Yoseph Serebrek (Hebrew).

Hillman, Penina, and Amnon Magen, eds. 1986. *Masada as an Educational Value: The Transcription of a Day of Deliberations on the Topic Dated October 31, 1985.* Efal, Yad Tabenkin: United Kibbutz Movement (Hebrew).

Hobsbawm, Eric, and Terence Ranger, eds. 1983. *The Invention of Tradition.* Cambridge: Cambridge University Press.

Hoenig, Sidney B. 1970. "The Sicarii in Masada: Glory or Infamy?" *Tradition* 11(1): 5–30.

Hoenig, Sidney B. 1972. "Historic Masada and the Halakhah." *Tradition* 13(2): 100–116.

Horowitz, Dan, and Moshe Lissak. 1989. *Overburdened Policy: Society and Politics in Israel.* New York: State University of New York Press.

Horowitz, Meir. 1988. "H. Leivick." In *Encyclopedia Hebraica,* vol. 21, pp. 732–33. Tel Aviv: Sifriat Poalim (Hebrew).

Horsley, Richard A. 1979a. "Josephus and the Bandits." *Journal for the Study of Judaism* 10(1): 37–63.

Horsley, Richard A. 1979b. "The Sicarii: Ancient Jewish Terrorists." *Journal of Religion* 455:62–63.

Horsley, Richard A., and John S. Hanson. 1985. *Bandits, Prophets, and Messiahs: Popular Movements at the Time of Jesus.* San Francisco: Harper and Row.

Hoy, Claire, and Victor Ostrovsky. 1990. *By Way of Deception.* Toronto: Stoddart.

Hunt, Lynn. 1988. "The Sacred and the French Revolution." In *Durkheimian Sociology: Cultural Studies,* ed. Jeffrey C. Alexander, pp. 25–43. Cambridge: Cambridge University Press.

Ichilov, Orit. 1976. "The Youth Movements in Israel as Agencies for Growing Up." In *Youth Frameworks in Israeli Society,* ed. Reuven Kahane and Ruth Suchi, pp. 349–58. Jerusalem: Hebrew University, Center for the documentation and Research of Israeli Society (Hebrew).

Ichilov, Orit. 1984. *The Political World of Children and Adolescents.* Tel Aviv: Yachdav (Hebrew).

Illan, Tzvi. 1968. *Following the Zealots to Masada.* Tel Aviv: Joseph Serebrek (Hebrew).

Illan, Tzvi, ed. 1972. *The Judean Desert and the Dead Sea,* a collection of papers presented at a meeting of the Society for the Protection of Nature, Ein Gedi Field School and the Society for the Protection of Nature (Hebrew).

Inbal, Leah. 1991. "Sudden Longings for Moshe Dayan." *Yediot Ahronot,* May 24, weekly magazine (*Seven Days*), pp. 4–6 (Hebrew).

In Masada and the Negev. 1944. Tel Aviv: The Histadrut, published by Mercaz Hanoar Haoved (Hebrew).

Irwin-Zarecka, Iwona. 1994. *Frames of Remembrance: The Dynamics of Collective Memory.* New Brunswick, N.J.: Transaction.

Ivianski, Zeev. 1977. "Individual Terror: Concept and Typology." *Journal of Contemporary History* 12:43–63.

Ivianski, Zeev. 1981. "Individual Terror. In *Encyclopedia of Social Sciences,* vol. 6, ed. David Kna'ni, pp. 409–14. Tel Aviv: Al Hamishmar (Hebrew).

Ivianski, Zeev. 1982. "The Moral Issue: Some Aspects of Individual Terror." In *The Morality of Terrorism,* ed. David C. Rapoport and Yonah Alexander, pp. 229–66. New York: Pergamon.

Ivianski, Zeev. 1987. "Lehi and the Limits to Terror." In *Struggle and Terror,* ed. Orna Makover-Katlav, pp. 24–59. Ramat Efal, Yad Tabenkin: Center for the Study of the History of the Defense Forces—Hahagana (Hebrew).

Jenkins, Philip. 1992. *Intimate Enemies: Moral Panics in Contemporary Great Britain,* New York: Aldine de Gruyter.

Jones, C. P. 1947. "Review" [of Eck's book]." *American Journal of Philology* 95:89–90.

Josippon, The Book of [Josephus Gorionides]. 1981. Ed. David Flusser. Jerusalem: Bialik Institute (Hebrew).

Kafkafi, Yitzhak, ed. 1975a. *The Years of Mahanot Haolim,* vol. 1. Tel Aviv: Hakibbutz Hameuchad (Hebrew).

Kafkafi, Yitzhak, ed. 1975b. *The Years of Mahanot Haolim,* vol. 2, Tel Aviv: Hakibbutz Hameuchad (Hebrew).

Kapferer, Jean-Noel. 1990. *Rumors: Uses, Interpretations, and Images,* trans. Bruce Fink. New Brunswick, N. J.: Transaction.

Kasher, Arieh, ed. 1983. *The Great Revolt.* Jerusalem: Mercaz Zalman Shazar (Hebrew).

Katriel, Tamar, and Aliza Shenhar. 1990. "Tower and Stockade: Dialogic Narration in Israeli Settlement Ethos." *Quarterly Journal of Speech,* 76(4):359–80.

Katz, Immanuel. 1987. *Lohamei Herut Israel (Lehi).* Tel Aviv: Beit Yair (Hebrew).

Katz, Shaul. 1985. "The Israeli Teacher-Guide: The Emergence and Perpetuation of a Role." *Annals of Tourism Research* 12:49–72.

Kedar, Binyamin. 1973. "The Masada Complex." *Haaretz,* April 22, p. 16 (Hebrew).

Kedar, Binyamin. 1982. "Masada: The Myth and the Complex." *Jerusalem Quarterly* 24:57–63.

Kedem, Menachem. 1987. *The Jews in the Days of the Second Temple.* Tel Aviv: Or Am (Hebrew).

Kedem, Menachem. 1988. *Questions and Answers in the Matriculations about the History of Israel.* Tel Aviv: Or Am (Hebrew).

Keinan, Amos. 1975. *Shoah 2.* Tel Aviv: Shocken (Hebrew).

Kirshenboim, Shimshon. 1988. *The History of Israel in the Days of the Second Temple.* Tel Aviv: Mishlav (Hebrew).

Kislev, Ran. 1991. "Masada beyond the Green Line." *Haaretz,* September 17, p. 1 (Hebrew).

Klosner, Joseph. 1925. *Israeli History,* vol. 4. Tel Aviv: Judaism and Humanity (Hebrew).

Klosner, Joseph. 1937. *Masada and Its Heroes.* Lanoar, Library of Eretz Israel, booklet 62, pp. 3–33. Tel Aviv: Omanut (Hebrew).

Klosner, Joseph. 1944. *When a Nation Fights for its Freedom: Historical Essays.* 3d ed., vol. 1. Tel Aviv: Hotzaa Medinit (Hebrew).

Klosner, Joseph. (1952, 1958, 1963): *History of the Second Temple,* vol. 5. Jerusalem: Achiasaf (Hebrew).

Kolitz, Zvi. 1971. "Masada—Suicide or Murder?" *Tradition* 12(1): 5–26.

Kol Makom Veatar ("Israel—Sites and Places"). 1989. 10th ed. Tel Aviv: Ministry of Defense and Carta (Hebrew). (See also the 1978 edition.)

Kossoff, David. 1973. *The Voices of Masada.* London: Vallentine Mitchell.

Kuhn, Thomas S. 1962. *The Structure of Scientific Revolutions.* Chicago: University of Chicago Press.

Ladouceur, David. 1987. "Josephus and Masada." In *Josephus, Judaism, and Christianity.* ed. Louis H. Feldman and Gohei Hata, pp. 95–113. Detroit: Wayne State University Press.

Lamdan, Yizhak. 1952. *Masada.* Tel Aviv: Dvir (Hebrew).

Lang, Gladys, and Kurt Lang. 1988. "Recognition and Renown: The Survival of Artistic Reputation." *American Journal of Sociology* 94:79–109.

Lankford, J. 1981. "Amateurs and Astrophysics: A Neglected Aspect in the Development of a Scientific Specialty." *Social Studies of Science* 11: 275–303.

Lankin, Eliahu. [1950] 1974. *The Story of Altalena's Commander.* Reprint. Tel Aviv: Hadar (Hebrew).

Lapide, P. E. 1964. "Masada." *Jewish Heritage,* 6(4): 28–29 (Spring).

Layton, Robert, ed. 1989. *Who Needs the Past? Indigenous Values and Archaeology.* London: Unwin Hyman.

Le Goff, Jacques, and Pierre Nora, eds. [1974] 1985. *Constructing the Past: Essays in Historical Methodology.* Reprint of French edition. Cambridge University Press.

Lewin, Israel Li. 1976. "The Zealots at the End of the Period of the Second Temple as a Historiographic Problem." *Cathedra* 1:39–48 (Hebrew).

Lewis, Bernard. 1975. *History: Remembered, Recovered, Invented.* Princeton: Princeton University Press.

Liebman, Charles S. 1978. "Myth, Tradition, and Values in Israeli Society." *Midstream* 24(1): 44–53.

Liebman, Charles S., and Eliezer Don-Yehiya. 1983. *Civil Religion in Israel.* Los Angeles: University of California Press.

Lifshitz, Moshe. 1987. *The History of the Second Temple.* Tel Aviv: Or Am (Hebrew).

Lincoln, Bruce. 1989. *Discourse and the Construction of Society: Comparative Studies of Myth, Ritual, and Classification.* New York: Oxford University Press.

Lissak, Moshe. 1972. "The Israeli Defence Forces as an Agent of Socialization and Education: A Research in Role Expansion in a Democratic Society." In *The Perceived Role of The Military,* ed. M. R. van Gils, pp. 325–40. Rotterdam: Rotterdam University Press.

Litai, Haim Lazar. 1963. *Warsaw's Masada: ZZW, The Jewish Military Organization of the Revolt in Ghetto Warsaw.* Tel Aviv: Jabotinski Institute (Hebrew).

Lively, Jack, ed. 1965. *The Works of Joseph de Maistre.* New York: Macmillan.

Livne, Micha. 1961. *A Pocket Book Guide to Masada.* N.p.: Micha Livne (Hebrew).

Livne, Micha. 1965. *Auxiliary Materials for the Guide in Masada.* Jerusalem: Israeli National Parks Authority and the Ministry of Tourism (Hebrew).

Livne, Micha. 1986. *Last Fortress: The Story of Masada and Its People.* Tel Aviv: Ministry of Defense (Hebrew).

Livne, Micha. 1990. "The Paths Going Up to Masada—Their Discovery and Localization." In *The Dead Sea and the Judean Desert, 1900–1967,* Idan Series, vol. 14, ed. Mordechai Naor, pp. 173–84. Jerusalem: Yad Yitzhak Ben-Tzvi (Hebrew).

Livne, Micha. 1986. "Masada." *Derech Eretz* 21 (January 22) ed. Irit Zaharoni: 25–32 (Hebrew).

Livne, Micha, and Zeev Meshel. 1969. "Masada in the Judean Desert." In *The Judean Desert: A Collection of Papers.* Tel Aviv: Kibbutz Movement, School of Tourism, Department for Yediat Haaretz (Hebrew).

Livne, Micha, and Zeev Meshel. 1966. *Masada.* National Park Authority. Jerusalem: Government Printing Press (Hebrew).

Livni, Eitan. 1987. *EZL—Operation and Underground.* Jerusalem: Edanim (Hebrew).

Lofaro, Michael, and Jo Cummings, eds. 1989. *Crockett at Two Hundred : New Perspectives on the Man and the Myth.* Knoxville: University of Tennessee Press.

Lowenthal, David. 1985. *The Past Is a Foreign Country.* Cambridge: Cambridge University Press.

Lowenthal, David. 1989. "The Timeless Past: Some Anglo-American Historical Preconceptions." *Journal of American History* 75:1263–80.

Luttwak, Edward N. 1976. *The Grand Strategy of the Roman Empire, from the First Century to the Third.* Baltimore: Johns Hopkins University Press.

Madrich Israel. 1979. *Israel Guide: A Practical Encyclopedia for Knowledge of the Land,* ed. Aryeh Itzhaki. Volume on *The Judean Desert and the Jordan Valley,* ed. Safi Ben-Yoseph. Tel Aviv: Ministry of Defense and Keter (Hebrew).

Magness, Jodi. 1992. "Masada—Arms and the Men." *Biblical Archaeology Review* 18(4): 58–67.

Maines, David R., Noreen M. Sugrue, and Michael A. Katovich. 1983. "The Sociological Import of G. H. Mead's Theory of the Past." *American Sociological Review* 48:161–73.

Masada N.d. Jerusalem: Israeli National Parks Authority, Government Printing House (Hebrew).

Masada, by Scouting. 1976. Ministry of Culture and Education, Center of Information, Publication Service. Jerusalem: Government Printing House (Hebrew).

Matza, David. 1969. *Becoming Deviant.* Englewood Cliffs, N.J.: Prentice Hall.

Mead, George Herbert. 1929. "The Nature of the Past." In *Essays in Honor of John Dewey,* ed. John Coss, pp. 235–42. New York: Henry Holt.

Meroz, Dafna. 1991. *Day Tours in Israel: A Guide To Family Outgoings,* vols. 1. Tel Aviv: Yediot Ahronot. Israeli Society for the Protection of Nature (Hebrew).

Meroz, Dafna. 1992. *Day Tours in Israel: A Guide To Family Outgoings,* vol. 2. Tel Aviv: Yediot Ahronot, Israeli Society for the Protection of Nature (Hebrew).

Meshel, Zeev. 1977. *Masada.* Holon: Airoax (Hebrew).

Meshel, Zeev. 1992. "Masada, the Battle on the Myth." *Kol Hair,* February 21, pp. 60–61 (Hebrew).

Miller, Tamar. 1984. "Masada—The Testimony of Josephus Flavius in Light of the Archaeological Findings." *Moreshet Derech* 7 (July-August): 7–13 (Hebrew).

Milner, Arthur. 1989. Masada. Ottawa: Arthur Milner.

Mosse, George L. 1990. *Fallen Soldiers: Reshaping the Memory of the World Wars.* New York: Oxford University Press.

Muhly, James D. 1987. "Solomon, the Copper King: A Twentieth Century Myth." *Expedition* 29(2): 38–47.

Mullen, Patrick B. 1972. "Modern Legend and Rumor Theory." *Journal of the Folklore Institute* 9(2/3): 95–109.

Nagel, E. 1961. *The Structure of Science.* New York: Harcourt, Brace.

Nagel, E., and J. R. Newman. *Gödel's Proof.* New York: University Press.

Naor, Aryeh. 1990. *David Raziel: The Life and Times of the Commander-in-Chief of the 'Irgun' Underground in Palestine.* Tel Aviv: Ministry of Defense (Hebrew).

Naor, Mordechai, ed. 1989. *Youth Movements, 1920–1960.* Idan Series, vol. 13, pp. 204–26 (Hebrew).

Naor, Mordechai, ed. 1990. *The Dead Sea and the Judean Desert, 1900–1967.* Idan Series, vol. 14. Jerusalem: Yad Yitzhak Ben-Tzvi (Hebrew).

Narkis, Uzi. 1983. "Judea Capta." In *Masada,* ed. Moshe Dayan, pp. 24–27. Paris: Armand and Georges Israel.

Negev, Avraham, and Yehuda Ziv (1975): *A Daily Guide for the Sites and Reservations.* Jerusalem: Jerusalemite Publishing House, pp. 170–74 (Hebrew).

Nerya, Rabbi Moshe Tzvi. 1961. " 'Suicide': The Heroes of Masada—in Light of the Halakha." *Or Hamizrach* (New York), issue A-B, pp. 8–12 (Hebrew).

Netzer, Ehud. 1983. "New Discoveries in the Winter Palaces from the Days of the Second Temple in Jericho." *Qadmoniot*, 1(57): 22–29 (Hebrew).

Netzer, Ehud. 1990. "Masada: The Survey, The Excavations, and the Reconstruction." *The Dead Sea and the Judean Desert, 1900–1967*, Idan Series, vol. 14, ed. Mordechai Naor, pp. 185–97. Jerusalem: Yad Yitzhak Ben-Tzvi (Hebrew).

Netzer, Ehud. 1991. "The Last Days and Hours at Masada." *Biblical Archaeology Review* 17(6): 20–32 (November/December).

Netzer, Ehud. 1992. "Masada: It Was Not an Exercise." *Maariv*, March 6, p. 13 in the "Views" department (Hebrew).

Netzer, Ehud. 1994. "Masada Ramp Thesis Is Still as Firm as Bedrock." *Jerusalem Post*, December 21, p. 7.

Neusner, Jacob. 1970. *The Life of Yochanan Ben-Zakkai ca. 1–80 C.E.*, Leiden: E. J. Brill.

Nir, Dov. 1970. *The Landscapes of Israel: A Guide for Trips in the land*, Tel Aviv: Masada (Hebrew).

Nisbet, Robert. 1978. "Conservatism." In *A History of Sociological Analysis*, ed. Tom Bottomore and Robert Nisbet, pp. 80–117. New York: Basic.

Niv, David. 1965–1980. *The Battles of the National Military Organization (Maarchot Hairgun Hatzvai Haleumi)*. 6 vols. Tel Aviv: Mossad Klosner (Hebrew).

Nora, Pierre. 1993. "Between Memory and History: On the Problem of the Place." *Zemanim* 45:4–19 (Hebrew).

Orlan, Haim. 1969. "Masada—The Historical Chapter We Are Being Forced into, as if . . ." *Hadoar* 49(18): 277 (Hebrew).

Orlan, Haim. 1969a. "More on Masada and Its Heroes." *Hadoar* 47:755–56 (Hebrew).

Orwell, George. 1961. *1984*. New York: New American Library.

Ozouf, Mona. 1988. *Festivals and the French Revolution*. Cambridge: Harvard University Press.

Pail, Meir. 1979. *The Emergence of Zahal (IDF)*. Tel Aviv: Zmora, Bitan, Modan (Hebrew).

Paine, Robert. 1991. *Masada between History and Memory*. Paper prepared for the "Politics of Memory" session, conference of the Canadian Historical Association, Memorial University of Newfoundland, June.

Paine, Robert. 1994. "Masada: A History of a Memory." *History and Anthropology* 6(4): 371–409.

Paz Guide to Roads and Tours in Israel. Jerusalem: Carta (Hebrew).

Pearlman, Moshe. 1967. *The Zealots of Masada*. London: Hamish Hamilton.

Peled, Rina. 1989. "Beitar Movement in Eretz Israel from Its Beginning till the 1950s." In *Youth Movements, 1920–1960*, Idan Series, vol. 13, ed. Mordechai Naor, pp. 105–18 (Hebrew).

Peres, Yeshayahu. 1921. *Eretz Israel and Southern Syria—A Book of Travels*. Jerusalem: Binyamin Hertz, pp. 224–26 (Hebrew).

Peres, Yochanan. 1969. "The Pioneering Youth Movement." In *The Social Structure of Israel. A Collection of Papers and Research Reports,* ed. S. N. Eisenstadt, Haim Adler, Rivka Bar-Yosef, and Reuven Kahane, pp. 482–95. Jerusalem: Academon (Hebrew).

Pfuhl, Erdwin H. 1986. *The Deviance Process.* Belmont, Calif.: Wadsworth Publishing Company.

Ponner, Y. [1921] 1970. "Yehuda Ben-Hizkiahu the Galilee." In *The Hebrew Play in the Period of the Hathia,* ed. G. Shaked. Reprint. Jerusalem: Mosad Bialik, pp. 40-42, 128, 217, 267–68, 347 (Hebrew). See also *Moznaim 1955,* vol. 4: pp. 4–5 (1955) (Hebrew).

Popper, K. R. 1950. *The Open Society and Its Enemies.* Princeton: Princeton University Press.

Porat, Dina. 1991. "Attitudes of the Young State of Israel toward the Holocaust and Its Survivors: A debate over Identity and Values." In *New Perspectives On Israeli History. The Early Years of the State,* ed. Laurence J. Silberstein, pp. 157–74. New York: New York University Press.

Porat, Yehoshua. 1990. "Recruiting or Defense." *Haaretz,* August 31, 1990, p. 9 (Hebrew).

Portelli, Alessandro. 1991. *The Death of Luigi Trastulli and Other Stories: Form and Meaning in Oral History.* Albany: State University of New York Press.

Prager, Moshe. 1971. "What Is Masada: An Archaeological Site or a Symbol for the Jewish Tradition?" *Beit Yaacov,* collection 4, 12(135–36): 7–10 (Hebrew).

Rab, Esther. 1979. "Smoked Poems." Tel Aviv: *Moznaim,* Sefer Hayovel (Hebrew).

Rabi, Yaakov. 1979. *Teshuvat Hashana.* Tel Aviv: Sifriat Poalim (Hebrew).

Rabinov, Baruch. 1969. "Hagana." *Encyclopedia of Social Sciences,* vol. 11, ed. David Kenaani, pp. 31–47. Tel Aviv: Sifriat Poalim (Hebrew).

Rabinowitz, Abraham. 1990. "Lots of Controversy: Six Years after the Death of Yigael Yadin, His Colleagues Have Begun Publishing the Fruits of His Fabulous Archaeological Career." *Jerusalem Post,* weekend magazine, Friday, March 16, pp. 6–9.

Rabinowitz, Danny. 1985. "Slaughtered Cows in the Desert." *Haaretz,* May 24, pp. 20–21 (Hebrew).

Rabinowitz, Louis I. 1970. "The Masada Martyrs According to the Halakha." *Tradition* 11(3): 31–37.

Rafter, Nicole Hahn. 1990. "The Social Construction of Crime and Crime Control." *Journal of Research in Crime and Delinquency* 27(4): 376–89.

Rakovski, Pua. 1939. "The Voice of a Hebraic Woman." In *Against Terrorism,* ed. R. Binyamin and Yaacov Peterzeil, pp. 84–85. Jerusalem: N.p. (Hebrew).

Rajak, Tessa. 1983. *Josephus: The Historian and His Society.* London: Duckworth.

Rapoport, David. 1984. "Fear and Trembling: Terrorism in Three Religious Traditions." *American Political Science Review* 78(30): 658–77.

Rapoport, Uriel. 1976. *A History of Israel in the Period of the Second Temple.* Tel Aviv: Amichai (Hebrew).

Rapoport, Uriel, ed. 1982. *Josephus Flavius.* Jerusalem: Yad Yitzhak Ben-Zvi (Hebrew).

Ratosh, Jonathan. 1976. *From Victory to Disaster.* Tel Aviv: Hadar (Hebrew).

Raz-Krakotzkin, Amnon. 1992. "The Real Brain-Washing." *Haaretz,* October 6, p. 4 (Hebrew).

Richmond, I. A. 1962. "The Roman Siege-Works of Masada, Israel." *Journal of Roman Studies* 52:142–55.

Roman, Yadin. 1987. "The Riddle Of Masada." *Eretz,* Autumn, pp. 18–74 (Hebrew).

Ron-Feder, Galila. 1982. *I Remember Masada.* Tel Aviv: Masada (Hebrew).

Rosenberg, Bruce A. 1974. *Custer and the Epic of Defeat.* University Park: Pennsylvania State University Press.

Rosenthal, Yehuda. 1968a. "About Masada and Its Heroes." *Hadoar* 38 (August-September): 693–95 (Hebrew).

Rosenthal, Yehuda. 1968b. "An Answer for a Critic." *Hadoar* 48:44–45 (Hebrew).

Roskies, David G. 1984. *Against the Apocalypse: Responses to Catastrophe in Modern Jewish Culture.* Cambridge: Harvard University Press.

Rosnow, Ralph L., and Gary Alan Fine. 1976. *Rumor and Gossip.* New York: Elsevier.

Rotenberg, Beno. 1960. *Following Kings and Rebels.* Ramat Gan: Masada (Hebrew).

Rotenberg, Beno. 1963. *Masada.* Tel Aviv: A. Lewin-Epstein (Hebrew).

Rotstein, Rephael. 1973. "The Bothering Myth." *Haaretz,* April 20, p. 16 (Hebrew).

Sahish, Yaron. 1993. "The Syrian-African Rift." *Jerusalem,* September 15, pp. 80–82 (Hebrew).

Sadeh, Pinhas. 1974. *A Trek in Eretz Israel.* Jerusalem: Schocken (Hebrew).

Safrai, Shmuel. 1970. *The Jewish People during the Days of the Second Temple.* Tel Aviv: Am Oved (Hebrew).

Samet, Moshe. 1989. *Moshe Montefiore: Reality and Myth.* Jerusalem: Carmel (Hebrew).

Schudson, Michael. 1989. "The Present in the Past versus the Past in the Present." *Communication* 11:105–13.

Schudson, Michael. 1992. *Watergate in American History: How We Remember, Forget, and Reconstruct the Past.* New York: Basic Books.

Schueftan, Dan. 1989. *Attrition: Egypt's Postwar Political Strategy, 1967–1970.* Tel Aviv: Ministry of Defense (Hebrew).

Schuman, Howard, and Jacqueline Scott. 1989. "Generations and Collective Memories." *American Sociological Review* 54:359–81.

Schwartz, Barry. 1982. "The Social Context of Commemoration: A Study in Collective Memory." *Social Forces* 61:374–402.

Schwartz, Barry. 1990. "The Reconstruction of Abraham Lincoln, 1865–1920."

In *Collective Remembering,* ed. David Middleton and Derek Edwards, pp. 81–107. London: Sage.

Schwartz, Barry. 1991. "Social Change and Collective Memory: The Democratization of George Washington." *American Sociological Review* 56(2): 221–36.

Schwartz, Barry, Yael Zerubavel, and Bernice M. Barnett. 1986. "The Recovery of Masada: A Study in Collective Memory." *The Sociological Quarterly* 27(2): 147–64.

Schwartz, Matthew, and Kalman J. Kaplan. 1992. "Judaism, Masada, and Suicide: A Critical Analysis." *Omega* 25(2): 127–32.

Segev, Tom. 1991. *The Seventh Million: The Israelis and the Holocaust.* Jerusalem: Keter (Hebrew).

Segre, Dan V. 1980. *A Crisis in Identity: Israel and Zionism.* Oxford: Oxford University Press.

Shaked, Gershon. 1993. "Between the Kotel and Masada." *Yediot Ahronot,* weekend literary supplement, July 23, pp. 30–31 (Hebrew).

Shalem, Natan. 1968. *The Judea Desert.* Brought to press by David Benvenisti. Jerusalem: The Leon Rekanati fund in conjunction with the Alscheich cultural fund and friends of the deceased (Hebrew).

Shalom, S. 1950. "The Cave of Joseph." In *All the Poems of S. Shalom,* vol. 3, pp. 171–253. Tel Aviv: Yavneh (Hebrew).

Shamir, Illana. 1988. *The History of the People of Israel for the Young Reader.* Tel Aviv: Omanut (Hebrew).

Shanks, Hershel. 1986. "Archaeology as Politics." *Commentary* 82(2): 50–52.

Shapira, Anita. 1992. *Land and Power (The Sword of the Dove).* Tel Aviv: Am Oved (Hebrew).

Shapira, Anita. 1994. "Historiography and Memory: The 1948 Latrun Case." *Alpaim* 10:9–41 (Hebrew).

Shapira, Rina, Haim Adler, Miri Lerner, and Rachel Peleg. 1979. *Blue Shirt and White Collar: A Study of the Social World of Graduates of Youth Movements in Israel.* Tel Aviv: Am Oved; Institute for Studies of Work and Society (Hebrew).

Shargel, Baila R. 1979. "The Evolution of the Masada Myth." *Judaism* 28:357–71.

Shashar, Michael. 1983. "Masada, Moshe Dayan, and the Destruction of a Myth." *Yediot Ahronot,* cultural, literary, and art Supplement, October 28, p. 4 (Hebrew).

Shashar, Michael. 1985. "Freedom and the Masada Myth," *Yediot Ahronot,* April 11, p. 25 (Hebrew).

Shashar, Michael. 1987. "Shmaria Guttman: The Creator of Masada Myth and the Exposer of Gamla in the Golan and Susia, on the book *Bamidbar.*" *Eretz* 1(1): 21–27 (Hebrew).

Shaskin, Roni. 1994. "Reality, Not Myth." *Nekuda* 179 (July): 7 (Hebrew).

Shatzberger, Hilda. 1984. *Interaction between the Jewish Political Tradition and the Jewish Underground Groups in Eretz Israel in the Mandate Period.* Master's thesis, Department of General History, Ramat Gan, Bar Illan University (Hebrew).

Shatzman, Israel. 1993. "The Roman Siege on Masada." In *The Story of Masada: Discoveries from the Excavations,* ed. Gila Hurvitz, pp. 105–20. Jerusalem: Hebrew University; Antiquities Authority: Society for Studying Eretz Israel and its Antiquities (Hebrew).

Shavit, S., ed. 1983. *The History of Israel and the Peoples,* vol. 2. Jerusalem: Ministry of Education, Center for Curriculum (Hebrew).

Shavit, Yaacov. 1984. *From Hebrew to Canaanite: Aspects in the History, Ideology, and Utopia of the 'Hebrew Renaissance'—From Radical Zionism to Anti-Zionism.* Jerusalem: Domino Press (Hebrew).

Shavit, Yaacov. 1986. "Truth Will Rise from the Land: Points in the Development of Public Jewish Interest in Archaeology (till the 1930s)." *Cathedra* 44:27–54 (Hebrew).

Shavit, Yaacov. 1987. *The Mythologia of the Zionist Right Wing.* Tel Aviv: Beit-Berl and the Moshe Sharett Institute (Hebrew).

Shavit, Yaacov. 1990. "Cyrus King of Persia and the Return to Zion: A Case of Neglected Memory." *History and Memory: Studies in Representation of the Past,* 2(1): 51–83.

Shavit, Yaacov. 1992. "Masada Will Fall." *Yediot Ahronot,* February 14, p. 27 (Hebrew).

Shils, Edward A. 1981. *Tradition.* Chicago: University of Chicago Press.

Shmueli, Moshe. 1963. *The History of Our People.* Jerusalem: Tarbut Vechinuch (Hebrew).

Shneler, Shmuel. 1989. "The Haredi Youth Movement Ezra." In *Youth Movements, 1920–1960,* Idan Series, vol. 13, ed. Mordechai Naor, pp. 121–23 (Hebrew).

Shochat, Azriel. 1956. *The History of Israel: The Period of the Second Temple.* Tel Aviv: Yehoshua Chechik (Hebrew).

Shomron, David ("Eli"). 1985. *We Were Recruited for Life.* Tel Aviv: Ministry of Defense (Hebrew).

Shorek, Yehiam. 1988. *The History of the People of Israel in the Days of the Second Temple.* Tel Aviv: Amichai (Hebrew).

Silberman, Neil Asher. 1989. *Between Past and Present.* New York: Doubleday, Anchor Books.

Silberman, Neil Asher. 1993. *A Prophet from amongst You: The Life of Yigael Yadin: Soldier, Scholar, and Mythmaker of Modern Israel,* Reading, Mass.: Addison-Wesley.

Silk, Joseph. 1980. *The Great Bang.* San Francisco: W. H. Freeman.

Simchoni, Y. N. [1923] 1968. "Introduction" and "Notes and Explanations." In *The History of the Wars of the Jews with the Romans,* by Joseph Ben-Matityahu (Josephus Flavius). Tel Aviv: Masada (Hebrew).

Slater, Jerome. 1991. "What Is the Significance of Israeli Historical Revisionism?" *Association for Israel Studies Newsletter,* Fall, pp. 17–23.

Smallwood, Mary E. 1976. *The Jews under Roman Rule.* Leiden: E. J. Brill.

Smith, Anthony D. 1991. *National Identity.* Reno: University of Nevada Press.

Smith, Morton. 1971. "Zealots and Sicarii: Their Origins and Relation." *Harvard Theological Review* 64(1): 1–19.

Spero, Shubert. 1970. "In Defense of the Defenders of Masada." *Tradition,* 11(1): 31–43.

Spero, Shubert. 1971. "The Defense of Masada." *Tradition* 12(2): 136–41.

Stern, Menachem. 1973. "Zealots." In *Encyclopedia Judaica Year Book,* pp. 135–51.

Stern, Menachem. 1983. "Sicarii and Zealots." In *Society and Religion During the Period of the Second Temple,* ed. Michael Avi-Yonah and Zvi Beres, pp. 167–96. Tel Aviv: Alexanderf Peli and Am Oved (Hebrew).

Stern, Menachem, ed. 1984. *The History of the Land of Israel: The Roman-Byzantian Period,* vol. 4. Jerusalem: Yad Yitzhak Ben-Zvi and Keter (Hebrew).

Stern, Menachem. 1987. "Yoseph Ben-Matitiahu, Historian of 'Wars of the Jews.' " In *Studies in Historiography,* ed. Joseph Salmon, Menachem Stern, and Moshe Zimmermann, pp. 41–51. Jerusalem: Zalman Shazar Center for Jewish History (Hebrew).

Stern, Menachem. 1989. "The Suicide of Elazar Ben Yair and His Men in Masada and the 'Fourth Philosophy.' " *Zion* 4(47): 367–97 (Hebrew).

Stern-Yair, Abraham. 1976. *In My Blood You Shall Live Forever.* Tel Aviv: Yair (Hebrew).

S.T.H: *Sefer Toldot Hahagana* (The History of the Hagana). 1954–1973. 8 vols. Tel Aviv: Maarachot (vols. 1–5), Am Oved (vols. 6–8) (Hebrew).

Stinchombe, Arthur. 1978. *Theoretical Methods in Social History.* New York: Academic Press.

Stone, Michael Edward, ed. 1984. *Jewish Writing of the Second Temple Period.* Assen: Van Gorcum.

Syon, Danny. 1992. "Gamla—Portrait of a Rebellion." *Biblical Archaeology Review* 18(1): 20–37 (February).

Syrkin, Marie. 1973. "The Paradox of Masada." *Midstream* 19(8): 66–70.

Tal, Yerach. 1990. "Paper Fortifications." *Haaretz,* July 19, p. 4 (Hebrew).

Talmi, Ephraim and Menachem. 1960. *Israel, Roads and Yeshuvim.* Tel Aviv: Izrael, pp. 309–10 (Hebrew).

Talmi, Ephraim and Menachem. 1966. *All the Land: A Geographical Lexicon of Israel.* Tel Aviv: Amichai (Hebrew).

Tamary, Dov. 1984. "Masada—A Redundant Ceremony." *Yediot Ahronot,* April 30, p. 25 (Hebrew).

Tepper, Yigael. 1984. "Notes for the Discussion about Education to Heroic Values." *Mebifnim* 3:410–17. (Hebrew).

Thackeray, Henry St. John. 1968. *Josephus: The Man and the Historian.* New York: Ktav.

Thelen, David. 1989. "Memory and American History." *Journal of American History* 75:1117–29.

"The Spirit of Masada." *Reconstructionist, a Jewish Bi-Weekly,* November 3, 1967, 33(13): 3–5.

Tomarkin, Yigael. 1988. "What Is There in Common between Mahler and the Table-Desk in S.A." *Haaretz,* October 7, 1988, weekly supplement, p. 23 (Hebrew).

Tuchman, Gaye, and Nina F. Fortin. 1984. "Fame and Misfortune." *American Journal of Sociology* 90:72–96.

Tudor, Henry. 1972. *Political Myth.* London: Macmillan.

Turner, Jonathan H., and Alexandra Maryanski. 1979. *Functionalism.* Menlo Park, Calif.: Benjamin/Cummings.

Turner, Jonathan H., and Alexandra R. Maryanski, 1988. "Is 'Neofunctionalism' Really Functional?" *Sociological Theory* 6(1): 110–21.

Turner, Victor W. 1968. "Myth and Symbol." In *International Encyclopedia of the Social Sciences,* ed. David L. Sills, vol. 10, pp. 576–582. New York: Macmillan.

Tzameret, Tzvi. 1989. "Brit Hasmoneans: An Educational-Fighting Youth Movement." In *Youth Movements, 1920–1960,* Idan Series, vol. 13, ed. Mordechai Naor, pp. 123–26 (Hebrew).

Tzoref, Efraim. 1960. *The Legend of Masada.* Tel Aviv: Yesod, pp. 9–24 (Hebrew).

Usque, Samuel. 1965. *Consolation for the Tribulations of Israel,* trans. Martin A. Cohen. Philadelphia: Jewish Publication Society of America.

Vidal-Naquet, Pierre. 1983. "Josephus Flavius and Masada." *Zemanim* 13:67–75 (Hebrew).

Vidal-Naquet, Pierre. 1991. *The Murderers of Memory.* Trans. Ada Paldor. Tel Aviv: Am Oved (Hebrew).

Vilnai, Zeev. 1935. *The Guide to Eretz Israel.* Jerusalem: Steimatzky (Hebrew).

Vilnai, Zeev. 1942. *The Guide to Eretz Israel, Jerusalem, Judea, and Samaria.* Jerusalem: Tour (Hebrew).

Vilnai, Zeev. 1964. *The Dead Sea and Its Israeli Beach.* Jerusalem: Tamar Regional Council (Hebrew).

Vilnai, Zeev. 1978. *Ariel—Encyclopaedia for the Knowledge of Eretz Israel.* Tel Aviv: Am Oved (Hebrew).

Views and Landscapes. 1984. Tel Aviv: Israeli Army, Chief Education Officer, Ministry of Defense (Hebrew).

Wagner-Pacifici, Robin, and Barry Schwartz. 1991. "The Vietnam Veterans Memorial: Commemorating a Difficult Past." *American Journal of Sociology* 97(2): 376–420.

Weinberg, S. 1977. *The First Three Minutes.* New York: Basic.

Weingarten, Y., and N. Teuber. 1936. *Our People in the Past and the Present.* Tel Aviv: Kedem (Hebrew).

Weinshall, Yaacov. 1978. *The Blood on the Threshold.* Tel Aviv: Yair (Hebrew).

Weiss, Hillel. 1994a. "Who Invents Masada?" *Haaretz,* May 30, p. 4 (Hebrew).

Weiss, Hillel. 1994b. "Secular Zionism Says Goodbye to Masada." *Nekuda* 178 (May): 44–47 (Hebrew).

Weiss-Rosmarin, Trude. 1966. "Masada and Yavneh." *Jewish Spectator* 31(9): 4–7 (November).

Weiss-Rosmarin, Trude. 1967. "Masada, Josephus, and Yadin," *Jewish Spectator* 32(8): 2–8, 30 (October).

Weitz, Yoseph. [1962] 1963. *Around Masada.* Jerusalem: Jewish National Fund (Hebrew).

Wiesel, Eli. 1988. "Judaism, History and Myth." *Yediot Ahronot,* September 20, special Yom Kippur magazine, pp. 3, 24 (Hebrew).

Yaakubovitz, Mordechai (Captain). 1953. *From Palmach to Zahal.* Tel Aviv: Amichai (Hebrew).

Yadin, Yigael. 1965. *Masada: First Season of Excavations, 1963–1964: Preliminary Report.* Jerusalem: Israel Exploration Society (Hebrew).

Yadin, Yigael. 1966. *Masada: Herod's Fortress and the Zealots' Last Stand.* London: Weidenfeld and Nicolson.

Yadin, Yigael. 1970. "Metzada." In *Encyclopaedia For Archaeological Excavations in Eretz Israel,* vol. 2, pp. 374–90. Jerusalem: Society for the Investigation of Eretz Israel and its Antiquity and Masada (Hebrew).

Yadin, Yigael. 1971. "Masada." *Encyclopedia Judaica,* vol. 11, pp. 1078–91. Jerusalem: Keter.

Yadin, Yigael. 1972. "Metzada." *Encyclopedia Hebraica,* vol. 24, pp. 104–6. Jerusalem: Peli-Hevra Lehotzaat Enziklopediot (Hebrew).

Yadin, Yigael. 1973. "1900 Years since the Fall of Masada." *Maariv,* April 16, p. 15 (Hebrew).

Yadin, Yigael. 1980. "Metzada." In *The Guide to Israel.* Jerusalem: Keter (Hebrew).

Yadin, Yigael and Gerald Gottlieb. 1969. *The Story of Masada by Yigael Yadin, Retold for Young Readers by Gerald Gottlieb.* New York: Random House.

Yaffe, Uri. 1967. *From Masada to Ramot Naftali.* Jerusalem: World Zionist Organization, Department for Culture and Education in the Diaspora (Hebrew).

Yediot Ahronot Guide for Vacation and Tours in Israel. 1965. Tel Aviv: Yediot Ahronot, pp. 187–89 (Hebrew).

Yellin-Mor, Natan. 1974. *Lohamei Herut Israel (Lehi).* Tel Aviv: Shikmona (Hebrew).

Yerushalmi, Yoseph Hayim. 1982. *Zakhor: Jewish History and Jewish Memory.* Seattle: University of Washington Press.

Yevin, Amichal Ada. 1986. *In Purple: The Life of Yair—Abraham Stern.* Tel Aviv: Hadar (Hebrew).

Yudkin, Leon I. 1971. *Isaac Lamdan: A Study in Twentieth-Century Hebrew Poetry.* Ithaca. N.Y.: Cornell University Press.

Yuval, Israel Yaacov. 1993. "The Revenge and the Curse, the Blood and the Libel." *Zion,* 58(1): 33–90. (Hebrew).

Zabludovski, Aryeh, and Yitzhak Moshe Immanuel. 1959. *Sefer Divrei Haya-mim*, part 2. Tel Aviv: Yehoshua Chechik (Hebrew).

Zaks, Yitzhak, and Mordechai Gavrieli. 1969. *A Guide for Trips in the Land.* Jerusalem: Eviatar, p. 90 (Hebrew).

Zeitlin, Solomon. 1965. "Masada and the Sicarii." *Jewish Quarterly Review* 55:299–317.

Zeitlin, Solomon. 1967. "The Sicarii and Masada." *Jewish Quarterly Review* 57:251–70.

Zeldes, Eliezer. 1935. *Practical History*, part 2. Tel Aviv: N.p. (Hebrew).

Zertal, Idith. 1994. "The Sacrificed and the Sanctified: The Construction of a Na-tional Martyrology." *Zemanim* 12 (48): 26–45 (Hebrew).

Zerubavel, Yael. 1980. *The Last Stand: On the Transformation of Symbols in Modern Israeli Culture.* Ph.D. Diss. Philadelphia: University of Pennsylvania.

Zerubavel, Yael. 1991a. "The Politics of Interpretation: Tel Hai in Israel's Collec-tive Memory." *American Jewish Society Review* 16:133–59.

Zerubavel, Yael. 1991b. "New Beginning, Old Past: The Collective Memory of Pioneering in Israeli Culture." In *New Perspectives On Israeli History,* ed. Lau-rence J. Silberstein, pp. 193–215. New York: New York University Press.

Zerubavel, Yael. 1994. "The Death of Memory and the Memory of Death: Ma-sada and the Holocaust as Historical Metaphors." *Representations* 45 (Win-ter): 72–100.

Ziv, Yehuda. 1983. *In the Path of the Travellers.* Tel Aviv: Ministry of Defense (Hebrew).

Zuta, H. A., and Y. Spivak. 1950. *The History of Our People. Part 1, Book 2.* Tel Aviv: Omanut (Hebrew).